Management Systems

in the Human Services

MANAGEMENT SYSTEMS

IN THE HUMAN SERVICES

Edited by Murray L. Gruber

Temple University Press  Philadelphia

CARNEGIE LIBRARY
LIVINGSTONE COLLEGE
SALISBURY, N. C. 28144

Library of Congress Cataloging in Publication Data
Main entry under title:

Management systems in the human services.

Includes bibliographical references and index.
1. Social work administration—United States—
Addresses, essays, lectures. 2. Management—Ad-
dresses, essays, lectures. I. Gruber, Murray L.
HV91.M276   361'.0068   80-21370
ISBN 0-87722-207-X

Temple University Press, Philadelphia 19122

© 1981 by Temple University. All rights reserved

Published 1981

Printed in the United States of America

Portions of this publication are reproduced from *A "PPBS"
Approach to Budgeting Human Service Programs for United
Ways,* copyright United Way of America 1972, by United
Way of America, Publisher, and pages 15–26 (inclusive) have
been reproduced here verbatim. These materials have been
reprinted by Temple University Press with the permission of
United Way of America.

36/. 0068
G 885

To my wife Irmgard

and my daughter Gabrielle

whose forebearance

made this possible.

114276

Contents

Humanizing Computerized Information Systems
Theodore D. Sterling

Acknowledgments

I owe many debts to many people. Among them are Eunice Shatz, Dean of the School of Social Work, University of Utah; Professors Sydney Bernard, Charles Garvin and Armand Lauffer, The University of Michigan School of Social Work; Professor Martin Birnbaum, Fairleigh Dickinson University Center for Social Work; and Professor David Gil, Brandeis University Florence Heller School for Advanced Studies in Social Welfare. Their criticism and suggestions, their advice and support were invaluable to me. Whatever the limitations of this work, they are mine alone.

Management Systems

in the Human Services

1. Introduction

MURRAY L. GRUBER

The search for effective management of the human services has emerged as a dominant motif of the current period. Its most immediate and direct cause is the turnabout in social perception from images of abundance to those of dismal scarcity. Magnifying this perception has been the dramatic rise in social spending during the last two decades. To be sure, not all sectors in the human services have gained equal shares—growth in the social services has been particularly meager—but overall, federal spending for health, education, and welfare has risen from about $20 billion in 1960 to $238 billion in 1979.[1] These dual developments, rising spending and shifting perceptions, have led to a revived concern for fiscal restraint and better management of resources. In the political realm, even the old distinctions between liberals and conservatives have been whittled away, and if liberals once opted for more spending, conservatives for frugality, the necessity to do more with less now seems clear to most.

Predictably, the stern logic of economics has ramified into the human services sector itself where it has worked many changes, not the least of which is a dramatic transformation in the outlook and practice of administration. The essence of this change is the quest for systematic and rational methods for managing resources and for making strategic and allocational decisions more effectively, a "science of administration." This reader is about that quest. It is specifically concerned with the introduction of modern analytic and informational technologies associated with the "systems view." More or less predicated on quasi-formalistic and quantitatively oriented models, the particular technologies discussed include: Planning-Programming-Budgeting-Systems (PPBS), Management by Objectives (MBO), Benefit-Cost Analysis, Zero-Base Budgeting (ZBB), and Management-Information Systems (MIS).

To many these tools promise administrative rationality—formal designs to systematize decision making, to use information better, to "reprogram" human service organizations, to develop better analytic capabilities, and to reveal what is being done with what results and at what costs.

But in the human services the new technologies have not been without challenge and misunderstanding. One problem is that they have come from such diverse fields as business administration, industrial engineering, military and defense analysis, water resource management, and other fields unlike the human services. Another problem resides in the lack of experience in applying the formalistic models of system management because their very formalism suggests a sense of definition and understanding more illusory than real. Third, there are limitations in the applicability of these tools in the sprawling, highly complex system of the human services. With these problems and difficulties in mind, this book, directed to students, scholars, and practitioners in the human services, takes account of the conceptual and the practical and is a corrective to two extremes, the outright rejection of the new tools or uncritical acceptance of them as exemplars of science and rationality.

At the outset, it may be useful to probe a bit more deeply into some of the thorny issues of organization in the human services. To do this, it is necessary to focus upon a few of the more important structural contours of the Welfare State before discussing some of the distinguishing characteristics of human service organizations themselves. This background will provide a foothold to problems of management, the ineluctable pressure to expand the orbit of managerial intervention, and the apparent logic of the systems view.

To begin with, the acts of social intervention that have led to the build-up of the Welfare State have been a historical necessity, but at the same time the vast array of programs and services for specialized needs and different population groups has grown up piecemeal, a series of improvisations creating a jerry-built structure of inelegant complexity. The series of "add ons" that has grown up is faithful to the political system within which it is found—never were the programs part of any coherent national plan, and wherever one looks, there is bedazzling pluralism. At the federal level within the Department of Health and Human Services, of the more than 300 programs, about a third are overlapping with each other or with programs in other departments. Emanating from categorical federal legislation, the matrix of categories for services to special groups (older Americans, the mentally ill, Native Americans, etc.) or specialized services (employment and training, family planning, vocational rehabilitation) had created, in Mott's words, a "bureaucratic jungle."[2] At state and local levels, the numbers of administrative agencies and service providers run into the hundreds with programs typically organized in terms of the categories of federal funding rather than holistic sets of human problems. Any single program is often enmeshed in different jurisdictions, different funding rules, and different eligibility requirements. Typically lacking is a single structure that channels services from funder to provider to user. Further complicating matters is the use of public funds for the delivery of services by voluntary or private agencies. Both from the standpoint of administration and the delivery of services, the whole system is extraordinarily dense, complex, and irrational, and simultaneous with attempts to rationalize it through such devices as "services integration," revenue sharing or national goal structures, each attempted reform must take account of the existing system so as to disrupt it as little as possible. The overall result is that the entire system resembles nothing more than a labyrinth of organized anarchy with each increment to the system piling up more and more requirements for administrative intervention in a process of cumulative causation.

A set of similar as well as distinctive problems of organization is found in service delivery agencies, and in the most fundamental sense they obscure accountability policy and concepts of organizational effectiveness, and complicate the burdens of management. In one sense, these burdens arise from the facts of scarcity which require that the production and distribution of human services will be accomplished economically. Scarcity constrains; and in this regard there is a close similarity between the human service organization and the profit-making enterprise. Beyond this similarity between the profit and nonprofit sectors in society, students of organizations emphasize certain fundamental differences between the two. The former, owing to "below the line" summation, have clear and unambiguous performance measures against which to test and sharpen their goals and objectives.[3] Human service organizations, on the other hand, operate within disorderly, messy environments in which competing and conflicting social and political goals abound. This makes difficult the task of ordering priorities and goals and the ways in which scarce resources shall be employed.

Partly as a function of the pluralistic and messy environments within which human service agencies operate and the attendant necessity to find centers of consensus, the stated purposes of human service agencies take on certain symbolic qualities, emblems of sacredness in the secular realm. To concert divergent interests pieties pass for precise purposes, and they mystify, that is to say, they mask the nature of actual operations. But were these pietistic, ambiguous generalities mere deceptions, the task of management would be far simpler.

In reality and unlike the profit-making enterprise, there is no easy operationalization of performance in the human services. To be sure, there is great diversity among the tens of thousands of agencies that deal with poverty, welfare, mental illness, family troubles, the aged, etc., but decisive similarities are found in the "messiness" of work in those many agencies whose central purpose is to influence the behavior of their clientele. Uncertainties, unknowns, and unpredictable events are perhaps the most common phenomena in the internal life of these agencies. This applies to the procedures or technologies applied, the reactions of the clients to whom they are directed, and especially to the outcomes.[4] Some key consequences are high worker discretion owing to the difficulties in proceduralizing work, the near impossibility of ordering activities in a tight chain of goals-means relationships, and for the purposes of internal coordination and management, the standard Weberian protocols of rules and regulations flounder on unknowns. Thus, it is difficult for agencies to control the performance of human service workers, and absent are operationally effective ranked preferences and performance measures at either the worker or organizational level. For how can one direct and control performance, rank priorities, and measure performance when events are unknown, goals are unclear, and behavior indeterminate? For these many reasons (the intangible texture of service, conflicting societal and system goals, tenuousness and unpredictability, and the difficulty of measuring outputs), decisions have been made intuitively in piecemeal, fragmented ways, not according to the procedures of rational or scientific analysis. The translation of purpose into resource allocation and budgetary decisions, perhaps the most critical function, is inevitably shot through with all of these problems.

At two levels then, in the theater of public policy planning, and at the level of organizational decision making, there is a maelstrom of disorder, uncertainty, and pluralism. Till now, the situation resembled nothing so faithfully as Lindblom's model of disjointed incrementalism and muddling through. In this view, the high costs of information, pluralistic politics, indeterminate ends, and constraints on analytic ability all call into question both the desirability and possibility of comprehensively rational problem solving.[5] Yet the costs of segmental problem solving and serial adjustments are high. For incremental tinkering and the absence of a view of the whole lead to an ever-expanding circle of detailed administrative intervention, a whole rigamorole of administrative coordination, detailed rules and regulations, and the enlargement of the administrative apparatus. Where lies the scaffold of rationality?

During the 1960s public sector decision makers intensified their search for answers to important public policy questions through formal and systematic analysis that would be sufficiently comprehensive to predict the combined effects of several lines of simultaneous action on one another. A variety of terms was employed for the intellectual phenomenon that promised a scaffold of rationality out of disorder: policy analysis, systems analysis, systems engineering, management science systems management, and systems science. With an abundance of meanings surrounding the "systems" view and with the distinctions between the various terms rather arbitrary, the absorption of this conceptual schema in the human services has not been without confusion and ambiguity.

In principle, the systems approach is opposed to incrementalism or the strategy of "cutting a problem down to size." Yet it makes no pretense of providing a complete theory of systems which is the realm of General Systems Theory (GST). Attempts to distinguish the various types of systems applications tend to confirm the interchangeability of terminology, and the fact that the distinctions are rather arbitrary. For example, Quade finds systems analysis and systems management closely akin to engineering because they are application-oriented and have common roots in "operations analysis."[6] The latter, renamed "Operations Research" (OR), was developed during World War II when British military executives turned to small teams of scientists to help incorporate the then new radar into the tactics and strategy of air defense. Among the major accomplishments were the development of the electronic digital computer and advanced feedback and control systems. In the postwar years, OR, systems management, and systems analysis moved forward with a common core of economic theory and mathematical methods for dealing with management and decision problems. Also advances in information processing continued to be an essential factor in coping with the complexities of systems problems.

For the human services, one of the more significant developments of the 1960s was the broadened application of the systems approach and its diffusion from military, private enterprise, and space technology applications to problems of urban planning, poverty, crime, public welfare, and other social problems.[7] What was needed, according to a new consensus in government, were better, more powerful analytic techniques for policy planning, operational efficiency, budgeting and resource allocation, and problems of strategic choice. More concerned with the logic of analysis than with the content of decisions, the basic framework for analysis could be applied both to "high level" public policy choices and to "lower level" management problems to define as fully as possible all significant aspects of a problem and its components, to formulate missions and objectives, to search for alternative ways of achieving the objectives, and to compare them in terms of some specified criteria. In one sense, the approach is a form of input-output analysis in which an organization is encouraged to analyze the logical relations between means and ends, between what it does and what the actual consequences are. Logically, one of the first requirements of formal analysis is the necessity to clarify objectives, to state them precisely, and to find quantitative measures for them to the extent possible. Then it is possible to specify alternative ways of achieving the objectives and to analyze the relations between different mixes of investment and varying levels of benefits. Throughout the entire process of sharpening and interrelating goals, objectives, means, criteria, benefits, and costs, there is a heavy emphasis on economic and quantitative tools, and the role of information as a major agent in the effort. Among the tools employed, Planning-Programming-Budgeting Systems (PPBS), Benefit-Cost Analysis, Management By Objectives (MBO), Zero-Base Budgeting (ZBB), and Management Information Systems (MIS) by no means exhaust the stock of systems tools, but they have a great deal in common and all draw heavily on systems thinking in one or another of its variant definitions.

The injection of systems thinking into the human services was decisively propelled by the expansion of social programs and social spending during the 1960s. Within a relatively short time much legislation had been passed for new social programs—the Area Redevelopment Act and the Manpower and Development Training Act, the Community Mental Health Centers program, the anti-poverty program, the Elementary and Secondary Education Act, Medicare and Medicaid, the Demonstration Cities and Metropolitan Development Act, and finally Title XX of the Social Security Act—causing a dramatic upsurge in expenditures for human services.

At the level of public policy and from the standpoint of efficient management, it was extraordinarily difficult to distinguish good programs from bad, effective from ineffective, owing to weak analytic capability and to the nature of the programs themselves. Like many traditional human services programs and the "soft" services that had been provided by social workers, the goals of many of the new programs were stated in such general terms that their effects could not be easily measured; consequently the information collected about the newer efforts was predominantly concerned with measures of effort or "inputs" rather than outputs or effectiveness or impact.

The lofty expectations generated by the New Frontier and Great Society would soon sour and generate deep skepticism, and the lexical coinage of "accountability" and "throwing dollars at problems" would come to betoken the curdled faith in social spending. Thus the "checkbook" approach would give way to such questions as these: What will programs do? Are they needed? What are the costs and benefits? How can human service agencies better evaluate their performance and thereby make sounder strategic decisions?

Systems approaches entered the human services with glittering promises, and although there has been a succession of disappointments in the federal government, the intellectual system, the managerial ideology, indeed the very meaning of rationality contained in the systems sciences pervaded the human services. A significant force in the spread of systems ideas and approaches has been the role of the federal government as a focal point for the in-gathering and the outward flow of new ideas. Thus, following the introduction of PPBS and benefit-cost analysis into federal civilian government in what was hailed as a "quiet revolution," these ideas spread rapidly downward to state and municipal governments and public and private agencies of all sorts.

Although the federal government played an important role in the diffusion of systems thinking, the itinerary of those ideas was far more serpentine. Developments in public welfare and social services planning are a case in point of multiple and intersecting channels of diffusion. At the federal level, for example, as early as 1966, Nicol addressed the question of income maintenance programs from the standpoint of "a public welfare systems model."[8] Simultaneously, at state and local levels, the General Planning Corporation, Lockheed Missiles and Space Company, and the Sperry Gyroscope Company were seeking to use systems technology to redesign public welfare agencies.[9] Parallel with these efforts, the American Public Welfare Association's Technical Assistance Project (TAP) was putting together a systems engineering/social work team to aid in the design of state public welfare departments. Noting that the process could be called systems analysis or operations research, TAP proposed the following formula for systems development based upon models developed in two states:

1. Formulate overall objectives for a public social service system.
2. Develop desirable criteria and characteristics of a public social service system by repeating the overall objectives down through layers of subobjectives to criteria using an objective-means iterative approach.
3. Using the criteria then developed, select the subset of alternative concepts and ideas pertinent to social services which best meet the criteria.
4. Using the criteria, select the functional, organizational structure which best translates the select concepts and ideas into practical, implementable form."[10]

Variously called an "input-output social service system model" and a "goal oriented guidelines" management system, the hierarchy of objectives and subobjectives would extend to all aspects of operation—social service program implementation, personnel practices, financial planning and allocation, organizational structure.[11] Fused with the approach known as "management by objectives," the imprint of the systems view was apparent. Yet despite its seeming rationality, this meticulous, systematic attempt to "blueprint" the rational organization ran afoul of the dense, "marblecake" quality of real organizational life. Moreover, to the extent that state agencies tried to follow the principles of "rational" work design, that is to say, specialization and differentiation, complexity was piled on complexity, the need for internal coordination mounted, and procedural specifications proliferated.[12]

In the federal government, up until the transition from Johnson's Great Society to Nixon's New Federalism, most debates on management and policy were dominated by PPBS and benefit-cost analysis, not management by objectives. In the Nixon administration, however, the powerful Office of Management and Budget (OMB) formally christened Management By Objectives as the administration's lead tool in holding federal agencies accountable for achieving objectives.[13] The strategy was also extended downward to state and local social service departments. For owing to a precipitous rise in federal expenditures for social services under the provisions of mandatory and open-ended federal matching to the states, questions of rational systems design and accountability once again pressed forward. Although the Congress would soon put a cap on federal social services funding effective fiscal year 1973, the social services were nonetheless burdened by broad, nonoperationalized goals, and an absence of measurable objectives and performance data in state social services programs. Consequently, within the Community Services Administration, Social and Rehabilitation Service of the Department of Health, Education and Welfare (DHEW), the search for a national "goal oriented" system of accountability that included social quantification measures came to rest on a system called GOSS (Goal Oriented Social Services). Consistent with the emerging MBO strategy of intergovernmental "coupling" from the top down, GOSS in concept resembled the early TAP system and was predicated on a hierarchical structure of specified program goals linked to more specific subobjectives in relation to which administrators could determine needed "service unit inputs." Also envisioned was a management information system to report results from the local to the federal level.[14] By 1974, as embodied in the Title XX Amendments to the Social Security Act, the goal-oriented system came to be known as "definition by objective" which meant that services would be defined by what they sought to achieve.

The model of rational management that had been persistently spreading throughout the human services for about ten years was in a sense officially ratified by a report of a Task Force of the National Conference on Social Welfare which included recommendations on expanding management technology in social service programs. In the interests of better delivery of services, the Task Force model includes such "innovations in management techniques and technologies" as goal-oriented case management, planning systems, project management, automated management information systems, and management by objectives as a two-way process,[15] the last perhaps to guard against the centralizing bias of rationalistic management and the mistakes of the past.

Returning to the central issues of choice, priorities, and design, a number of different threads and tools have emerged in the prevailing paradigm of rationality. Of the various tools discussed, ZBB is not strictly speaking a "systems technology." Yet the systems approach has enormous range and is a kind of all-purpose term for rational means-ends analysis, and under its embrace ZBB forms part of a cohesive system. From the standpoint of conceptual bonding, it is designed to show the link between agency purposes and agency spending, and it is but another servant of accountability. Its accent may vary somewhat, but its cornerstone is the prevailing concept of rationality in which reason is rendered equivalent to a comprehensive analysis of objectives, to a ranking of those objectives, and then to a choice according to some specified criterion, in this case "efficiency." Like PPBS and MBO, ZBB was rapidly installed throughout the federal bureaucracy as still another presidential administration continued searching for tools with which to render decision making more technically rational. In the most theoretical sense, ZBB together with the other semiformalistic, quantitative tools forms a coherent pattern in which systems analysis supplies the broad framework of the system and identifies the results wanted, systems engineering creates a design that incorporates the optimized technology, and systems management defines the overall responsibility for the whole procedure.[16]

Propelled by scarcity and dissatisfaction with the performance of human services programs and carried forward under the rubric of science, the central concepts and operations of the prevailing paradigm of rationality have worked their way through myriad channels of information and technology transfer, and are by now deeply imprinted in the intellectual and organizational systems in the human services. With the necessity for better management clearly established, there also has been much hyperbole about "systems," and especially in relation to numerous disappointments and failures, an excessively optimistic view of the potential benefits. Observing the reactions of urban planners to PPBS, for example, Downs observed somewhat cynically that it was as if a group of experimental biologists had successfully crossed a talking parrot and a Bengal tiger and produced a strange new animal. No one knew exactly what it was but when it talked they listened.[17]

However, it would be inaccurate to suggest that there has been wholesale and uncritical acceptance of the new tools. Within the human services and allied disciplines, there could be heard a critical minority. There were those who challenged the claims to science, rationality, and precision in systems applications. As a general theoretical model applicable to all kinds of systems from neurophysiological to social, some saw the intellectual foundations of systems theory as leading to a superficial vagueness in which the term system purported to explain so much that its definitional parameters could not be located. On the practical side, there appeared to be some merit in the criticism that the methods dissolved in the very piecemeal fragmentation they were designed to overcome. For example, Hoos has argued that because the techniques are quantitative, "they can deal with only the measurable aspects of programs under way or under consideration—dollars spent in relation to pupils taught, housing units built, miles of road laid, or whatever. Due to its nature, the method of analysis forces the question into the form it can answer."[18] Downs, along similar lines, invokes the metaphor of a horse and rabbit stew. Because of their tractability (the rabbit), some variables are selected for meticulous treatment, but the incommensurable aspects are enormous (the horse) and these are neglected.[19] Others, tracing the evolution of systems management partly to Taylor's scientific management, view it as a technocratic system and quarrel with systems management on the basis of its underlying value frame, that is, a relentless search for ends defined by managers and a technical elite.[20] More to the point perhaps is whether or to what extent the management and policy analysis tools developed in other sectors can be effectively used in the human services.[21] In general, the formalistic, quantitative mode has proven most successful in situations where goals have been clear, easily measured, and consensual, conditions that do not prevail in the human services. One expressed concern has been that in the zealous quest for "blueprints" and quantification the human dimension would be squeezed out. In a somewhat similar vein, but at a different level, is the view that systems management seeks to bend and perhaps even to usurp for its own interests the supremacy of the political process.[22]

In the current attempts to apply management science to the human services, a number of dilemmas and problems emerge. Insofar as the administrator of a human service agency must be concerned with problems of choice based on efficiency and effectiveness criteria, the new tools may have value. Likewise, an administrator is also engaged in policy analysis to the extent that administration is concerned with the connections between objectives and alternatives, and again one sees potential applications of systems management approaches. Yet simultaneously, human service agencies are embedded in dense, interorganizational fields that not only constrain agency operations but also require the administrator to deal with the political dimension, to negotiate consensus, and for the sake of support, to trade-off one good for another. Moreover, to institute more or less formalized, quantitatively oriented systems in human service agencies involves complex and delicate matters of change in both the formal and informal life of the agency, issues that are sometimes neglected by the "black box" approach of systems management that tends to be preoccupied with "inputs" and "outputs," to the neglect of the "insides" of the box.

The problems are compounded because all the management tools with which this book is concerned have had their conceptual and methodological development entirely outside the human services. Social work, for example, is a synthetic field in which there has been much borrowing of concepts, approaches, and methods from a variety of other disciplines and that has often proven enriching. But cross-fertilization is problematical in the sense that ideas and tools need to be honed and adapted, all the more so when they are being imported from such dissimilar fields as business administration, industrial engineering, military and defense analysis, among others. However, to date, a time when attention is being focused on making the practice of administration more sensitive to efficiency and effectiveness criteria, there has not yet appeared a relevant, comprehensive "literature of adaptation" that attempts to translate into the human services the analytic and quantitatively oriented systems in a measured and careful fashion stripped of hyperbole and rhetorical excess. Consequently, there exists much confusion, ambiguity, and often disappointment in the attempted application of systems approaches in the human services. In addition, the literature on the new technologies is rather dispersed, not always easily accessible to the student, scholar, or practitioner in the human services.

This volume, designed to fill an important need in administration and management and to clear away some of the confusion, ambiguity, and misapplication of the new tools, aims to provide the needed conceptual mapping of the tools themselves together with examples of actual attempts to apply them in human service organizations. No claims are made that their application will transform human service agencies into well-oiled, smoothly running machines. In fact, unless administrators employ such methods judiciously, they may create or amplify organizational problems. Perhaps what is needed most of all is much greater illumination between the two extremes of polemical assault, on the one hand, and bandwagon enthusiasm, on the other. This volume therefore attempts to bring into focus the best from the fields of systems analysis and management coupled with representative applications designed to identify and illuminate important implementation issues and consequences. Thus, each of the succeeding five sections takes up in sequence, Planning-Programming-Budgeting Systems, Management by Objectives, Benefit-Cost Analysis, Zero-Base Budgeting, and Management Information Systems. In each of the sections, introductory notes are designed to provide the reader with the background and evolution of the methods discussed, some of the major types of issues, questions, or problems to which the tools address themselves, plus observations on the contributions and problems contained in the application articles. Finally the book presents a variety of well-reasoned criticisms and some possible alternatives to the future management of the human services. It is hoped that the new methodologies can be applied with the wisdom and good judgment befitting the complexities in the human services, or as Wallace Sayre once put it, that the "triumph of technique over purpose" can be avoided.

NOTES

1. The basis for distinguishing a "social service" from a "human service" is often not clear. Generally, the former is a subset of the latter and it is often equated with the domain of social work. While this idea is connoted in the use of the term "social services," the explicit reference is to those services included in the federal budget category, "social services," for example, services to individuals to promote independence and self-support and to reduce institutionalization, services for disabled, elderly, and other special groups, and community services, especially for the poor.

2. Paul E. Mott, *Meeting Human Needs: The Social and Political History of Title XX* (Columbus, Ohio: National Conference on Social Welfare, 1976), p. 12.

3. Drawing attention to differences between human service organizations and profit-making enterprises should not obscure important similarities between the two. In general, setting goals in the administrative or overhead units of private firms is no less problematical than the goal-setting process in human service agencies. Nor is the private firm the sole repository of efficiency, for there too one finds poor budgetary and planning controls, weakness in analytic capability, ineffective decision-making procedures, outmoded ways of dealing with information flow, and computerized information processing fiascos. Moreover, in a mixed economic system with semiadministered markets and prices, and multiple forms of government intervention, it can hardly be still asserted that "the market" operates as a singular determinant of efficiency and effectiveness.

4. Among those who have conceptualized dimensions of organizational technology are Eugene Litwak, "Models of Bureaucracy Which Permit Conflict," *American Journal of Sociology*, vol. 67 (2) September 1961, pp. 17–18; Charles Perrow, "A Framework for the Comparative Analysis of Organizations," *American Sociological Review*, vol. 32 (3) April 1967, pp. 194–208; Jerald Hage and Michael Aiken, "Routine Technology, Social Structure and Organizational Goals," *Administrative Science Quarterly*, vol. 14 (3) September 1969, pp. 366–75; James D. Thompson, *Organizations in Action* (New York: McGraw Hill, 1967). In general, the attempt is

made to link technology as a variable to the structure and functioning of the organization.

5. Charles E. Lindblom, "The Science of 'Muddling Through,'" *Public Administration Review*, vol. 19 (2) Spring 1959, pp. 79–88; David Braybrooke and Charles Lindblom, *A Strategy of Decision: Policy Evaluation as a Social Process* (New York: Macmillan, 1963); Charles E. Lindblom, "Still Muddling, Not Yet Through," *Public Administration Review*, vol. 39 (6) November-December 1979, pp. 517–26.

6. E. S. Quade, *Analysis for Public Policy Decisions* (New York: American Elsevier Publishing Co., 1975), esp. pp. 21–23.

7. For a variety of perspectives and applications see C. West Churchman, *The Systems Approach* (New York: Dell Publishing Co., 1968); Alvin W. Drake, et al., eds., *Analysis of Public Systems* (Cambridge, Mass.: MIT Press, 1968); Lawrence E. Lessing, "Systems Engineering Invades the City," *Fortune*, vol. 77 (1) January 1968, pp. 155–57, 217–22; Harold Geneen, president of ITT Corp., as quoted in John McHale, "Big Business Enlists for the War on Poverty," *Transaction*, vol. 2 (4) May-June 1965, p. 5; James A. Kalish, "Flim-Flam, Double-Talk and Hustle: The Urban Problems Industry," *Washington Monthly*, vol. 1 (10) November 1969, pp. 6–16; New York City—Rand Institute Research in 1970–1971, *Operations Research*, vol. 20 (3) May-June 1972, pp. 474–515; Ida R. Hoos, *Systems Analysis in Public Policy: A Critique* (Berkeley, California: University of California Press, 1972).

8. Helen O. Nicol, "Guaranteed Income Maintenance: A Public Welfare Systems Model," *Welfare in Review* vol. 4 (9) November 1966, pp. 1–12.

9. See Hoos, *Systems Analysis*, pp. 113, 202–206.

10. Jack C. Bloedorn, et al., *Designing Social Service Systems* (Chicago: American Public Welfare Association, 1970).

11. Bloedorn, et al., *Service Systems*, esp. pp. 25–36.

12. For some interesting examples of this general problem, see *Detailed Design of a Social Service Delivery System for the Bureau of Social Welfare, Department of Health and Welfare, State of Maine* (Chicago: Technical Assistance Project, American Public Welfare Association, July 1970); *Michigan Department of Social Services Delivery System Design and Implementation Requirements Workbook* (Lansing: Michigan Department of Social Services, January 1973). In the Michigan plan some of the specializations added were "client processing," "client programming," "service inventory management." As a result of the dysfunctions generated by excessive specialization, the department's largest unit reversed this approach with the establishment of a "generalist" model.

13. John Walsh, "Office of Management and Budget: New Accent on the 'M' in OMB," *Science*, vol. 183, January 25, 1974, pp. 286–90.

14. For a detailed description of these developments see Mott, *Meeting Human Needs*, esp. pp. 4–23.

15. National Conference on Social Welfare, *The Future for Social Services in the United States: Final Report of the Task Force* (Columbus, Ohio: National Conference on Social Welfare, 1977), pp. 64–71.

16. These distinctions are suggested by Guy Black, *The Application of Systems Analysis to Government Operations* (New York: Frederick A. Praeger, 1968), pp. 6–10. Many in the systems sciences agree that each is related to the other and that the distinctions are rather arbitrary.

17. Anthony Downs, "PPBS and the Evolution of Planning," in *Planning 1967* (Chicago: American Society of Planning Officials, 1967), pp. 91–99.

18. Hoos, *Systems Analysis*, p. 70.

19. Anthony Downs, "Comments on Urban Renewal Programs," in Robert Dorfman, ed., *Measuring Benefits of Government Investments* (Washington, D.C.: The Brookings Institution, 1965), pp. 342–51.

20. Murray Gruber, "Total Administration," *Social Work*, vol. 19 (5) September 1974, pp. 625–36; Rino Patti, "The New Scientific Management: Systems Management for Social Welfare," *Public Welfare*, vol. 33 (2) Spring 1975, pp. 23–31; Winifred Lally, "Social Services: Our Commitment," *Public Welfare*, vol. 33 (2) Spring 1975, pp. 7, 11–21.

21. Aaron Wildavsky, "The Political Economy of Efficiency: Cost-Benefit Analysis, Systems Analysis, and Program Budgeting," *Public Administration Review*, vol. 26 (4) December 1966, pp. 292–311; Hoos, *Systems Analysis*; Gruber, "Total Administration"; Patti, "The New Scientific Management"; Arnold Gurin, "Conceptual and Technical Issues in the Management of Human Services," in Rosemary C. Sarri and Yeheskel Hasenfeld, eds., *The Management of the Human Services* (New York: Columbia University Press, 1968), pp. 289–308.

22. Wildavsky, "The Political Economy of Efficiency"; Aaron Wildavsky, *Budgeting—A Comparative Theory of Budgetary Processes* (Boston: Little Brown, 1975); Jeffrey D. Straussman, *The Limits of Technocratic Politics* (New Brunswick, N.J.: Transaction Books, 1978).

PART I

Planning and Programming:

The PPBS Approach

Introductory Note

To a large degree the planning and budgeting processes in human service organizations are ill-coordinated and poorly designed for accountability. This is because budgets have been developed traditionally and presented in terms of objects of expenditure, or "inputs," in systems parlance. In this form, the budget focuses much attention on what is purchased and too little attention on what the funds are intended to accomplish. In other words, budgets do not often show the link between agency spending and agency purposes—between the resources an agency uses and its missions or tasks, now called "outputs." It is also rare that alternative methods to achieve objectives are elaborated and analyzed, that interdependencies between programs are taken account of, or that total costs and benefits are specified.

On what basis, then, are decisions made to allocate X dollars to Program A instead of to Program B? An assortment of factors other than the application of efficiency and effectiveness criteria are operative in such an allocational decision. For example, budgetary allocations are used as powerful political inducements to gain the support of internal and external interests; the budgetary base is zealously protected; the power of sunken costs tends to perpetuate the past; and various kinds of professional precepts and "rules of thumb" are invoked in budgetary decisions.

These constraints on rationality in planning and budgeting have made human service organizations prime candidates for one of the most widely publicized but least understood management tools, the Program-Planning-Budgeting-System (PPBS), a formalized approach introduced by President Lyndon Johnson into civilian government in 1965. Stripped to its core, that system was designed to link resources to purposes, inputs to outputs in a program, and by planning ahead for several years, to contribute to a better appraisal of what budgetary decisions would mean to an agency's program. Emphasizing a comprehensive view, PPBS exemplified the systems analytic perspective in administration and policy making.

Injected into federal civilian government from the Department of Defense, PPBS was heralded as a triumph of economic logic and rationality. To true believers, PPBS was the "most basic and logical planning which exists."[1] On the other hand, critics found much wrong with the system and some like Wildavsky argued that no one really knew how to do PPBS because it could not be stated in operational terms.[2] Partly, controversy over PPBS arose because when confronted with skepticism about the large claims for the system, advocates insisted that those claims could be realized only through installation of the system in a complete and tightly integrated way. Consequently, with its demise at the federal level, PPBS is mostly remembered for being procedurally rigid, excessively mechanistic, and for inflicting masses of paperwork of dubious value. The extreme formalism of systems analysis generated opposition, and in addition, some saw in PPBS a dangerous tendency to centralize power at the top of an organization, plus a naive attempt to quantify those things that cannot be reduced to numbers, a kind of technocratic arrogance in the name of analysis and accountability.

Despite the demise of PPBS at the federal level, and notwithstanding the controversiality of the system, its component ideas have proven enormously attractive and have become widely diffused throughout state and local governments as well as operating agencies in health, education, and social services. For example, a 1972 study of nearly 2,000 public and private institutions of higher education found that 30 percent had implemented PPBS concepts.[3] Also indicative is the experience of the states: within a few years of the federal introduction of PPBS more than half the states had been impelled to consider or attempt to implement PPBS, but by mid-1970, it was not yet fully operative in a single state. Moreover, Schick's five state analysis showed great variability in the implementation of PPBS with some states emphasizing the reconfiguration of budgetary data, others concentrating on performance measures in the form of workload, output, and efficiency data, some concentrating on the measurement of program needs, and in a few instances of attempts to determine effectiveness in meeting objectives.[4]

Within the human services, the early response to PPBS ideas was one of fairly general acclamation and lofty expectations, but these were later tempered by greater realism and subsequently waned. As a system PPBS proved difficult to implement owing to the great problems in specifying adequate measures of effectiveness, to difficulties in producing output or effectiveness data, and to the administrative problems in organizing and managing the analytic and evaluative components of PPBS. Because of the variety of problems encountered in implementing PPBS as a total system, partial system approaches now appear more practical for many organizations. Measured against the ideals of completeness embodied in systems analysis, hybrid approaches fall short; however, the potential value of PPBS may lie in just such adaptations of the formal system.

Steering a middle course between total skepticism of PPBS and inflated expectations of its potentials, the readings in this section will clarify the conceptual contours of PPBS plus a variety of operational issues. They will also distinguish the reconfiguration of budgetary data from the analytic or evaluative function of PPBS while looking at some partial system approaches to PPBS.

The General Terrain of PPBS. A classic but less doctrinaire and formalistic statement of PPBS principles is presented by Charles L. Schultze, former director, Bureau of the Budget. Schultze clarifies many of the problematic and potentially more troublesome aspects of PPBS, especially the criticism that PPBS places undue emphasis on quantification and thereby ignores "human factors and intangibles." As Schultze points out in his discussion of the meaning of "systematic analysis" in PPBS, the word "analyze" does not require quantification or measurement. Contrary to much common misconception, systematic analysis, says Schultze, is not co-extensive with quantitative analysis.

In the social services, especially the voluntary sector, PPBS concepts and applications were significantly advanced by the dissemination efforts of the national office of the United Way of America. Encouraging the adoption of PPBS by its member agencies, the United Way established a services identification system (UWASIS),[5] a comprehensive attempt to identify and define both voluntary and public programs which culminated in a four-level program structure. This structure moved from a very broad set of goals statements in descending hierarchy to increasingly more specific ones. With the framework of program structures in place, the stage was set for the introduction of PPBS to United Way budgeting. In "PPBS for United Way Organizations," the national agency explains the steps involved in PPBS and clarifies the meaning of "Planning," "Programming," and "Budgeting." Of particular interest is the relative flexibility of the approach, the emphasis on confining the analytic segment to "feasible alternatives," rather than to a comprehensive analysis of alternatives to achieve stated goals, and especially in light of the limited analytic capability of the many voluntary agencies, the relative lack of attention to the analytic segment of PPBS.

Establishing a Program Structure. The next reading by Paul L. Brown is interesting on two counts, the reconfiguration of the traditional line-item or object class budget, and the use of a participatory process. Line-item budgets, as Brown points out, must be converted into a program structure, a process known as the "crosswalk" or "conversion matrix." However, program structures are not received wisdom, nor are there any clear-cut rules for their development. Brown looks at this issue in a state level agency for Special Education, and by example, indicates the formidable conceptual problems in defining a program structure. Although these problems are typically handled at the upper levels of the organization, and indeed, PPBS has been severely criticized for its centralizing tendencies, there would not appear to be any inevitability to this tendency. As Brown demonstrates, it is possible to begin analysis at lower organizational levels, and to develop a program structure through a "bubble up" process. Again, absent is any attempt to implement the more difficult analytic aspects of PPBS.

PPBS in Service Delivery. As indicated, the technical features of PPBS include data aspects and analytic aspects. The former emphasize such factors as the realignment of the accounting code with the program structure, while the latter deal with the examination of goals, objectives, alternative programs, and measurements of outputs or effectiveness. Whichever aspects have been emphasized in the adoption of PPBS, insufficient attention has been given to the processes of organizational change that are involved. Most early advocates of PPBS simply assumed that a technically optimal PPB system would require organizations to be shaped in the interests of that system. And because PPBS was seen as a neutral tool, the role of technical analysts would dominate decision making and presumably make it more rational. "PPBS in a Community Mental Health Center" by M. Basheerudin Ahmed and David D. Stein is an interesting challenge to these assumptions. In this case illustration, systems analysis of alternatives was foregone in favor of a needs assessment and priority determination process that involved staff and community residents in the identification of new programmatic alternatives. Thus, rather than locating PPBS deep within the technical core of the organization, surveys were conducted off catchment area residents who had been involved in some way with the center, as patients, clients, or community advisory board members. Attempts were then made to integrate the data into a "basic PPBS framework."

A decade and a half has now elapsed since PPBS was introduced into federal civilian government and debate about its usefulness still continues. The original conception of PPBS fell of its own dead weight, its rigid formalism and self-defeating paperwork system. PPBS also failed because systems analysts and economists created a polarization between "rationality" and politics, exalting the one, denigrating the other, thereby failing to integrate PPBS into the political process. Whatever its defects, PPBS still remains enormously attractive particularly because of the current emphasis on "accountability." Serious problems remain, however. Even though the system has loosened, and some interesting participatory approaches have been developed, the more elastic does PPBS become, the more elusive its core methodology. Currently, the preoccupation is with program structures and the formalisms of program clarity and specificity, but the difficult analytics of PPBS remain a Gordian knot. Because of that, the collection of data appears to center on various measures of effort and "input" as well as a preoccupation with accounting procedures and paperwork, a far cry from the original intentions of the system. Thus, rationality, the original panacea offered by PPBS, seems to have been replaced by the trappings of budget reform. Whether PPBS will ultimately prove useful in altering expenditure decisions must remain an open question.

NOTES

1. Sen. William Proxmire, 91st Congress, 1st Session *Congressional Record*, vol. 115 (85) May 23, 1969, p. 1351.
2. Aaron Wildavsky, *Budgeting, A Comparative Theory of Budgetary Processes* (Boston: Little Brown & Co., 1975).
3. Lawrence Bogard, "Management Institutions of Higher Education," in *Paper On Efficiency In The Management Of Higher Education* (New York: Carnegie Commission on Higher Education, 1972), p. 11.
4. Allen Schick, *Budget Innovation In The States* (Washington, D.C.: The Brookings Institution, 1971); for an excellent analytic framework for the analysis of PPBS variants see James E. Frank, "A Framework for Analysis of PPBS Success and Causality," *Administrative Science Quarterly*, vol. 18 (4) December 1973, pp. 527–43.
5. *People And Programs Need Uniform And Comparable Definitions—UWASIS, United Way of America Services Identification System* (Alexandria, Va.: United Way of America, 1972).

2. The General Terrain of PPBS

What Program Budgeting Is

CHARLES L. SCHULTZE

Much has been published on PPB [Planning, Programming, Budgeting]. Learned articles have treated it sometimes as the greatest thing since the invention of the wheel. Other articles attack it, either as a naive attempt to quantify and computerize the imponderable, or as an arrogant effort on the part of latter-day technocrats to usurp the decision-making function in a political democracy. . . .

"What PPBS Is," statement of Charles L. Schultze to the Subcommittee on National Security and International Operations of the Committee on Government Operations, U.S. Senate, 90th Congress, 1st Session, August 23, 1967.

PPB is neither. It *is* a means of *helping* responsible officials make decisions. It is *not* a mechanical substitute for the good judgment, political wisdom and leadership of those officials.

The need for PPB, along the lines we are trying to establish, stems from two sources:

First, the resources of the government are always less than we need to accomplish all the good and useful things that we would like to do. Therefore, among competing claims on resources, we must choose those which contribute most to our national objectives, and we must execute our choices effectively and efficiently in order to free scarce resources for other good and useful things.

Second, government programs rarely have an automatic regulator that tells us when an activity has ceased to be productive or could be made more efficient, or should be displaced by another activity. In private business, society relies upon profits and competition to furnish the needed incentives and discipline and to provide a feedback on the quality of decisions. The system is imperfect, but basically sound in the private sector—it is virtually nonexistent in the government sector. In government, we must find another tool for making the *choices* which resource scarcity forces upon us.

Now to say that wise choice ultimately depends on good judgment is not the same thing as saying that good judgment *alone* makes for wise choices. Forced to choose among irrelevant alternatives, on the basis of misleading facts, and without the benefit of solid analysis, even the best judgment can do little but grope intuitively in the dark. PPB is a means to improve the decision-making process, in order to assist the final judgment, not to supplant it.

While I realize that the major outlines of PPB are familiar to you, let me summarize briefly its five major elements, as I see them, and then concentrate in some detail on several general aspects of PPB. . . .

The Nature of the PPB System

As the *first* step PPB calls for a careful specification and analysis of basic program objectives in each major area of governmental activity. The key to this part of the operation is forcing federal agencies to back away from the particular program they are carrying on at the moment and to look at their objectives. What are they really trying to accomplish? The objective of our intercity highway program, for example, is *not* to build highways. Highways are useful only as they serve a higher objective, namely transporting people and goods effectively and efficiently and safely. Once this is accepted as an objective, it then becomes possible to analyze aviation, railroads and highways to determine the most effective network of transportation. But so long as we think of the ultimate objective of the highway program as simply laying concrete, this comparison of different transportation systems is impossible.

At the same time, while we want to view our objectives broadly we are not helped at all by stating them too broadly. Highways or transportation, for example, generally may contribute to the good life and to national unity, but to take these as our sole stated objectives does not tell us much, if anything, useful about the desirable rate of highway building, the character of the highways, their locations, or their relations to other elements of our transportation system. In the case of highways, we want a specification of objectives broader than "laying concrete" but narrower than "improving our national life." As a matter of fact, there is a constant interaction between the decision process and our knowledge of our true objectives. Often, the more we learn about *how* to reach an objective, the more clearly we begin to understand the objective itself.

The *second* step, under the PPB system, is to analyze insofar as possible, the *output* of a given program in terms of the objectives initially specified in the first step. Again, for example, in the case of highways, we must ask not primarily how many miles of concrete are laid, but more fundamentally what the program produces in terms of swifter, safer, less-congested travel—how many hours of travel time are eliminated, how many accidents are prevented.

The *third* step is to measure the *total costs* of the program, not just for one year, but over at least several years ahead. In this year's budget, for example, $10 million in budget funds are requested for the Atomic Energy Commission to design a 200 billion electron volt atom-smasher. But the total cost of constructing this machine will amount to $250 million or more. We have commonly had some estimate of the total capital cost in mind when we have embarked on construction projects. This has not happened systematically, however. And we can't stop here. Once the machine is built, the annual operating costs will run $50 to $100 million per year. This is not to say that because of these costs we should decide to abandon the project. But it does mean that we should be aware of all the costs when we make the initial $10 million decision, not just the capital costs but the follow on operating costs as well. Or, to cite the highway example again, in deciding how to build an expressway through a downtown area we must take into account not only the cost of the expressway, but also the cost of relocating the displaced residents and, in a qualitative sense, the effects of the freeway on the areas through which it is to run.

All of this sounds obvious. Yet, too often large federal investment decisions have been made on the basis of the first-year costs alone—or made without taking into account all of the indirect associated costs.

The *fourth* and crucial step is to analyze *alternatives*, seeking those which have the greatest effectiveness in achieving the basic objectives specified in the first step or which achieve those objectives at the least cost. In the highway case, for example, we should be comparing the effectiveness of additions or improvements to highways with that of additions or improvements to aviation and railroads as a means of providing safe and efficient transportation. This does not mean that we pick only one. Of course, we should not. But we do need to decide, at least roughly, which combination of alternatives is the preferred one.

By this process we hope to induce federal agencies to consider particular programs not as ends in themselves—to be perpetuated without challenge or question. Rather, they must be viewed as means to higher objectives and subjected to competition with alternative and perhaps more effective programs. It is this competition among alternatives which is crucial as a means of testing the effectiveness and economy of existing and proposed programs.

The *fifth* and final element of this approach is establishing this method and these analytic techniques throughout the government in a *systematic* way, so that, over time, more and more budgetary decisions can be subjected to this kind of rigorous analysis.

Merely writing up academic papers is not enough. The analysis has to be an integral part of the budgetary decisions. The programming concept is the critical link that relates planning to budgeting, converting planning from paper exercise to an important part of the decision process.

Some Special Considerations

There are several aspects of this system which warrant special attention, in part because they have been subject to some criticism. Let me elaborate briefly on two of those aspects:

1. *Multi-year programs.* PPB, particularly as it is presented in brief summaries and—I must admit—as we first conceived it, puts heavy stress on *forward programming*—on laying out for five or ten years ahead a program of action in each major area of federal activity, be it highway construction, foreign assistance, or aid to elementary education.

Clearly, one cannot address the problem of the urban ghetto solely in terms of what can be done in a single fiscal year. If we restrict ourselves to such a narrow outlook, we will simply be rushing around putting band-aids on festering wounds. We cannot attack the problem of water supplies for the arid sections of the nation solely in terms of individual projects, or a slate of public works authorizations for a single year. Nor can we deal with problems of rising medical costs and scarcity of medical manpower by devising a series of one-year programs. After all, it takes 10 to 14 years to turn a high school graduate into a doctor. And a P. L. 480 program which ignored the long-run necessity to increase food production in the developing countries could, as we have begun to realize, do more harm than good.

A reasonable decision-making process must, therefore, provide the decision maker with a perspective longer than a single year. Ad hoc solutions are often extremely valuable. But in dealing with deep-rooted problems pure "ad hocery" can become a destructive force rather than a tool for good. And so PPB lays great stress on forward planning as an essential aid to decision-making.

But here we come up against a dilemma. When the chips are down, no president, no cabinet officer or budget director—or congress for that matter—is really willing to commit himself in advance to decisions in 1967 about the specific level of federal programs in 1970 or 1972. Nor should he be. There is nothing inherent, for example, in the nature of a P. L. 480 program which requires us to decide this year how much food aid we should provide in 1971 or 1972. The Elementary and Secondary Education Act—for which we have requested $1.6 billion in 1968—could be funded at several very different levels in 1971, depending on the fiscal situation, competing needs, and our evaluation of the merits of the program at that time. Some of our programs are frankly experimental, and we want to examine the results before we *commit* to full-scale activities—even though for *planning* purposes, we might assume a full-scale commitment. In other words, for most programs, our decisions today do not necessarily bind us to a particular level of those programs several years ahead. And there is no use pretending that we need make these decisions before we have to—indeed, making such decisions prematurely would be harmful.

At the same time, *some* of the decisions about this year's budget *do* imply legal or moral commitments about future budgetary levels. In the example I noted earlier, this year's decision about the 200 Bev accelerator clearly implies specific capital and operating outlays for many years to come.

A decision to shift the mix of airlift vs. sealift in transporting and supplying our conventional forces abroad, carries with it a whole series of implications about future budgetary levels. It is essential that we know, program by program and, at least roughly, for the budget as a whole, what costs we are firmly committed to next year from this year's budget decisions. Unless we know this, we can find ourselves unknowingly foreclosing future options by current decisions.

How do we sort out realistically this tangle of conflicting needs and problems with respect to multi-year planning and budget figures? We have begun to approach it as follows:

Each federal agency, for each of its major programs, is asked to present and evaluate those programs in terms of long-run objectives. To the fullest extent possible, programs are to be analyzed and this year's budget request justified in the context of forward planning toward basic targets.

But these long-run plans are not to be considered *commitments* on the part of the agency head. As you might expect, the sum total of all the forward plans of all federal agencies tends to exceed, by far, any reasonable projection of available resources. Consequently, the acceptance or rejection of this year's budget request is *not* to be considered an acceptance or rejection by the president of future plans. Rather, the forward planning is a means of evaluating current decisions in the context of a comprehensive analysis of problems and alternative solutions. It is an aid to current decision-making, not a premature commitment to future decisions.

At the same time agencies will be required to specify the future-year budgetary consequences of current decisions. For example, HEW may present a program for assisting the construction of medical schools in the context, say, of increasing the supply of doctors 35 percent by 1975. Analysis of the rationale behind the 1975 target and knowledge of the future budgetary costs of reaching it are an aid to making current decisions. But the program, within reason, can be accelerated or decelerated in succeeding years as conditions require. Hence, acceptance of *this year's* program implies no commitment about the specific rate of progress toward the target in later years. The future year costs of reaching the target are treated as planning aids, not immutable decisions. On the other hand, if the particular program for medical school construction envisaged entering into advance five-year commitments to match medical schools' own construction outlays with federal funds, then we would insist on having an estimate of the federal costs over the full five years. For in this case, the current year's decisions will definitely commit the expenditure of federal funds over five years—there would be no options left open, on the downward side at least. And these kinds of future year estimates, we must have.

In short, then, we are encouraging multi-year *planning*; we do *not* consider the forward years' part of the plan as a decision or commitment; except where current decisions bind us to future year outlays.

2. *Mathematics, statistics, computers and the decision process.* While our approach to the PPB in the past may, perhaps, legitimately be criticized for lack of precision about forward planning, there is another frequently heard criticism of PPB which stems, I believe, from a straight misconception as to what PPB is all about.

This criticism takes a number of forms. But basically it charges that PPB and cost-effectiveness analysis set up a bias in decision making: by concentrating on the cost accounting elements of an issue and ignoring those human factors and intangibles which cannot be quantified; or, conversely, by naively attempting to put numbers on these essentially imponderable elements, thereby misleading the decision maker.

Often this criticism is expressed in terms of an attack on PPB for trying to "computerize" what is essentially a political and judgmental process. Or sometimes it is expressed in terms of "not letting the statisticians and cost accountants take over."

I might interpolate, . . . that on the basis of my experience in government, which is limited, I will admit, this fear of the statisticians and analysts taking over ranks about twenty-eighth on my list of fears, perhaps just below my fear of being eaten alive by piranhas. I have many fears of government, and this is not one of them so far.

Quite frankly . . . these kinds of criticisms—however sincere—reflect a complete misunderstanding of the issue. And sometimes they simply reflect chagrin that particular pet projects do not show up well under the light of cost-effectiveness analysis.

PPB *does* call for systematic analysis of program proposals and decisions, concentrating upon those decisions which have budgetary consequences. But systematic analysis does not have to be and is not coextensive with quantitative analysis. The word "analyze" does not, in any man's dictionary, have the same meaning as the words "quantify" or "measure," although analysis often includes measurement.

Systematic analysis is an aid to policy debate. Too often these debates revolve around a simple list of pros and cons. There are no means of making progress in the debate, since participants simply repeat, in different words, their original positions. Systematic analysis is designed to improve this process by uncovering the irrelevant issues; identifying the specific assumptions and factual bases upon which alternative recommendations rest; and, tracing out the knowable consequences and costs of each alternative.

By this means, systematic analysis is designed to narrow the debate, to focus it on the important issues, and—I underline and stress this—to separate those points about which the judgments of reasonable man can disagree from those which are demonstrably true or false.

Now such analysis often does, and must, involve quantitative estimates. Most of our decisions—in fact, all of our budgetary decisions—willy-nilly involve quantitative consideration. For example, take the question of how many doctors to train and how much aid to give to medical schools. We can debate this simply in terms of arguing more or less budget dollars for the program. Alternatively, we can calculate the current and projected ratio of doctors to population, examine the relationship between the doctor/ population ratio and various indices of health, review the distribution of doctors throughout various areas in the nation, estimate the costs of training doctors, and a host of similar factors. We cannot, of course, measure precisely, or even close to precisely, the national advantages to be gained from a program of aid to medical schools, nor can we account for all of the costs. But we can isolate, in a quantitative form, a number of the key elements involved in the program. The debate then can proceed in terms of weighing fairly specifically the advantages the nation gains from alternative increases in the supply of doctors against the costs of achieving each alternative.

Handled properly, a well-constructed numerical estimate can be worth a thousand words. And, in PPB, we seek to encourage quantitative estimates, as part of the systematic analysis of budgetary issues.

But this, most emphatically, does not mean that quantitative estimates are the only elements of systematic analysis. The latter is far broader than the former. Human factors and intangible elements in a decision must not be ignored. And that which cannot reasonably be measured should not be.

In short . . . PPB does not represent an attempt to "computerize" decision-making or to measure the immeasurable or to ignore the intangible. It merely seeks to subject to systematic analysis both the tangible and the intangible elements of a program decision.

Prospects and Problems

Let me turn to our prospects for PPB and some of the problems we are facing.

As you know, it was two years ago this month when the president instructed that PPB be installed in all major civilian agencies. Not surprisingly, the application of PPB to twenty-one agencies so far (thirty-six agencies ultimately) dealing with a variety of national problems, has resulted in great differences in technique and result. Performance so far has been spotty, with great disparities between agencies and between constituent parts of agencies. This is due in part to differences in the extent to which agencies have worked out means of adapting and using PPB, and in part to the difficulty of the substantive questions involved.

From each agency we are requiring this year three formal kinds of submissions:

1. A *Program Memorandum* for each of its major program categories. These memoranda contain the major recommendations of the agency head for the coming budget; identify the major issues involved in the recom-

mendations, in terms of a selection from among alternative choices; explain the basis for the recommended choice among those alternatives.

Realistically, we cannot yet expect that every choice be backed up by a full analytic approach. Analytic staffs are just being developed in many cases; and there are thousands of issues. But we have required that where the analytic base is lacking, the Program Memorandum at least contain a clear statement of the reasons which were employed in choosing the particular recommendations involved.

2. *Special studies* of individual issues. These studies, addressed to issues of particular importance, form the analytic background for many of the recommendations in the Program Memorandum. Work on these studies should be a year-round affair, not something confined to the few weeks or months before the budget is developed.

3. A *Program and Financial Plan* which lays out in tabular form the costs and, wherever possible, the outputs of agency programs. This is a multi-year table. For future years, the entries show the future-year implications of present decisions—i.e., they do not reflect future decisions but only the future consequences of present decisions.

Some of the major problems we face are: maintaining a schedule that will permit PPB material to be used in the development of the budget. (One of our problems here is the crowding together of the analytic discussion of major issues and the detailed budgetary decisions which follow out major program decisions. Ideally, we would like to schedule this so that we first make major program decisions and then translate them into detailed budget issues, but, given the human frailties of the agency and Budget Bureau staffs involved, the decisions tend to get crowded together. It is a massive problem to sort them out, because we must do all of it in three or four months. This is a real problem and we have not licked it yet.); linking broad program analysis to the budgetary decision process in terms of detailed appropriation requests: HEW alone, for example, has 116 separate appropriations; securing appropriations for, and developing, experienced PPB staffs appropriately placed within the agencies to improve the quality of their planning processes; the difficulty of obtaining relevant data; the problem of defining program benefits in concrete and specific ways; the application of PPB to programs which require participation by federal, state and local governments; finally, convincing harassed and skeptical agency officials of the utility of PPB in their operation.

The list of problems is formidable, but I believe we are making progress. The Program Memoranda this year appear to be more useful than last, in terms of form and focus, if not in terms of analytic content. I think that a number of the documents this year will at least provide useful summaries of program strategy.

I look forward to substantial improvements next year in terms of schedule, understanding of the role and desired character of the Program Memoranda, and perhaps more important, in terms of their analytic content. Analytic staffs have been assembled and have had a chance to shake down; a number of data collection efforts and long term study efforts should reach fruition; and we are learning how to state program issues in a way that facilitates analysis and comparison. We have not yet by any means achieved my expectations for the system. That is partly because I have such high expectations for it.

Ultimately I expect we will realize those expectations. . . .

PPBS for United Way Organizations

UNITED WAY OF AMERICA

Background[1]

For many years, the method of accounting commonly utilized by voluntary human services agencies was "line-item," i.e., *object accounting*. These agencies recorded expenditures for the "things" bought, such as equipment, rental, salaries, travel, printing. This, then, became the financial information reported to the public. Budgeting followed the same "line-item" approach. In preparing their budget requests, agencies reviewed how much was spent for each line-item in prior years, projected the amounts to be spent for each line in the current year, and then used those figures, plus a factor for inflation and other cost increases, as the basis for their budget requests for the ensuing year. This type of budgeting is also known as *incremental budgeting*. Under this system whatever is already in the budget is more or less frozen—carried forward with no questions asked—and the focus is on current increments to that budget. The opposite of that system is what is known as *base-zero budgeting* where nothing is taken for granted, everything is questioned and examined.

With the publication of the *Standards* in 1964, the concept of *functional accounting* was introduced to United Way organizations. Functional

Reprinted with permission from *A "PPBS" Approach to Budgeting Human Service Programs for United Ways* (United Way of America, 1972), pp. 15–26.

accounting requires that agencies record and report their financial activities in terms of "programs" or "services" they provide, as contrasted with the practice of line-item accounting referred to above. This concept has been steadily gaining acceptance among human service agencies and United Way organizations. Incentive for adoption of the *Standards*–including functional accounting—has recently come from the Federal Government. The United States Civil Service Commission ruled[2] in early 1972 that agencies receiving funds from any of the Combined Federal Campaigns (CFCs) must conform with the *Standards* by the end of 1972. Thus, beginning with the program year 1973, the adoption of the *Standards* will be obligatory for United Ways and their member agencies who wish to participate in CFCs.

Functional budgeting is the distribution of all revenue and expenditures to general management, fund raising (if any), and the separately identifiable programs operated by an agency. Within each of the functional categories, income and expenditures are reported by object or line item, as in the conventional system. However, the ultimate report distributes overhead costs (management and general and fund raising) among program costs in order to arrive at an accurate accounting of the total costs of all of the agencies' programs.

Program budgeting as represented by the PPBS theory, is the next logical step in the direction of responding to the current concern for judicious management and prudent allocations of resources. As costs of supporting existing programs spiral upward and as new needs for human services emerge, United Ways come under increasing pressure to make difficult choices among competing demands for funds. Program budgeting is a tool for making rational the decision-making process as to which programs to fund, for what reasons, at what levels.

Program budgeting differs from line-item budgeting in that it focuses on the purpose(s) for which an agency is requesting funds. It is also a variation from the concept of functional budgeting because, while the use of functional budgeting does lead an agency indirectly to identifying the purpose(s) for which services are offered and funds requested, these requests, nonetheless, are merely an itemization of the dollars required to continue a given program or to install a new one. The important elements indigenous to the concept of program budgeting, namely, (1) a careful analysis of alternatives to a given program and (2) the linking of the program costs to potential program products (or results), are missing from the functional budgeting process. These two elements are built into the program budgeting process. The program budgeting process starts with the delineation and definition of the purpose(s) or objective(s) of the particular program selected—what is it that the chosen program is expected to accomplish?

The dollar amounts requested, though important, are considered only in relation to achieving a desired and agreed-to purpose.

Program budgeting (and accounting) adds, in effect, the dimension of annual evaluation of the programs which have been classified for budgeting purposes. It provides a procedure which enables the providers of services (agencies) and the providers of funds (United Ways) to collaborate on defining the objectives of the programs operated by each agency, to consider alternatives for reaching these objectives, and to accept or reject the alternatives for any given logical reasons. The end result is intended to be the achievement of continual relevancy to community needs and effectiveness of programs, through an annual evaluation intrinsic to the budgeting system itself.

In the ensuing pages, an attempt will be made to apply the PPBS theory . . . to the United Way system as functioning in a typical American community. By the United Way system is meant to include all those directly and indirectly involved in or affected by, the United Way movement in any given community, such as donors, consumers, and service deliverers. However, attention is primarily focused here on the two main actors—the distributors of funds, the United Way allocating instrumentalities, and the providers of services, the human service agencies. This is not an effort at how to implement PPBS in United Ways. It is not a manual nor a handbook of program budgeting. The attempt here is merely to show that it is possible for a United Way system to install program budgeting. Although the terms PPBS and program budgeting were used interchangeably in the first part, for the remainder of this paper, the term program budgeting will be used exclusively. The individual elements and steps in the program budgeting process are grouped, for convenience, as follows:

A. Planning
    1. Develop budgetary guidelines
    2. Identify and define goals
    3. Develop needed information
B. Programming
    1. Examine current programs
    2. Analyze feasible alternatives
    3. Define desired program changes
C. Budgeting
    1. Specify needed financial support
    2. Review budget requests
    3. Modify budget
    4. Allocate funds

Planning

The planning function is performed by both the United Way and agencies. The following activities are described without reference to sequence as they are interrelated and interdependent, and the sequence may vary in different situations.

DEVELOP BUDGETARY GUIDELINES

Agencies using program budgeting require, and United Ways expecting agencies to adopt program budgeting must provide, budgetary guidelines. Budgetary guidelines furnish vital assistance to agency personnel preparing agency budgets. In fact, they are absolutely essential if the budget request is not to be merely an incremental increase over the prior year's allocation. These guidelines should be communicated to the agencies early in the budget-making process. There are three major components to budgetary guidelines: assumptions; constraints; and priorities.

Assumptions. Assumptions are statements setting forth the social, economic or other external conditions which will most likely affect the community and should, therefore, be considered in developing the budget.

Constraints. Constraints are existing or projected conditions that will limit the range, level or method of operating for agencies. Since, as a rule, they cannot be bypassed, they should be recognized in the budget process.

Priorities. Priorities are statements setting forth the program areas which are considered most important and which a community, through its United Way, has decided to emphasize during the coming year.

Two aspects of priorities should be understood. First, they reflect the current concerns within a United Way's total and continuing field of interest. Thus, they represent an excellent way to begin the implementation of recommendations resulting from a priorities study, community survey, or other similar project.[3] Second, a priority is not a decision as to which programs will be approved and thus does not in any way preempt the budget review and approval cycle. It would be much easier to implement United Way's priorities if agencies were involved in the priorities-setting process.

The number and explicitness of the guidelines depend upon the local situation. These can be a few broad statements of policy or numerous very detailed parameters. The primary purpose of the guidelines is to assist the agencies, and this objective should be considered in the development of the guidelines. Finally, in formulating the guidelines, it is advisable to consult with agencies.

IDENTIFY AND DEFINE GOALS

The key element in program budgeting is the identification and definition of goals in clear and succinct terms.

A goal, in the context of a human services agency, is the statement of broad intent whereby the agency communicates to the public the problems it expects to solve, the conditions it expects to ameliorate, or the needs and aspirations it attempts to fulfill. The major tool available for goal identification and definition is UWASIS, which provides a conceptual framework for the entire range of human services, yet identifies most programs and services individually. A word about the use of UWASIS in goal definition is in order.

The UWASIS structure is designed to provide goal statements for most human endeavors on four different levels, each with increasing specificity. The top level—that of six broad human goals—is the most general. The bottom level—that of 171 programs—is the most specific. While most agencies will find it convenient to use the third level—that of the 57 services—for defining their goals, certain multi-service agencies may find it more appropriate to use the second level, that of 22 services systems. On the other hand, a single-purpose agency may find it more appropriate to go down to the fourth level—the programs level in UWASIS—to find a goal statement. For example, a blood bank agency will find its goal statement at the fourth, or programs, level in UWASIS, namely, ". . . to provide total blood and component supply to all persons in need of blood transfusion therapy."[4] A general rule might be: the broader the scope of services provided by an agency, the higher the level it might choose in UWASIS to find the appropriate goal statements, and vice versa.

Each participating agency should examine its current philosophy and purpose, and establish the goals it feels are appropriate. Hopefully, each goal will encompass one or more of the program services (functions) the agency is presently conducting. As a matter of practicality and common sense, agencies should ensure that its goals are not inconsistent with those of its local United Way, as explicated in the aforementioned budgetary guidelines. Further, goals should be identified and defined for all services operated by the agency, and not just those funded by a United Way. Since program budgeting is a way of improving an agency's total operations, the process described herein is applicable to all of the agency's services. Finally, agencies' goals reflect, as a rule, long-range concerns. They do not necessarily change from year to year unless the community's needs or the character of the agency change substantially. The above process would be followed in the first year a United Way and its agencies undertake program budgeting. In subsequent years, the agency need only review its goals to ensure that they are still consonant with the community's needs. Revision would be made when necessary.

The United Way for its part is obligated to the agencies and the community at large, to enunciate its goals and objectives. It is imperative that the United Way's goals emanate from a process of participation involving all segments of the community—business and industry, organized labor, minorities, professions, government, etc.—but, most importantly, the lay and professional representatives of member agencies. The spirit of partnership between the United Way and member agencies in developing the United Way's goals can be one of the major keys to the success of the program budgeting process in any community. A close and preferably structured interchange could result in harmonizing the goals of United Way and its agencies. But the responsibility for this task in the final analysis rests with the United Way, as indicated in the previous section.

DEVELOP NEEDED INFORMATION

Major inputs into the United Way's goal development process comes from a systematic development of information which get at: who is doing what, to whom, to solve which problems, and with what kinds of results. This type of information is essential for needs-delineating and priorities-planning, the two fundamental elements in establishing United Way's goals. It goes without saying that, in any priorities-planning process, the United Way must fully involve member agencies.

There are two kinds of data an agency needs in order to determine the type and size of program it should undertake to fulfill declared goals. The first is the size and characteristics of the group that requires particular services. This is called the target population. The other is the approximate costs that are presently incurred in pursuit of this goal.

Knowing the target population helps an agency executive determine the scope of the program necessary, and assists him in analyzing program alternatives with respect to the level of penetration of the program. Further, if other agencies are serving the same or a related need, a determination should be made of the coverage they provide.

Likewise, the estimate of expenditures, that will be incurred for each program and in pursuit of each goal in the current year, reveals the degree of community support that presently exists. It also helps the agency in the evaluation of potential programs and alternatives, particularly with respect to total cost and cost per unit served. These two factors represent yet another perspective for the analysis of program alternatives. Furthermore, knowledge of existing costs can be of substantial help for a determination of how much it will cost to provide a program in an ensuing year. Agencies using the *Standards*, and those which have chosen goals which are the end-result of the program services identified in their financial reports, will have already defined the expenditures for each program and the program goal(s).

Programming

The agency is now ready to identify and define the program it wants to conduct in order to accomplish its goals. Program budgeting, however, involves more than asking for monies by program. It is a process that promotes the choice of the *best* programs, a choice which the agency arrives at through a process of self-study. Also, it is a process enabling agencies to assess whether its current or proposed program(s) complement or duplicate similar or related programs under other agency auspices.

Three elements are identified.

EXAMINE CURRENT PROGRAMS

With respect to existing programs, the agency should include in its narrative: (a) a brief description of different activities forming the essential elements of the program; (b) the different categories of personnel utilized in conducting those activities; (c) the numbers and characteristics (e.g., age, sex, ethnic background, income level, etc.) of individuals served; (d) some measure of time span over which these individuals were served; (e) some indication of facilities and/or equipment and materials utilized in providing the program(s); and (f) the total cost of the program(s). Also, to the extent feasible, agencies should include in its program(s) narrative some measure of actual results achieved (e.g., "permanent housing was found for 250 families hitherto without homes"), if indeed, such are measurable. Finally the narrative for each program should be in sufficient detail so that its value and appropriateness can be determined in relation to other alternatives.

ANALYZE FEASIBLE ALTERNATIVES

The systematic identification and analysis of alternative ways of achieving stated goals is the cornerstone of program budgeting. In order to demonstrate to itself and to others why it chose the program(s) it did, the agency should identify and analyze feasible alternatives it considered and rejected and identify the advantages and disadvantages of each in such detail that the rationale for the selection is almost self-evident.

The following are examples of criteria that might be considered in such an analysis:

Feasibility. Is the alternative economically, socially, or politically feasible at this time?

Timing. Is this the "right time" for this type of program?

Legal Constraints. Are there legal barriers? For instance, in some communities, a family planning program might be prohibited by law.

Benefits. What benefits would the potential recipients of the services receive as a result of the alternatives?

Effectiveness and Efficiency. How effective is the alternative in achieving the desired impact. Is it an efficient use of available manpower and other resources?

Availability of Appropriate Manpower. How appropriate is the alternative for the agency's current staff? Do they have the necessary training, experience and expertise to implement the alternative program(s)? Are the necessary types of personnel available?

Capital and Operating Costs. How does the alternative program(s) compare in terms of initial and continuing financial requirements?

Possibility of Other Funding. Is the alternative likely to produce partial financial support from non-United Way sources, such as government agencies or program fees?

The above criteria are merely some of the factors which might be considered during an analysis of programs and program alternatives and should not be considered a uniform checklist for all agencies.

Questions are often raised as to the need for the documentation of in-depth analysis of alternatives considered but rejected. There is no hard and fast rule. Large organizations insist on documentation. Without documentation, it is difficult to demonstrate to the funding body that the agency has, in fact, gone through the analytical process. Here, again, it is a matter of negotiation between the United Way and the agencies as to what extent documentation is desired. The important point is that the agency abide by the spirit of the principle of rigorous program analysis in determining final programs.

DEFINE DESIRED PROGRAM CHANGES

The final step in the determination of an agency's program is for the agency to define any changes it wishes to introduce in its overall program. From time to time, an agency may determine that it is essential and appropriate to introduce changes in its overall total program. This decision might be prompted by changing community conditions, shifting priorities within a United Way, or a change in the beliefs of an agency. Thus, a separate step is included in the program budgeting process for the consideration of substantial changes in an agency's overall program. These changes may occur in terms of: (a) addition of one or more entirely new programs; (b) elimination of one or more existing programs; or (c) substantial modifications in existing program(s).

Consideration of program changes starts with an identification of the benefits the clientele group will experience because of the new or improved program. Then the agency identifies the alternative ways these same benefits can be achieved and the advantages, disadvantages and cost of each alternative. In the same vein as the prior step, the benefits, advantages and disadvantages, and program description should be dealt with in enough detail to demonstrate clearly why the change is proposed and why the particular alternative was chosen. In other words, it should reflect considerations similar to those described in the preceding step. However, in this instance, documentation of the agency's program analysis is absolutely essential to sound decision-making. The principles of program budgeting require it.

It should be noted that the three steps outlined above do not question the agency's choice or existence. Rather, they represent a framework that helps to assure that the agency has thought through its program choices. For many agencies, this will not be easy. There are programs that have been operated for long periods of time, and there are programs for which agencies may assert that no alternatives exist. Naturally, the appropriateness of programs and the potential number of alternatives vary considerably from agency to agency and from United Way to United Way. The important, indeed critical, element in the process, however, is that an agency considers *what* it is trying to accomplish (the goals), *how* it is trying to achieve this objective (the program description), and *whether* there are different ways (the alternatives) to achieve the desired objective. The intensity with which the agencies ask themselves, and attempt to answer, these questions reflects their appreciation for imaginative and prudent management.

Budgeting

Four steps are considered under budgeting: (1) specification of desired financial support; (2) reviewing budget requests; (3) budget modification; and (4) allocation of funds.

SPECIFY NEEDED FINANCIAL SUPPORT

As stated earlier, one of the major purposes of program budgeting is to enable United Ways and agencies to determine the amount of allocations with which the agencies can accomplish their goals in providing needed services to people in the community. Thus, once an agency has considered all the preliminary factors, i.e., goals, size and nature of the target group, expenditures presently incurred, *best* program, etc., its fiscal requirements for providing the programs can be specified. Since the agency has previously identified the kinds of resources necessary to operate a program, it can now estimate the quantities of each resource required and the dollars necessary to obtain them. Further, these financial requirements can be expressed in terms of the object expenditure categories contained within the community's standard chart of accounts. If, for example, a United Way has prescribed a chart of accounts based upon the *Standards,* each agency would state how much it needs for salaries to conduct a program, how much it needs for employee health and retirement benefits to conduct a program, etc. In the event that more than one program is operated in order for a goal to be achieved, the requests for various programs can also be aggregated into the total amount an agency is requesting to meet a goal. Similarly, the totals for all the goals, plus the amount budgeted for management and general activities, fund raising and dues or support payments to a national organization represent the agency's entire budget.

REVIEW BUDGET REQUESTS

Any allocation process requires that a budget be reviewed by an individual or group different from the preparer. In program budgeting, this review consists of an analysis by the appropriate United Way allocating instrumentality. The review is conducted from two points of view: (a) program goals and (b) program costs. From the point of view of the program goals, the United Way considers if the programs are in accord with the budgetary guidelines, if they will contribute toward the accomplishment of the accepted agency goals, if they will provide sufficient coverage considering the size of the target population, if the programs are feasible and the "best" choices among the alternatives. If a program change has been requested, the United Way considers if the benefit is clearly identifiable, if it is desirable and within the budgetary guidelines, and if the alternatives to desired program changes have been sufficiently explored and whether the chosen alternative makes sense.

The other review should be from the fiscal point of view. Have the agencies asked for sufficient staff and dollars, or too much? Are the requests within the budget guidelines? Are they computed correctly?

MODIFY BUDGET

The individual budget reviews, plus a compilation of all the budget requests and a comparison of this amount to the available monies—projected or actual—may indicate need for budget modificaitons. A United Way must consider not only what to support, but also the level of support that can be sustained in view of the total dollars requested for all programs from all agencies and United Way's own resources. Viewed in this context, a United Way allocator has two choices: to grant the agency request in toto or to allocate a reduced amount. In the event that an agency's budget request cannot be met, the United Way allocator may adopt one of two courses. The United Way may suggest specific changes in the agency's program in line with an allocation reduction. This, however, is a less desirable course and should be avoided if it can be helped. The preferred practice in this regard is for the United Way to estimate the dollar amount it might be unable to provide and then inquire of the agency how it would handle the reduction in United Way's allocation. This way agencies experience greater freedom of action in devising the necessary adjustments. This, however, does not preclude a United Way from specifying which goals should or should not be affected by the program adjustments. Under the circumstances, the agency is left with four options: eliminate all or part of the program; reduce the level of services planned under one or more programs; attempt to operate the planned program more efficiently by making certain shifts and adjustments in the use of its resources; attempt to make up the difference in allocation from sources outside of United Way.

The budget review process resulting in either reduction or increase in allocation should occur preferably before the campaign. This is because judgments can be exercised solely on the basis of the community's needs and priorities, established jointly by the United Way and the agencies, on the one hand, and careful analysis of all programs offered by all agencies, including a review of alternatives considered and rejected, on the other. The advantage of precampaign budget review and conditional allocation is that the decisions are not influenced by the exigencies of available dollar amounts. Theoretically, however, the timing has no bearing on the mechanics of the budget review and allocations process, since the judgments exercised are based on a careful analysis of what human services are needed in the community and to what extent they might be realistically expected to be funded. Albeit, final allocation must conform with the campaign results. However, the major decisions as to programs and program levels will have already been made. Since there is a difference of opinion and experience with regard to precampaign budgeting, it must be stressed that there is no hard rule in this matter. A preference is expressed here for stated reasons. United Ways and their agencies should have the option to decide this issue in close consultation with each other.

ALLOCATE FUNDS

This is the final step in the program budgeting process. The process ends when a United Way allocates the funds requested in the budget submission—or the resubmission, if required. The essential element to bear in mind for this final task in the agency budgeting-United Way allocating process is that the actual allocation amount—especially if it is less than the agency's requested amount—must be based upon specific details of the program(s) adjustments. In other words, the dollars allocated must match the program blueprint, as revised to fit a dollar figure different from the original budget request. The reason for this final note of caution is that sometimes, due to time pressures and other demands on the allocating instrumentalities, there is a temptation to utilize the original budget request as the basis for final allocation even though the support level is lower compared with the original agency request.

Conclusion

The growing complexity of modern life and the public's demand for services geared to contemporary human care needs have made the task of policy makers, planners, and United Way leaders—lay and professionals from funds as well as agencies—increasingly difficult. The range of problems and the possible range of responses have called into question old methods of establishing priorities, designing programs, controlling budgets and managing operations. The "old ways" were perhaps adequate for the conditions which prevailed at the time they were developed. It is now recognized that there are a number of weaknesses inherent in traditional approaches to budgeting: vagueness of United Way and agency goals-objectives; limited or no analysis of alternatives (at least not structured); partial costing of programs; inadequate or no consideration of future year implications of current decisions; short review and decision span; emphasis on expenditure control instead of performance–input orientation; minimal formal planning. The techniques of PPBS, or program budgeting, as discussed in this paper, can go a long way toward correcting many of these weaknesses.

United Way organizations shifting to program budgeting will discover that substantial benefits accrue from the disciplined thinking inherent in the system. Some United Ways are already on the path of program budgeting. So, also, are some of the voluntary national social agencies and their local affiliates. Program budgeting offers the following specific aids to managers of service institutions and agencies: the conceptual discipline for defining what the institution is doing; the process of sorting out expenditures so as to identify the direct and allocated costs; the process of relating the various types of funding to the purposes for which they were intended and of identifying the uses to which unrestricted funds are being put; the means for estimating with confidence the cost consequences of expanding or contracting any program and the related impact on other programs and facilities; the means for examining the financial implications of a program over a span of time; the concept (and, some time in the future, the means) of measuring the results of programs by some common denominator.[5]

It is suggested that United Way organizations desirous of installing program budgeting adopt a planned but gradual approach. A United Way may choose to start out on a *demonstration* basis with a few selected agencies willing and motivated to try it out. One approach to the incremental method might be to introduce program budgeting in one "service system." As the *demonstration* proves successful, more agencies are likely to consider switching to program budgeting. This switch will necessitate, at least initially, that United Ways provide considerable training and assistance to agencies adopting program budgeting. One of the prerequisites might be that functional budgeting has been installed and that it is operating reasonably smoothly for a majority of agencies. Finally, United Ways, having adequate staff resources, might want to try yet another approach to assisting member agencies. This approach would permit United Way staff to participate in the agency sessions in which programs alternatives and program changes are defined and examined, and to review the various documents from an analytical—as opposed to content—point of view.

Those who have grasped the spirit and the underlying principles of program budgeting will appreciate the degree of flexibility and simplicity inherent in the system. Installing program budgeting is like buying a house. One could buy an extravagant mansion or a villa; one could also buy a simple modest dwelling. The basic purpose of both types is the same—to provide shelter.

NOTES

1. The term "United Way Organizations" is used throughout this paper in a generic sense to apply to all local federated fund-raising, planning and allocations organizations by whatever names they might be identified, e.g., United Fund, Community Chest, United Crusade, United Appeal, United Community Services, Social Planning Council, etc. It also applies to allocating and/or planning bodies in communities where these are separate and independent from the fund-raising bodies. It includes agencies funded by these bodies.

2. See memorandum on this subject, dated February 29, 1972, from William Aramony, National Executive, United Way of America, to United Way Executives. The ruling requires certification on behalf of local United Ways themselves and their individual member agencies to the effect that the "Standards" have, in fact, been adopted. See also "Manual on Fund-Raising within the Federal Service," particularly Chapter 5, Sections 5.46f and 5.46j.

3. In some communities priorities plans might be for United Way dollars exclusively. In others, the United Way priorities might be in some way related to the total community priorities plan. In either case some coordination needs to take place between United Way's priorities and those set by other planning bodies in the community.

4. *People and Programs Need Uniform and Comparable Definitions—UWA-SIS, United Way of America Services Identification System* (Alexandria, Va.: United Way of America, 1972), p. 61.

5. Roderick K. McCleoud, "Program Budgeting Works in Nonprofit Institutions," *Harvard Business Review*, vol. 49 (5) Sept.-Oct. 1971, pp. 46–56.

3. Establishing a Program Structure

An Operational Model for a Planning-Programming-Budgeting System

PAUL L. BROWN

Purpose

One of the basic purposes underlying a PPB system is an attempt to furnish the most meaningful information to the decision makers. This includes all people who must make decisions about how functions are carried out. Thus efforts should be made to build a structure that can provide the necessary information for internal administration and result in an improvement in the ability of the governor, the legislature, the press and the general public to understand the budget and the services provided.

An Approach to Classifying Programs

One of the characteristics of PPBS is that it is goal-oriented. It focuses on the fundamental purposes for which government should exist and then relates all activities to one of these fundamental purposes. One of the first problems that must be faced is how to define these fundamental purposes. Some advocate stating the broad governmental purpose first and then identifying all the efforts that should be undertaken to fulfill that purpose. Others propose to start at the bottom and group all existing activities by some functional arrangement until they are all accounted for in terms of some stated objectives. The proponents of the top-to-bottom approach express their concern that the "bubble-up" approach contains the inherent danger that each administrative subdivision will continue its traditional

Excerpted from "An Operational Model for a Planning-Programming-Budgeting System," a paper presented to the Post Audit Seminar, Lexington, Kentucky (July 17, 1970), pp. 3–6, 12–24, by permission of the author.

Reprinted with permission from Fremont J. Lyden and Ernest G. Miller, eds., *Public Budgeting: Program Planning and Evaluation*, 3d ed. (Chicago: Rand McNally, 1978), pp. 185–97.

activities without challenge or change. This is a very real danger. However, I find some real problems of application in a methodology that works exclusively from the top down. For example, the Committee for Economic Development in its publication *Budgeting for National Objectives* recommends that the broad goals and objectives be stated and that agency activities be regularly subjected to a searching review to see that they conform to broad goals and government objectives. That committee developed definitions for several program levels. I tried working with some of the definitions and found it extremely difficult to arrive at very meaningful statements. For example, in Table 3–1 I have attempted to apply the definitions to the general area of education.

What disturbs me about this broad approach from the top down is that many of these definitions become almost truisms. They have to be refined through several levels before they become meaningful for immediate budgetary or operational purposes. These immediate purposes are areas in which we must make decisions today. We do not have the luxury of declaring a moratorium for three to five years until a new structure can be developed and refined. Maybe it is more proper to speak in broader global terms on the national level, but many state programs are already homogeneous entities which just need proper identification for ease in categorization, and a workable program structure could be established. I see more of a payoff in concentrating initial attention at a lower level of activity than the goals and objectives of government.

I am not convinced that a proper description of the objective cannot be started at an intermediate level, be properly evaluated, measured, and combined with statements for higher levels to reach a unified goal which can then be evaluated and worked back down. In this way objectives and subobjectives could be formulated, and perhaps better measurements could be developed more rapidly. The measurements would be designed to answer such questions as what is to be accomplished, who is the target population, how much change is desired, when and where is the outcome expected, and what information must be generated to determine just how effectively the stated purpose for carrying on an activity is being fulfilled? I do not wish to imply that the broad goals and objectives should be ignored. Indeed, they should not be. I am merely offering an alternative approach which is more workable in the short run and should result in essentially the same structure in the long run. I think my approach has the added benefit of being able to utilize some of the PPBS methodology for today's decisions as we go along.

Thus, by way of getting started on the development of a PPB system, at least at the state level, I subscribe to starting an analysis at the departmental level rather than at the "role of government" level. The final application

Table 3–1.
Definitions of the Committee on Economic
Development Applied to Education

Definition	Use for education
1. Goal: Statements of highly desirable conditions toward which society should be directed.	1. Everyone should be given the opportunity to be educated to the highest level of their capability to learn.
2. Objectives: The stated purpose of an organization or individual capable of planning and taking action to gain intended ends.	2. To educate everyone to the highest level of their capability to learn.
3. Programs: Time-phased plans for allocating resources and for specifying the successive steps required to achieve the stated objectives.	3. Identify operations for elementary, secondary, vocational and higher education.
4. Program Objectives: The specific results to be attained by the planned commitment of resources.	4. To provide higher (or elementary or vocational as the particular program warrants) educational opportunities for all.

is going to take a number of years and there is little danger that the major activities of a department are going to be terminated in the near future. For example, workable alternatives to operating educational institutions and mental hospitals will have to be developed if indeed there are alternatives. Therefore, for the time being, I suggest a concentration of attention on the role these major programs play in meeting our society's needs, how effective they are in these roles, and the relationships of their programs to each other.

Developing the Rationale for Defining Programs

Identifying the basic programs carried on by the state and determining what operations should be included in the programs is no easy task. Operations can be structured many different ways. It is necessary to develop a systematic approach that can be easily understood and universally applied. To accomplish this project the director of the Office of Budget and Management released an analyst from all other duties, assigned him as project director to plan, coordinate and direct the conversion, and provided a full-time systems analyst to aid in the design and control of forms and their related data flow systems. The professional budget analysts in the Bureau were then made part of the team. This approach enabled the project to gain the advantage of the ideas of all the members of the staff and yet provided unity of direction and decision making. With this organizational approach we found we were able to move very rapidly, converting the entire state to a program budget in less than a year.

The initial responsibility of this team was to study and define:

1. Just exactly what is program budgeting?
2. What are its objectives?
3. Can conversion be accomplished on a mass basis or must it be a gradual development over a period of years?

The purposes of program budgeting have been stated in a variety of ways. Perhaps the shortest, but probably one of the clearest, is that of Mosher in his book, *Program Budgeting: Theory and Practice with Particular Reference to the U.S. Department of the Army*. He states, "The program budget should be designed to furnish the most meaningful information for top administrative and political review" (p. 237).

Designing a program budget with this objective in mind makes the task one of analyzing the information needs of governmental decision making. The underlying assumption behind this statement is that the way material is presented to the governor and the legislature significantly influences the kind of decisions they will make. It is assumed if we present detail they tend to make decisions on detail. If we present program data identifying major policy issues they tend to make decisions on policy. This no doubt seems overly obvious; yet most of the arguments we have received have been that no matter how well we develop the format, the decision maker won't feel comfortable until he has gotten down to something small that he can understand more easily, and therefore, the whole concept of improving decision making is fallacious. Certainly we cannot be 100 percent effective, for old habits and individual differences exist, but we feel we have improved the decision making significantly.

Our view was that the first responsibility of the central budget office was to develop and present a synthesis of agency plans which would enable the constitutional intent of control of governmental activity by elected representatives to be implemented. We felt that all appropriations had to be built and all programs had to be defined with this end in mind. Convenience for agency administrators, the central budget office, or the central accounting agency should certainly be considered, but definitely, it should be subordinated to one of the basic needs of effective democratic government. We feel that one of those basic needs is the final determination of policy by elected representatives responsible to their electorate. This concept, that our budget format or synthesis should be a format which would best enable the governor and the legislature to make effective policy decisions on planned governmental programs, became our criterion for developing a program definition rationale.

The first thing we noted in developing a rationale for defining programs was that our appropriation structure did not conform to the general areas or units within which agencies planned their programs. The budget was not a formulation of agency plans, but rather a mechanical exercise in which the agencies took the dollar formulation of plans and recategorized the dollars according to the often meaningless appropriation accounts of the budget. The budget had become a reformulation of the dollars rather than a dollar formulation of the plans. The key policy decisions on planned programs were made prior and external to the budget formulation. As a result important policy decisions often lay buried in the mass of detail characteristic of the line-item budget.

Our solution to the problem was to attempt to find a program definition rationale which would define programs according to the categories and framework within which agencies planned. Appropriations could then be made to carry out these plans. We noted that agencies, especially the larger welfare and educational agencies, plan in two basic ways. They construct, sometimes very informally, long-range goals or plans based on growth, decline, or change in the nature of the population being served. Often cost per unit formulas are used to project the fiscal effect of change in the group to be served. It is here that many major policy issues are decided, that is, what groups or what percent of each group will be served, or what projections of growth, decline or change in the population will be assumed correct? It was important that our program structure would enable us to include and express these plans. We also noted, however, that these long-term program plans are translated into short- and long-range operational plans which correspond roughly to organizational units or subunits. Most of the remaining policy decisions are made here, that is, what will be the best administrative techinque for serving this group, and what geographical area will we serve? We felt that our program definition should enable us to include and express these operational plans, for it is usually in these organizational units that the detail of a budget originates.

We also wanted our program definition to facilitate coordination and synthesis between programs of different agencies. We hoped to be able to prepare and present "policy plans" on the demand of the chief executive. For example, it would be much easier for the chief executive to prepare a synthesized package plan to eliminate water pollution if the budget were expressed in planned programs that could identify the overall efforts in water pollution abatement. In effect a plan could be based and constructed around a policy—the elimination of water pollution. We felt that ease of synthesis could only be achieved if we developed a common language for all programs which could be used by all.

Thus, our basic criterion for a program definition rationale was whether it enabled every agency to define its programs according to the categories and framework within which they planned. This would enable us to present to the governor and the legislature planned programs and the policies inherent in them translated into the language of dollars. Our subcriteria which implemented the above goal were that the definition rationale should: (1) enable agencies to express policies inherent in their long-range program plans based on projections of changes in the population to be served (numbers, composition, and the like); (2) enable agencies to express the policies inherent in the operational, organizational plans; (3) enable the budget office to synthesize plans of separate agencies into comprehensive programs or plans implementing a specific policy.

The basic rationale that was developed for defining programs centered attention on what service a legitimate state activity provides and who is to receive these services. The most important advantage of this rationale is the estimation of total impact of the services being provided for any particular clientele. Such an approach bridges the two basic orientations, the inner direct "what," with the outer directed "for whom." The concept, simple as it sounds, is an innovation in budgeting, making it conform to the realities of political allocation of resources.

Thus, we had developed a common language for program definition which we called the *what, for whom* and *how* program definition. Briefly, this definition involves taking an agency's operations and asking, "What are you doing?"; after this question has been answered, we ask, "For whom are you doing it?" This gave us a basic program definition, and one which was easy to follow.

After we had the basic program identified, we needed to get more specific and identify program sublevels. For the first sublevel we again used the same "what for whom" rationale, but added the ingredient of asking "what more specifically is done" or "for whom more specifically is it done?" After the "what for whom" had been answered for two levels of program operation, the next question was "how are you doing it?" For example, what administrative techniques or activities are performed to carry out the services? This original approach has now been refined to use a basic building block, the program element, which is described below.

The next determination that is prompted by the information on how you are doing something is "how well are you doing it?"—that is, how well are

CARNEGIE LIBRARY
LIVINGSTONE COLLEGE
SALISBURY, N. C. 28144

you performing each one of these activities of community services, institutional treatment, and so forth? We had to draw a practical line somewhere on the extent of our conversion. As I mentioned before, we decided to convert the entire state in one conversion process because the time was opportune. We wanted to go as far as necessary to get a program budget and to get an appropriation structure that conformed to the programs. But since there was the danger of such a major undertaking collapsing under its own weight, we decided to stop with "how" and not go immediately into "how well."

The distinction between "how" and "how well" is, in our own language, where program budgeting ends and performance budgeting begins. We felt that it was enough in the initial conversion phase to define the major services being provided and how they were carried out, and that later, following the conversion to program budgeting, we could more scientifically identify "how well they were doing something" by the development of performance information on how extensive, how efficient, or how effective a program was operated. We thought we had to make this distinction because "how they were doing something" involved the time-consuming task of identifying the units of accomplishment for all of the sometimes indeterminate programs in state government. As we all know, identifying workload units, identifying the cost, distinguishing the fixed from the variable costs that go into these work units, are a time-consuming process. We felt that in using mass conversion techniques we had to postpone the performance element at this time and just define the major program areas.

Successful operation of a program budget requires a very careful definition of the programs and program sublevels carried out by a state agency. Programs are the basis for appropriations, and it is most important that programs and other breakdowns be defined so as to produce the most effective appropriation structure. All efforts put into a careful definition of programs will be rewarded with a successful appropriation structure in the years to come.

Wisconsin's Basic Program Structure

The basic concept of our program budget is to relate costs of government activity to services provided. This concept established our approach to grouping agency services. The Wisconsin program structure consists of a grouping of the basic units of governmental operations, starting with the most general and proceeding to the most specific. It includes the following general categories:

1. Functional Areas
2. Programs
3. Subprograms
4. Activities

Following is an explanation of these basic units with specific examples of how agency programs are classified in terms of these units.

1. *Functional Areas.* A program structure of state government should outline the basic purposes of state government and should be divided into program areas which are broadly encompassing and self-contained, yet easily definable in relation to each other. Each functional area has a purpose, goal or end product which is intrinsically different from those of other functional areas.

Wisconsin functions have been categorized as follows:

Commerce
Education
Environmental Resources
Human Relations and Resources
General Executive Functions

2. *Programs.* The major functional areas are in turn divided into programs carried out by state agencies. In the context of the program budget structure, programs are defined as: "A broad category of similar services for an identifiable group or segment of the population for a specific purpose." Programs are thus defined in terms of what services are provided for a group with similar disabilities, needs or attributes, or "What is done for whom?" For example, in our public instruction department one program we have identified is:

What	*For Whom*
Education and Related Services	Handicapped Children

3. *Subprograms.* Subprograms are defined as "A breakdown of the program into units which identify more specific services or a more specific segment of the population."

Programs are thus categorized into subprograms to the point where the subprograms defined serve a more specific group because it has only one basic disability, attribute or need, or "What for whom more specifically." For example, in the major program of (What) Education and Related Services for (Whom) Handicapped Children, the term handicapped identifies a group with broadly similar attributes. However, this group can be divided into subprograms because there are meaningful groups served within the general category of handicapped children: They are distinguishable because they have a more specific disability or attribute than "handicapped." For example:

What	*For Whom*
Program I: Education and Related Services	Handicapped Children

What	*For Whom* *(more specifically)*
Subprogram A: Education and Related Services	Crippled Children
Subprogram B: Education and Related Services	Visually Handicapped children
Subprogram C: Education and Related Services	Deaf Children

This identification of subprograms should make it possible to divide the program to the degree that the group served has a reasonably homogeneous disability or attribute. The decision-maker can now decide on the allocation of resources among competing groups.

Further categorization into subprograms is unnecessary. A further breakdown of Educational and Related Services for Visually Handicapped Children into services to the slightly blind, moderately blind, and totally blind is meaningless to those who are attempting to make a policy decision, for it would be based on the degree of disability not a kind of disability. The degree of disability does not identify an actually distinct interest group. More value will be gained by concentrating on the administrative techniques which accommodate the individual needs of the persons with the group which has a basic disability, such as being visually handicapped.

4. *Activities.* Activities have been defined as: "the administrative techniques employed to carry out the programs." Subprograms would, therefore, be broken down into the activities which illustrate *how* the service is performed for the group. For example:

What	*For Whom*
Program I. Education and Related Services	Handicapped Children

What	*For Whom* *(more specifically)*
Subprogram A. Education and Related Services	Crippled Children

How
Activity 1. Orthopedic Hospital Services
Activity 2. Financial Aids to Individuals
Activity 3. Aids to Orthopedic Schools
Activity 4. Transportation Aids

What	*For Whom* *(more specifically)*
Subprogram B. Education and Related Services	Visually Handicapped Children

How

Activity 1. Resident Instruction
Activity 2. Aids to Special Classes

MODIFICATIONS OF THE STRUCTURE

In the general approach and examples cited above, subprograms constitute a further clarification of the group (Whom), while the services (What) remained constant. This approach will be applicable to many programs, especially those in the health and welfare functions. In some cases, however, the group already constitutes a homogeneous group, and the most meaningful further breakdown would be a clarification of the type of service or the means by which it is accomplished. Following are some potential methods of developing meaningful breakdowns under these circumstances:

1. When a variety of related services is performed for one homogeneous group, it may be more meaningful to define subprograms by more specific statements of "what" is done rather than more specific statements of "for whom" it is done. The Department of Administration is an example of meaningful subprograms being more specific breakdowns of "what is to be done." It might be classified as follows:

What	*For Whom*
Program I. Administrative Services	All State Agencies

What *(more specifically)*	*For Whom* *(assumed the same)*
Subprogram A. Accounting Services	

      B. Architectural and Engineering Services
      C. Budget and Management Services
      D. Data Processing Services
      E. Operational Services
      F. Personnel Services
      G. Printing Services
      H. Property Management
      I. Purchasing Services
      J. State Planning Services

2. In some circumstances, both the services (What) and the group for whom it is performed (Whom) already constitute a reasonably homogeneous unit. In these cases it may be most meaningful to break down the program immediately into activities, instead of further clarifying the services or the group. A good example is civil defense operations. It is a single

type of service and it is performed for everyone in the state. Civil defense might, therefore, most meaningfully be divided into the "hows" (activities) of administrative techniques.

		What	*For Whom*

Program I. Preparation for Disasters   *(everyone implied)*

	How

Activities   A. Shelter Development
          B. Food and Clothing Storage
          C. Storage of Medicines
          D. Transportation Planning
          E. Communications Development
          F. Monitoring Radio Activity
          G. Training of Emergency Personnel
          H. Administration

Caution must be execised in the use of this approach of immediately categorizing programs into activities instead of further clarifying the service or the group for whom the service is performed. Program budgets are aimed at assisting the governor and legislature in making policy decisions on the type of state services and the level to be provided for the recipient of the services. Seldom do the governor and legislature make policy decisions about the administrative means of providing services. This last approach of immediately categorizing programs by administrative techniques should be used only when it is clear that further clarification of the group or the service is completely without meaning to the governor and the legislature.

FURTHER BASIC CONSIDERATIONS

As an agency's operations are reviewed there is no uniform level of development which should be sought. In some cases, a program identification may be all that is desired. In other cases, it may be advisable to break out the activities into subclassifications. Basically we should be attempting to construct an overall structure that will enable us to identify and consider the lowest program sublevel that is presented as an autonomous building block that we can consider as a program element. Around this program element we should attempt to define the basic purpose of this element; determine what kind of performance indicators need to be developed to assess the adequacy of the program to carry out that basic purpose; and include this element as an identifiable entity in our accounting system, our reporting systems, our statistical systems, etc.

One of the primary advantages in the identification of these basic building blocks is the ability to develop a broader executive program budget which makes it possible to identify major problem areas and/or specific target groups served by related programs in separate agencies. An example of this type of executive program budget might be in the area of recreation. Today, we may not have any program which we would formally identify to focus on recreation. However, there are several activities which we are carrying on which pertain to recreation. Such activities appear, for example, under hunting and fishing, game management, parks, forests, and open-area development. We also might want to identify other areas of concern which we should be preparing to meet. An area to consider could be educating people on how to use an increased amount of leisure time that will develop through shorter working weeks, earlier retirement, and so forth.

A fully developed program structure should enable us to pull out all of these activities that are related to a specific executive program budget that we might want to develop; line them up; determine what basic purpose each of these activities is designed to serve; determine how effectively they are meeting this basic purpose; and determine whether or not the purposes of the various activities are in conflict or whether the administrative techniques used to carry out the activities are in conflict. If it is decided that the program is important enough to warrant making it a special program, we could then pull these basic building blocks out of the various programs and assign them to a new program. However, if we did not care to alter the program structure we could still pull them out for informational purposes to look at them in a different context or a different frame of reference. Consequently, our attention must be directed toward defining the rationale that will enable us to properly define these program elements. Proper identification is necessary to insure that these elements are really the building blocks around which we want to concentrate our efforts in building our management information systems.

4. PPBS in Service Delivery

PPBS in a Community Mental Health Center

M. BASHEERUDDIN AHMED and DAVID D. STEIN

During the last few years, many businesses and organizations have faced serious belt-tightening as a result of shifting national and local priorities, inflation, and a general state of affairs where technological development has demanded greater expenditures than the economy has been able to accommodate. In particular, social service and educational programs have been hard hit by repeated budget cuts and increasing demands by funding bodies to account in fiscal and programmatic terms for the utilization of resources.

In the mental health field, agencies dependent upon governmental funding have been required to account rigorously for their services in order to justify current operations and expansion. Skilled administrators, budget experts and management systems personnel are being sought to fill positions created in these agencies to meet the need for greater accountability. This trend represents a new harsh reality for professionals who are not accustomed to precise analysis of their work.

This paper relates how a comprehensive community mental health center reacted to demands for more precise accounting and adapted a Planning-Programming-Budgeting System (PPBS) to its needs. . . .[1] The system itself is an exemplar of rational thought and analysis. Yet, in its application, many irrational elements are encountered. The problems in its application by the Defense Department during the early 1960's and in the War on Poverty were due not only to its complicated nature, including detailed fiscal and program decisions, but also to the highly developed resistance of many people to lay bare for scrutiny their basic values and assumptions. . . .[2] If we lived in a world where decisions were made solely, or even primarily, on the basis of rational judgment, merit and expertise perhaps everyone would be willing to work with a PPBS type system. But when the decision-making processes in our society are interwoven with

Reprinted with permission from *Administration in Mental Health* 3, no. 1 (Fall 1975): 79–85.

political considerations, racial and class prejudice, and other obstacles to rationality, PPBS can be expected to meet resistance.

The experience of the Sound View-Throgs Neck Community Mental Health Center with PPBS has caused us to look at previously hidden or tacit assumptions. Although considerable heated debate has resulted from our use of PPBS, it is the kind of debate that is healthy for an organization. Examples of the issues that arose will be discussed below as we explain how and why the center moved toward the use of PPBS and, in particular, how it was utilized in the preparation of an expansion grant for children's services.

Budget Concepts

The traditional line-item budget can be defined as an instrument of administrative control. It rigidly regulates expenditures, limiting the discretion of the director. The line-item budget bears no relationship to organizational goals and objectives. This makes it difficult to estimate the cost of a specific program designed to achieve certain goals.

The line-item budget is organized according to categories such as personnel, other than personal services, equipment and rent. It is basically a description of lines used for hiring professional, paraprofessional and support service personnel in any given program. There is no requirement to report the activity of this personnel. Therefore, no comparisons can be made to establish cost effectiveness. The basic information used in preparing the budget request includes the budget for the current year, actual expenditures and an estimate of salary adjustments, promotions, and other increments. On certain occasions the funding agencies provide guidelines for a fixed percentage as a cost of living increase.

New programs are generally provided under an *expansion budget*, with separate budgets required for each new program. Mental health agencies do not generally receive advance guidelines from funding sources. As a result, directors have to guess about whether additional funds are likely to be available for expansion, and the kind of new programs most likely to attract support. This encourages efforts to seek funds for their own sake instead of concentrating on previously determined priority programs. Thus, survival pressures conflict with sound management and program direction.

A program budget can be defined as a financial plan that clearly outlines organizational goals and provides a basis for the analysis of costs, activities and outputs. Feldman[3]. . . points out that the program budget can be used as a measure of organizational goals, activities, and functioning. It can be used as a management tool, not merely as a control device. McLeod[4]. . . has indicated that program budgeting permits disciplined organization of the economic data relative to a decision about the allocation of resources. This budgeting approach provides information about program costs and helps to evaluate the financial impact of a program's expansion or contraction. It can also help with estimates of a program's future economic demands.

Ideally, under PPBS, each agency should first develop a master plan, including a careful assessment of consumer needs, the nature of the community being served, and its own administrative structure and functions. Methods for coordinating the overall program and a delineation of consumer and provider roles in program planning, development, operation, and evaluation are detailed in the plan. Program priorities and the projects to accomplish them are specified and alternaiive approaches are analyzed. Consideration should also be given to possible alternate providers of service where appropriate.

After the master plan has been carefully developed, budget program accounts are defined. Budget program accounts are a categorical system of program functions. They must be accompanied by specific operational objectives for each program offered by the center so that services can be evaulated in terms of goal attainment. For example, in developing outpatient programs for children the following objectives may be considered: providing mental health services to a specific number of children in a previously unserved group; or a reduction of hospital admissions through crisis intervention. In order to progress toward the achievement of its objectives, the center operates certain programs, each offering one or more kinds of services. By measuring accomplishment in terms of specific objectives programs purporting to achieve the same results can be compared between centers.

Once the budget program accounts are set, the center allocates a percentage of its total human and material resources to each. These allocations determine the relative amount of the total budget devoted to each function or program. For example, if a budget program account is set up for alcoholism and 10 percent of the total budget is allocated to it, then that is the amount to be used for alcoholism programs during that year. If drug abuse has no assigned account, the organization should *not* be providing any drug abuse services.

For each budget program account, the center must specify the goals to be achieved in operational terms, the activities planned to achieve these goals, the number of people to be served, the staff assigned to each activity, and the costs. Although this is a tedious process, it provides the information necessary to compare dollar costs with achievements. In this way, a center's program is appraised by determining whether the amount of service originally budgeted was provided and at what cost. To the extent that it can be ascertained, the impact of these services would constitute the prime measure of accountability.

It is not possible to measure the performance of every program within a mental health agency in quantifiable terms. In such cases, objectives, activities, treatment modalities, number of clients served and costs are combined into a single statement of program effectiveness. This may consist of a description of the actual work done during the period, the relative stages of development of various activities and anticipated dates of completion. In programs such as consultation and education, the product can be measured by the number of sessions provided, classified according to the nature of the group served. Wherever possible, this approach should be refined to meet the requirements of the more precise budget program account system described above.

Each program will have both direct and indirect costs. Direct costs are those that are directly attributable to a specific program. Indirect costs such as rent and electric are allocated to each program using a standardized formula. Total program cost should be controlled by the program director, who must balance direct and indirect costs so that they do not exceed the amount of money allocated to operate the program. This dollar amount is directly related to the priority value of the program within the organization's specified plan.

Saul Feldman[5]. . . has pointed out that an effective program audit can be used as one standard to evaluate efficiency. Such an audit is a quantitative method of assessing the extent to which the mental health center has achieved its objectives in terms of both cost and productivity. Evaluation of the services of a mental health center, however, must go far beyond considerations of efficiency. Feldman has further commented that quantitative accomplishment constitutes only a limited yardstick of performance, measuring only efficiency rather than effectiveness in any value sense. Yet, it is felt that established priorities and defined objectives are inferential indicators of these broader values.

Application of PPBS to SVTN-CMHC and Its Children's Services

In 1972, the New York City Department of Mental Health and Mental Retardation adopted PPBS as its primary instrument for evaluating agencies, hospitals and clinics. Unfortunately, the city chose to utilize only part of the system. It required reports on the performance of professional and paraprofessional staff including their activities and kinds of services provided, number of clients served, time spent and costs. These efforts were not related to specific service objectives. Thus, "apparent success" could be achieved by having the lowest salaried staff members see the largest number of clients. A "cost-activity" ratio in such a case would be extremely low. The city did not seek to determine the quality of the services provided. To its credit, the Department of Mental Health and Mental Retardation has promised that as soon as it "debugs" the system, it will incorporate the full complement of PPBS categories.

The Sound View-Throgs Neck Community Mental Health Center (SVTN-CMHC), in an effort to learn the new PPBS "language," arranged for a two-day workshop on the rudiments of the system. Expert consultants led intensive, practical training sessions for the center's top and middle management staff. With the basics of PPBS understood, staff members were able to apply the concepts to the center's operations. Some additional follow-up consultation further enhanced our understanding of this very complicated system.

We learned that in order to use PPBS it was necessary to reassess our priorities and reallocate our resources. This process might lead to major shifts of staff from one program to another, hiring new staff, retraining others, or even encouraging some staff to leave. It was finally decided to examine our priorities in those areas where the center provided either limited services or none at all. In that way, minimal strain would be placed on staff and desired services could be developed and delivered without long delay. This assessment of service gaps involved substantial community involvement.

In essence, we surveyed all staff members and catchment area residents who had been involved in some way with the center, as patients, clients, or community advisory board members. We also surveyed Spanish-speaking residents reached through local Hispanic clubs. They were asked what they thought were the most important services the center should offer. The survey results were tabulated and categorized. A second questionnaire based on these results was then distributed to the same people asking them to select three areas that should receive priority in utilizing existing funds and seeking additional grants. The checklist included only those areas in which the center was already offering minimal services that might need to be expanded.

In summary, staff gave highest priority to children's services, crisis intervention, services to teenagers and families. Community respondents chose drug addiction services, services for teenagers, families, and children, and assistance to neighborhood groups. Services for youth were emphasized by both staff and community. The community choices of drug addiction and neighborhood group assistance appear to reflect community concerns most visible and salient to those who live in the area.

The more difficult task of deciding whether the center's allocation of resources to the operating programs and services should be changed was deferred, pending an assessment of the center by an outside management consultant. Although it is logically possible to change priorities and develop new programs within a center, there are many constraints on such a process. Certain components are mandated by legislation and must be included in any community mental health center. Some of these, such as inpatient care, are very expensive and this limits the extent to which priorities can be reordered. It is our expectation, therefore, that any changes in our program priorities are likely to be moderate.

Master Plan

Although the SVTN Center did not draw up a formal master plan as outlined above, many of the steps were carried out informally. For example, community and staff views were assessed as in the surveys briefly described above. The priority given to services for children was supported by other human service agencies in the community. These included public health nurses, schools, day care and head start centers. A study by the Joint Commission on the Mental Health of Children[6]. . . showed (when extrapolated to our area of service) that approximately 7,000 children, 18 years of age or less, were in need of some kind of professional mental health care. We now had to translate this obvious need into specific programs. When funds became available in 1972 for children's services under Part F of the CMHC Act the Center submitted a grant proposal.

Rationale for Proposed Programs

Our first task was to determine a rough dollar ceiling for the proposed programs, one that would have a reasonable chance of success. Funding bodies were not able to offer specific guidelines because national priorities were in a state of flux, and no one could know how many centers would apply for the newly released funds. In addition, local and national bodies had conflicting priorities, even within the area of children's services.[7]. . . It was generally suggested that we submit a request for a "couple of hundred thousand dollars." Given this figure, we set about determining the exact nature of the programs to be proposed by the center.

SVTN-CMHC has always provided a substantial consultation and education service with ten to fifteen full-time staff members working with community groups, agencies and schools. These services include children and operate essentially within a framework of primary prevention and organizational development. Since we were clearly not meeting the need for direct services to children we decided to focus our grant proposal on this area. Further, New York City officials had clearly indicated to us a preference for direct services. We were also aware that we would be perceived more positively by others in the community if we offered additional direct services. This would help soften some previous criticism that our consultation and education program was a luxury. A joint staff and community committee was created to discuss the kinds of direct service programs that would most effectively meet the needs of young people in the area, one that would complement our current efforts, as well as the programs of other agencies.

The Proposed Programs

Under PPBS, it is possible to prepare a grant proposal with a variety of programs so interlinked that a review committee would have difficulty eliminating part of the proposal without adversely affecting other parts. An applicant can adopt this strategy if grant approval appears to be a good prospect since it minimizes the possibility of cutting down the proposed programs. If, on the other hand, approval is in doubt, the applicant is in a better position by proposing relatively independent programs so that at least some may be funded. The center chose the latter strategy, and we were very pleased to have our entire proposal funded.

In brief, two programs were designed for preschool children. One was for high risk children of low-income families with at least one parent with a history of mental illness. This program focused on improving the cognitive, social, and emotional interaction pattern between parent and child. The other preschool program was a nursery for disturbed youngsters including two or three days a week of outpatient therapeutic treatment and activity.

The most severely disturbed nonhospitalized school-age youngsters in our area are on waiting lists for special education programs or receiving home tutoring. For this group, we proposed a Psycho-Educational Day Care Center (renamed the Children's Day Treatment Center), staffed by SVTN clinicians working with trained teachers and paraprofessionals assigned by the Board of Education. For children with moderate-to-severe problems, we proposed treatment by clinical staff in our outpatient units and counseling services within the school setting. These were expansions of existing center programs.

We also proposed a program to serve adolescents involved with the court system. Outpatient psychiatric care, guided peer-group interaction, vocational testing, training and placement were the major elements of this program.

PPBS Analysis of Proposed Programs

Within the basic PPBS framework, the grant proposal was prepared so that the cost of the program could be related to the number and kind of staff, the activities to be performed, the number of clients served, and the objectives to be reached. Each program included the treatment modalities and activities to be used in attaining the objectives. Among these were individual, group, family, play and activity therapy, psychodiagnostic testing and medication. The number of staff needed and the number of clients to be served by each method were listed in parallel columns. Our formula required staff to spend approximately two-thirds of their time in direct contact with clients and one-third in other activities such as conferences or administrative tasks. The reverse was true for staff with management responsibilities.

Funding agencies have become particularly interested in knowing the number of contacts with clients per unit of cost. To provide this information, we first computed the total time spent in a particular activity or modality of treatment and then determined how many units of that activity were provided within that time. For example, a group session averages one and a half hours. If fifteen hours per week are spent in group therapy, then ten group sessions took place in that week. If each group has six patients, sixty patients were seen during that week in group therapy.

This process is repeated to obtain the number of clients seen in all direct service programs. It is then possible to relate that number to dollar costs. Our grant of just over $500,000 was projected to generate 50,000 contacts representing 30,000 hours per year. This reflected a very efficient operation as compared with our existing services or those in other centers.

Other benefits of using PPBS include easy extrapolation from the grant proposal in the preparation of job descriptions, ready justification for every staff position in each component because a staff member's activities are clearly related to program objectives, and guidance in determining the disciplines and qualifications of staff needed to perform the described activities.

Conclusion

Our experience at the center with PPBS has been invaluable in helping us think more systematically about our overall program. We have not yet been able to apply this system rigorously, particularly in service areas where traditional ways of working are entrenched. But we have noticeably sharpened our thinking. We can now state in *program budget* terms the performance of our children's program and we expect to analyze other center programs in the same way.

NOTES

1. Fremont J. Lyden and Ernest G. Miller, *PPB, A Systems Approach to Management* (New York: Markham Press, 1972).
2. Joe B. Alexander, "The Planning-Programming-Budgeting System in the Mental Health Field," *Hospital and Community Psychiatry*, vol. 23 (12) December 1972, pp. 357–61.
3. Saul Feldman, "Budgeting and Behavior," in Saul Feldman, ed., *The Administration of Mental Health Services* (Springfield, Ill.: Charles C. Thomas, 1973), pp. 29–55.
4. Roderick K. McCleod, "Program Budgeting Works in Nonprofit Institutions," *Harvard Business Review*, vol. 49 (5) September–October 1971, pp. 46–56.
5. Feldman, "Budgeting," pp. 29–55.
6. Joint Commission on Mental Health of Children, *Crisis in Child Mental Health: Challenge for the 1970s* (New York: Harper and Row, 1970).
7. M. Basheeruddin Ahmed and David D. Stein, "Community and Staff Development of Child Psychiatric Services for Community Mental Health Centers," *Hospital and Community Psychiatry*, in press.

PART II

Organizational Objectives and MBO

Introductory Note

The vague and nonoperationalized goals common to human service organizations pose serious problems for accountability policy and the measurement of organizational effectiveness. Management By Objectives (MBO) is a tool designed to deal with these problems, and in principle its procedures are straightforward enough. Members of the organization identify goals, and then goals are factored into objectives. Feasibility is established, action plans are developed, and effort is coordinated toward achieving goals and objectives. Results are tracked, evaluated, and fed back to organizational members, and in light of those results, another cycle of planning and assessment begins anew.

MBO was officially adopted by the federal government in 1973 when President Nixon introduced it to heads of twenty-one federal agencies via a presidential memorandum. As a system-wide strategy, MBO was intended as a vehicle for continuous program review, high-level program choices, and ultimate integration with the budget cycle. Although attempts were made to avoid some of the rigidities of its predecessor, PPBS, it was nonetheless a strategy for hierarchical control, and like PPBS it generated an enormous paperwork burden.[1] MBO also reached its zenith early but then quietly faded from federal government. Despite that, MBO persistently appears in organizations throughout the human services enterprise, a popular but confusion-ridden system.

Although MBO may appear to be conceptually simple, in practice there is great variability in execution, misunderstanding of the system, faddish pretensions of its cure-all capabilities, hence a tendency to legitimize almost any real or fancied improvement under its banners. In some agencies MBO vaguely suggests results measured against expenditures, while in others it is merely a style of thinking that gives ritualized expression to agency accountability. Sometimes it refers to an approach to supervision and worker development; other times it is suggestive of a system-wide managerial strategy. The variant conceptions are numerous, and it appears to be intrinsic to MBO that there is not much consensus on what it is and how it ought to be used. For example, in the private enterprise sector where MBO has had most of its conceptual and technical development, it has become an all-purpose term meaning almost anything one chooses it to mean. Indicative of this variety, Carroll and Tosi in their study of over eighty private firms using MBO identified about ten different approaches.[2]

Partly, the problem of accurately defining and describing MBO lies in its different intellectual stems. One major variant of MBO owes intellectual debts to the systems approach filtered through Taylorism and efficiency engineering, both of which were dominated by economic logic and the search for maximum efficiency through the redesign or "reprogramming" of work. To this was conjoined the intellectual structure of Fayol and Urwick's classical school of administration which emphasized the importance of upper management in planning, organizing, and controlling work. Herein lay the early fusion of what would later become one dominant mode of MBO—an emphasis on productivity and output plus a one-way flow of decision making, that is, from the top down. In the 1930s, for example, it was under the rubric of productivity measurement that MBO type activities were undertaken in government and influential was the Ridley and Simon monograph, *Measuring Municipal Activities*, in which was stressed the need for defining objectives so as to measure productivity.[3] Later, the First Hoover Commission in 1948 emphasized the importance of defining governmental objectives and measuring progress toward them. The productivity movement waxed and waned, but over the years its precepts took hold in a number of federal agencies and were incorporated into MBO ideas. Implicit in these approaches was a "top down" orientation within a formalistic framework emphasizing the monitoring of each successively lower level by its superordinate one. Compliance was the engine of movement.

When some two decades or so later MBO was formally adopted in federal government, it had a strong predilection for the systems approach, scientific and systematic analysis, measurement and quantification. Indeed, surrounding MBO and emanating from the loftiest pinnacles of power down through the Office of Management and Budget and on to HEW, the dominant assumption was that bureaucratic reform and efficiency in government would be achieved through the tools of rational management.

By the time of the Nixon administration federal costs for state social services programs had risen rapidly but accountability was vexed by the lack of clear and measurable objectives in those programs. The system known as Goal Oriented Social Services (GOSS), a form of management by objectives, would require states to report progress in terms of the GOSS goal structure. GOSS would also be linked to a vertical information system and to the planning and budgeting systems within state level departments of public welfare. It should be noted that one distinguishing feature of the rationalistic approach to MBO is that it is a systems strategy, not a mere tactic of management, and that it tends to seek interlinkage with other organization systems and procedures such as budgeting, information and evaluation subsystems. Along these lines, however, the Comptroller's Office in HEW noted of GOSS that it was "such an elaborate structure that the states could not possibly cope with it."[4]

In distinction to the foregoing approach to MBO, there is a variant that owes much to social scientists who adopted a psycho-logical orientation rather than an econo-logical one. In the principles of "Scientific Management" and "rational man" theories of organization some social scientists saw a variety of organizational dysfunctions: production-centered, dependency-producing, and submission-oriented leadership styles.[5] For Douglas McGregor, a key to organizational effectiveness was found in MBO as a performance appraisal technique with major emphasis on worker growth, problem-solving team development, open communications and high feedback.[6] In this variant the qualitative nature of work is stressed, management control and accountability systems tend to be looser. The importance of common philosophy, cohesion, and social processes for decision making tend to eclipse rule-oriented compliance. The assumption is that under the *proper* organizational conditions, organizational cement is found in the internalization of objectives by members of the system. Although this approach has not been especially popular in government, there are some exceptions worth noting. For example, in the early years of the Social Security Administration (SSA) narrow efficiency and/or economy criteria were renounced, and partly as a result SSA developed an image as a humane and helping organization. Another interesting example was found in IRS where in one of the regional offices the commissioner eschewed measurement and specificity as guides for MBO because the agency was already awash with numbers and computers.[7]

With the current popularity of MBO in human service agencies, it is important to examine how it may be employed for maximum benefit and wherein lie its hazards. In execution, there are many hybrid approaches to MBO with features from the two major variants criss-crossing with each other. We therefore present a number of variations on the MBO theme to identify both the potential benefits as well as the costs. We begin, however, with Peter Drucker who popularized the term "management by objectives."[8]

Management and Objectives. Public service organizations, says Peter F. Drucker in "A User's Guide to MBO" need MBO even more than private enterprise owing to the multiplicity of vague and conflicting goals in the former. Yet, it is precisely this need that may lead to abuse, the confusion of procedure for the substance of management and objectives. In attempting to develop clarity about what MBO *is*, Drucker discusses a number of important issues: dealing with priorities and posteriorities, the problem solving core of MBO, the role of management and the functions of participation plus the question of measuring or at least judging performance. In the final analysis, however, Drucker develops a meta-principle for MBO; it too must be known by its results.

A Participatory Systems Approach. Robert M. Spano and Sander H. Lund describe the use of MBO in a hospital social services unit and illustrate a hybrid approach. As an overall strategy, MBO would be linked to other systems—the Management Information System, the departmental budget, and perhaps ultimately to higher administration in the organization. Emphasizing open communications, a participative orientation, and qualitative rather than quantitative objectives, the implementation of MBO nevertheless provoked staff dissatisfaction with "bureaucratic paperwork," one of the more common criticisms of MBO. Although the authors perceive the MBO program as a success, the costs involved were high ones owing to many staff resignations during the first year of the program.

MBO as a Supervisory Tool. Whether or not MBO is used as a management system in an agency, its utilization for supervisory purposes is becoming more widespread. Supervision By Objectives (SBO) says Donald Granvold can contribute to accountability and the legitimation of achievement in the delivery of social services. In an interesting variant of MBO, one that departs from Drucker's prescription that organizational objectives should not be assumed as "givens," Granvold focuses on individuals within the context of the supervisory dyad. He discusses different types of objectives in supervision, how to establish objectives, and how to write them. Specific examples of objectives are given together with worksheets for their development. Although there is a strong emphasis on quantification, there is nevertheless an attempt to incorporate personal development aims together with production objectives. Once again, notwithstanding that the MBO process is encapsulated within the supervisory process as distinct from its use as a complete management system, the "paperwork problem" is seen to occur.

Evaluating MBO. In the search for ways to improve the efficiency and effectiveness of human service agencies, MBO has become a popular tool. Serious questions, however, have been raised about its effectiveness. It has, for example, been argued that despite the best of intentions, when used as a supervisory tool and coupled with performance appraisal, MBO usually intensifies hostility, mistrust, and resentment between managers and subordinates. To counteract these tendencies Harry Levinson has urged that MBO be improved by examining the underlying assumptions about motivation, by incorporating group decision making, goal setting and appraisal, and above all, by keeping in the foreground the question, "How do we meet individual and organizational purposes?"[9]

To date, there is not much in the way of rigorous evaluation of the effectiveness of MBO, nor of the conditions that contribute to successful or unsuccessful implementation. Like many other management tools, MBO's achievements as a tough-minded instrument of rationality rest, paradoxically enough, on testimonial evidence and salesmanship. An interesting exception is Donald D. White's study of managers in a hospital, their attitudes toward an MBO system, and the factors that predict those attitudes. Although not identified as such, the MBO approach employed appears to have been more a management system than a supervisory system, and according to the data, at five different levels of the organization, managerial attitudes were found to be positive toward MBO. Some of the factors involved the attitudes of managers' superiors toward the system, contribution of MBO to communications flow, and the facilitation of personnel being "in on decisions." The study is silent on the issues that are involved in MBO as a supervisory tool, but worthy of note is the fact that the lower in the managerial hierarchy, the less favorable were attitudes toward MBO. Whether those in subordinate positions are generally less positive toward MBO is an open question. For erstwhile users of MBO, this study does provide some important leads. As for the larger questions of effectiveness, MBO may sometimes contribute to organizational integration, but there is as yet no accumulation of evidence that the costs of implementing MBO are balanced by any measurable output benefits.

NOTES

1. For two views of the Nixon MBO see Frank P. Sherwood and William J. Page, Jr., "MBO and Public Management," *Public Administration Review*, vol. 36 (1) January–February 1976, pp. 5–12; also Chester A. Newland, "Policy/Program Objectives and Federal Management: The Search for Government Effectiveness," *Public Administration Review*, vol. 36 (1) January–February 1976, pp. 20–27.

2. Stephen J. Carroll and Henry W. Tosi, Jr., *Management by Objectives: Applications and Research* (New York: Macmillan, 1973).

3. Clarence E. Ridley and Herbert A. Simon, *Measuring Municipal Activities*, 2d ed. (Chicago: The International City Manager's Association, 1943).

4. Paul E. Mott, *Meeting Human Needs: The Social and Political History of Title XX* (Columbus: National Conference on Social Welfare, 1976), pp. 22–23.

5. For example, Rensis Likert, *New Patterns of Management* (New York: McGraw-Hill Book Co., 1961); and Chris Argyris, *Personality and Organization: The Conflict Between System and Individual* (New York: Harper & Row, 1956).

6. Douglas McGregor, *The Human Side of Enterprise* (New York: McGraw-Hill Book Co., 1960).
7. Sherwood and Page, "MBO," pp. 5–12.
8. Peter F. Drucker, *The Practice of Management* (New York: Harper & Row, 1954).
9. Harry Levinson, "Management by Whose Objectives," *Harvard Business Review*, vol. 48 (4) July–August 1970, pp. 125–33.

5. Management and Objectives

What Results Should You Expect?
A User's Guide to MBO

PETER F. DRUCKER

MBO has a longer history in governmental institutions than most of its present-day practitioners realize. The basic concepts are strongly advocated by Luther Gulick and his associates in the mid and late 1930s, in their studies of the organization and administration of the federal government. Yet, the concept of management by objectives and self-control originated with the private sector. It was first practiced by the DuPont Company after World War I. By the mid-1920s, Alfred P. Sloan, Jr., of General Motors used the term "Management by Objectives and Self Control" systematically and with great conceptual clarity.

Yet today MBO seems to have become more popular in public service institutions that it is in the private sector; it is certainly more discussed as a tool of the public, especially the governmental administrator.

There is good reason for this popularity of MBO in the public sector. Public service institutions need it far more than any but the very biggest and most complex businesses. Public service institutions always have multiple objectives and often conflicting, if not incompatible objectives. While no institution, including business, has truly satisfactory measurements, the measurements generally available to government agencies and other public service institutions, especially in the budget area, rarely have

Reprinted from *Public Administration Review* © 1976 by The American Society for Public Administration, 1225 Connecticut Avenue, N.W., Washington, D.C. All rights reserved.

anything to do with performance and goal attainment. Even a fairly small governmental agency, such as one of the smaller and less populous states or a medium-sized city, is a "conglomerate" of greater diversity and complexity than even ITT.

The resources of public service institutions are people, and the outputs are rarely "things." Therefore, direction toward meaningful results is not inherent in the work or in the process itself. Misdirection, whether by the individual employee or by the administrator, is at the same time both easy and hard to detect. Public service institutions are prone to the deadly disease of "bureaucracy"; that is towards mistaking rules, regulations, and the smooth functioning of the machinery for accomplishment, and the self-interest of the agency for public service.

Public service institutions, in other words, paricularly need objectives and concentration of efforts on goals and results—that is management. These are, of course, precisely the needs management by objectives and self-control (MBO) promises to satisfy. But the same reasons which make MBO potentially so productive for the public service institution also make it only too easy for the institution to mistake MBO procedures for the substance of both management and objectives. Indeeed, they may encourage the fatal error of misusing MBO as a substitute for thinking and decision making.

Therefore, the administrator in the public service institution needs a "users' guide." He needs to know whether he uses MBO correctly or whether he misuses it. He needs to know, above all, the results MBO yields if used properly. That, I am afraid, is what few of the texts and manuals spell out. Yet only when these results have been achieved has MBO really been applied.

MBO is both management by *objectives* and *management* by objectives. What is needed, therefore, are two sets of specifications—one spelling out the results in terms of objectives and one spelling out the results in terms of management.

What Are Our Objectives? What Should They Be?

The first result, and perhaps the most important one which the administrator needs to aim at in applying MBO, is the *clear realization that his agency actually has no objectives*. What passes for objectives are, as a rule, only good intentions.

The purpose of an objective is to make possible the organization of work for its attainment. This means that objectives must be operational: capable of being converted into specific performance, into work, and into work assignments. However, almost no public service agency has operational objectives. To say our objective is "the maintenance of law and order" or "health care" is operationally a meaningless statement. Nothing can be deduced from these statements with respect to the goals and the work needed. Yet these statements are already a good deal more operational, more nearly true objectives, than is commonly found in the objectives statements of public service agencies.

The first result to be expected from managment by *objectives* is the realization that the traditional statement of objectives is inadequate, is indeed in most cases totally inappropriate. The first work to be done is to identify what the objectives should or could be.

The moment this question is raised, however, it will also be realized— and this is the second result to be obtained—that *objectives* in public service agencies are ambiguous, ambivalent, and multiple. This holds true in private business as well.

The hospital, while complex, is still a very small institution compared to most governmental agencies. Yet its objectives are by no means clear. "Health Care" sounds plausible, most hopsitals have nothing to do with health care. They are concerned with the treatment and care of the sick. Clearly, the most intelligent and most effective way to produce health care is the prevention of sickness, rather than its treatment and cure. To the extent that we know how to provide health care it is not, bluntly, the task of the hospital at all. It is done by public health measures such as vaccination, providing pure drinking water, and adequate treatment of sewage. Hospitals, in effect, are the result of the failure of health care, rather than agencies to provide it.

Yet even if the hospital defines its objectives very narrowly, as do the hospitals in the British Health Service, as the "treatment of the sick" (repair of damage already done), the objectives are still cloudy. Is the hospital, as in the traditional concept of the American community hospital, the private physician's plant facility and an extension of his office? Is it, in other words, the place where the physician takes care of those patients whom he cannot take care of in his own office or in his own private practice? Or should the hospital as so many American hospitals have attempted, be the "health care center" for the community, through such activities as the well-baby clinic, counselling service for the emotionally disturbed and so on? Should the hopsital also become the substitute for the private physician and provide the physician's services to the poor—the objectives of the outpatient department in the American big city hospital today? If the hospital defines its function as care of the sick, what then is the role and function of the maternity service? Giving birth to a baby is, after all, no sickness, but a perfectly normal and indeed perfectly healthy occurrence.

Similarly, when the police department tries to make operational the vague term "maintenance of law and order" it will find immediately that there is a multiplicity of possible objectives each of them, ambiguous. "Prevention of crime" sounds very specific. But what does it really mean, assuming that anyone knows how to do it? Is it, as many police departments have traditionally asserted, the enforcement of all the laws on the statute book? Or is it the protection of the innocent lawabiding citizen, with respect both to his person and to his property? Is it safety on the streets or safety in the home, or is it both? Is the primary task the eradication and prevention of corruption within the police force itself? The latter may sound quite peripheral, if not trivial. Yet, in a recent major study of the job of chief of police, sponsored by one of the agencies of the federal government, the experienced police chiefs guiding the study maintained that to rid police forces of corruption was the first, and most important, objective in maintaining law and order.

In attempting to reduce pious intentions to genuine objectives, the administrator will invariably find that equally valid objectives are mutually incompatible or at least, quite inconsistent.

The classical example is the American farm policy of the last forty years. Strengthening the American farmer was the stated objective from the beginning, before New Deal days. Does this mean protecting the family farmer? Or does it mean making the American farmer efficient, productive, and capable of world market competition? Congress, in writing farm legislation, has always used rhetoric indicating that the purpose of farm policy is to protect and preserve the small family farmer. However, the actual measures then enacted to achieve this purpose have primarily been aimed at making farming a more efficient, more productive, and more competitive industry, in which the small family farmer has practically no place and may indeed be an impediment to the attainment of the goal.

Thus the most important result of management by *objectives* is that it forces the administrator into the realization that there cannot be one single objective, notwithstanding the language of policy statements, whether acts of Congress or administrative declarations. To call realization of this fundamental problem a result of management by *objectives* may seem paradoxical. Yet it may be the most important result, precisely because it forces the administrator and his agency to a realization of the need to think and of the need to make highly risky balancing and trade-off decisions. This should be one of the results management by *objectives* strives for, which have to be attained if MBO is to be an effective tool which strengthens the performance of the institution.

The next area in which management by *objectives* has to attain results is that of *priorities* and *posteriorities*.

Public service institutions, almost without exception, have to strive to attain multiple objectives. At the same time each area of objectives will require a number of separate goals. Yet no institution, least of all a large one, is capable of doing many things, let alone of doing many things well. Institutions must concentrate and set priorities. By the same token, they must make risky decisions, about what to postpone and what to abandon—to think through posteriorities.

One basic reason for this need to concentrate is the communications problem, both within the institution and among the various external publics. Institutions which try to attain simultaneously a great many different goals end up confusing their own members. The confusion is extended twofold to the outside public on whose support they depend.

Another cogent reason for concentration of goals is that no institution has an abundance of truly effective resources. We have all learned that money alone does not produce results. Results require the hard work and efforts of dedicated people; such people are always in short supply. Yet nothing destroys the effectiveness of competent individuals more than having their efforts splintered over a number of divergent concerns—a function of the frustration that results from giving part-time attention to a major task. To achieve results always requires thorough and consistent attention to the problem by a least one effective man or woman.

Finally, and this may be the most important factor, even a unitary, or a simple goal often requires a choice between very different strategies which cannot be pursued at the same time; one of them has to be given priority, which means that the other one assumes secondary status or is abandoned for an unspecified time.

One example of this dilemma, which is familiar to every experienced administrator, is the educational policy in developing countries. That a trained and schooled population is desirable, and is indeed a prerequisite for social and economic development, would be accepted by practically all students of development. However, should primary emphasis be given to the education of a small, but exceeding capable, elite? Or should the main drive be on "mass literacy"? Few countries can pursue both goals simultaneously—they must make a choice. If the first course is followed, there is the risk of educating people to be highly skilled and at great expense to the country. The consequences are that the society cannot utilize the expertise it has paid for and cannot provide meaningful jobs for those individuals. The result is then a "brain drain" in which the potentially most productive, most expensive resources of a poor country leave to find opportunities elsewhere for the application of their knowledge.

If the second alternative is being followed, there is the risk of educating large masses of people who are no longer satisfied with traditional employment and/or traditional subsistence standards of living. These people cannot find the jobs they have been trained for and have been led to expect, simply because institutions capable of employing them do not emerge, and the leadership is missing.

To set priorities is usually fairly simple, or at least seems politically fairly simple. What is difficult and yet absolutely essential, is the risk-taking and politically dangerous decision as to what the posteriorities should be. Every experienced administrator knows that what one postpones, one really abandons. In fact, it is a sound rule not to postpone but to make the decision not to do something altogether or to give up doing something. For in strategy, timing is of the essence. Nothing is usually less productive than to do ten years later what would have been an excellent and worthwhile program ten years earlier.

If an illustration is needed, the fate of so many of President Johnson's programs would supply it. What made so many of these programs fail is not that they were the wrong programs, or even that they were inadequately supported. They were, in large measure, five or ten years too late. These programs had been postponed, and when the time came to do them, that is when Congress was willing to consider them after long years of resistance, they were no longer "right" programs.

In addition, public service institutions find "abandonment of yesterday" even more difficult than businesses. Business, of course, does not like to abandon. The product or service that no longer serves a purpose, no longer produces results, no longer fulfills a major need, is usually also the product or service which the people now at the top have spent the best part of their working lives to create and to make succeed. However, in business enterprise, the market eventually forces management to face up to reality and to abandon yesterday.

The Ford Motor Company held onto the Edsel as long as it could—far longer than economic reality justified. The American public had abandoned the Edsel long before Ford management was willing to accept the verdict. Eventually, however, even a very large, strong, and stubborn company had to accept reality.

No such pressure exists as a rule in the public service institution. Indeed, if we had had ministries of transportation around in 1850 or 1900, we might now have in every country major research projects, funded with billions of dollars, to reeducate the horse. In any public service institution, whether government agency, hospital, school, or university, any activity and any service almost immediately creates its own constituency: in the legislature, the press, or the public. Yet nothing is quite as difficult to do as to maintain the moribund. It requires greater energies, greater effort, and greater abilities to sustain an obsolete program than to make effective the responsive and productive program.

Thus, the public service agency is always in danger of frittering away its best people as well as a great deal of money on activities which no longer produce, no longer contribute, have proven to be incapable of producing, or are simply inappropriate.

Therefore, essential to management by *objectives* in the public service agency is the establishment of priorities, decisions concerning areas for concentration.

Equally essential is the systematic appraisal of all services and activities in order to find the *candidates for abandonment.* Indeed it is wisdom in a public service agency to put each service and activity on trial for its life every three or four years and to ask: if we had known what we now know at the time we established this service, would we have gotten into it? If the answer is no, one does not say, what do we have to do to make it viable again? One does not even say, should we consider getting out of it? One says, how fast can we get out?

Goals of abandonment and schedules to attain these goals are an essential part of management by *objectives,* however unpopular, disagreeable, or difficult to attain they might be. The great danger in large institutions, especially in public service institutions, is to confuse fat with muscle and motion with performance. The only way to prevent this degenerative disease is a systematic procedure for abandoning yesterday, setting specific and courageous goals for abandonment.

In this respect, the Budget Reform Act of 1974 may represent the biggest step forward in public administration in many decades, though it still remains to be seen, of course, whether the act will produce the desired results. This act entrusted the General Accounting Office with the duty of appraising existing programs and projects in the federal service based on their suitability, stated objectives, and appropriateness.

But will the Congress that wrote the act be willing to face up to its abandonment implications?

The next results are *specific goals*, with specific *targets*, specific *time-tables* and specific *strategies*. Implicit in this is the *clear defintion of the resources* needed to attain these goals, the efforts needed, and primarily the *allocation* of available resources—especially of available manpower. A "plan" is not a plan unless the resources of competent, performing people needed for its attainment have been specifically allocated. Until then, the plan is only a good intention; in reality not even that.

Finally, management by *objectives* needs to bring out as a clear result of the thinking and analysis process, how performance can be *measured*, or at least *judged*.

It is commonly argued that public service institutions aim at intangible results, which defy measurement. This would simply mean that public service institutions are incapable of producing results. Unless results can be appraised objectively, there will be no results. There will only be activity, that is costs. To produce results it is necessary to know what results are desirable and be able to determine whether the desired results are actually being achieved.

It is also not true that the activities of public service institutions cannot be measured. "Missions" are always intangible, whether of business enterprise or of social service institutions.

Sears Roebuck and Company defined its mission in the 1920s as being the "buyer for the American Family." This is totally intangible. But the objectives which Sears then set to accomplish this mission (e.g., to develop a range of appliances that most nearly satisfy the largest number of homeowners at the most economical price) was an operational objective from which clear and measurable goals with respect to product line, service, assortment, price, and market penetration, could be derived. This in turn made possible both the allocation of efforts and the measurement of performance.

"Saving souls" as the mission of a church is totally intangible. At least, the bookkeeping is not of this world. However, the goal of bringing at least two-thirds of the young people of the congregation into the church and its activities is easily measured.

Similarly, "health care" is intangible. But the goals for a maternity ward which state that the number of "surprises" in delivery must not be more than two or three out of every hundred deliveries; the number of postpartum infections of mothers must not exceed one-half of one percent of all deliveries; eight out of ten of all premature babies born live after the seventh month of conception must survive in good health are not intangible, but fairly easy to measure.

To think through the appropriate measurement is in itself a policy decision and therefore highly risky. Measurements, or at least criteria for judgment and appraisal, define what we mean by performance. They largely dictate where the efforts should be spent. They determine whether policy priorities are serious or are merely administrative doubletalk. For this reason it needs to be emphasized that measurements need to be measurements of performance rather than of efforts. It is not adequate, indeed it is misleading, to use measurements that focus on efficiency of operation, rather than on the services the agency delivers to somebody outside, whether another public service agency or the public. Measurement directs effort and vision. One of the central problems of public service agencies, indeed of all organizations, is the tendency to direct efforts and vision toward the inside, that is toward efficiencies, rather than toward the purposes on the outside for which every public service institution exists.

With measurements defined, it then becomes possible to organize the *feedback* from results to activities. What results should be expected by what time? In effect, measurements decide what phenomena are results. Identifying the appropriate measurements enables the administrator to move from diagnosis to prognosis. He can now lay down what he expects will happen and take proper action to see whether it actually does happen.

The actual results of action are not predictable. Indeed, if there is one rule for action, and especially for institutional action, it is that the expected results will not be attained. The unexpected is practically certain. But are the unexpected results deleterious? Are they actually more desirable than the results that were expected and planned? Do the deviations from the planned course of events demand a change in strategies, or perhaps a change in goals or priorities? Or are they such that they indicate opportunities that were not seen originally, opportunities that indicate the need to increase efforts and to run with success? These are questions the administrator in the public service agency rarely asks. Unless he builds into the structure of objectives and strategies the organized feedback that will force these questions to his attention, he is likely to disregard the unexpected and to persist in the wrong course of action or to miss major opportunities.

Organized feedback leading to systematic review and continuous revision of objectives, roles, priorities, and allocation of resources must therefore be built into the administrative process. To enable the administrator to do so is a result and an important result, of management by *objectives*. If it is not obtained, management by *objectives* has not been properly applied.

What Is Management? What Should It Be?

Management by objectives, similarly, has to attain a number of results to be properly applied.

The first result is *understanding*. *Management* by objectives is often described as a way to obtain agreement. But this is gross oversimplification. The decision which MBO identifies and brings into focus: the decisions on objectives and their balance; on goals and strategies; on priorities and abandonment; on efforts and resource allocation; on the appropriate measurements, are far too complex, risky, and uncertain to be made by acclamation. To make them intelligently requires *informed dissent*.

What MBO has to produce as the first *management* result is understanding of the difficulty, complexity, and risk of these decisions. It is understanding that different people, all employed in a common task and familiar with it, define objectives and goals differently, see different priorities, and would prefer very different and incompatible strategies. Only then can the decision be made effectively.

The decisions to be made are also of such complexity and of such importance that the responsible administrator would not want to make them without understanding them. The full complexity of any issue can only be understood on the basis of informed dissent. "Adversary proceedings" are not the best way, as a rule, to make these decisions. Informed dissent is essential where people of good will and substantial knowledge find out how differently they view the same problem, the same mission, the same task, and the same reality. Otherwise, symptoms rather than the underlying problem will be attacked; trivia rather than results will be pursued.

It is almost fifty years since Mary Parker Follett applied the early insights of perception psychology to point out that people in an organization who seem to differ on the answers usually differ on what the right question is. The issues, with which the administrator in the public service institution deals, are of such complexity and have so many dimensions that any one person can be expected to see only one aspect and only one dimension rather than the total concept.

However, effective action requires an understanding of complexity. It requires an ability to see a problem in all its major dimensions. Otherwise, a maximum of effort will produce no results, but more commonly wrong and undesired results.

Management by *objectives* is an administrative process rather than a political process. This makes it all the more important to focus on understanding as the first management result—bringing out the basic views, the basic dissents, the different approaches to the same task and the same problem within the organization.

The major departments of the federal government that have been created in the last twenty years: the Department of Defense, the Department of Health, Education, and Welfare (HEW), the Department of Transportation, and the Department of Housing and Urban Development (HUD) are commonly criticized for being ineffectual as well as administrative labyrinths. They are often contrasted, to their detriment, with older agencies such as the Department of the Interior or the Department of Agriculture, which, it is alleged, are so much more effective. The reason usually given for the lack of effectiveness of these newer agencies is "lack of direction" or "internal division." What made these older agencies effective, especially in the New Deal days when they reached a peak of effectiveness, was, however, the intelligent use of informed dissent on the part of the men who led them. Harold Ickes in Interior or Henry Wallace in Agriculture took infinite care to produce informed dissent within the organization and thus to obtain understanding for themselves and to create understanding for their associates. Thus, when decisions on goals and priorities were made unilaterally by the top man himself, and by no means democratically, they were understood throughout the organization; the top man himself understood what alternatives were available as well as the position of his people on them.

Similarly, the Japanese system of "decision by consensus" is often cited these days as an example for the American decision maker. However, the Japanese do not make decisions by consensus, rather they deliberate by consensus. The seemingly long gestation period of a decision in Japanese organizations is devoted to bring out the maximum understanding within the organization and to enabling those who are going to have to participate in the subsequent action to express their own views of the issue and their own definitions of the question. Consequently, they find out where their colleagues and associates stand, what they feel, and how they feel. Then a decision can be reached which the organization understands, even though large groups within it do not necessarily agree or would have preferred a different decision. Perhaps the greatest strength of the Japanese process is that priorities can actually be set and be made effective.

The second management result of management by objectives is to produce *responsibility* and *commitment* within the organization; to make possible *self-control* on the part of the managerial and professional people.

The advocate of MBO likes to talk about participation. This is a misleading term, or at least an inadequate term. The desired result is willingness of the individual within the organization to focus his or her own vision and efforts towards the attainment of the organization's goals. It is ability to have self-control; to know that the individual makes the right contribution and is able to appraise himself or herself rather than be appraised and controlled from the outside. The desired result is commitment, rather than participation.

For this reason the usual approach of MBO towards goal-setting for the individual or for the managerial component is inadequate and may even do damage. Usually MBO says to the individual manager, here are the goals of this institution. What efforts do you have to make to further them? The right question is, what do you, given our mission, think the goals should be, the priorities should be, the strategies should be? What, by way of contribution to these goals, priorities, and strategies, should this institution hold you and your department accountable for over the next year or two? What goals, priorities, and strategies do you and your department aim for, separate and distinct from those of the institution? What will you have to contribute and what results will you have to produce to attain these goals? Where do you see major opportunities of contribution and performance for this institution and for your component? Where do you see major problems?

Needless to say, it is then the task of the responsible administrator to decide. It is not necessarily true, as so many romantics in management seem to believe, that the subordinate always knows better. However, it is also not necessarily true that the boss always knows better. What is true is that the two, subordinate and boss, cannot communicate unless they realize that they differ in their views of what is to be done and what could be done. It is also true that there is no *management* by objectives unless the subordinate takes responsibility for performance, results, and, in the last analysis, for the organization itself.

The next results are *personnel decisions*. As stated earlier, MBO requires allocation of resources and concentration of effort. *Management* by objectives should always result in changing the allocation of effort, the assignment of people and the jobs they are doing. It should always lead to a restructuring of the human resources toward the attainment of objectives. It is not true, though administrative routine believes it, if only subconsciously, that every existing job is the right job and has something to contribute. On the contrary, the ruling postulate should be: every existing job is likely to be the wrong job and neeeds to be restructured, or at least redirected. Job titles may be sacred and in every large organization there is an unspoken, but fervent belief that the Good Lord created section chiefs. In reality, job substance changes with the needs of the organization, and assignments, that is the specific commitment to results, change even more frequently.

Job descriptions may be semi-permanent. However, assignments should always be considered as short-lived. It is one of the basic purposes of managerial objectives to force the question, what are the specific assignments in this position which, given our goals, priorities, and strategies at this time, make the greatest contribution?

Unless this question is being brought to the surface, MBO has not been properly applied. It must be determined what the right concentration of effort is and what the manpower priorities are, and convert the answer into personnel action. Unless this is done, there may be objectives, but there is no management.

Similarly important and closely related are results in terms of *organiza-tion structure*. If the work in organizations over the last forty years has taught us anything, it is that structure follows strategy. There are only a small number of organization designs available to the administrator.[1] How this limited number of organization designs is put together is largely determined by the strategies that an organization adopts, which in turn is determined by its goals. *Management* by objectives should enable the administrator to think through organization structure. Organization struc-ture while not in itself policy, is a tool of policy. Any decision on policy, that is any decision on objectives, priorities, and strategies, has consequences for organization structure.

The ultimate result of *management* by objectives is *decision*, both with respect to the goals and performance standards of the orginization and to the structure and behavior of the orginization. Unless MBO leads to decision, it has no results at all; it has been a waste of time and effort. The test of MBO is not knowledge, but effective action. This means, above all, risk-taking decisions.

The literature talks about MBO often as a "tool for problem solving." However, its proper application is as a means of problem definition and problem recognition. Perhaps even more important, it is a means of problem prevention.

Thus, MBO is not a procedure to implement decision, a systematic attempt to define, to think through, and to decide. Filling out forms, no matter how well designed, is not management by objectives and self-control. The results are!

MBO is often called a tool of planning. It is not the same things as planning, but it is the core of planning. MBO is usually called a manage-ment tool. Again, it is not all of management, but it is the core of manage-ment. It is not the way to *implement* decisions on policy, on goals, on strategies, on organization structure, or on staffing. It is the *process* in which decisions are made, goals are identified, priorities and posteriorities are set, and organization structure designed for the specific purposes of the institution.

It is also the process of people integrating themselves into the organiza-tion and directing themselves toward the organization's goals and pur-poses. The introduction of MBO into public service institutions, especially into governmental agencies during the last few years, may thus be the first step toward making public service institutions effectve. So far it is only a first step. What has been introduced so far, by and large, is the procedure, and there is danger in procedure being mistaken for substance. Yet the great need of the public institution is not procedure. Most of them have all the procedures they need—the great need is performance. Indeed, performance of the public service institution may be the fundamental, the central, need of modern society. Management by objectives and self-control should help fill a good part of this need. However, its success depends upon the administrator: in applying MBO he or she must obtain the right results, both with respect to *objectives* and to *management*.

NOTE

1. Peter F. Drucker, *Management: Tasks; Responsibilities; Practices* (New York: Harper & Row, 1974), chapters 41–48.

---

6. A Participatory Approach

Management By Objectives in a Hospital Social Service Unit

ROBERT M. SPANO and SANDER H. LUND

There is a rich tradition in the social sciences that distinguishes formal organizations from other human service groups by the dedication on the part of organization members to attain collectively accepted goals. Building on this literature, Peter Drucker,[1] a prominent management consultant, has promulgated an administrative technique called "Management By Objectives" (MBO) wherein organizations are directed through formulation and evaluation of express program objectives. Management By Objectives has been adopted successfully by many business organizations but has received relatively little attention in the human services.[2] The purpose of this paper is to help fill this gap by describing the installation of an MBO system in a hospital social service department. The mechanics of the system will be presented, the advantages will be highlighted, and it will be shown how the usual MBO format was modified to fit a human service milieu.

Reprinted from *Social Work in Health Care* 1, no. 3 (Spring 1976): 267–76, with the permission of the publisher. © 1976 by The Haworth Press. All rights reserved.

Setting

The setting for this venture was the Social Service Department of the University of Minnesota Hospitals. Founded in 1909, the department employs 22 full-time MSWs, 2 BA staff, and 1 case aide, and provides a full range of services to the hospital's patients and their families. In 1974, 10,000 clients were served by the department.

Management By Objectives

As the name implies, Management By Objectives involves direction of an organization through the periodic establishment and review of formal objectives. Objectives are typically derived from and serve to expand a statement of the organization's mission and are in turn elaborated by subordinate goals, which represent the specific outcomes that must occur in a given time period if the objectives and larger mission are to be achieved. Goals and objectives are formulated with input from staff at all levels of the hierarchy. Evaluation, in Management By Objectives, consists of comparing the actual outcome with the original goal and using this information to judge organizational effectiveness and formulate new goals.

At the University of Minnesota Hospitals Social Service Department a modified version of Management By Objectives was used to derive a four-tiered organizational goal structure (Figure 6–1). As can be seen, there are two changes in the usual MBO format: (a) derivation of a mission statement from a formal department philosophy, and (b) inclusion of "department functions" between the mission statement and objectives. The philosophy is an attempt to incorporate the department's value system into its formal operation. The functions serve as a mechanism to insure that attention is paid to all appropriate professional standards.

PHILOSOPHY

At the apex of the goal structure is the Social Service Department's philosophy. Derived from literature reviews, community meetings, hospital policies, and staff discussion, it is a statement of the department's overall dedication and serves as background for examination and revision of the goal structure. The philosophy attempts to give continuity and subjective meaning to the department's operation by providing a sense of its fundamental, but not previously articulated, value system. The importance of this can be that unlike private operations, which tend to be accountable only to themselves, public service providers have a multiplic-

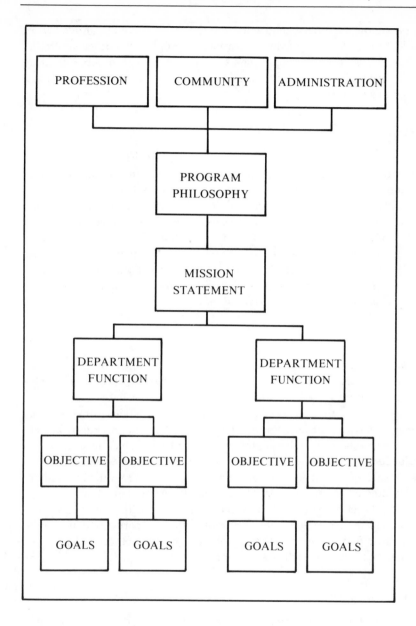

Figure 6–1.
University of Minnesota Hospitals Social Service Department Goal Structure Format

ity of "significant others," and as a result the values served by an agency are subject to many points of view. A formal philosophy can mitigate potential turmoil by insuring that a program's values are subject to public scrutiny and by providing a channel for integrating legitimate external input into a program's operation.

MISSION STATEMENT

The philosophy serves as a platform for development of the department's mission statement, which is a brief description of its fundamental reason for existence. The following mission statement was formulated by the director of the department based upon the philosophy and upon his understanding of the role of professional social work in the provision of medical services:

MISSION: *It is the mission of the Social Service Department to enhance the delivery of comprehensive health services by providing social services to the patients and their families of the University of Minnesota Hospitals and to assist in resolution of social and emotional problems related to illness, medical services and rehabilitation.*

FUNCTIONS

Subordinate to the mission statement are the department functions. Each function is a discrete activity, or cluster of activities, that the Social Service Department must perform adequately if its mission is to be realized. The list of functions is based upon a series of recommendations from the Social Service Department Director Search Committee, and provides rubrics to link the setting of objectives to the department's mission. Unless there is a major redirection of the department, the mission statement and functions will rarely be revised. The objectives, however, are evaluated and reformulated on an annual basis. The current department functions are to: (1) provide direct patient services; (2) maintain liaison with community agencies; (3) foster professional development of staff; (4) participate in hospital programs; (5) provide educational programs; (6) conduct research projects; (7) administer and coordinate programs.

OBJECTIVES AND GOALS

Each objective is a separate event, or group of related events, that must occur in a specified time period if a function is to be adequately served. An objective consists of: (a) the title of the objective; (b) the staff responsible for activities in regard to the title; (c) a statement of current activities in regard to the title; (d) a statement of the outcome expected in regard to the title;

and (e) the date at which the expected outcome is to occur (Figure 6–2). In cases where attainment of an objective involves a series of related outcomes, each such outcome is presented as a separate goal under that objective. Objectives and goals were formulated by department staff, under review of the director. There was at least one staff committee for each function, and in many cases temporary subcommittees were established as well.

Installation of the System

During the fall of 1972, the senior author [Spano] was selected by the Social Service Department Director Search Committee to take charge of the University of Minnesota Hospitals Social Service Department. Concurrent with this appointment, the department was receiving administrative encouragement to expand its community and hospital activities, and there were signs that staff desired a more direct involvement in the development of departmental policy. Consequently, a request by hospital administration for a statement of the new director's goals served as a stimulus to supplant the previous administrative system, which focused power on the office of the director, with Management By Objectives. It was hoped that this move would both tighten the linkage with higher administration and provide a rational structure for the management of new programs, while at the same time serving as a mechanism for significantly increasing staff influence in the department's overall operation.

Following the request for his goals, the director met with staff, explained his desire to implement an MBO system, and called for committees to be formed in each function area to establish departmental objectives and goals. Seventeen out of twenty-four staff volunteered, and within one month a goal structure containing forty-two objectives and goals was constructed. The director reviewed the goal structure, met with committee chairpersons to discuss his reactions and negotiate revisions, and forwarded the final document to hospital administration. Accompanying the final version was a cover letter that stated the director's belief that the goal structure represented both a work plan for the department and a contract with hospital administration.

One year later, each staff committee reported on the attainment of the objectives and goals in its function area, and the junior author was retained to review these reports and help compose the annual report. The results were positive: During the first year, thirty-one of the thirty-three objectives and goals scheduled for attainment had actually been achieved. The completed annual report was sent to hospital administration, and staff

DEPARTMENT FUNCTION: PARTICIPATION IN EDUCATION PROGRAMS

Function Objectives	Responsible Staff	Current Level of Functioning	Expected Level of Functioning	Completion Date	Outcome Level
FORMULATE TEACHING ROLE IN APPROPRIATE UNIVERSITY AND HOSPITAL COURSES.	Formal Teaching Role Committee	Minimal use of staff as consultant teachers; usually on informal basis with no departmental recognition.	Recognition and sanction by department of work done now.	June, 1974	Recommendations made as to recognition and sanction of present work.
			Establish committee to evaluate further department involvement in teaching.		Committee appointed; evaluation of further teaching will be continued.
PARTICIPATE IN TRAINING OF STUDENTS IN ALLIED HEALTH CARE DISCIPLINES.	Formal Teaching Role Committee	Minimal: occurs primarily in departments of Neurology and Psychiatry.	Documentation and evaluation of role in Neurology and Psychiatry.	January, 1975	Volume and direction of teaching in this area has been documented.
CONSULTATION TO OTHER HEALTH CARE DISCIPLINES.	Formal Teaching Role Committee	Provided informally and on request; has low department priority.	Improve and expand consultation.	January, 1975	It has been suggested that a coordinator for educational consultation be appointed; procedures have been set up to process requests for consultation.
STUDY THE POSSIBILITY OF FACILITATIVE ASSISTANCE TO RELATIVES OF PATIENTS IN ICU'S & WAITING ROOMS.	Two Students	Need for assistance has been brought to attention of department for investigation.	Determine potential involvement of department, either on its own or in conjunction with other departments.	April, 1974	Study complete and presented to department and administration.

Figure 6–2.
Administrative Portion of the Social Service Department's 1974 Goal Structure

committees were reconvened to initiate the second iteration of the MBO goal-setting process.

REACTION TO THE SYSTEM

The MBO system was a striking departure from the previous administrative style, and drew attention from a variety of sources. The reaction of the Social Service Department staff was mixed. Some staff eagerly seized the opportunity to make their priorities heard in the operation of the program. Other staff saw the system as bureaucratic paperwork, and treated it as a nuisance to be avoided. A few appeared to view it as a threat, and resisted the implicit accountability that accompanies formulation and evaluation of program goals. After the first year of operation, ten staff members had left the department and had been replaced by individuals whose values were congenial with the new system. In addition, goal setting was established as an integral part of each staff person's annual performance review.

The reaction of the University of Minnesota Hospitals' administration was uniformly favorable. Shortly after submission of the first annual report, the director was requested to present the full system at a meeting of the hospitals' department chiefs, and subsequently the University of Minnesota Hospitals implemented Management By Objectives in all administrative units. . . .

FUTURE DEVELOPMENTS

The values and objectives of a public human service organization are often a matter of conflict and negotiation. The next stage in the development of the Social Service Department's MBO system will involve periodically surveying groups and individuals with a continuing interest in the department's development. Sources of input will include clients, legislators, community agencies, hospital administrators, and professional social work organizations. A panel of individuals representing each group will be contacted annually to get both input on future priorities and feedback on the degree to which past priorities have been satisfied. The results of the surveys will be incorporated into the department's overall goal structure.

The second future development will be integration of the MBO format with the department's Management Information System. Developed by the director and an independent evaluation consultant, the system is an automated staff accountability mechanism wherein all personnel report their professional activities in specific function categories.[3] The function categories used in the system are based upon standards developed by the Southern Regional Educational Board and may be modified so they are consistent with the department functions presented previously. Particularly when linked to decentralized budgeting, this creates the potential to determine the expense required to support objectives in each function area and allows the director to make programmatic decisions based on cost-effectiveness information.

Discussion

Like most formal organizations, human service programs typically have two distinct, and occasionally conflicting, needs: (a) rational and orderly allocation of limited resources, and (b) creation of an atmosphere that allows maximum use of diverse staff talents. Students of Frederick Taylor's[4] "Scientific Management" school argue that the basic requirement of organization is "structure," and contend that effectiveness can best be assured through construction of a formal supervisory hierarchy with sanctions allocated according to the degree that staff meet specific and detailed role expectations. However, disciples of Chester Barnard[5] and Elton Mayo's[6] "Human Relations" approach to management believe that "participation" is essential to organization, and counter that open communication, decentralized decision making, and personalized task expectations are the key to optimal functioning.

The authors believe that organizational needs for "structure" and "participation" are not mutually exclusive. The Management By Objectives system presented here is an attempt to develop the three "structural" administrative functions mentioned by Allen Schick (i.e., planning, management, control),[7] while at the same time using human relations theorist Douglas MacGregor's[8] Theory Y assumption of management to allow maximum staff impact on the course of the Social Service Department's development.

The first structural requirement of organization mentioned by Schick, "planning," involves anticipating future needs, deciding on the resources necessary to meet these needs, and formulation policy to govern allocation of the resources. In the Planning, Programming, and Budgeting sytem (PPB) advocated by Schick, planning represents an attempt to project the activities of an organization ahead through time by formulating organizational objectives. The core of this process, of course, is identical with Management By Objectives. The very act of establishing objectives compels consideration of future contingencies, and the existence of an organizational goal structure provides a natural framework for examining the relationship of an organization's activities to its basic dedication.

"Management" according to Schick is the means through which resources are organized in the attainment of program objectives. In the same way that "planning" corresponds to the MBO process of forming objectives, "management" represents the setting of operational goals to attain them. This is the step in which each rather global objective is transformed into the clear, realistic, and concrete event(s) that will signal its attainment. An integrated goal structure of organizational goals facilitates the management function by providing a vehicle for distribution of resources and monitoring of staff task responsibilities. Such a structure also provides a coherent description of the organization's operating structure, which facilitates identification of weaknesses and redundancies.

"Control" according to Schick is the function insuring that specific activities are performed in an efficacious and efficient manner. Regarding Management By Objectives, "control" relates to evaluation and feedback, and involves assessing goal attainment and using such information to monitor organizational development. MBO enhances the control function in two ways. First, of course, it provides a means of evaluating performance. Predetermined goals, stated clearly and concretely, are effectiveness standards that avoid the potential biases of unstructured post hoc judgment. Second, Management By Objectives provides a catalyst for improving organizational communication. An open statement of organization reduces conflicts due to idiosyncratic interpretation of the organization's mission.

Subscribing to MacGregor's Theory Y assumption of management, which holds that under appropriate circumstances human beings will actively seek increased responsibility, the authors believe that inflexibility and excessive centralization of power can deny formal organizations the full creative potential of their personnel. Under the present Management By Objectives system this problem is mitigated through the direct staff establishment of goals, an arrangement that provides a mechanism for controlled opening of a hierarchy. Placing responsibility for goal setting on staff, rather than merely enforcing strict task instructions, increases flexibility and nurtures personal growth at the same time that it creates a structure for formal staff accountability. Staff are simultaneously provided with an opportunity to take a personalized approach to their work and accorded public responsibility for both the level of their expectations and the quality of their output. In the long run, this increases the energy and inspiration leveled against any particular problem, and tends to increase morale and efficiency as well, since staff tend to be most committed to goals of their own formulation. At the same time, MBO opens a useful channel of reciprocal communication between staff and administration, providing for open debate on issues directly related to improved organizational functioning. This dialogue helps clarify organizational priorities and places them "up front" where they may be examined by staff, consumers, and community.

NOTES

1. Peter F. Drucker, *Managing For Results* (New York: Harper & Row, 1954).
2. Rodney Brady, "MBO Goes to Work in the Public Sector," *Harvard Business Review*, vol. 51 (2) March–April 1973, pp. 65–74.
3. James Baxter, "An Automated Professional Staff Accounting System" (Unpublished Manual, University of Minnesota Hospitals Social Service Department, 1974).
4. Frederick Taylor, *Scientific Management* (New York: Harper & Row, 1947).
5. Chester Bernard, *The Functions of the Executive* (Cambridge, Mass.: Harvard University Press, 1938).
6. Elton Mayo, *The Social Problems of Industrial Civilization* (Cambridge, Mass.: Harvard University Press, 1945).
7. Allen Schick, "The Road to PPB: The Stages of Budget Reform," *Public Administration Review*, vol. 26 (4) December 1966, pp. 243–58.
8. Douglas MacGregor, *The Human Side of Enterprise* (New York: McGraw-Hill Book Company, 1960).

7. MBO as a Supervisory Tool

Supervision By Objectives

DONALD K. GRANVOLD

Management By Objectives (MBO) is the predominant management philosophy and style adopted by administrators to satisfy contemporary efforts to be accountable. Although this preoccupation has been most evident in business and industry, social service organizations, in response to the "age of accountability," have begun implementing MBO in various forms. Ideal-

Reprinted from *Administration in Social Work* 2, no. 2 (Summer 1978): 199–211, with the permission of the publisher. © 1978 by The Haworth Press. All rights reserved.

ly, the MBO approach necessitates organization-wide commitment and implementation. In settings in which MBO is not being implemented as the management system, however, the supervisor can nevertheless incorporate the concepts and procedures of MBO in fulfilling his middle-management responsibilities. Supervision By Objectives (SBO) is advanced in this paper as the social work supervisor's contribution to accountability and the legitimation of "achievement" in the delivery of social services.

Authors generally agree that the management process involves planning, organizing, directing, and controlling. These responsibilities are aimed at converting human resources into the attainment of organization objectives. This transformation is dependent, to an extent, upon the skill of the supervisor in achieving congruence between desired worker performance and actual worker performance. . . .[1] Managerial behaviors that have received empirical support for their contribution to worker performance include: the setting of objectives, feedback or knowledge of results, and worker participation in decision making. A series of highly controlled experimental studies have yielded the following results: (a) goal setting itself increases performance more than does feedback alone; (b) feedback or knowledge of results can improve performance; (c) the effects of feedback on performance are influenced by the quality of the feedback—the more specific, relevant, and timely the feedback, the greater the positive effects on performance; and (d) participation, or the influence that an individual has on decisions that affect him, can affect performance levels and job satisfaction. . . .[2] The SBO approach to supervision incorporates these managerial behaviors and, thereby, presumably contributes to minimizing worker performance discrepancy (the disparity between actual performance and desired performance).

This paper is designed to inform the reader how to supervise by objectives. The discussion of SBO addresses types of objectives, establishing objectives, guidelines for writing objectives, and advantages and disadvantages. Examples of objectives are given throughout, including two complete SBOs.

Types of Objectives

In a social agency, the social work supervisor is responsible to see that organization goals are effectively addressed through service delivery. Inherent in this process are issues of scheduling, quality, and efficiency of service. The implementation of SBO in addressing these responsibilities involves the development of managerial and worker objectives. Although there are many variations in the implementation of MBO and the process of determining objectives, there are essentially two forms of objectives: performance objectives and personal development subjectives.

PERFORMANCE OBJECTIVES

Performance objectives are designed to measure the completion of job tasks against established production standards and may be aimed at maintaining or improving given performance levels. Raia . . . further categorizes performance objectives as addressing (a) routine objectives in key results areas, (b) special activities, and (c) innovative and creative activities.[3]

Performance objectives designed to *maintain* a given level of unit productivity in a key results area might be written as a managerial SBO as follows: "To sustain the rate of foster home licensing at 100 homes per year"; "To provide 500 hours of direct counseling services per month."

Performance objectives designed to *improve* the level of unit productivity in key results areas might be stated as follows: "To increase by 20% the number of foster homes licensed this year over last year's 85 homes licensed"; "To increase by 1,000 hours the amount of direct counseling service provided this year over last year's 7,200 hours."

Although these objectives are written from the manager's perspective, corresponding worker objectives may be developed as a means of achieving them. For example, as a means of achieving an increase of 1,000 hours of direct counseling service this year, a worker's objective may read as follows: "To increase from 22 to 25 hours per week my time spent in providing direct counseling services."

Special activities may result from changes in priorities, emergencies, special projects, or in response to management decisions.[4] . . . For example, the receipt of a new grant providing supplemental funds for the "meals on wheels" program may facilitate the expansion of the program. The objective might read as follows: "To increase by 10% the number of people served meals in catchment area IV."

The solution of persistent problems and the introduction of new ideas for achieving better results form the basis for innovative and creative objectives.[5] . . . In stimulating innovation and contributing to improved service delivery/organization functioning, the supervisor may develop objectives for himself or call upon his workers' creativity in writing innovative objectives. For example, it may be determined that one of the problems in treating youth in a residential treatment center is that parents are nonsupportive of the program partially due to their lack of involvement. In evaluating resources, it is determined that there is adequate living space to accommodate families for weekend visitations to campus. The objective might be written as follows: "To develop and implement a family visitation program designed to bring families to campus at a rate of two families per month."

PERSONAL DEVELOPMENT SUBJECTIVES

Personal development subjectives differ from performance objectives in that (a) they are addressed to the individual's skill development and professional interest and (b) subjectives are statements of specific verifiable/measurable events or activities which, if accomplished, *presumably* lead to the achievement of a desired result.[6]. . . The effectiveness of service delivery in the social agency is highly dependent upon the competency of the social worker. The improvement of worker competency is addressed through personal development subjectives. These subjectives may be oriented either to the enhancement of skill for functioning in the current position or for the purpose of supervisor or worker preparation for alternative career direction or advancement. A supervisor might write a subjective for his professional growth as follows: "To develop grantsmanship through successfully completing a series of three grant-writing courses through the Center for Labor and Management from January 1, 1978 to January 1, 1979."

The supervisor's commitment to worker development might take the form of the following subjective: "To ensure that all unit social workers attend one continuing education course each 6 months."

A worker might write a subjective for the improvement of his own professional competency as follows: "To gain competency in interviewing through the development of microcounseling skills by March 1, 1978."

Establishing Objectives

The development of managerial and worker objectives relies upon validating the relationship between organization goals and specific objectives. This validation is accomplished as the supervisor evaluates objectives for (a) relevance (the extent to which the objective is addressed to the overall goals of the unit/organization), (b) timeliness (the extent to which the objective represents the best choice evaluated against competing alternatives), and (c) quality (the extent to which the objective is stated in measurable, tangible, or verifiable terms). The following interrelated procedures serve to ensure validation of objectives and proper implementation:

1. Identify the key results areas of the job and the corresponding skills/actions.
2. Assess worker knowledge/skill in each performance area.
3. Set objectives for key results areas consistent with the above assessment.
4. Rank objectives by priority.
5. Develop acceptable performance standards for each area stated in terms of measurable outcome criteria where possible.
6. Develop action plans for objective attainment, with target dates assigned.
7. Modify or reorder objectives prior to implementation as indicated through supervision/consultation.
8. Implement objectives and monitor performance/progression.
9. Final review.

The process of implementing SBO (a) provides the worker with an opportunity to participate in goal setting and in the establishment of criteria for performance appraisal, (b) contributes to the quality of the interaction between supervisor and workers, and (c) provides a mechanism for the definition of measurable outcome criteria for job tasks.

IDENTIFICATION OF KEY RESULTS AREAS AND OBJECTIVE SETTING

In capitalizing on the potential benefits of SBO, the supervisor must ensure that key areas of worker responsibility are explicitly stated and the requisite competencies for effective performance defined in behaviorally measurable terms. The supervisor and the worker must jointly participate in the identification of job tasks, assessing worker competency in job-related skill areas, defining objectives in mutually agreed-upon key responsibility areas, assigning priorities, developing action plans and target dates, and in the establishment of objective measurement criteria for each objective. Raia . . . indicates that the setting of objectives tends to be most successful when the individual himself assumes the responsibility for initiating the process and interacts with the supervisor in a creative and problem-solving manner.[7] It is the supervisor, however, who is accountable to see that objectives are appropriately established, which implies supervisory modification and review.

The ultimate goal of initial objective setting is the identification of those functions or activities that are considered by worker and supervisor to offer the highest potential for improved worker performance and unit effectiveness.

ESTABLISHING PRIORITIES

Given the various types of objectives and the range of job tasks constituting key results areas, it is necessary to establish an ordering of objectives. A triadic classification system of priorities is typically utilized. Top priority is assigned to objectives that are considered essential to the job. Second-order objectives are considered important, although not as essential as top-priority objectives. Third-order objectives are least in importance and, although they may be highly desirable for improved performance, are not considered critical to the performance of the job. Priority groupings are frequently identified as "must do," "should do," "nice to do." It is in the establishment of priorities that supervisor and worker perspectives may be in conflict.

ESTABLISHING PERFORMANCE STANDARDS

SBO requires the development of standards of performance for each key results area. Raia . . . notes that "the whole idea of accountability in management is based upon measurable standards which involve such factors as quantity, quality, cost, and time."[8] These factors are as relevant for the delivery of social services as they are for business and industry. Social service delivery has not often been viewed in quantifiable terms, and, likewise, managerial and worker performance have not been quantified. The predominant rationale for resisting quantification is the belief that one cannot put numbers on quality. The challenge is to identify those factors that lend themselves to measurement and that presumably represent reliable indicators of successful performance.

Whenever possible, then, performance standards should be stated in specific and quantifiable terms. Quantification explicates expectations and facilitates outcome measurement. These advantages and benefits of quantification are considered to outweigh the inherent limitations.

DEVELOPING ACTION PLANS

An integral part of the SBO process is the specification of action plans as a means of providing order to objective attainment. The specification of successive actions leading toward objective attainment guides the individual in "mapping out" his route. The procedure of evaluating various alternative action plans, defined as programming by Morrisey . . . , allows for problem solving before action is taken.[9] Raia . . . suggests a seven-step procedure to facilitate the development of an action plan:[10]

1. Specify what is to be accomplished.
2. Define the major activities required to support the objective.
3. Establish the critical relationships between the major activities.
4. Clarify roles and relationships and assign primary responsibility for each activity.
5. Estimate time lines for each major activity and its subactivities.
6. Identify additional resources required for each activity.
7. Verify deadlines and modify the action plan.

Although performance appraisal is accomplished against objectives in SBO, action plans may ultimately be evaluated to identify those activities that contributed positively or negatively to outcome. Utilized in this manner, the process of goal attainment may be monitored or revised for improved results.

Guidelines for Writing Objectives/Subjectives

Objectives must incorporate a clear statement of desired results, activities leading to objective attainment, time targets, and resource factors. It is also desirable to include a statement of the area of accountability (key results area) and the priority of the objective. The following criteria may serve as guidelines for writing objectives:

1. Begin the objective/subjective statement with the word "to," followed by an action verb, as in the following examples:
   a. Objectives
      (1) To increase the number of adoptive placements.
      (2) To decrease the rate of turnover in staff.
      (3) To maintain the number of unit hours of direct counseling services.
   b. Subjectives
      (1) To improve staff relations.
      (2) To develop an in-service training program calendar.
      (3) To implement a family treatment program.
2. Identify present and future performance levels where possible. An objective should reflect quantifiable change from a designated baseline. The objective "to decrease by 10% the average interim period between abuse complaint and home investigation" is meaningless without an established baseline. This applies to all objectives involving quantifiable change.

3. A specific target date should be included with the objective along with interim dates specified for action plans. It is important that worker and supervisor are in mutual agreement regarding the length of time in which to complete the objective. Interim dates serve as guideposts in monitoring progress toward objective attainment.

4. State the objective in measurable, tangible terms whenever possible. If quantification is not possible, use subjectives. Carroll and Tosi . . . make the distinction between measuring an objective and determining a subjective as follows: "If we are unable to quantify or specify the goal level adequately, we simply assume that the desired goal level will be achieved if a particular event or set of activities takes place."[11]. . .

5. Objectives should be challenging yet attainable. Although success must be attainable, objectives must be designed to motivate the individual to higher levels of performance.

6. Specify cost and resource factors. Money, materials, manhours, and other resources associated with the accomplishment of the objective should be estimated and weighed in the determination of priorities.

7. Avoid using words and expressions whose concept lacks measurability. Schoderbek . . . provides the following list of words to be avoided:[12] acceptable, adequate, appropriate, as soon as possible, comprehensive, decisive, effective, efficient, good, innovative, orderly, pertinent, progressive, quality, realistic, regular, sound, timely, tolerable, workable.

8. Personalize objectives as much as possible, recognizing differing abilities, experiences, and training.

9. State objectives in writing with file copies for the supervisor, the worker, and other relevant individuals.

10. Focus objectives on a few highly relevant and critical areas of responsibility. Particular attention should be given to ensure that the objective is within the scope of the writer's responsibilities.

11. Express the objective in a clear and concise manner.

12. The objective should be consistent with organization policies, procedures, and scope. Innovative objectives must be scrutinized to identify conflicts with organization operations and policy.

13. Give consideration to group objectives where teamwork projects are appropriate. In such cases, the contribution of each member should be spelled out as clearly as possible.

Figures 7–1 and 7–2 are examples of complete SBOs. Figure 7–1 is a worker performance objective written by a social worker in a residential treatment center. Figure 7–2 is a unit performance objective written by a supervisor in a public agency foster home certification unit. Included in each objective are: (a) area of accountability; (b) quantifiable objective statement with target date; (c) action plans with interim dates; (d) priority code; (e) rating scale of ultimate performance evaluation; and (f) space for comments on the completion of the objective.

Advantages and Disadvantages

The major advantages of SBO are related to accountability. The method is designed to facilitate reciprocal accountability between worker and supervisor in which there is explication of expectations and jointly predetermined criterion measures of performance appraisal. Reddin . . . identifies the benefits to the subordinate as knowledge of expectations, knowledge of performance, measurement criteria, clarification of responsibility, and increased job satisfaction.[13] Supervisor benefits include strengthened relationships with staff, greater motivation of workers, the elimination of weak appraisal methods, and the provision of a coaching framework. These advantages to worker and supervisor are of obvious benefit to the organization as well.

The predominant disadvantage of SBO is the expenditure of time and energy in developing, revising, and reviewing objectives. The paperwork itself may be a frustration to supervisor and staff. The method also requires that staff be trained in implementing the procedures. In addition to teaching the skills for the effective use of SBO, some time may be required in addressing staff resistance to the quantification of service delivery.

An argument often expressed against the MBO approach to management is that the objectives of social agencies are defined in intangible terms. Interestingly enough, the same exception is true for business in many cases. Drucker . . . notes that "achievement is never possible except against specific, limited, clearly defined targets, in business as well as in a service institution. Only if targets are defined can resources be allocated to their attainment, priorities and deadlines set, and somebody be held accountable for results. But the starting point for effective work is a definition of the purpose and mission of the institution which is almost always intangible."[14]. . .

The relationship between intangible goals and measurable objectives is, at best, based upon presumption—the presumption that achievement of measurable objectives contributes to the realization of the purpose and

SUPERVISION BY OBJECTIVES
WORK SHEET

DATE 8/1/77 _____   NAME D. Granvold

Objective	Action Steps to Achieve Objectives	Results Achieved
Area of Accountability: Recruitment/Certification Objective: To increase by 20% the number of foster homes certified this fiscal year over last year's 85 homes certified. Review date 6/30/78.	1. Working with workers x and y, develop a foster home recruitment brochure by 9/1/77. 2. Workers x, y, z develop a series of special interest "stories" on foster care needs for news media by 9/30/77. 3. Contact news media (radio, tv, newspaper) and arrange a series of articles/public service announcements by 10/1/77 4. Offer foster home training/screening programs in surrounding communities in the county beginning 11/1/77. 5. Meet with local Council of Ministers to solicit their involvement/support by 11/15/77. 6. Develop a spring recruitment campaign involving Foster Parents' Association. 7. Evaluate progress of certification by 4/1/78.	

Priority Code   Rating Scale
 ①   5 – Outstanding
 2   4 – Well above standard
 3   3 – Fully satisfactory – normal expectations

2 – Generally satisfactory – some improvement needed
1 – Unsatisfactory – definite improvement needed

Figure 7-1.
Worker Performance Objective Written by a Social Worker in a Residential Treatment Center

DATE 8/1/77

SUPERVISION BY OBJECTIVES
WORK SHEET

NAME T. Wilson

Objective	Action Steps to Achieve Objectives	Results Achieved
Area of Accountability: Direct Service Objective: To increase from 3 to 6 hours per week the average number of hours expended in family treatment by 6/30/78.	1. Develop procedures for selecting families with greatest potential to benefit from family treatment. 8/16/77 2. Evaluate current caseload applying procedures in #1 in selecting potential cases. 8/30/77 3. Meet with supervisor to set priorities among cases selected. 9/15/77 4. Arrange with administration a change in work schedule to facilitate evening treatment. 9/30/77 5. Discuss with supervisor approaches to involving family in treatment of child. 10/15/77 6. Develop a statement for families defining advantages of family treatment for improved behavior in children. 11/1/77 7. Contact families selected. 11/30/77 8. Develop a procedure for evaluating effectiveness of family treatment. 1/1/78 9. Check increase in average family treatment hours. 2/15/78 10. Complete analysis of evaluation data. 6/30/78	

Priority Code
　①
　2
　3

Rating Scale
　5 - Outstanding
　4 - Well above standard
　3 - Fully satisfactory

　2 - Generally satisfactory-some improvement needed
　1 - Unsatisfactory

Figure 7-2.
Unit Performance Objective Written by a Supervisor in a Public Agency Foster Home Certification Unit

mission of the organization. The value of the SBO method, then, is dependent upon the supervisor's validation of the assumptions supporting the relationship between specific objectives and organization goals.

In conclusion, the SBO method, with its inherent disadvantages, has the potential to enhance the managerial effectiveness of the social work supervisor. The viability of the method has received significant support; the effectiveness of its implementation rests with the supervisor.

NOTES

1. R. F. Mager and P. Pipe, *Analyzing Performance Problems or "You Really Oughta Wanna"* (Belmont, Calif.: Fearon, 1970).
2. S. J. Carroll Jr., and H. L. Tosi, Jr., *Management by Objectives: Applications and Research* (New York: Macmillan, 1973), pp. 4–7.
3. A. P. Raia, *Managing by Objectives* (Glenview, Ill.: Scott, Foresman, 1974), pp. 48–50.
4. Ibid., p. 49.
5. Ibid., pp. 49–50.
6. G. L. Morrisey. *Managing by Objectives and Results* (Reading, Mass.: Addison-Wesley, 1970), p. 47; Raia, *Managing*, p. 25.
7. Raia, *Managing*, p. 52.
8. Ibid., p. 55.
9. Morrisey, *Objectives and Results*, p. 68.
10. Raia, *Managing*, pp. 70–77.
11. Carroll and Tosi, *Management by Objectives*, p. 81.
12. P. P. Schoderbek, *Management by Objectives* (Iowa City: University of Iowa, 1973).
13. W. J. Reddin, *Effective Management by Objectives: The 3-D Method of MBO* (New York: McGraw Hill, 1971), pp. 195–99.
14. Peter F. Drucker, *Management* (New York: Harper & Row, 1973), p. 140.

8. Evaluating MBO

Factors Affecting Employee Attitudes toward the Installation of a New Management System

DONALD D. WHITE

Management programs, such as Management By Objectives and System IV, are increasing in popularity among both writers and practicing managers. Characteristically, they embody many of the practices and concepts set forth by behavioralists; e.g., participative decision making, goal setting, and increased responsibility and self-control for subordinates.Drucker..., Odiorne . . . , and Likert . . . , as well as other proponents, have popularized these systems and detailed their value to the total organization and the individual.[1] Yet, practicing managers are well aware that employee attitudes toward any newly introduced system ultimately may be responsible for its success or failure.

The purpose of this research was to assess the reaction of participating managers to a recently installed management system and to determine what factors might be responsible for positive or negative attitudes toward it. Specifically, variables related to the system itself or to its effect on selected aspects of organizational life were examined.

Little in the way of systematic research has been done to identify factors related to employee attitudes toward Management By Objectives-type systems per se. However, at least three studies have uncovered seemingly important variables of this nature. Doris M. Cook . . . concluded that attitudes were directly related to the frequency with which feedback was provided.[2] In a separate study, Carroll and Tosi . . . found that subordinate influence in the goal-setting process did not appear to be an important factor affecting attitudes toward a Management By Objectives system.[3] Finally, a study by Ivancevich, Donnelly, and Lyon . . . concluded that need satisfaction of participants was influenced by an MBO program.[4] In addition, their research suggested that the influence of top level managers

Reprinted from *Academy of Management Journal* 16, no. 4: 636–46, with permission from Academy of Management Publications.

in the organization was an important factor in improving perceived need satisfaction.

The Present Study

The present study was conducted in a state health-care facility. The institution employed 1,025 persons. Of those employed, 195 were managers who worked in departments directly responsible for patient care and rehabilitation. (Personnel in departments providing supporting services, e.g., food service, grounds, were excluded from the sample.) The organizational hierarchy in the departments studied consisted of six levels of supervision. The primary data-gathering device, a forty-one item questionnaire, was administered to the 195 managers. One hundred and fourteen respondents reported having contact with or knowledge of a Management By Objectives program which had been introduced at the facility some eighteen months earlier. Questionnaires submitted by these persons constituted usable sets of data and served as the basis for much of the final analysis.

Included in the questionnaire were eight classification questions, twelve open-ended questions, and twenty-one scale items using bipolar adjectives. Scale items were designed to reveal the extent to which the management system was responsible for affecting selected organizational conditions. Additional information was gathered through interviews with a representative sample of those managers participating in the study. Statistical techniques employed included simple correlation analysis, factor analysis, and multiple correlation analysis.

Management By Objectives is treated in the literature as a management system in and of itself. However, the explicit elements of MBO along with organizational members' perceptions of its novelty may cause participants to view Management By Objectives as a unique program. Therefore, the terms "system" and "program" are used interchangeably herein.

Attitudes of Employees and Their Immediate Superiors

Table 8–1 reveals that employee attitudes toward the MBO program definitely were favorable. Fewer than four percent of the managers responding suggested that they viewed MBO unfavorably. At the same time, 68.9 percent of the respondents indicated that they had favorable or very favorable attitudes toward the program.

Managers who were asked to indicate what they believed their superiors' attitudes were toward the Management By Objectives program indicated

Table 8–1

Managers' Attitudes Toward the Management By Objectives Program

Interval and Description	Department					Total Responses	Percent of Totals
	I	II	III	IV	V		
1 Very unfavorable	1					1	1.0
2		3				3	2.9
3	2	8	7	3	8	28	27.2
4	5	12	6	7	10	40	38.8
5 Very favorable	4	8	10	5	4	31	30.1
Total Number Responding	12	31	23	15	22	103[a]	100.0
Average Response[b]	3.9	3.8	4.1	4.1	3.8	3.9	

[a]Eleven managers failed to respond.

[b]Average response calculated by multiplying the numerical value shown below intervals on the scale of the appropriate question times the number of responses per interval. Values for each interval were then totaled and the results divided by the total number of responding managers in the Unit or organization, respectively. Average response figures are used for relative rather than absolute value comparisons.

overwhelmingly (80 percent) that their superior's attitude toward the program was favorable. Furthermore, one half of those persons who said their superior's attitude was favorable went so far as to indicate that the superior's attitude actually was very favorable (see Table 8–2). In addition, it was noted that average response figures for all units were higher for "perceived attitude of superior" than comparable figures reflecting the respondent's own attitude.

The average response figure representing the respondent's own attitude toward MBO was 3.9 for all managers. However, the average response figure regarding perceived attitude of the respondent's superior was 4.2. These figures were interpreted to mean that subordinates perceived their superiors to have better attitudes toward MBO than they, themselves, had toward the program. Such a finding was not unexpected. It seems natural for managers to believe that attitudes of superiors toward a program such as MBO would be equal to, or better than, their own attitudes since the superior may have been perceived as "pushing" the concept initially.

Differences in average response figures according to department were attributed to intradepartmental factors such as difficulties encountered

Table 8–2

Subordinates' Perceptions of Their Superiors' Attitudes Toward the Management By Objectives Program

Interval and Description	Department					Total Responses	Percent of Totals
	I	II	III	IV	V		
1 Very unfavorable	1	1				2	1.9
2				1	1	2	1.9
3		5	4	1	6	16	15.4
4	4	11	10	9	8	42	40.4
5 Very favorable	7	16	10	4	5	42	40.4
Total Number Responding	12	33	24	15	20	104[a]	100.0
Average Response	4.3	4.2	4.3	4.1	3.9	4.2	

[a]Ten managers failed to respond.

during installation of the system. In addition, staffing differences within departments may have negatively affected installation. Line positions in departments I, II, and III were staffed with nonprofessional employees. However, departments IV and V employed professional educators and nurses, respectively.

Responses also were analyzed by the manager's level in the hierarchy (see Table 8–3). Average response figures were relatively similar when organizational levels were grouped (i.e., levels two through four and levels five and six). A more detailed analysis indicated a significant relationship between managers' attitudes toward MBO and level in the hierarchy ($r = .33; p < .01$). However, personal interviews revealed that supervisors' attitudes toward the program actually were not consistently higher than attitudes of their subordinates (as was perceived by subordinates) throughout the entire organization.

Reasons for Dissatisfaction with the MBO System

As reported, there was only a small number of persons who were dissatisfied or apathetic toward the MBO System. However, employees who were not satisfied with the system expressed similar reasons for their

Table 8–3.
Managers' Attitudes Toward the Management By Objectives Program

Interval and Description	Organizational Level[a]						Total Responses	Percent of Totals
	1	2	3	4	5	6		
1 Very unfavorable						1	1	1.2
2					2	1	3	3.6
3		1	6	3	7	7	24	28.6
4	3	4	2	8	5	7	29	34.5
5 Very favorable	2	3	6	6	4	6	27	32.1
Total Number Responding	5	8	14	17	18	22	84[b,c]	100.0
Average Response	4.4	4.2	4.0	4.2	3.6	3.7	3.9	

[a]Level 1 is Department Head.
[b]Eleven non-responses.
[c]Nineteen staff managers responsible to Department Heads were excluded.

neutral or negative attitudes. For example, individuals recognized the need for cooperation from peers and support from superiors in establishing and achieving meaningful objectives. Unfavorable attitudes were expressed when the necessary integrated efforts were perceived not to be forthcoming. Unrealistic objectives also discouraged a number of managers. Perceived achievability of objectives was an important factor governing formation of attitudes about the MBO system in two ways. First, a number of managers stated that adequate resources simply were not available to accomplish objectives. In such cases, negative attitudes often were developed by workers as soon as objectives were received. Thus, use by some managers of a directive approach to goal setting was evidenced. Had greater participation in the formulation of objectives taken place, more realistic goals or strategies to achieve needed objectives might have resulted and dissatisfaction might have been minimized. On the other hand, low budgets, inadequate help, and lack of needed equipment are not uncommon complaints in any organization.

Second, some objectives that were accepted by subordinates as being realistic were not always achieved. Although failure to achieve some goals was not unexpected, lack of achievement was discouraging to a few managers. In these cases, expectation levels were higher than could be realized; consequently, some managers became disappointed. Other employees commented that the entire program of Management By Objectives simply did not meet their expectations in terms of anticipated changes and improvements in their own work areas.

Additional factors which may have produced less than favorable attitudes toward the program were overemphasis on achieving objectives and too little understanding of the MBO program as a whole.

Reasons for Favorable Attitudes toward the MBO System

Figures in Table 8–2 indicate that attitudes of employees throughout the organization were strongly in favor of the Management By Objectives system. Reasons for satisfaction with the system were assessed in two ways. First, statements by managers whose attitudes toward the Program were favorable were reviewed. Second, coefficients of correlation were computed for sets of data relating attitude toward the MBO program to a number of selected variables. These variables included perceived effects of the management program and conditions for which it was believed to be responsible.

STATEMENT OF MANAGERS

Managers had an opportunity to explain their perceptions of the system directly, through open-ended questions and personal interviews. The most commonly reported reasons supporting favorable statements toward Management By Objectives dealt with benefits derived from its use. Managers who commented on the benefits of the MBO program generally suggested that achievement of objectives was profitable to personnel as well as to patients. Improved living and working conditions and reduced resident population were cited as examples of achievements which were fully or partially credited to MBO. Comments regarding results produced by the Program often referred to motivational aspects of goal setting.

Organization of resources in terms of established priorities was cited as another factor that influenced positive attitudes toward the Program. Knowing what was expected of their respective organizational units reportedly caused supervisors to look closely at manpower, material, and time resources in order to determine how goals could be accomplished. A feeling of being organized, along with increased clarity of responsibilities, apparently caused managers to feel more secure in their positions.

Finally, increased contacts with other members of the department and more meaningful communication with those persons were said to influence

Table 8–4.
Selected Variables Correlated with Managers' Attitudes Toward the MBO System

Independent Variables	Coefficient of Correlation (r)	Coefficient of Determination (r^2)	Level of Significance
Greater exposure to MBO	.37	.14	.01
Frequency of goal-setting meetings	.23	.05	.02
Frequency of progress-review meetings	.35	.12	.01
Increase in contact with superior with MBO	.28	.08	.01
Satisfaction with changes in number of formal contacts with superior	.27	.07	.01
Suggestions encouraged in goal-setting meetings	.26	.07	.01
Relative number of suggested goals accepted by superior	.21	.04	.05
Increased control over own activities	.42	.18	.01
Clarification of own responsibilities	.31	.10	.01
Increased responsibility as a result of MBO	.20	.04	.05
Satisfaction with change in amount of responsibility	.39	.15	.01
Feeling in on decisions as a result of MBO	.40	.16	.01
Satisfaction with feelings in on decisions	.52	.27	.01
Increased influence on superior as a result of MBO	.31	.10	.01
Increased influence in the department	.33	.11	.01
Satisfaction with the amount of information received about department operations	.25	.06	.02

Table 8–4—Continued.

Independent Variables	Coefficient of Correlation (r)	Coefficient of Determination (r^2)	Level of Significance
Satisfaction with the amount of information received about state home operations	.24	.06	.02
Positive effect on communication	.46	.21	.01
Increased quantity of workload	.17	.03	.10
Perceived attitudes of superior toward MBO	.65	.42	.01

positively attitudes toward MBO. Better relationships growing out of improved interpersonal communication was credited by one supervisor with increasing his respect for ". . . those in authority as well as my own subordinates." Also, the belief that Management By Objectives was supported fully by top management personnel was reported to be a reason for favorable attitudes toward the system.

STATISTICAL SIGNIFICANCE OF SELECTED FACTORS

Table 8–4 describes the coefficient of correlation (r) and the coefficient of determination (r^2) for the dependent variable (managers' attitudes toward the MBO Program) and the respective independent variables along with the level of significance of the relationships.

According to figures shown in Table 8–4, all items examined were significant at the .01 level except the following: (1) frequency of goal-setting meeting; (2) relative number of suggested goals accepted by the superior; (3) increased responsibility as a result of the MBO program; (4) satisfaction with the amount of information received about unit or state home operations; (5) increased quantity of workload as a result of the MBO program. The fact that at the .01 level these variables were not related to managers' attitudes toward the Management By Objectives program is notable in itself. For example, a more significant positive value of r logically might have been expected when attitudes toward MBO were correlated to "relative number of suggested goals accepted by the supervisor." On the other hand, a significant negative value of r might have been anticipated when the variable, "increased quantity of workload," was introduced.

Although all other variables listed in Table 8–4 were significant at the .01 level, some factors accounted for a greater amount of variance than did others. Consequently, variables were categorized as weak, intermediate, or strong predictors of employee attitudes toward the MBO program. (The term, "predictor," is used to describe the degree of covariation between two variables. Independent variables described as strong or intermediate predictors may have a predictive value. Cut-offs for the three categories of predictors were set according to natural groupings of the coefficients of determination and are as follows: weak, $r^2 \leq .08$; intermediate $r^2 > .08$ and $\leq .18$; and strong, $r^2 > .18$.)

Weak predictors. Variables which accounted for only a small amount of total variance were classified as weak predictors and included the following: (1) suggestions encouraged in goal-setting meetings; (2) Increase in formal contacts with superiors; (3) Satisfaction with change in amount of formal contacts. A statistically significant relationship existed between these variables and employee attitudes toward the program. However, since the amount of variance explained by each factor was very small, discussion is not deemed warranted.

Intermediate predictors. Intermediate strength predictors showed more substantial relationships with the attitude variable. The frequency with which progress-review meetings were held appeared to have relevance as a predictor of satisfaction with the program. A positive correlation ($r = .35$) was recorded for the two factors, supporting earlier findings of Cook.[5] . . . Significantly, "frequency of progress-review meetings" was a more reliable predictor of attitude than was "frequency of goal-setting meetings." The importance of feedback provided in the meetings rather than the opportunity to set performance objectives seems to be reflected in the significant difference for the two items. Not unexpectedly, exposure to the program also ranked as an intermediate predictor.

Increase or decrease in responsibilities as a result of the program was found to be a weak predictor of attitudes toward MBO. However, "satisfaction with change in the amount of responsibility" explained a greater amount of variance in the attitude factor. Together, the two variables accounted for 16 percent of the variance in the dependent factor. Therefore, they constituted an intermediate predictor when viewed in conjunction with one another. Although clarification of responsibilities was cited by administrators as an important factor governing attitudes toward MBO, "effect of the MBO system on clarification or responsibilities" ranked only as an intermediate predictor on the basis of the statistical analysis. Thus, the variable was not found to be as strong a predictor of attitudes toward the program as the comments from managers would seem to have indicated.

Three variables related to effectiveness of subordinate participation in the organization all ranked as intermediate strength variables. "Feeling more in on decisions as a result of MBO," "increased influence on the superior," and "increased influence in the department as a whole," each accounted for no less than ten percent of the variance in the dependent variable (by simple correlation). Carroll and Tosi . . . found that subordinate influence in the goal-setting process did not appear to be an important factor affecting attitudes toward a Management By Objectives-type program.[6] If either "increased influence on the superior" or "feeling more in on decisions as a result of the program" are considered to represent subordinate influence in the goal-setting process, then Carroll and Tosi's finding was not supported by this study. However, if the variable, "perceived acceptance of suggested goals," is considered as a lone indicator of subordinate influence in the goal-setting process, their hypothesis would appear to be upheld since that particular variable accounted for only four percent of the variance in the attitude variable. Further investigation of the relationship between subordinate participation in goal setting and attitudes toward MBO-type programs seems warranted.

The highest ranking intermediate predictor was "effect of the Program on a manager's control over his own activities." Although 18 percent of the variance in the dependent factor was accounted for by this variable, increased control over their own activities was not mentioned by managers as a reason for favorable attitudes toward the MBO program.

Strong predictors. Two variables were found to be strong predictors of managers' attitudes toward the Management By Objectives program. A set of two additional variables constituted a third strong predictor. A substantial relationship existed between attitudes toward the program and the perceived attitude of the respondent's superior toward the MBO program. The variable accounted for 42 percent of the variance between the two factors for the enterprise as a whole. When Departments I, II, and III were viewed independently of Departments IV and V, 50 percent of the variance was explained. (An earlier study at the subject facility revealed that the Program was installed less satisfactorily in Departments IV and V than in Departments I through III.) Correlation analysis does not provide a cause-effect explanation of relationships. However, dispositions of managers toward MBO logically were concluded to be largely dependent upon perceptions of how their superiors viewed the program. Stated another way, subordinates who believed their superior had a positive attitude toward the MBO system were, themselves, likely to have a positive attitude toward the program.

Notably, no managers mentioned the enthusiasm of their immediate superior as a factor influencing their own attitudes toward the system. Two persons did suggest that support from the top of the organization was a factor influencing their attitude. Thus, perceived attitude of the superior toward the program appeared to be an unconscious, yet extremely important, influence on individuals' perceptions of MBO.

Another factor which ranked as a strong predictor of attitudes toward MBO was the perceived effect of the program on communication. Persons who saw the management program as contributing positively to communication were likely to have favorable attitudes toward it. Twenty-one percent of the variance was accounted for by the variable and 35 percent of the variance was explained when Departments IV and V were excluded from consideration.

The last variable classified as a strong predictor was the "degree of satisfaction with feeling 'in on' decisions in the department." When this factor was related to "effects of the MBO program on feeling in on decisions," the two variables accounted for 28 percent of the variance in the attitude factor. Although Management By Objectives cannot be credited alone with satisfaction resulting from feeling in on decisions, it did increase managers' feelings of being more in on decisions. In turn, feeling more in on decisions generally was satisfying to managers. Therefore, the effect of the program on causing managers to feel more in on decisions in their departments indirectly contributed to favorable employee attitudes toward the system.

Conclusions and Implications

Employees throughout the five departments studies generally had favorable attitudes toward the Management By Objectives system. Stated reasons for positive attitudes included resulting benefits for staff and patients, contribution to planning and utilization of resources, and effects on interpersonal communication in the enterprise. Failure to realize established goals was the primary reason given for dissatisfaction with the system. Other factors cited in connection with unfavorable attitudes toward MBO included lack of needed cooperation from supervisors and overemphasis on achieving objectives.

A number of variables were discovered to be statistically significant indicators of attitudes toward the program. However, a manager's perception of his superior's attitude toward MBO was found to be the strongest predictor of his own attitude toward the program. Particularly noteworthy was the finding that NO single item or factor approached in significance that of perception of superior's attitudes. The conclusion may be interpreted as supporting the earlier findings of Ivancevich, Donnelly, and Lyon . . . regarding the impact of upper-level managers on such a program.[7] Perceived contribution of Management By Objectives to communication and satisfaction with feeling in on decisions in the department (when related to the effect of MBO on feeling in on such decisions) also were found to be strong indicators positively related to attitudes toward the system.

Porter and Lawler . . . have concluded that continuous monitoring of attitudes might help to identify an employee's disposition toward a "novel social situation" with which he has been confronted (e.g., a newly installed management system).[8] This study has identified specific criteria or signals which will aid in the monitoring process. Indicators suggested herein may assist upper-level managers in planning for the installation as well as administering management systems similar to Management By Objectives.

NOTES

1. Peter F. Drucker, *The Practice of Management* (New York: Harper & Row, 1954); George S. Odiorne, *Management by Objectives* (New York: Pitman, 1965); Rensis Likert, *The Human Organization* (New York: McGraw-Hill, 1967).
2. Doris M. Cook, "The Impact on Managers of Frequency of Feedback," *Academy of Management Journal*, vol. 11 (3) September 1968, pp. 263–77.
3. Stephen J. Carroll and Henry L. Tosi, "Relationship of Goal-Setting Characteristics as Moderated by Personality and Situational Factors to the Success of the 'Management by Objectives' Approach," *Proceedings, American Psychological Association*, 77th Annual Meeting, 1969, p. 600.
4. John M. Ivancevich, James H. Donnelly, and Herbert L. Lyon, "A Study of the Impact of Management by Objectives on Perceived Need Satisfaction," *Personnel Psychology*, vol. 23, 1970, pp. 139–51.
5. Cook, "Impact on Managers."
6. Carroll and Tosi, "Goal Setting Characteristics."
7. Ivancevich, Donnelly, and Lyon, "Management by Objectives."
8. Lyman Porter and Edward Lawler, *Managerial Attitudes and Performance* (Homewood, Ill.: Irwin, 1968).

PART III

Evaluating Alternatives:

Benefit-Cost Analysis

Introductory Note

The logic of benefit-cost analysis is essentially simple and consists of attempts to estimate certain costs and gains that would result from alternative courses of action. Presumably, human behavior has always been guided by some such calculation. Today, with much more powerful tools of rational calculation, benefit-cost analysis is being applied with greater frequency to comparisons of alternative health programs, educational measures, mental health programs, and many others. Typically the criteria of goal achievement are translated into monetary units so that the economic benefits of a program can be compared to the costs.

This is one of the most controversial features of benefit-cost analysis in the human services. The reason for employing benefit-cost analysis is to overcome the lack of a market for the human services, for when the price mechanisms of the market do not or cannot carry out their functions of evaluating different courses of action, different policies, or the consequences of alternative inputs and outputs, benefit-cost analysis suggests an attractive solution. Consider that in the private sector of the economy markets and the amount of profit in a firm provide the measures of efficiency or effectiveness—profit provides that single agreed upon metric that can be used to focus policy in respect to investment, product development, and marketing efforts. As a measure, profitability has its limits, to be sure, providing no useful data on the social costs of an enterprise,[1] but it does yield that single summary number called the "bottom line" that permits a comparison of the expected profitability of not only like products and services but also of incommensurables.

Social agencies, on the other hand, are handicapped by the lack of agreement on criteria for allocating resources and for measuring the outputs of these resources. For example, if a public welfare department attempts to choose criteria for the evaluation of day-care programs, several possibilities might be selected including the social and cognitive benefits that may accrue to the child, a mother's employability enhanced by the provision of day care, perhaps in the long run economic independence for this mother and savings to the public fisc. In which direction lies social "profitability"?

Undoubtedly, tight resources and skepticism about the efficacy of the human services have generated an upsurge of interest in benefit-cost analysis. Nevertheless, the value of being able to identify the benefits and costs, say of alternative juvenile corrections programs, or of alternative programs for the elderly would seem to be beyond dispute. For unless we can identify more desirable alternatives, how can administrators and policy makers choose better rather than worse, how can we know where political and administrative processes may be leading to poor decisions?

Conceptually, the antecedents of benefit-cost analysis harken back to attempts to estimate the monetary value of human life. Probably the earliest such systematic work dates back to 1699 when Sir William Petty assessed the capital value per capita of the English population. Then toward the end of the nineteenth century, Max Von Pettenkoffer stated that the monetary value of health to a city consisted of the average loss of wages while sick and the costs of medical care (leaving aside the losses due to premature death). Pettenkoffer also discussed the public and private benefits to be gained from the implementation of public health programs, and his work can be thought of as a primitive form of benefit-cost analysis.[2]

These endeavors have a line of continuity with those contemporary assessments that fall under the rubric of the "human capital" approach. This approach views expenditures in health, education, child welfare, employment training programs and the like, as *investment*, not consumption expenditures. In other words, currently or potentially productive persons are regarded as capital and or wealth, and attention is directed to gains and losses in that capital or wealth measured in terms of dollars.[3] Manifestations of the human capital approach are found in attempts to measure decrements and increments to national productivity owing respectively to mental illness and its alleviation.[4] This mode of thought is deeply embedded in discussions and analyses of the human services, where, for example, expenditures for children's programs and for education are commonly justified on the basis of their contributions to national productivity.

For all the compelling attractiveness of benefit-cost analysis, limitations intrinsic to the method condition its utility in the social services. As William Gorham, an early advocate pointed out, the method proved inapplicable to the "grand decisions" of social policy:

> If I was ever naive enough to think this sort of analysis possible, I no longer am. The benefits of health, education and welfare programs are diverse and often intangible. They affect different age groups and different regions of the population over different periods of time. No amount of analysis is going to tell us whether the Nation benefits more from sending a slum child to school, providing medical care to an old man or enabling a disabled housewife to resume her normal activities.[5]

But benefit-cost analysis is not bound to "grand decisions," and if the accumulated experience to date provides any guide, the informational and decision technologies of management science and economics may be more handicapped in such large systems as the federal government than in smaller state and local organizations. Whatever the organizational level, however, there are common methodological elements and principles involved in performing benefit-cost analyses.

The Economic Calculus. With unusual clarity, Roland McKean lays bare the crucial methodological considerations involved in benefit-cost analysis. Of first importance is comprehensiveness or systems analysis in terms of objectives, the analysis of interrelated alternatives and specification of costs and gains. Also significant in the calculus are "opportunity costs"— spending money one way preempts the opportunity to spend it another way, hence opportunity costs consist of the benefits of lost chances to do things and should be factored into the analysis. Moreover, costs and gains accrue over a period of time and must be "discounted" in analyzing options even if there is no fully agreed upon method for discounting, and notwithstanding the fact that fairly small variations in the discount rate can often lead to major differences in conclusions. The issue of criteria surrounds the entire discussion. What criteria will be used to point to the best choice? McKean specifies three different types of criteria and points out that the use of benefit-cost *ratios* may be a *criterion error*.

The Economic Calculus in the Human Services. Technical difficulties of considerable magnitude confront administrators and policy makers who seek to quantify goals and objectives, benefits, and costs. Quantification in terms of the dollar metric compounds the problems, for "a dollar is a dollar" when it comes to *aggregate values*, but in the case of *distributive values*, costs and benefits do not accrue equally because the aim may be to provide more services to one group than another, to one geographic area than another. In proposing that benefit-cost analysis be linked to program-evaluation, Stanley Masters, Irwin Garfinkel, and John Bishop discuss this problem and suggest that the decision-making utility of benefit-cost analysis will be increased if benefits and costs are assessed from the point of view of various individuals, groups, and organizations. Of particular importance to the authors is the necessity for social programs to serve a *redistributive* function with more benefits going to the poor and more costs paid by those who are well off. Also discussed is the highly problematic question of treating nonmonetary values. Recognizing that it is often impossible to put dollar values on important program benefits, the authors propose two solutions: (1) With numerous cautions and caveats, they examine the circumstances under which cost-effectiveness studies may be useful, and (2) they suggest that benefit-cost analyses may be constructed out of the

explicated value judgments of the analyst to which policy recommendations are attached.

The succeeding discussion by Morris and Ozawa also acknowledges
some of the problematical aspects of benefit-cost analysis, but on balance,
the authors argue vigorously for its use in the human services. Questions of
cost determination, benefit attribution, and data analysis are explored
within the context of decision making in public service. For application at
the level of the agency or program, John A. Morris and Martha N. Ozawa
develop a five-step model of benefit-cost analysis in which they introduce
an ingenious value-weighted mechanism as a substitute for the dollar
metric in determining benefits. The model is then demonstrated through a
simulation in a hospital setting where the question is whether to undertake
a new planning technique known as Goal Planning. Absent from the model
are specifications of opportunity costs and a decision criterion. The authors
nonetheless argue that benefit-cost analysis can be systematic, precise, and
objective.

Benefit-Cost Analysis in Child Welfare and Mental Health. Joseph Halpern and Paul R. Binner illustrate the range of application of benefit-cost
analysis, methodological variation from the prior approaches, and the
problem of perspective in valuing benefits. In the context of mental health
programs, and consistent with human capital approaches, the "output
value" method described by Halpern and Binner seeks to specify in dollar
terms the value of program "products" relative to program costs. With the
aim of achieving more economic allocational decisions, they address the
fundamental question of investment: in which patients should treatment
resources be invested? They answer: in those patients whose expected
productivity is greatest where productivity is measured by a patient's
earnings for the year prior to entry to the program. A better measure of
economic benefits would be the discounted or present value of expected
future earnings. Presumably, this measure might reflect program effect,
whereas prior earnings would not. In general, however, the rationale for
using a person's dollar value remains highly controversial and yields biased
results: resources would be shifted away from those whose earnings are
low—the old, the young, the poor, and the unskilled. Because of the
difficulties in attributing an economic value to most programs other than
those specifically intended for employment development, cost-effectiveness analysis might be a useful alternative to benefit-cost analysis.

Any overall assessment of the current status and value of benefit-cost
analysis must acknowledge that the attempt to allocate, assess, and measure all program costs and benefits in terms of tangible and intangible
benefits is a worthy ideal, and perhaps no more than common sense. In
practice, however, completeness is decomposed and proves illusory, and

in the attempt to replace intuition and unexplicated value judgments with science and precision, arbitrary dollar values are attached to the diminution of suffering. Although benefit-cost analysis may be a promising tool, contrary to claims made for it, it belongs in the realm of philosophy and normative theory, perhaps even ideology, more than in the niche of science.

NOTES

1. In economics these are referred to as "negative externalities." Air and water pollution, nuclear and occupational hazards are some of the forms of negative externalities. The increase in costs of services when a firm moves into an area is another form of negative externality as is the increase in per capita costs to those remaining when a firm moves out.
2. Alan L. Sorkin, *Health Economics* (Lexington, Mass.: Lexington Books, 1975), pp. 102–103.
3. Theodore W. Schultz, "Investment in Man: An Economists View," *Social Service Review*, vol. 33 (2) June 1959, pp. 109–17; Charles W. Schultze, "Investment in Human Capital," *American Economic Review*, vol. 51 (1) March 1961, pp. 1–7.
4. See for example, Rashi Fein, *Economics of Mental Illness* (New York: Basic Books, 1958).
5. William E. Gorham, *Hearings, The Program-Planning-Budgeting System: Progress and Potentials,* Joint Economic Committee, Congress of the United States, 90th Congress, First Session, September, 1967, p. 83.

9. The Economic Calculus

Cost-Benefit Analysis

ROLAND N. MC KEAN

"Cost-benefit analyses" are attempts to estimate certain costs and gains that would result from alternative courses of action.[1] For different applications, other names are often used: "cost-effectiveness analysis" when

Reprinted from Roland N. McKean, *Public Spending* (McGraw-Hill, 1968), pp. 135–45, with the permission of the publisher.

courses of action in defense planning are compared; "systems analysis" when the alternatives are relatively complex collections of interrelated parts; "operations research" when the alternatives are modes of operation with more or less given equipment and resources; or "economic analysis" when the alternatives are rival price-support or other economic policies. The term "cost-benefit analysis" was originally associated with natural-resource projects but has gradually come to be used for numerous other applications. The basic idea is not new: individuals have presumably been weighing the pros and cons of alternative actions ever since man appeared on earth; and in the early part of the nineteenth century, Albert Gallatin and others put together remarkably sophisticated studies of proposed U.S. government canals and turnpikes. But techniques have improved, and interest has been growing. All these studies might well be called economic analyses. This does not mean that the economist's skills are the only ones needed in making such analyses or, indeed, that economists are very good at making them. It merely means that this analytical tool is aimed at helping decision makers—consumers, businessmen, or government officials—economize.

In recent years, the Bureau of the Budget, the National Bureau of Standards, many other U.S. agencies, and governments and agencies in other nations have been exploring possible uses of cost-benefit analysis.[2] Sometimes the analyses are essentially simple arithmetic. Sometimes high-speed computers are used—as they were, for instance, in the search by a Harvard group for the best way to use water in the Indus River basin in Pakistan. One of the major applications of cost-benefit analysis will continue to be the comparison of alternative natural-resources policies— proposals to reduce air and water pollution, to divert water from the Yukon to regions further south, to do something about the rapidly declining water level in the Great Lakes, and so on. But other applications are appearing with growing frequency—comparisons of such things as alternative health measures, personnel policies,[3] airport facilities, education practices, transportation systems, choices about the management of governmental properties, and antipoverty proposals.

All such analyses involve working with certain common elements: (1) objectives, or the beneficial things to be achieved; (2) alternatives, or the possible systems or arrangements for achieving the objectives; (3) costs, or the benefits that have to be foregone if one of the alternatives is adopted; (4) models, or the sets of relationships that help one trace out the impacts of each alternative on achievements (in other words, on benefits) and costs; and (5) a criterion, involving both costs and benefits, to identify the preferred alternative. In connection with each of these elements there are major difficulties. Consider a personal problem of choice that an individual might try to analyze—selecting the best arrangements for his family's transportation. Spelling out the relevant objectives, that is, the kind of achievements that would yield significant benefits, is no simple task. The objectives may include commuting to work, getting the children to school, travel in connection with shopping, cross-country trips, and so on. Part of this travel may be across deserts, along mountain roads, in rainy or icy or foggy conditions. The family may attach a high value to the prestige of traveling in style (or of being austere, or of simply being different from most other people). Another objective that is neglected all too often is a hard-to-specify degree of flexibility to deal with uncertainties. Adaptability and flexibility are particularly important objectives if one is examining alternative educational programs, exploratory research projects, or R&D policies. Overlooking any of the relevant objectives could lead to poor choices.

The second element, the alternative ways of achieving the benefits, also deserves careful thought, for selecting the best of an unnecessarily bad lot is a poor procedure. In choosing a family's transportation system, the alternatives might include various combinations of a compact automobile, a luxury automobile, a pickup truck, a jeep, a motor scooter, an airplane, a bicycle, the use of a bus system, and the use of taxicabs.

In many problems of choice, the alternatives are called "systems," and the analyses are called "system analyses." This terminology is quite appropriate, because the word "system" means a set of interrelated parts, and the alternative ways of achieving objectives usually are sets of interrelated parts. At the same time, the word "system" is so general that this usage is often confusing. In defense planning, for example, the term "system" can be used to refer to such sets of interrelated parts as the following:

Guidance mechanism ——————→ Guidance system
Missile Structure
Nose cone
Fuel } Missile X, also a system
Warhead

Installations
Other missiles and installations
Decoys } Strategic retaliatory system
Bombers and installations
Active defenses
Command and control

All three of these systems are collections of interrelated parts. How large should systems be for their comparison to be called a "systems analysis" or for their comparison to be a useful aid? There are no correct answers; one must exercise judgment in deciding how large the systems should be to provide worthwhile assistance in tracing out the costs and benefits. (In effect, one must weigh the costs against the benefits of preparing alternative cost-benefit analyses.) Where interrelationships are relatively important, one is usually driven to consider large systems. Thus to choose between two engines for a supersonic airliner, one can hardly compare thrusts alone and make an intelligent selection, for weight, reliability, cost, noise, etc., may have diverse effects on overall desirability. The power plants must be fitted (at least on paper) into rival aircraft designs, and thence into airline and airport systems to see their net impact on the real objectives and the full costs. Moreover, other components of the projected systems may have to be modified so as not to use either engine stupidly. Suppose one engine would make possible the use of relatively short runways. To use an aircraft with this power plant in an intelligent way, one might have to modify many parts of the proposed airports, traffic patterns, ground installations for instrument-landing systems, and even proposed airline schedules. Hence one would end up comparing rather broad systems having many common components but also having several components that differed.

So much for the alternative systems to be compared. The third element of cost-benefit analysis, cost, is crucial because it really reflects the alternative benefits that one might obtain from the resources. It is just as foolish to measure costs incorrectly or to neglect part of them as it is to measure benefits incorrectly or neglect part of them. If selecting a luxury car entails building a new garage or paying higher insurance premiums, these are part of the costs of choosing that alternative. If one already has an adequate garage, the value foregone by using it (but *not* the cost of building a garage) is the relevant cost.

"Models," the fourth element of cost-benefit analysis, are simply crude representations of reality that enable one to estimate costs and benefits. If a person figures, "With the bus I could average 10 miles per hour, traverse the 5 miles to work in one-half hour, spend five hours per week commuting to work, and would stand up 50 percent of the distance on 50 percent of the trips," he is using a model. If he says, "With Automobile X, I would get a motor tune-up every 5,000 miles and would therefore spend $50 per year on that item," he visualizes these events and uses a set of relationships, that is, a model, to estimate this cost. When one tries to perceive how something would work, it has become convenient and fashionable to say, "Let's build a model," though one could simply say, "Let's devise a way to predict what would happen (or a way to estimate costs and benefits)."

The fifth element of cost-benefit analysis is the criterion or test of preferredness by means of which one points to the best choice. People tend to make a variety of criterion errors.[4] One error, the use of the ratio of benefits to costs, is such a perennial favorite that it merits a brief discussion. Suppose at first that both benefits and costs can be measured *fully and correctly* in monetary terms and that one must choose among the following three discrete (and not mutually exclusive) alternatives:

	A	B	C
Cost	$100	$100	$200
Benefit one year later	$150	$105	$220
Ratio of benefits to costs	1.5	1.05	1.10

Suppose further that the constraint is that funds can be borrowed at 6 percent. Which projects should be undertaken, and what is the criterion? A and C, both of which yield more than 6 percent, should be undertaken, and the proper criterion is to maximize the present value of net worth or, its surrogate, to undertake projects wherever the marginal benefit exceeds the marginal cost. Note that the criterion is *not* to maximize the ratio of benefits to costs, which would restrict one to Project A. If the constraint is a fixed budget of $200, Projects A and B should be selected. Again, maximizing the ratio of benefits to costs would limit one to Project A.

Or consider two discrete and mutually exclusive alternatives (for example, two sizes of a dam):

	A	B
Cost	$100	$200
Benefit one year later	$150	$260
Ratio of benefits to costs	1.50	1.30

If funds can be borrowed at 6 percent, Project B should be undertaken. One should not choose A simply because the benefit-cost ratio is larger. Ratios are not irrelevant—every marginal productivity is a ratio—for one often seeks to *equalize* certain ratios as a condition for achieving a desired maximum. But the ratio itself is not the thing to be maximized.

The issue takes on a good deal of importance when the benefits can only be suggested by physical products or capabilities. In these circumstances, presumably in desperation, people frequently adopt as a criterion the maximization of some such ratio as satellite payload per dollar, hours of student instruction per dollar, or target-destruction capability per dollar. But the benefit-cost ratios of rival proposals simply cover up the relevant information. Take another example from the choices that confront the individual. If one is selecting a hose with which to sprinkle his lawn, one may have the following options:

	⅝-IN. DIAMETER	1-IN. DIAMETER
Cost	$3	$5
Benefit (water put on lawn per hour)	108 gallons	150 gallons
Ratio of benefits to costs	36/1	30/1

The ratios are irrelevant. The pertinent question is whether or not the extra capability is worth the extra $2. Less misleading than showing the ratio would be showing the physical capabilities and the cost à la consumers' research. Or, where it makes sense to do so, one can adjust the scale of the alternatives so that each costs the same or achieves the same objectives. Then one can see which system achieves a specified objective at minimum cost, or achieves the greatest benefit for a specified budget. This is not a perfect criterion, for someone has to decide if the specified budget (or objective) is appropriate. But at least this sort of test is less misleading than a benefit-cost ratio.

With regard to this fifth element of cost-benefit analysis, discussing the correct way to design criteria may seem like discussing the correct way to find the Holy Grail. In a world of uncertainty and individual utility functions, judgments must help shape choices, and no operational test of preferredness can be above suspicion. Moreover, analyses vary in their quality, which is hard to appraise, and in their applicability to different decisions. For these reasons, responsible decision makers must treat cost-benefit analyses as "consumers' research" and introduce heroic judgments in reaching final decisions. In a sense, then, it may be both presumptuous and erroneous to discuss having a test of preferredness in these quantitative analyses.

Criteria should be considered, nonetheless, in connection with such analysis. First, cost-benefit analysts do apply criteria, especially in designing and redesigning the alternatives to be compared. They delete features that appear to be inefficient, add features that appear to be improvements, and probe for alternative combinations that are worth considering. This screening of possibilities and redesign of alternative systems entails the use of criteria, and these should be explicitly considered and exhibited.

Second, whether or not they ought to, analysts often present the final comparisons in terms of a criterion. Thus while it may be wrong to talk as if a definitive criterion is an element of every analysis, these warnings about criterion selection should be emphasized.

Needless to say, in reaching decisions, one should attempt to take into account *all* gains and *all* costs. Some people feel that there are two types of gain or cost, economic and noneconomic, and that economic analysis has nothing to do with the latter. This distinction is neither very sound nor very useful. People pay for—that is, they value—music as well as food, beauty or quiet as well as aluminum pans, a lower probability of death as well as garbage disposal. The significant categories are not economic and noneconomic items but (1) gains and costs that can be measured in monetary units (for example, the use of items like typewriters that have market prices reflecting the marginal evaluations of all users); (2) other commensurable effects (impacts of higher teacher salaries, on the one hand, and of teaching machines, on the other hand, on students' test scores); (3) incommensurable effects that can be quantified but not in terms of a common denominator (capability of improving science test scores and capability of reducing the incidence of ulcers among students); and (4) nonquantifiable effects. Examples of the last category are impacts of alternative policies on the morale and happiness of students, on the probability of racial conflicts, and on the probability of protecting individual rights. In taking a position on an issue, each of us implicitly quantifies such considerations. But there is no way to make quantifications that would necessarily be valid for other persons. This sort of distinction between types of effects does serve a useful purpose, especially in warning us of the limitations of cost-benefit analysis.

One should recognize, too, that cost-benefit analysis necessarily involves groping and the making of subjective judgments, not just briskly proceeding with dispassionate scientific measurements. Consider the preparation of such analyses to aid educational choices. No one says, "This is the educational objective, and here are the three alternative systems to be compared. Now trace out the impacts of each on cost and on achievement of the objective, and indicate the preferred system." What happens is that those making the analysis spend much time groping for an *operational* statement of the objective, such as a designated improvement in specific test scores without an increase in the number of dropouts or nervous breakdowns. A first attempt is made at designing the alternative ways of realizing this objective. Preliminary costs are estimated. Members of the research team perceive that the systems have differential impacts on other objectives, such as flexibility, or student performance on tests two years later, or student interest in literature. Or the rival arrangements may elicit different reactions from teachers, parents, and school boards, affecting the achievement of other objectives. The analysts redesign the alternatives in the light of these impacts, perhaps so that each alternative performs at least "acceptably" with respect to each objective. Next it appears that certain additional features such as extra English-composition courses might add greatly to capability but not much to cost. Or the research team's cost group reports that certain facilities are extremely expensive and that eliminating them might reduce costs greatly with little impairment of effectiveness. In both cases the systems have to be modified again. This cut-and-try procedure is essential. Indeed, this process of redesigning the alternatives is probably a more important contribution than the final cost-effectiveness exhibits. In any event, the preparation of such an analysis is a process of probing—and not at all a methodical scientific comparison following prescribed procedures.

An appreciation of cost-benefit analysis also requires an awareness that incommensurables and uncertainties are pervasive. Consider the impacts of alternative educational policies that were mentioned above. These effects can perhaps be described, but not expressed in terms of a common denominator. Judgments about the extent of these effects and their worth have to be made. Some costs, such as the monetary measures of foregone benefits, perhaps additional sacrifices in terms of personality adjustment and ultimate effectiveness, or undesirable political repercussions that yield costs, cannot validly be put in terms of a common denominator. Furthermore, because of uncertainties, whatever estimates can be prepared should in principle be probability distributions rather than unique figures for costs and gains. The system that performs best in one contingency may perform worst in another contingency. Finally, costs and gains occur over a period of time, not at a single point in time, and there is no fully acceptable means of handling these streams of costs and gains in analyzing many options.[5]

These difficulties are present because life is complex, and there is no unique correct choice. The difficulties are not created by cost-benefit analysis. Moreover, they do not render quantitative economic analysis useless. They simply mean that one has to be discriminating about when and how to use various tools. In general, the broader choices made by higher-level officials pose relatively great difficulties regarding what value judgments to make and what the physical and social consequences of alternative actions would be. Consider, for example, the allocation of the U.S. budget among various departments or the allocation of funds among such functions as the improvement of health, education, or postal service. Cost-benefit analysis gives relatively little guidance in making these choices, for in the end the decision maker's task is dominated by difficult personal judgments. Cost-benefit analysis may help somewhat, for it is the appropriate framework in terms of which to *think* about these broad choices, and it can usually provide *some* improved information. When personal judgments must play such a huge role, however, the improved information may not be worth much.

Consider another example of such broad choices: the government's allocation of its R&D effort between basic research and applied development. To choose between these two alternatives, officials must rely heavily on personal judgments about the consequences and judgments concerning the value of those consequences. Values cannot be taken as agreed upon, and physical-sociological effects cannot be predicted with confidence. Quantitative analysis can probably contribute only a little toward the sharpening of intuition here. Or consider the allocation of effort between improving medical care for the aged and improving it for the young. Suppose one could made extremely good predictions of the effects, which would of course aid decision makers. The final choice would be dominated in this instance by value judgments about the worth of prolonging the lives of elderly persons, the worth of lengthening the lives of persons in great pain, the worth of saving the lives of weakened or physically handicapped children, the relief of different kinds of distress, and so on.

Another broad or high-level choice that brings out these difficulties is the allocation of funds to, or for that matter within, the State Department. In the tasks of diplomacy it is hard to visualize taking a set of value tags as being clearly stated, let alone agreed upon. And disagreement is quite understandable in predicting the effects of alternative courses of action on the probabilities of stable alliances, provocations, little wars, nuclear wars, and so on. Positive science has provided few tested hypotheses about these relationships.

As one proceeds to narrower or lower-level problems of choice, these difficulties frequently, though not always, become less severe. (Actual decisions, of course, vary continuously in the extent to which they present these difficulties, but it is often economical to think in terms of such categories as broad and narrow or high-level and low-level choices). Within such tasks as education and health improvement, there are lower-level choices for which quantitative analysis may be very helpful, but there are also many middle-level choices that are fraught with difficulties. Should more effort be placed on the improvement of mental health even if it means less emphasis on the treatment of conventional ailments? Should effort be reallocated from higher education toward the improvement of elementary-school training, or vice versa? Or, as an alternative policy, should government leave such allocative decisions more than at present to the unin-fluenced choices of individual families? Cost-benefit analysis cannot do much to resolve the uncertainties about the consequences of such decisions, about their relative worths to individual citizens, or about whose value judgments should be given what weights.

Within applied research and development, a choice between specific projects might appear to be a low-level choice that economic analysis could greatly assist. In such instances, it is true that values can sometimes be taken as agreed upon. In selecting research and development projects for new fuels, for instance, the values to be attached to various outcomes are not obvious, yet they are probably not major sources of divergent views. Perhaps the principal difficulty is the inability to predict the physical consequences, including "side effects," of alternative proposals. Here too, cost-benefit analysis may be destined to play a comparatively small role.

One can list many problems of choice that seem to fall somewhere in this middle ground—that is, where cost-benefit analysis can be helpful but not enormously so. It would appear, for instance, that the selection of anti-poverty and welfare programs depends heavily on consequences that one cannot predict with confidence and on value judgments about which there is much disagreement. Similar statements apply also to the selection of foreign-aid programs, urban-development proposals, or law-enforcement programs—the comparison of different methods of curbing the use of narcotics, say, or of different penal institutions and procedures. In education, many decisions that may appear to be low-level or relatively simple—for example, the selection among alternative curricula or teaching methods or disciplinary rules—are inevitably dominated by judgments about the consequences of these policies and about the value tags to be attached to those consequences.

It is in connection with comparatively narrow problems of choice that cost-benefit analysis can sometimes play a more significant role. In these instances, as might be expected, the alternatives are usually rather close substitutes. Science can often predict the consequences of governmental natural-resource investments or choices affecting the utilization of water or land, and people can often agree on the values at stake—at least to a sufficient extent to render analyses highly useful. Competing irrigation plans, flood-control projects, swamp drainage and land reclamation ventures, and water-pollution control measures are examples of narrow problems of choice in which cost-benefit analysis can help.

Cost-benefit analysis also promises to be helpful in comparing certain transportation arrangements. The interdependencies of transportation networks with other aspects of life are formidable, yet with ingenuity extremely useful studies of some transportation alternatives can be produced.[6] Numerous transportation alternatives have been the subject of such studies: highways, urban systems, inland waterways, modified railway networks, the utilization of a given amount of sea transport, air transport fleets and of course many lower-level choices, such as alternative road materials, construction practices, airport facilities, and loading arrangements. In some instances, of course, the interdependencies may be too complex for analyses to be very valuable; transportation alternatives that affect a large region and its development yield chains of consequences that are extremely difficult to trace out.

At best, the difficulties of providing *valuable* information are awesome. . . . There can always be legitimate disagreement about any of these policy decisions, and analyses must be regarded as inputs to decisions, not as oracular touchstones. Nonetheless, to think systematically about the costs and gains from alternative policies is surely more sensible than to rely on haphazard thought or intuition. Such analyses can bring out the areas of disagreement so that people can see where their differences lie. Even with considerable divergence in judgments, they can screen out the absurdly inferior alternatives, focusing the debate on subsets of relatively good alternatives. For some choices, cost-benefit analysis provides information that can help officials agree upon a course of action that is preferred or accepted by most citizens. And for all choices, it is the right framework to use in organizing the evidence and one's thoughts and intuitions regarding alternatives. Even in deciding which research project to undertake, or how much time to spend on it, a researcher consults rough cost-benefit T-accounts. In deciding anything, a person should weigh costs and gains. Preliminary weighing may suggest that the use of a tentative rule of thumb or "requirement" is preferable to further or repeated analyses, but he should not initially pull some mythical requirement out of the air.

NOTES

1. For more detail on many of these points, see Charles J. Hitch and Roland N. McKean, *The Economics of Defense in the Nuclear Age* (Cambridge, Mass.: Harvard University Press, 1960).
2. For pertinent references, see Alan R. Prest and Ralph Turvey, "Cost-Benefit Analysis: A Survey," *Economic Journal*, Vol. 300 (75), December 1965, pp. 683–735. See also Robert Dorfman, ed., *Measuring Benefits of Government Investments* (Washington, D.C.: The Brookings Institution, 1965).
3. Joseph A. Kershaw and Roland N. McKean, *Teacher Shortages and Salary Schedules* (McGraw-Hill Book Company, New York, 1962).
4. Hitch and McKean, *Economics of Defense*, chap. 9.
5. Ibid., chaps. 10 and 11.
6. See especially J. R. Meyer, J. F. Kain, and M. Wohl, *The Urban Transportation Problem* (Cambridge, Mass.: Harvard University Press, 1965); and T. M. Coburn, M. E. Beesley, and D. J. Reynolds, *The London-Birmingham Motorway: Traffic and Economics* Road Research Laboratory Technical Paper 46, D.S.IR. (London: H. M. Stationery Office, 1960).

10. The Economic Calculus in the Human Services

Benefit-Cost Analysis in Program Evaluation

STANLEY MASTERS, IRWIN GARFINKEL,

and JOHN BISHOP

Benefit-cost analysis is a highly useful, though often misunderstood, method for evaluating many activities, including social programs. All activities have benefits and costs. Consider this paper. There are clearly time and effort costs for both the writers and the readers. We hope that there will be benefits as well: a few professional Brownie points for the writers, and increased understanding for both readers and writers. This mundane example illustrates an important point. Benefit-cost analysis has wide applicability, and amounts to no more than an attempt to look carefully and systematically at the benefits and costs of an activity or program.

In addition to comparing the benefits to the costs for a particular program, this type of analysis involves comparing (implicitly if not explicitly) the benefits and costs of alternative programs or activities. Such comparisons are essential because a fundamental premise of benefit-cost analysis is that choices are necessary—that neither the time nor the material resources are available to do all good things. When choices are necessary it is only reasonable, if one values rationality, to choose activities or programs where the benefits are highest relative to the costs.

Although this rationale for benefit-cost analysis sounds uncontroversial, perhaps even incontrovertible, specific benefit-cost studies often stimulate bitter opposition. In part, this is to be expected and is unavoidable. No matter how a study comes out, some interest group will be politically opposed to the policy recommendation implied by, if not contained in, the study. Other reasons for the controversiality of some benefit-cost studies will be discussed below.

This paper explains the rudiments of benefit-cost analysis and discusses how we believe such analysis should be done. First, we discuss benefits.

Reprinted from *Journal of Social Service Research* 2, no. 1 (Fall 1978): 79–93, with permission of the publisher. © 1978 by The Haworth Press. All rights reserved.

Second, we discuss costs. Third, we consider the analysis of both from the viewpoints of several interested parties.

Valuing Benefits

A variety of important issues are involved in evaluating the benefits of a program. First, the goals of the program must be identified. A clinic, for instance, is likely to be trying to improve the health of its patients, a job-training program to improve the employment and earnings opportunities of its trainees. Second, a methodology must be developed for evaluating the extent to which the program is accomplishing these goals. Finally, the benefits must be converted to some common denominator so that they can be added together and compared with the overall costs.

The identification of goals is an important issue. It is also a difficult one that does not lend itself to easy generalizations but requires a case-by-case analysis. (Side effects, both positive and negative, also need to be investigated.) Articulating goals in measurable terms is particularly problematic for much of social work practice, which is directed at improving individual, group, or community functioning. Most practitioners are quite capable of recognizing improvement when they see it; specifying beforehand which behavioral changes should be identified as the goals of a program is much more difficult.[1] . . . In order to keep our exposition simple enough to make the major points readily understandable, we shall concentrate here on a relatively straightforward program and goal—that of a training program whose primary aim is to increase the earnings opportunities of program participants. The goal that we have postulated, increased earnings, is a relatively easy one to measure. It is quantitative, with dollars as the measuring unit. Even in this relatively easy case, however, there are still important difficulties in determining program benefits. For example, we usually want to know the effect of the program not only on the earnings of participants immediately after the program but also for years into the future.

Two problems arise in this regard. First, analysts cannot usually wait several years to complete the study. Thus, they will normally have to guess what is likely to happen to the future earnings differentials between program participants and nonparticipants. Similar problems occur in many areas, including programs to reduce weight or to stop smoking. Second, it is generally believed that benefits in the future are not as valuable as benefits right now. Monetary benefits, in particular, can be invested and thus lead to larger future benefits. Thus, some discount factor has to be applied to the benefits expected from future earnings before adding them to the more immediate benefits. (Future costs also have to be discounted. Although the choice of an exact discount rate has been the subject of a large and rather inconclusive literature in economics, discounts in the 5–15 percent range are generally used.)[2]

BENEFITS NOT MEASURED IN DOLLARS

Next let us consider how to evaluate benefits when the initial outcome is not directly measured in dollars. These benefits fall into two categories: (a) those that are not measured in dollars but are susceptible to objective quantification of some kind; and (b) those that are inherently nonquantifiable.

Continuing with our example of a training program, an instance of the first type might be reduced criminal activity. For those training programs aimed primarily at ex-offenders or delinquent youth the program goal is not only to increase participants' long-run employment and earnings but also to reduce their criminal activity. Criminal activity is inherently difficult to measure, but arrest rates are a frequently used proxy. Let us assume that a program has been found to reduce arrest rates. How is this benefit to be translated into dollar terms so that it can be added to the benefits from higher earnings in order for the combined benefits to be compared with the program's costs? The reduction in the number of arrests for program participants will reduce the costs of our law enforcement system (e.g., fewer police should be needed), of the courts (e.g., fewer judges should be needed), and of the correctional system (e.g., fewer prisons should be needed). The process of calculating the dollar savings thus achieved is cumbersome but not analytically intractable.

Instances of inherently nonquantifiable factors are being beaten up or living in fear of being robbed. All would agree that reductions in such factors are benefits, but they typically receive little emphasis in benefit-cost studies simply because they are nonquantifiable.

How should program evaluators (and policy makers) proceed given that, for so many programs, it is difficult, if not impossible, to put a dollar value on certain important program benefits? In cases where it is possible to show that the benefits are greater than the costs even if some of the benefits are disregarded, the problem can be avoided, at least to some extent. Initial postprogram earnings gains as a result of a training program, for example, might be larger than the costs. In this case, we would not need specific dollar estimates of future earnings gains or other less easily quantified benefits, such as possible reductions in criminal activity, in order to show that the program was worthwhile. This approach can be useful in many programs—such as drug treatment and mental health—where increased earnings are one indicator of successful treatment of participants. Dollar estimates would still be necessary, however, in deciding how to allocate funds to several programs, all of which had large benefits relative to their costs.

In cases where the most important benefits are not convertible into dollars and cannot be handled as just described, there are two possible approaches.

Cost-effectiveness analysis. The first approach, from the perspective of an individual agency, is to use cost-effectiveness rather than benefit-cost analysis. The cost-effectiveness approach is useful in the special case where the agency's mission and total budget are fixed. In our training example, the mission might be to run training programs to increase the earnings of the poor, working within an annual budget of, say, $200,000. Then the issue would be which kinds of jobs to train people for (construction skills, typing, or automotive repair), what people to train (the old or the young, those with or without recent work experience, the poor strictly defined or those who need training under a more flexible definition of need), and how to do the training (classroom or on-the-job training). The objective would be to determine which approaches would lead to the greatest earnings gains per dollar spent—and thus to the greatest total earnings gains to be had for $200,000 per year. This cost-effectiveness approach would work equally well if the goal were reductions in infant mortality at a clinic for pregnant women, better school performance for a child counseling clinic, or reductions in crime for a police department.

Although it can sometimes allow an individual agency to avoid having to put a dollar value on its benefits when it allocates its own funds, cost-effectiveness analysis only works if the agency has a single goal. Even then cost-effectiveness analysis will not help if there are a variety of subgoals and no single index, such as dollars, to weight the relative importance of the subgoals. For example, cost-effectiveness analysis might help a mental health agency with the single objective of improving the mental health of the residents in a certain geographical area to decide whether to use short- or long-term casework or psychiatric treatment interventions for certain kinds of mental health problems. But it would be of no use in judging which kinds of mental health problems should be given budget priority. And even when there is a single goal and single measure, cost-effectiveness still leaves the problem unsolved of how society should allocate funds to different agencies with different missions.

Presenting a range of estimates. A second approach has wider applicability. Rather than placing a great deal of emphasis on a single benefit-cost ratio, the program evaluator spells out as clearly as possible the various benefits and costs of a program, and indicates what evidence there is that may be relevant in assigning dollar weights to those benefits and costs that are not initially measured in dollars. In some cases, such as family counseling, none of the benefits may be easily reduced to dollars. In fact, they may not even be readily quantifiable.

The evidence needed is of three types: (a) descriptions of the various ways in which people are served or benefited; (b) counts of the number of people benefited in each way; and (c) evidence useful in assigning dollar values to these benefits. For example, in considering whether to mount an inoculation campaign against some new flu strain, the analyst should seek to estimate who would be inoculated and what effects such inoculations would have on the total incidence of the disease in the community. The value of fewer people becoming ill should include estimates of the output that would have been lost because they could not work. Obviously, the dollar value of the benefits is much greater since the disease is unpleasant and also keeps people from their normal tasks outside the work place. However, the value of reducing such discomfort is difficult to determine. We believe that the analyst should indicate his or her own assessment of this value and then show how sensitive the results would be to a wide range of alternative assessments. Policymakers—government officials, legislators, and ultimately the voters—would thus be given a menu of alternative value judgments and the policy recommendations that are attached to each one. In this way the analyst can provide the policymaker with guidance on technical matters without impinging upon the policymaker's job of making the value judgments.[3] . . . This procedure focuses attention on the need for such value judgments rather than on coming up with one "objective" result.

To summarize, we believe that benefit-cost analyses would not only have a deservedly better reputation but would be more useful if, in addition to an accounting of the readily quantifiable benefits and costs, they routinely contained (a) educated best guesses about unmeasured benefits and costs, (b) explicit assessments as to their relative worth from a value judgment point of view, and (c) explicit discussions of the policy implications that follow from alternative best guesses and value judgments. In addition, we believe that it would be useful to include explicit statements about the values held by the author. These additions would not only make the reader aware of the possible biases but would also force the writer to treat seriously the inevitable interrelations among scientific analysis, value judgments, and policy recommendations. (We take our inspiration from Gunnar Myrdal's argument that social science research, by its very nature, cannot be value free.) Consequently, the investigator should begin with a value premise or set of value premises in order to separate factual knowledge from values.[4] . . .

Designs for Estimating Benefits

Let us return to our example of a training program, where the benefits are quantifiable and measured in dollars. Even in this relatively easy case where a good metric is available, there are empirical problems in measuring a program's benefits. If we simply compare the earnings of program participants immediately before and after the program, the program effects are likely to be distorted. This is because earnings prior to the program are likely to be abnormally low,[5] and earnings immediately after the program may be either artificially high or low depending on the extent and efficiency of placement efforts by program operators.

CONTROL GROUPS—RANDOM ASSIGNMENT

To avoid these difficulties most evaluations of training programs compare the earnings gains of program participants to those of comparable people who did not receive training during the program period. Ideally, these groups should be indistinguishable from each other in every respect except their program experience. Such groups can be constructed by defining a given group of persons as eligible for the program and then selecting, on a strictly random basis, some for program participation (the experimentals) and some as the comparison group (the controls).

Such random assignment has, however, rarely been used in training program benefit-cost studies—in large part because this method of allocating people to the program seems less equitable to many people than alternatives such as "first come, first served." In its absence, various comparison groups have been used—a common one being those selected for the program who failed to show up. Unfortunately, those who do not show up are likely to be different in important ways from those who do. For example, those who do not report to the program may be less motivated than those who do report. If this is the case, the trainees would have done better than the comparison group even if there had been no program. Alternatively, the no-shows may be people who obtained good jobs in the interval between applying for training and the start of the program. In this case trainees are likely to do less well than the comparison group even in the absence of the program. Such differences are called selectivity biases, and can lead to potentially serious distortions in the results, often in favor of the program. All studies without randomly assigned control groups will and should be suspect.

Program evaluations should, therefore, institute a random assignment process whenever possible. This is difficult because program operators in general dislike the idea of random assignment, at least in part because it seems unfair that the opportunities should be awarded, so to speak, simply by luck. Unless the program budget and staff are large enough to serve everyone who wants to participate, some rationing device will necessarily operate. Of these, random selection appears as just as the others and has, in addition, extra benefits.

A look at other possible ways of rationing the opportunity to participate is instructive. First come, first served, the most common rationing device, creates a long waiting list and results in services going only to those who can afford to wait for the help. The fear of long waiting lines, alternatively, may cause agencies to avoid appropriate outreach efforts to make the whole potential client population aware of the service—resulting in services being focused on only the most vocal and aware. Another common approach is to let professionals choose whom to serve. This often results either in "interesting" cases becoming the focus of attention, in clients with middle-class characteristics being given preference, or in client access being determined by interagency bureaucratic politics. A third response to an insufficient budget is to try to serve everybody by depreciating the quality of the service. This approach risks spreading resources so thinly that no one receives any appreciable benefits. The benefit of the random assignment method of rationing the service, which other methods do not have, of course, is that it will yield research results that enable services to be improved for all. It has also been proven that if a program is set up with a research evaluation as a primary objective and the funding agencies are prepared to insist on random assignment, there are not usually any prohibitive administrative problems with it.

We are not arguing that the only evaluation studies worth doing are based on random assignment. For example, regression analysis can be used to control for measurable differences between program participants and those in some nonrandom comparison group. We do believe, however, that the researcher should make every effort to utilize a true experimental design before turning to alternative quasi-experimental designs. If the research community becomes more vocal about the advantages of random assignment, we believe that an increasing number of evaluations can be based on a rigorous experimental design.

STATISTICAL SIGNIFICANCE

Once a control (or comparison) group has been established, the next issue is how to compare the earnings of the two groups. A point estimate can be obtained by subtracting the earnings of the control group from the earnings of the experimental group. The problem, however, is to understand how seriously policymakers should take this estimate of the differential in earnings that results from the program experience. Problems of possible selectivity bias have already been mentioned. Here we discuss a second problem, which is especially important if the sizes of the two groups being compared are small—that the experimental-control differential may be due to chance rather than a real effect of the program. To guard against the danger of placing importance on differentials that could easily have resulted from chance, evaluation studies normally put considerable emphasis on the "statistical significance" of the results. The standard use of statistical significance starts with a presumption (the null hypothesis) that the program is not having any effect and then tests to see whether the data support or refute it. Experimental-control differentials that are not statistically significant are then interpreted as showing no effect. In most studies an experimental-control differential is regarded as statistically significant if there is no more than a 5 percent probability that it could have occurred by chance.

This procedure evolved within the framework of academic research, and is most suitable in that context—where the issue is largely whether other scholars should take the time to pay close attention to a colleague's new results. In the context of program evaluations with direct policy implications, however, we regard other techniques as preferable.

First, the presumption of no effect means that lack of statistical significance is interpreted as showing that the program has no effect. In our view, if an ongoing program that has passed previous political tests is being evaluated in order to make decisions as to its continuation, it makes at least as much sense to take the opposite tack. This entails starting with the presumption (null hypothesis) that the program effects are favorable enough to yield benefits that are at least equal to costs and testing that presumption against the data. For a null hypothesis of this type, lack of statistical significance is interpreted as showing that the benefits are at least equal to the costs. Which null hypothesis to use is a value judgment. Science gives us no guide. Traditional practice biases the results against finding an effect. The alternative approach that we are suggesting, of course, carries the opposite bias. The best approach in this instance is to test both null hypotheses.

Alternatively, the emphasis could be placed not on whether the results stand up to some specific level of statistical significance, but rather on the best point estimate of the effect and on the confidence interval surrounding that estimate. Although we cannot be very confident that there is a true program effect if the results are not statistically significant, the confidence interval may also indicate a moderate chance that the program effect could be very large. A 95 percent confidence interval is generally agreed to be reasonable; thus, if samples similar to the one being used in the evaluation were drawn repeatedly, then in 95 percent of the samples the true experimental-control differential would fall within the two values spanning the interval. What we want to emphasize is that policymakers need and should be provided with a wide range of relevant information, rather than having to rely completely on the results of standard tests of statistical significance.

The alternatives discussed thus far are variations of the classical approach to statistical decision making, based on the concept of statistical significance. A more radical alternative is to shift away from the concept of statistical significance entirely and use the Bayesian decision theoretic approach instead. This Bayesian approach takes explicit account of the researcher's a priori expectations and of the costs of making an incorrect decision (e.g., terminating a program when it is successful or continuing it when it is not successful). It is also possible to determine the optimal sample size for the analysis, given these assumptions. For research that is intended to lead to policy decisions, we believe that this Bayesian approach has much to recommend it. As in the case of our recommendations with regard to nonquantifiable benefits and costs, the Bayesian approach has the advantage of forcing the researcher to make all his or her assumptions explicit and to come to an explicit recommendation as to the policy implications of the analysis.

Analyzing Costs

Thus far our discussion has focused mainly on the analysis of program benefits. In analyzing the costs of a program the obvious place to start is with the expenditures of the agency running it. If we are interested in total costs to society, other costs must then be added. These costs represent time or physical resources devoted to the program that might be directed instead to alternative worthwhile activities.

An important yet frequently neglected cost is the time spent by participants in the program. For example, participants in a training program could normally earn some income if they looked for a job immediately instead of spending their time in the training program. The amount of earnings foregone by participants in this way can often be substantial. Other costs that will not appear as agency expenditures are goods and services provided free by other organizations or individuals. A training program, for example, might use public school facilities after hours without being charged for them. Yet the program is likely to increase wear and tear on these facilities and may require extra expenses for utilities, custodial services, and so forth. Volunteer labor by altruistic individuals should also be included in assessing total costs, at least if we assume that the individuals involved would be willing to work on alternative charitable undertakings.

The factors discussed thus far are examples of how agency expenditures are likely to underestimate a program's total costs. There are also factors working in the opposite direction, however. For example, evaluations are often made of new programs, since these are generally the ones of most concern to policymakers. A new program may be established with a clear understanding that it will be evaluated at a budget review time (e.g., one or two years in the future) and with the likelihood that its future will depend on how effective it appears to be. (Long-established programs, in contrast, that have survived budgetary competition in the political arena and have a well-established political clientele may be less likely to be evaluated by outside analysts.)

New programs, especially ones that require the formation of new organizations, are likely to have start-up problems as they learn to operate effectively. To the extent that these result in higher costs per participant, evaluations will be biased against new innovative programs. If the results of such evaluations are then extrapolated to relatively similar, older programs, this bias will be extended to programs in general. When new programs do not require much new overhead (e.g., new education programs in existing schools), then the difference between new and ongoing programs may run the other way—the greater enthusiasm of program personnel for what is new and exciting may increase program benefits in the short run.

In our view, analysts should consider a program's long-run potential and not just its current benefits and costs. Although we do not believe that analysts should avoid evaluating new programs, we do believe that when such evaluations are made the analysts should try to estimate how the benefits and costs can be expected to change once the program has been in operation long enough to operate at "normal" effectiveness.

Benefits and Costs
from Different Viewpoints

Thus far we have implicitly assumed that the benefit-cost analyst should consider all benefits and costs to anyone in society. It is important to realize, of course, that the benefits and costs are often going to be quite different for different organizations or groups of people. By counting a dollar's worth of benefit and cost as a dollar, no matter who receives it or bears the cost, we are treating society as if it were one big family. We are ignoring the distributional effects of programs from one group to another. Although we believe that all benefits and costs should be considered, we also want to know who receives the benefits and who pays the costs. Of particular importance to us is that more benefits go to the poor and more costs be paid by those who are well-off.

Let us return to our example of a training program. One useful breakdown of benefits and costs is that of participants and nonparticipants. Since everyone is either a participant or a nonparticipant, the sum of these benefits and costs represents the aggregate benefits and costs to society as a whole. The major benefits and costs of our hypothetical training program are presented in this format in Table 10–1. Note that training allowances are a benefit to participants, but a cost to nonparticipants. Thus if one accepts the value judgment that a dollar is worth a dollar no matter who gets it, training allowances are neither a net cost nor a net benefit to society.

Economists doing benefit-cost analysis have focused most of their attention on the societal perspective. Although we believe that this perspective is useful, we do not believe it deserves as large a share of the limelight as it currently receives. For example, nonparticipants (e.g., average taxpayers and voters) are likely to want to know what the program is costing them and what benefits, if any, accrue directly to them (such as reduced welfare payments to participants or reductions in criminal activity), as well as the

Table 10–1.
Benefits and Costs from Three Perspectives

Participant	Nonparticipant	Society
	Benefits	
1. Net postprogram earnings gain[a]	1. Participants increased tax payments and/or decreased welfare payments	1. Greater output as reflected in post-program gross earnings gain
2. Training allowance	2. Aiding the employment of the poor[b]	2. Aiding the employment of the poor
	Costs	
1. Foregone earnings	1. Training allowance	1. Instructional costs
	2. Instructional costs	2. Foregone earnings

[a]After adjusting for increase in taxes and decreases in welfare payments.
[b]In contrast to the other items in the table, this benefit, which occurs if participants are poor, cannot be valued in dollars.

effects of the program in aiding the poor. Also, the agency running the program should know how much the program is helping the agency accomplish its mission and at what cost (political, perhaps, as well as budgetary).

We believe that a much greater understanding can be gained by looking at benefits and costs from alternative perspectives, rather than by focusing exclusively on the perspective of society as a whole. The political process is acutely concerned with who gains and who loses from different programs and policies. Assessing benefits and costs from the point of view of various individuals, groups, and organizations should thus increase the relevance of the benefit-cost approach for both understanding and influencing political decisions concerning social programs.

Conclusion

We have tried to outline what benefit-cost analysis is, including both its strengths and weaknesses. As a general framework for thinking about programs and other policy alternatives it is a very useful approach, with wide applicability to human services as well as in most other policy areas. Since resources are always scarce it makes sense to look systematically at the benefits and costs of alternative programs. Benefits and costs should be evaluated from a wide variety of perspectives, including that of the agency, program participants, all nonparticipants, and society as a whole. In order to compare benefits to costs and make comparisons across programs, quantitative measures of benefits, in dollar terms are very useful. But benefits should not be assumed to be zero simply because they cannot be easily converted to dollars or because they have not been found to be "statistically significant." The approach we advocate would in our opinion be common practice if benefit-cost analysts were expected to trace out explicitly the alternative policy implications that followed from the combination of their empirical findings and alternative value judgments.

As we have indicated, benefit-cost analysis is a way of thinking about programs and policies. Like law or public relations, it has some relevance for all programs and policies, and can be used wisely or superficially. The worth of a study will depend not only on how well practitioners know benefit-cost techniques but, perhaps of greatest importance, on their imagination and on how well they know the program and the policy problem to which it is addressed. If done mechanically by someone with little knowledge of the program being evaluated—its goals, its history, and its relation to other programs and institutions—then benefit-cost studies may not be very useful and may in some cases actually be counterproductive. If done with care and sensitivity, however, such analyses can often be useful to those who run programs, make funding decisions, and who simply want to learn more about what works and what does not work—both in order to test different social, political, and economic theories, and also to use this knowledge to develop new programs and policies.

NOTES

1. Irwin Garfinkel, "The Economics of Social Work," *Social Work*, vol. 19 (5) (September 1974), pp. 596–606.
2. Robert H. Haveman, *The Economics of the Public Sector*, 2d ed. (New York: John Wiley & Sons, 1976), pp. 161–65. For a good general elementary discussion of benefit-cost analysis, see pp. 151–70.
3. For an alternative approach, see Robert H. Haveman, *Determinants of Performance in Public Employment Projects: Evidence from the Dutch Employment Program* (Discussion Paper 396–77) (Madison, Wisc.: University of Wisconsin, Institute for Research on Poverty, 1977).
4. Gunnar Myrdal, "Appendix II: A Methodological Note on Facts and Valuations in Social Science," *An American Dilemma* (New York: Pantheon Books, 1972), pp. 1035–65.
5. Those with very low earnings are the most likely to meet eligibility earnings. Many of those with very low earnings may have earnings that are only temporarily low. Youth, for example, are likely to obtain higher earnings as they grow older, regardless of whether they participate in the training program.

Benefit-Cost Analysis and the Social Service Agency: A Model for Decision Making

JOHN A. MORRIS, JR. and MARTHA N. OZAWA

Benefit-Cost Analysis at the Program Level: A Model

David W. Dunlop states that the chief usefulness of benefit-cost analysis is to provide "a conceptual framework for at least enumerating the possible

Reprinted from *Administration in Social Work* 2, no. 3 (Fall 1978): pp. 271–82, with the permission of the publisher. © 1978 by The Haworth Press. All rights reserved.

benefits and costs, in the form of a balance sheet, which can then be used (at least in a qualitative way) in making programmatic decisions."[1]. . . It is within the context of providing a "conceptual framework" for decision making that we propose the following model. We know that a full-scale benefit-cost analysis would be beyond the technical and financial resources of almost all small social service agencies, and yet they are frequently confronted with decisions that demand reliable data. Why should they be denied an analytical tool? As Kast and Rosenzweig . . . suggest,[2] adequate planning (based on sound information) and good decision making are inseparable.

In order to be useful, an analytical tool should be as simple as possible (without sacrificing validity) and should provide maximum flexibility for the user. It should highlight the data, not obscure it in arcane codes and jargon, and should account as clearly as possible for areas of uncertainty. The model presented here has attempted to satisfy these criteria.

The proposed model consists of these five steps:

1. *Clear statement of objectives.* Insofar as possible, objectives should be specific and operationalized.
2. *Determination of costs.* All known or anticipated costs are to be included, including spillover costs if foreseen (expressed in dollar values).
3. *Determination of benefits.* Using criteria given below, a value weight on a ten-point scale (with ten as the highest value) is assigned to correspond to each objective.
4. *Data and analysis.* The average (mean) of all value scores for a given project is divided by the cost per unit of service in that project. This yields a rate of return for that project, which can then be compared to similar scores for other alternatives.
5. *Decision.* Information from the benefit-cost analysis is combined with other relevant data, and a plan of action is selected.

STEP 1: OBJECTIVES

The most important step in this analytic model is the establishment of clear, concrete objectives. It is impossible to determine in advance the benefits to be derived from an undertaking if goals are fuzzy. In this context, benefits simply do not exist without goals.[3]. . .

STEP 2: COSTS

All costs for each alternative (which includes the alternative "No change") are computed according to a standardized unit of service delivered (e.g., therapy hour, interview, etc.). Unless the proposal involves capital outlay for new buildings and the like, most social service agencies can restrict their view to personnel and material costs. Personnel costs can be determined simply by arriving at hourly wages, then determining how many hours (or fractions thereof) are involved in the delivery of the service unit.

STEP 3: BENEFITS

It is in the computation of benefits that the model departs from traditional benefit-cost procedures. In the place of dollar values, benefits here are to be determined by the use of scores that reflect perceived value weights. A ten-point scale is used to provide a reasonable range, without excessive complexity; ten is the highest score. For example, Project A is expected to do much to achieve objective x, and so it might be given a value score of eight, whereas Project B is likely to do little to achieve objective y, and so is assigned a score of two. When all scores have been assigned, they are averaged, and the mean is the figure used in analysis. (This procedure will become clearer via the simulation below.)

Since this assignment of benefit scores forms a crucial link in the proposed paradigm, we present some normative criteria for assigning these scores. These are by no means exhaustive, and it is expected that they will be revised and expanded in field trials.

First, value weights must be grounded in reality. If there is research information available to suggest that a proposed activity will indeed be effective in meeting a stated goal, it can support a fairly high value score. In the absence of such information, more conservative scores would be used.

Second, value scores must be closely linked to stated objectives. If there is much enthusiasm for a project (perhaps because of its novelty value), and yet its relationship to a stated objective is strained, it would have to be assigned a relatively low score.

Third, value scores should ideally take into account the probability of successful initiation and implementation. If the proposed project would be helpful in achieving stated objectives but stands no chance of approval by a governing administrative body, this necessarily affects the scoring.

Finally, value scores should reflect broad input from those who will be affected. Values assigned by one analyst have less integrity than scores agreed upon by all staff (and clients where feasible).

STEP 4: DATA ANALYSIS

Once costs and value weights are determined, their relationship must be interpreted. What is sought is a figure that suggests the effectiveness of the investment in terms of objectives desired: a standardized value score. The following simple equation yields such a figure:

$$\frac{\text{Mean value score}}{\text{Cost per unit of service}} = \text{Standardized value score.}$$

The standardized value score derived is a qualitative or suggestive number and has no absolute predictive power; its only meaning is in relationship to another standardized value score for an alternative project. No ideal score is posited here.

STEP 5: DECISION

The decision-making step necessarily reflects the norms of the program or agency engaging in the analysis, and will logically reflect its dominant values. The judgment of the decision maker(s) retains its primacy, as these data "prove" nothing. Hopefully, the decision will reflect an intelligent use of any additional insight that the benefit-cost procedure can provide. We shall return to the role of the decision maker momentarily, but we hope that the following simulation will first help the reader get a clearer idea of the model.

Simulation

SETTING

The simulation is set in a 150-bed, inpatient treatment facility for alcohol- and other drug-dependent persons. The facility is licensed by the Joint Commission on Accreditation of Hospitals (JCAH) and therefore must prepare individualized treatment plans for all residents (clients). The treatment plan is prepared by an interdisciplinary treatment team, comprised of: one social worker (annual salary of $12,000), one psychologist (annual salary of $14,000), one recreation therapist (annual salary of $13,000), two occupational therapy aides (annual salary of $8,000 each), and a registered nurse (annual salary of $13,500). The team conducts treatment planning sessions (called "staffings") for an average of eight residents per week. At the time the model is investigating, each staffing requires thirty minutes of treatment team time and one hour of clerical time. No special supplies are needed, and overhead costs are ignored for this analysis.

Staff have been dissatisfied with treatment planning and feel that the plans are too similar and not genuinely "individualized." There is frequent difficulty with follow-through on the treatment goals. The social worker proposes that the team investigate a new planning technique known as Goal Planning.[4] Because it is known that this method will require more time per staffing, some team members are skeptical but agree to undertake a systematic analysis prior to making their decision.

STEP 1

Team members arrive at four objectives for the staffing procedure. (Note that the statements of objectives contain, parenthetically, underlying assumptions.)

1. The creation of a clear, simple, individualized treatment plan that would meet or exceed JCAH standards.
2. The eliciting of maximum input from the resident in identifying issues for treatment. (A consequent increase in commitment to therapy is anticipated.)
3. The assurance of maximum input from all team members in the plan design. (A consequent improvement in follow-through is anticipated.)
4. The assurance of maximum effectiveness of staff time, an already overburdened commodity.

STEP 2

Initially, the cost per resident staffing under prevailing conditions was determined to be $20.46.[5] Goal Planning would double the amount of treatment team time but eliminate clerical services, and therefore the cost per staffing would be $32.93.[6] Since consultants will have to be employed, consulting and training costs are also included (prorated over a one-year period). Including these costs, the new procedure has a per-staffing cost of $38.43.[7]

STEP 3

All members of the treatment team next participate in assigning value scores to each condition, contingent upon their perception of how well the method would perform to meet the stated objectives. The present condition obtained a mean value score of 4.75, whereas the proposed condition (Goal Planning) obtained a mean value score of 8 (see Table 10–2).

Table 10–2.
Value Scores by Objective Desired

Objective	Mean Value Score[a] for Each Objective	
	Present Condition	Proposed Condition
1	6	9
2	2	9
3	6	8
4	5	6
Total	19	32
Grand Mean	4.75	8

[a]Represents average score obtained from all staff involved in rating process.

STEP 4

Completing the equation of mean value score divided by cost per unit of service delivered, the standardized value score for the present condition is .232 (viz., $4.75 \div 20.46 = .232$). The standardized value score for the proposed condition is .207 (viz., $8 \div 38.43 = .208$). The two conditions, then, offer roughly similar rates of return, with the proposed condition yielding a slightly lower rate.

STEP 5

In the example given, the final decision made is to implement the Goal Planning program. Although this may appear paradoxical, it serves to demonstrate the role of benefit-cost analysis in the decision process. The staff involved felt that the slight increase in cost was more than justified in light of the marked increase in ability to achieve stated objectives. The important point is that they were able to make this decision with a fairly clear idea of what was involved. The benefit-cost analysis had provided relevant data.

These same data could have been used to support the opposite decision under different circumstances. The decision makers might have felt that the margin of gain was insufficient to justify undertaking the proposed program (at least at the present time), and so they would have explored other alternatives. Probabilities for successful implementation and initiation might also have been considered at this point, and have contraindicated any change in status.[8]. . .

Discussion and Conclusions

After reviewing the history of cost-benefit analysis, and having briefly sketched its methodology, we have addressed an area where benefit-cost analysis has been underutilized: the mezzosystem of agencies, projects, and programs. With a view toward responding to Turem's . . . call for an "increased management stance" in social work,[9] we have proposed a model for using cost-benefit analysis in program planning and decision making. The model makes use of traditional concepts but introduces a value-weighted scoring mechanism for assessing desired benefits.

It has been our intent to offer a heuristic device for the decision maker(s). Whether cost-benefit analysis is used in the Department of Defense or in a small social service agency, it serves the same purpose.

Although we recognize that there are potential weaknesses in a paradigm that introduces a major subjective element such as the value-weighted scores, we also recognize that such value judgments permeate every level of even the most sophisticated analyses.[10]. . . A certain advantage is gained, in fact, by having such value choices made explicit and not couched in deceptively "empirical" estimates.

We submit that a foundation tenet of rational management is the acknowledgment of goals and values with maximum clarity and view the paradigm suggested here as an aid to that clarity.[11]. . .

Alan Williams . . . raises these three questions about benefit-cost analysis: (a) Is it systematic? (b) Is it objective? and (c) Is it precise?[12] We answer—as he did—that all of the questions can be answered in the affirmative in principle. In practice, however, an analysis may not be systematic, objective, or precise. The effectiveness of the tool is dependent upon the honesty and skill of the user and the quality of data available for analysis. Like any other device, it can be abused and its conclusions rendered useless by inaccurate or biased inputs.

But used responsibly, benefit-cost analysis has great potential not only in terms of national and regional policy development but also at the agency or program level as well. The critical variable in decision making will remain the judgment of the decision maker(s). This tool can enhance the quality of the decisions made by helping that judgment to resemble more closely an ideal: the *informed* judgment.

NOTES

1. N. Dunlop, "Benefit-Cost Analysis: A Review of Its Applicability in Policy Analysis for Delivering Health Services," *Social Science and Medicine*, vol. 9 (1975), p. 137.
2. F. E. Kast and J. E. Rosenzweig, *Organization and Management* (St. Louis: McGraw-Hill, 1974), p. 438.
3. L. Merewitz and S. Sosnick, *Budget's New Clothes* (Chicago: Markham, 1971), p. 179.
4. Goal Planning is a treatment planning strategy developed by Robert A. Scott and Peter S. Houts of the Hershey Medical Center, Hershey, Pennsylvania. References to consulting fees and training expenses are fictitious.
5. This figure is arrived at by dividing the total annual wages (viz., $68,500.00) by 2,080 (i.e., 52 weeks × 40 hours per week), thus obtaining the cost per hour of the whole treatment team: $32.93. One-half hour of treatment time costs $16.46, and one hour of clerical time costs $4.00; therefore, the cost per staffing under present conditions is $20.46.
6. This figure is simply the single hour cost for the entire team, as derived above: $32.93.
7. The consulting fee is $1,500.00. Training time needed is 3 full working days (24 hours) for the entire team. The cost for removing these staff members from normal duties is $790.32 (viz., $32.93 × 24 = $790.32). Added to the consulting fee, total costs are $2,290.32 (viz., $1,500.00 + $790.32 = $2,290.32). At eight staffings per week for 52 weeks (8 × 52 = 416), the cost per staffing is $5.50 (viz., $2,290.32 ÷ 416 = $5.50). Added to the basic cost per staffing hour ($32.93), the total cost per staffing under Goal Planning is $38.43 (viz., $32.93 + $5.50 = $38.43).
8. For a formula designed to complete the probabilities of successful initiation and implementation, see R. E. Peterson and K. K. Seo, "Benefit Cost Analysis for Developing Countries," *Economic Development and Cultural Change*, vol. 24 (1975), pp. 185–97.
9. J. Turem, "The Call for a Management Stance," *Social Work*, vol. 19 (1974), pp. 615–23.
10. W. J. Baumol, "On the Discount Rate for Public Projects." In R. H. Haverman and J. Margolis, eds., *Public Expenditure and Policy Analysis* (Chicago: Markham, 1970), pp. 273–90; K. E. Boulding, "Economics as a Moral Science," *American Economic Review*, vol. 59 (March 1969), pp. 1–12; and P. Peacock, "Cost-Benefit Analysis and the Public Control of Public Investment." In J. N. Wolfe, ed., *Cost Benefit and Cost Effectiveness* (London: George Allen & Unwin, 1973), pp. 17–29.
11. In chapter 7, Kast and Rosenzweig (*Organization and Management*) give an excellent review of the role of goals and values in organizational life.
12. A. Williams, "Cost Benefit Analysis: Bastard Science? And/Or Insidious Poison in the Body Politick?" In J. N. Wolfe, ed., *Cost Benefit and Cost Effectiveness* (London: George Allen & Unwin, 1973), p. 35.

11. Benefit-Cost Analysis in Child Welfare and Mental Health

A Model for an Output Value Analysis of Mental Health Programs

JOSEPH HALPERN and PAUL R. BINNER

. . . This paper presents an evaluative framework that relates specifically to the program and fiscal concerns of the mental health administrator. Applicable to any program or component, the framework focuses on estimating the economic value of a program's output and relating this value to the costs of achieving the output. It is simpler than a full cost-benefit analysis, which would require a much more comprehensive picture of all the costs and benefits involved. It focuses on just two of the basic, direct benefits of any mental health program and relates these to immediate program costs.

This analysis stresses the practical virtues of an evaluation that translates results into economic terms readily understood by funding sources and other outsiders. The data required and methods used are simple enough to be applied in a wide variety of mental health settings without extensive additional resources. Most programs already have most of the types of information required. Finally, specific operational definitions will be suggested for the concepts employed. They are only some among a number that could be used. Depending on the availability of other data and on specific needs, different definitions could be employed without necessarily violating the logic of the analysis proposed.

Such a unitary evaluative measure, albeit rudimentary, should be useful for comparing the productivity of various kinds of programs, the results for different kinds of patients, or even the interactions between kinds of programs and types of patients. Many of the items of information used are nominal or ordinal and therefore do not require a high degree of scaling precision or sophistication. The initial measure can be modified and improved as experience dictates and as more precise or complete date become available.

Reprinted with permission from *Administration in Mental Health* 1 (Winter 1972): 40–51.

The remainder of this paper is concerned with the development of this framework and also provides the results of a preliminary application of the framework to data available at the Fort Logan Mental Health Center.

II. The Framework

This framework seeks to relate two basic measures of a program's performance: (1) an estimate of the value of what the program has produced, and (2) an estimate of the costs involved in achieving that product.

Out of a variety of products that a mental health program might produce (i.e., custody for the dangerous; asylum for the disturbed; preventive intervention for a high risk group; or consultation to community caretakers) perhaps the most important single "product" is the patient who is returned to function in the community. Out of the variety of costs involved in achieving this return to the community (i.e., welfare or other social agency costs involved in helping or supporting the family; medical or treatment costs prior to admission to the program; police, court or prison costs involved in coping with disturbed behavior; lost or reduced earnings due to impairment of functioning, or impaired functioning by other family or community members influenced by the patient's disturbed behavior), the factors most immediately involved and most directly related to the administrator's influence are the program costs expended in behalf of the patient.

These two elements—the value of the patient returned to the community and the costs of the program—will be given specific operational meanings.

Estimating the value produced. A variety of values may be attached to returning an individual to function in his community. Two of these are especially relevant to this analysis: (1) his value as an economically productive member of his community, and (2) the value that can be attached to his degree of improvement while enrolled in the program.

The first component acknowledges the most direct way in which an individual produces value for his family and his community.

The second component recognizes the value inherent in the improved functioning and lessened misery enjoyed by the individual. The production of this improved state is the main reason for the existence of the program. It is critical that some estimate of its value be included to make any economically oriented evaluation meaningful.

The value of a patient as an economically productive member of society may be estimated in a number of ways. Ideally, this measure should be based on his actual earnings during a given period *after* his return to the community. Unfortunately, many programs do not know the earnings performance after discharge. Approximation could be based on the earnings reported for a given period *prior* to admission. This estimate would be conservative, in that the earnings level would tend to be diminished because of impairment. Presumably, if the program is successful, earnings would increase after discharge. However, some patients may continue to be severely impaired even after the program has done all it can. Lacking either pre- or posttreatment earnings information, estimates might be made on the basis of variables such as education and occupation (i.e., social class) and then related to local or national earnings expectations for such individuals. These could be discounted to allow for the impairment. For instance, patients in the Fort Logan Mental Health Center tended to earn approximately half as much as other employed individuals in the Denver metropolitan area. Such group averages could not be applied directly to individuals; but they could be useful for estimating this component of the economic productivity of a program.

Certain special subgroups of patients present unique problems in estimating the value of their economic productivity. The housewife performs economically valuable duties but receives no wages. Some men are involved in nonwage tasks, such as tending the yard, repairing the house, or maintaining the household. For such persons, economic value has been linked commonly to the cost of domestic labor,[1] . . . although there are compelling reasons to argue that they provide much more than the services of a domestic.

Other special subgroups are children and students, who are not yet producing earnings. Their economic value to the community may have to be estimated from the assumed value of part or all of their future earnings. Geriatric patients, on the other hand, ordinarily have no further potential for earnings. Their economic value might be estimated on the basis of their lifetime earnings, with their right to receive treatment seen as a form of society's interest on their past economic contribution to the community.

A variety of logical schemes may need to be developed to provide estimates of the economic productivity of the individual. The data for at least a rudimentary estimate probably are well within the reach of most programs. It also is apparent that all the data needed even for an ideal solution could be acquired if the resources were available to do so. How precise the economic-productivity evaluation needs to be is itself an economic question; the degree of precision is contingent on the willingness of the funding source to pay for it. (If this linkage could be made clear to the funding source, some of the incongruity between increased demands for better evaluation and lack of support for it might be reduced.)

The degree of improvement sustained by the patient while he was enrolled in the program also lends itself to a variety of estimates. These could be as simple as a rating scale with values attached to each degree of improvement. The values could be assigned arbitrarily by a single individual and would represent his particular value system. Or they might be arrived at by a consensus among staff members, representatives of the funding source, patients, patients' relatives or friends or some combination of these groups.

The scheme could be refined further by taking into account the degree of impairment suffered by the individual at the time he entered the program. This would allow any analysis to be sensitive to the mix of patients served and would give differential credit for working with patients of different degrees of impairment. Again, an estimate of impairment might be based on simple ratings at time of admission or it might be a relatively sophisticated score based on the weighted composite of various characteristics of a patient.

One such score was developed by Bloom . . . to predict the amount of resources a patient would use in treatment.[2] Bloom identified demographic items routinely collected on admission forms as well as some personality variables from a mental status examination at our mental health center. When combined to produce a weighted score, these items predicted— with considerably better than chance success—the amount of resources utilized (i.e., the amount of time the patient would spend in various treatment-statuses weighted by the estimated cost of each status). The score reflected the relative impairment of the patients; the more impaired patients required the most resources in treatment.

Ratings assigned for impairment at time of admission and those assigned for degree of response at the time of termination can be combined into a matrix, such as shown in table 11–1. The matrix offers estimates of the relative value of each level of accomplishment. The values can be used in assigning an economic value to each of the treatment outcomes.

An estimate of what each level of achievement should be worth in economic terms may be assigned arbitrarily by a single judge, or groups of judges. Various schemes might be proposed for developing the estimates. To keep the value assigned to the subjective improvement in line with those assigned for economic productivity, a value equivalent to the average earnings of the group of patients studied could be used. We thought it undesirable to value the same subjective improvement of a rich patient much higher than that of a poor patient; therefore, an average productivity measure for the group is proposed. This value could be assigned to either the average response level for the group or to some level of response in the matrix. Once the value of the anchor point was established, the value of each cell in the matrix can readily be computed.

In summary, the framework calls for a value to be placed on two components of the product: (1) the economic productivity of the patient, and (2) the degree of improvement obtained.

The formula for deriving these values for our data is as follows. The economic productivity of the patient is estimated from the earnings he reports for the twelve months prior to admission. For housewives, a minimum wage for a forty-hour week is assigned. (Since no children, students or geriatric patients were in the group studied, no formula was developed.) The value determined by this formula will be referred to as the patient's Estimated Economic Productivity.

The value of the degree of improvement is estimated by multiplying the Estimated Response Percentages from Table 11–1 by the Average Economic Productivity of the group of patients studied. This yields a construct of Estimated Response Value for the degree of improvement attained. In formula format, the method used for estimating the value of the product produced by the program is as follows:

1. Estimated Economic Productivity = 12 months prior earnings of individual
2. Average Economic Productivity = 12 months prior earnings of reference group
3. Estimated Response Value = Estimated Response Percentage × Average Economic Productivity (2)
4. Estimated Output Value = Estimated Economic Productivity (1) + Estimated Response Value (3)

Table 11–1.
Estimated Response Percentage Matrix

Level of Impairment at Admission	Level of Response at Discharge				
	1	2	3	4	5
	Regressed	No Change	Slight Improvement	Moderate Improvement	Marked Improvement
Slight 1	−10%	0	10%	40%	70%
Moderate 2	−10%	0	20%	50%	80%
Marked 3	−30%	0	30%	60%	90%
Severe 4	−40%	0	40%	70%	100%

As has been stressed several times before, these particular definitions are only some among any number that might be developed. Since the primary purpose of the present paper is to explain and illustrate the framework for the evaluation proposed, rather than the presentation of firm data, no specific defense will be offered for the particular definitions used.

Estimating the costs incurred. The impact of any particular disability may be measured by the costs of social agency and correctional services treatment, and by reduced income and subjective losses. The cost that concerns the mental health program administrator most directly, however, is the cost of services provided to the client. These services might involve only direct treatment costs. Or they also might include an allocated portion of the costs of all the indirect and supporting services offered by the program. In the latter case, the direct-service products of the program would be priced to cover all expenditures of the program. Cogent arguments can be made to either include or exclude these allocated costs. Whatever the decision, it will need to be explained and justified to the satisfaction of the funding source or other relevant audience.

The formula in this study uses a procedure that allocates the cost of all indirect and supporting services to the direct services of the program. The time each patient spent in each of various patient statuses (inpatient, day hospital, family care, outpatient, etc.) was multiplied by the cost of each of these statuses. This computation resulted in the Estimated Resource Investment for each patient. In formula format, the method used for estimating the costs incurred is as follows:

5. Estimated Resource Investment = sum of time in each
    status × cost of each status

It is important to bear in mind that the intent of this analysis is not to achieve a highly accurate and complete estimate of all the costs and benefits of a program. The intent is to devise a reasonable and equitable set of procedures that allow the assignment of a relative economic value to each discharge and a relative economic cost to the services provided. This permits, for example, comparisons of programs from year to year as well as comparisons of different components of a program within the same year with the same measures. The translation of program activities and results into economic weight permits the aggregation of different facts about input, process, and output into a unitary measuring system; it focuses analysis on the value rather than the volume of activity or output. Even this small step should be an important improvement over simply counting the numbers of patients admitted, attended, or discharged, and relating these to the amount of money spent. As has been indicated, those who are willing to pay the price should be able to buy greater precision than will be achieved by the measures proposed.

Thus far, we have discussed the general framework and the specific formulas for estimating both the economic value of the products of a mental health system and the economic costs incurred in the effort to produce these results. The next step will be to examine some of the kinds of questions that might be addressed within such a conceptual framework.

Evaluating the program's functioning. One of the most basic questions that might be asked within the framework is, "What rate of return is being realized on the costs invested?" Since the answer is a relative rather than absolute one, it would be formulated as follows:

6. Output Value Index =

$$\frac{\text{Estimated Output Value (4)}}{\text{Estimated Resource Investment (5)}}$$

This measure could be applied to the same program over a period of time, to see if the return is increasing or declining, or it might be used to compare different programs or subparts of the same program. It also might be applied to different groups or subgroups within the population served.

Another question might be, "How effective is the program?" If effectiveness is defined as the extent to which the program is accomplishing a goal relative to the maximal possible accomplishment, our framework suggests the following answer. It will be recalled that the measure of program productivity proposed was the Estimated Output Value. This was defined as:

Estimated Output Value = Estimated Economic
Productivity + Estimated Response Value

It may be recalled also that the Estimated Response Value was defined as:

Estimated Response Value = Estimated Response Percentage
× Average Economic Productivity

For the value representing the extent to which the goal is being attained, i.e., the Estimated Response Percentage, we now substitute the maximum possible value that could be attained for each level of impairment. This gives a measure of maximal possible accomplishment. These values may readily be obtained from the matrix in Table 11–1. They are the values assigned for "marked improvement" for each level of impairment. If the Maximum Response Percentage is substituted in the formula defining the Estimated Response Value (3), we derive a formula defining the Maximum Response Value, as follows:

7. Maximum Response Value = Maximum Response
Percentage × Average Economic Productivity

If the Maximum Response Value is substituted for the Estimated Response Value in the formula defining the Estimated Output Value (4), this gives a formula defining the maximum Output Value Possible, as follows:

8. Output Value Possible = Estimated Economic Productivity
(1) + Maximum Response Value (7)

The question of how well the program is accomplishing a goal relative to the maximal possible accomplishment could be answered as follows:

9. Effectiveness Index =
$$\frac{\text{Estimated Output Value (4)}}{\text{Output Value Possible (8)}}$$

Just as with the Output Value Index (6), this measure could be applied to the same program over time, different programs or subprograms operating at the same time, or different parts of the population served.

A third general question would be, "How does the amount of work to be done relate to the amount of resources available?" A workload index . . . may be used to examine this relationship.[3] This index summarizes the direct service workload experienced by a mental health system in terms of the input, process, and output components of the system. Input work consists of the patient evaluations that do not result in an admission as well as the admissions. Process work consists of the average number of patients enrolled in the program and the average number attending. The output work consists of the number of patients discharged from the system. These three components may be combined, on the basis of estimated relative weights, to form a single work estimate. When related to the amount of resources available, as represented by the average number of full-time equivalent (FTE) positions available to do the work, this provides a work-load index:

10. Workload Index =
$$\frac{\text{(input + process + output work)}}{\text{resources available (FTE's)}}$$

The Workload Index increases with the amount of work to be done relative to the resources available to do them. This index could also be related to the Output Value Index (6) to see if a higher Workload Index is related to a greater or lesser return on the program investment or to the Effectiveness Index (9) to see what the relationship might be between workload and program effectiveness. Most likely, neither program efficiency (Output Value Index) nor program effectiveness relate to workload in a simple linear fashion. Program managers need to have some idea as to just what these relationships might be.

III. Preliminary Results

This framework has been applied to 583 individuals admitted to the Adult Psychiatry Division of the Fort Logan Mental Health Center in 1967–68 and discharged by June 30, 1970. The concepts have been defined as indicated previously. The definitions, all preliminary, will undergo change and refinement as the work progresses. Perhaps the most serious limitation of the present data is that the response values are all based on a single individual's judgment, as shown in the matrix in Table 11–1. These, too, will undergo some change. Nevertheless, while the absolute value reported will change, the data will help illustrate the kinds of answers that might be given to some basic program questions.

Rate of return. The question of what rate of return is being shown by the program lends itself to a number of answers. For the group as a whole, the data show an average of $2,444.39 of resources invested with an average output value of $3,298.84, or an output value index of $1.35. Assuming the data were firm, this would tell the program manager that he was realizing $1.35 worth of benefits for every $1 he invested in his program.

If he carried his inquiry into the subparts of his program, he would see that not all of his teams were equally productive. Table 11–2 shows that the return on investment for individual teams within the division ranges from

Table 11–2.
Output Value Analysis Measures by Team

Team Number	Aver. Econ. Product.	Est. Econ. Product.	Est. Resource Invest.	Est. Response %	Est. Response Value	Output Value	Output Value Possible	Effectiveness Index	Output Value Index
1	1218.00	3337.58	2093.30	0.32	392.72	3730.30	4366.52	0.76	1.78
2	1218.00	3349.16	2161.88	0.38	462.60	3811.76	4357.25	0.79	1.76
3	1218.00	3791.06	2911.25	0.34	409.17	4200.23	4851.10	0.76	1.44
4	1218.00	1592.66	2421.48	0.30	365.38	1958.03	2714.81	0.65	0.81
5	1218.00	3378.31	1667.65	0.30	370.41	3748.71	4404.91	0.75	2.25
6	1218.00	3499.51	2811.82	0.34	409.09	3908.60	4528.44	0.76	1.39
7	1218.00	2173.96	2366.90	0.47	578.19	2752.15	3243.95	0.77	1.16
8	1218.00	1962.67	2271.80	0.41	499.41	2462.09	3055.39	0.72	1.08
9	1218.00	2426.25	4108.28	0.35	430.09	2856.34	3560.51	0.69	0.70

$2.25 for Team 5 down to $.70 for Team 9. It is interesting to note, however, that Team 9 obtains a higher rate of response from its patients than does Team 4, i.e., 35 percent as compared to 30 percent. The difference between these two units appears to be mainly in the amount of resources invested to obtain the response, i.e., $1,667.65 for Team 5 as compared to $4,108.28 for Team 9. The economic productivity of their patient groups differ considerably, too; Team 5's average is $3,378.31 and Team 9's $2,426.25. Since economic productivity plays such an important part in determining the output value figure, Team 9 cannot hope to recover the investment in treatment, even though patient response is superior. The investment simply exceeds the possible value of the product. Even if receiving the best possible response from all their patients, Team 9 would still have spent more than the maximum output value possible.

Just as the teams differ in their productivity, the rate of return achieved by the program differs markedly for different kinds of patients. For instance, the highest rate of return by age . . . is for the 35–44 age group, while the lowest is for the 55–64 age group. While economic productivity helps determine this, the resources invested are again an important factor. Interestingly, the return on men and women . . . is very similar, i.e., $1.30 for men as compared to $1.38 for women. The formula for valuing housewives played a key role in the result. Among diagnostic groups, . . . the highest return ($3.29) is for psychoneurotics, excluding depression; and the lowest ($.32) is for mental deficiency. Other differences relate to such variables as the number of times the patient is admitted, social class, employment status, education, admission status, and the county of residence.

The productivity of a program is a complex function of both the staff strategy and the patient mix. Unlike the proprietor of a commercial venture, however, the administrator of a mental health program may not be able to maximize his return on investment. In fact, he may have to follow strategies that lower his return, if he is to serve those who need his help most. Using our framework and formulas, however, he should be able to understand and explain more clearly what he is doing with his program. He should also be in a position to make certain decisions and their consequences more explicit.

Degree of effectiveness. How effective the program is requires an equally complex answer. The overall effectiveness index for the 1967–68 cohort is .75. However, an index number like that has little meaning, unless compared to other index numbers. Effectiveness by age group . . . ranged from .78 for the 35–44 age group to .70 for the 17–24 group. For men and women . . . it covered a similar range, .69 for men and .78 for women. By diagnosis . . . it ranged from .94 for paranoid reaction and other psychosis down to .68 for mental deficiency and transient situational disorders, personality pattern disorders, and special symptoms. Again, there was a range of index numbers.

Workload index. For the one year available, there appears to be no clear relationship between the Workload Index and either the productivity (output value produced) or the Effectiveness Index of the team. Whether this is due to an actual lack of relationship or to flaws in the measures used is not known. Certainly, it would be very valuable to a manager if such relationships could be established. This area will be the subject of further studies.

One final point deserves some discussion. Specifically, it has been implied throughout that the quality of any evaluative scheme would be some function of the support level provided by funding sources. While the framework provided here is designed to operate as is, it certainly would be useful to have accurate post-discharge information for the purpose of validating certain of the output value measures. It should come as no surprise that accurate followup studies frequently are difficult to perform and typically are expensive. One possibility, for validating the framework, would be to use some subset of the patient population where followup costs are within an economically feasible range.

Summary and Conclusions

This paper has presented a framework for the evaluative analysis of mental health programs. The framework relates specifically to the program and fiscal concerns of the mental health administrator.

This framework seeks to relate two basic measures of a program's performance: (1) An estimate of the value of what the program has produced, and (2) an estimate of the costs involved in achieving that product. Out of a variety of products that a mental health program might produce, perhaps the most important single "product" is the patient who is returned to function in the community. Out of the variety of costs involved in achieving this return to the community, the most immediately involved and most directly related to the administrator's influence are the program costs expended in behalf of the patient.

The value of the patient returned to the community and the costs of the program involved are operationally defined. The value of the returned patient is defined in terms of the patient's estimated economic productivity and the value of his response to the program. Costs are measured by weighting the time he spent in each treatment status by the estimated cost of each status.

The framework was applied to a group of admissions to the Adult Psychiatry Division of Fort Logan Mental Health Center. A number of indices were computed from the data generated. The Output Value Index illustrated the variety of insights into the productivity of the program that might be possible with such a measure. Productivity seemed to relate to both the kinds of patients served and the kinds of program strategies employed. The Effectiveness Index gave a similar picture of patient and program differences. The relationship between workload and the productivity and effectiveness indices proved to be complex and less clear than some of the other findings.

The primary purpose of presenting the results is to illustrate the kinds of answers that might be obtained from the data prepared. While the results are still tentative, because the definition and values used are still expected to change, the internal consistency and apparent reasonableness of the results obtained are very encouraging.

It would appear that the framework proposed and the data generated hold considerable promise for giving the mental health program administrator at least partial answers to the kinds of questions frequently posed by his funding or governing bodies. The framework offers a method whereby he can analyze his programs and make decisions on the allocation of his efforts based on explicit measures of the productivity and effectiveness of his programs. . . .

NOTES

1. D. Rice, *Estimating the Cost of Illness*. Department of Health, Education, and Welfare Health Economics Series, No. 6, PHS. Publications No. 947–6 (Washington, D.C.: Superintendent of Documents, U.S. Government Printing Office, 1966).

2. B. L. Bloom, "Predictions and Monitoring of Resource Utilization in a Community Oriented Hospital." In *Demonstrations of Statistical Techniques*. Boulder, Colo.: Western Interstate Commission for Higher Education, 1969).

3. Ibid.

PART IV

Effort Level Decisions and

Zero-Base Budgeting

Introductory Note

Zero-base budgeting (ZBB) is a tactical tool of administration whose popularity lies in the hope it gives of bringing budget growth under control by supplanting the deficiencies of incremental budgeting. E. Hilton Young's statement nearly fifty years ago could hardly be more applicable today:

> It must be a temptation to one drawing up an estimate to save himself trouble by taking last year's estimate for granted, adding something to any item for which an increased expenditure is foreseen. Nothing could be easier or more wasteful and extravagant. It is in that way obsolete expenditure is enabled to make its appearance year after year long after reason for it has ceased to be.[1]

ZBB is a system which in principle can be integrated with other systems such as PPBS and benefit-cost analysis as a way of filling in analytic gaps. Under PPBS, once *major* policy decisions have been made, there are many detailed decisions about functions and operations for which ZBB may provide analytic capability. For example, PPBS (and benefit-cost analysis) might assist in determining whether in a given catchment area, community mental health centers should be large and centrally located, or small and dispersed. But when it comes to such line-operational concerns as the levels of effort required for each of the mandated functions in a comprehensive community mental health center, ZBB picks up. Also, unlike PPBS that was designed as a long-range or multi-year management system, ZBB is a short-run budgeting and planning tool, and demands that programs be reviewed from the ground up each year.

ZBB is thus designed to counter the bureaucratic inertia and wastefulness that appears built-in to incremental budgeting. Justification of each expenditure from a base of zero permits the analysis of competing claims and tends to foreclose the possibility of obsolete programs continuing indefinitely. Incremental budgeting, on the other hand, begins with the prior period's operating and expenditure levels as an *established base*, it directs attention to incremental changes in the budget, and it seeks to justify changes at the margin. Thus, at each budget review, only a small fraction of the total dollars budgeted are really analyzed.

At first glance, ZBB appears to be an eminently practical tool to combat the extravagance and irrationality of incrementalism. On the other hand, a number of theoretical and practical arguments have been put forward in defense of incremental budgeting. Incremental analysis of budgets assumes that substantial portions have already been committed owing to prior political agreements and obligations. For example, at the federal level, incremental analysis assumes that about three-fourths of the federal government's expenditures are for such "noncontrollables" as interest on the public debt, medical care, social security obligations, and the like. The public, moreover, has come to depend on a variety of long-established programs, and although there may be opposition to the overarching conception of "welfare," who would be ready to curtail the extensive network of child welfare services including foster homes, adoption services, child protection, and institutional facilities? Not only would annual reconfirmation of programs be sternly resisted by program beneficiaries and their advocates, but involved as well are "sunken costs" in facilities and personnel who have been trained and employed. Such practical arguments are buttressed by more general propositions about the efficacy of incrementalism. Thus, Lindblom has argued that democracies are made up of widely differing factions that compete for the public's interests, and even were those interests not contradictory, the inability to know the future coupled with uncertain outcomes of government actions requires that choices be made in small, manageable steps.[2]

The debate between advocates of incrementalism and comprehensive rationality will no doubt continue, but whatever the merits of the former, political and economic debate is now dominated by a psychology of limits and scarcity, powerful pressures toward the application of zero-base concepts. Although ZBB concepts are not new, they have only gained currency in the last few years owing primarily to their compatability with the current mood, and secondarily to the working out of a detailed methodology for their implementation by Peter Pyrhh in Texas Instruments. Following Pyrhh's development of the methodology, it was adopted by Governor Jimmy Carter for use in Georgia. Actually, however, the zero-base review was first used in government nearly two decades ago. As Director Bell of the Bureau of the Budget then put it, "I think we should in a real sense reconsider the basic funding for each program—justify from zero in the budgetary phrase."[3] The following year, the U.S. Department of Agriculture Office of Budget and Finance stated: "All programs will be reviewed from the ground up and not merely in terms of changes proposed for the budget year."[4] Despite substantial effort to implement the zero-base review, a study by Wildavsky and Hamman showed two major problems with the method. First, it proved impossible to compare all programs with each other. Second, a high volume of paperwork was generated. The major positive effect seemed to be the feeling among officials that they were proceeding rationally.[5]

Although there is dispute about the efficacy of ZBB, the Georgia experience gave it impetus, and at the National Governor's Conference in 1974, Jimmy Carter described its reputed benefits in that state's government. According to Carter, "decision packages" covering every existing or proposed function in each agency in state government were ranked in order of importance, planning and budgeting were linked for the first time, and significant economies were achieved.[6] Following Carter's election to president, ZBB was rapidly implemented in the federal bureauracy and since then debate on budgetary monitoring and cost control has been dominated by the zero-base concept that is now cascading downward to state and local agencies.

The ZBB Process. From the federal perspective, the shortcomings of traditional budgeting and the potential benefits of the ZBB process are discussed by Victor Kugajevsky, director of the Office of Special Initiatives, Social and Rehabilitation Service, HEW. According to Kugajevsky, the ZBB approach facilitates clear identification of priorities, a structured search for improved efficiency and productivity, accountability for inputs and outputs, and overall, more rational budget formulation. Kugajevsky discusses the meaning of "decision packages," the heart of the ZBB process, and provides a general overview of the basic steps in ZBB. A simplified example of a ZBB analysis is presented in schematic format.

Implementing ZBB. Focusing on decision packages, Terrell Blodgett describes in detail the crucial administrative considerations and steps involved in implementing ZBB. The approach is a practical one including such "start-up" issues as the need for administrative training workshops, the question of whether to begin on a pilot-project basis, the necessity to define decision units, and the kind of forms to use. The author, an experienced city manager and ZBB enthusiast, cautions that ZBB, like any other management tool, can create the illusion of efficiency, or it can serve as a useful control. Of crucial importance is the way in which ZBB is implemented.

Problems of implementation are brought sharply into focus by Shirley M. Buttrick and Vernon Miller's description of ZBB in action in a school of social work. "An Approach to Zero-Base Budgeting" describes the application of ZBB principles in an attempt to determine staffing or "effort levels" required to support an "irreducible minimum" program. As with PPBS, the analytic aspects of ZBB—decision variables, policy parameters for data collection and analysis, definition of outputs—proved highly problematical. Additionally, the faculty opposed implementation of the zero-base review.

ZBB and Program Evaluation. The thorny problems of the analytics involved in ZBB are pursued by Joseph S. Wholey in "Evaluating Program Performance." As Wholey points out, ZBB may have little utility without an adequate data base or measures of performance on which to base budget decisions. Yet many agencies may lack the resources for sophisticated evaluation of programs. Nevertheless, says Wholey, useful evaluation work can be accomplished through a strategy of relatively quick and inexpensive evaluation efforts that produce successive increments of information. The elements of this strategy are evaluability assessment, rapid-feedback evaluation, outcome monitoring, and finally, intensive evaluation. Wholey distinguishes the four approaches in terms of data employed, likely time frame and costs, and decisions to which the evaluation may be linked.

Problems of Analysis and Review. A less sanguine approach is taken by Paul H. O'Neil, Deputy Director, Office of Management and Budget. In testimony before a Congressional task force examining S.2925, zero-base review and sunset legislation, O'Neil underscores the necessity for linkage between ZBB and program evaluation and highlights the problems involved therein. Securing program impact data is difficult enough; for ZBB to be of value, production functions, that is, varying dollar investments must be related to program impacts. Following O'Neil's thesis, ZBB would require not only impact evaluation of a Head Start, or of after-care for ex-mental patients, but also specification of the relationship between effort levels and outcomes. Thus, the magnitude of cost for ZBB may itself prove burdensome. Although O'Neil's perspective is from the federal level, the issue of ZBB costs will be applicable to most organizations in terms of the relativity of cost to organizational resources.

NOTES

1. E. Hilton Young quoted in A. E. Buck. *The Budget in the Government of Today* (New York: Macmillan, 1934), p. 172.
2. Charles E. Lindblom, "The Science of Muddling Through," *Public Administration Review*, vol. 19 (2) Spring 1959, pp. 79–88.
3. Quoted in Leonard Merewitz and Stephen H. Sosnick. *The Budget's New Clothes* (Chicago: Markham, 1971), p. 60.
4. Ibid.
5. Aaron Wildavsky and Arthur Hamman, "Comprehensive Versus Incremental Budgeting in the Department of Agriculture," in Fremont J. Lyden and Ernest G. Miller, eds., *Planning, Programming, Budgeting: A Systems Approach to Management* (Chicago: Markham, 1969), pp. 140–62.
6. Jimmy Carter, "Planning a Budget from Zero," A speech delivered at the National Governor's Conference, June 1974. Claims for ZBB have been sternly challenged by Robert N. Anthony, "Zero-Base Budgeting is a Fraud," *Wall Street Journal*, April 27, 1977, p. 26.

12. The ZBB Process

Zero-Base Budgeting

VICTOR KUGAJEVSKY

The new buzz word that is forcing managers to: (1) dig into old files and determine how they justified an activity five years ago; and (2) study how the scene has changed since then is ZBB—zero-base budgeting.

It is receiving so much attention today because many experts say ZBB can increase an organization's resources from 15 to 30 percent without increasing the budget. Dozens of private firms—Xerox, Texas Instruments, Ford Motor Co., etc.—have used ZBB and found it cuts costs and raises profits by 10 to 20 percent.

The potential payoffs of ZBB are: controlled budget growth; clear identification of priorities—those funded and those not; better targeting of resources; funding new priorities from resource reallocations; structured search for improved efficiency and productivity; accountability for outputs and inputs; rational and participative budget formulation.

Perhaps more than any other government activity, health and welfare programs are feeling the pressure of continuously expanding demands for service, rising costs and shrinking revenues. To make matters worse, efficient management of health and welfare programs is not commonplace.

Because most states administer many of these programs from the same administrative unit, we will look at the potential role of ZBB in both areas. Before doing this, however, it is useful to look at the situation in health and welfare programs today. H. Mahler of the World Health Organization estimates that if every American were provided with the full range of health services which current technology can deliver, the costs would exceed the nation's gross national product. In health programs the combination of open-ended "cost plus" federal financing of Medicare and Medicaid, together with the continuing output of new and expensive technology (e.g. CAT scanners) and the infinite demand for better health care, guarantee an ever-escalating cost curve for health expenditures (at present rates they would double every five years). Add to this less than

Reprinted with permission from *The Social and Rehabilitation Record* 1, no. 2 (May 1977): 9–13.

adequate administration, fragmentation and other factors, and you get a health care system which is costly, inefficient, and unable to consistently deliver a high quality product or service at an affordable price. Examples of efficient consumer measures rarely used by the hospital industry are group-purchasing, shared services, and general productivity management and optimum bed utilization techniques.

The nation's welfare programs, such as Aid to Families with Dependent Children and Food Stamps are in somewhat better shape but far from being efficient. While ZBB can help solve many of the problems which contribute to the poor administration of welfare programs, one problem stands out as the most easily solvable: program priorities which are seldom clearly chosen and left fixed long enough to make any significant progress.

Traditional Budgeting vs. ZBB

ZBB forces managers to examine carefully the fiscal rationale behind the whole program or activity. Traditionally, last year's budget base is never questioned. It is assumed that when funds were provided the rationale was sound or funds would not have been allocated. In addition, it is assumed that the circumstances which necessitated this program have not changed. Therefore, if a program had a $10 million budget last year, when it comes up for review it almost automatically gets a $10 million base for next year.

Budget review tends to focus on additions to last year's base and requests to fund new programs. Thus, much of what passes for budgeting is merely a calculation of the amounts to be added to last year's budget. Instead of using the budget as a tool for planning and executing objectives, traditional budgeting is mainly a process of adding or subtracting from last year's spending level to balance next year's spending with available revenues.

Under the traditional budget review process the choice was to accept, reject, or arbitrarily modify the request; the budget reveiwer was effectively denied the option of trading off a requested increase in one activity against a reduction in another. A good budgeting system should give decision-makers options together with the best possible description of the cost and consequences of each option. Zero-base budgeting provides precisely these capabilities in a way that no other budget planning system can.

This is because there are several procedural shortcomings in traditional budget systems—the uncritical acceptance of last year's program activities, the inadequacy of the information developed; the lack of comprehensive analysis; and the inability to divide spending options. ZBB, on the other hand, shows policymakers clear expenditure options and the consequences of selecting one rather than another; . . . uncovers low priority activities and shows the consequences of reducing or eliminating them; lists programs or activities in a clearly discernible order of importance; . . . lays out alternative methods of doing things and alternative levels at which they may be done.

The Decision Package

The heart of the ZBB process is the "decision package." (See example on following page). This is usually a single-page document which describes a program activity in terms of: (1) purpose; (2) method of performing the activity; (3) alternative methods; (4) consequences of not performing the activity; (5) measures of performance and outputs; and (6) costs and benefits.

The decision package is prepared by the manager of the unit or function which is described in the package—this is where the "participative" aspect of ZBB occurs. Program managers, normally quite divorced from budgeting, get involved on the ground floor in building a ZBB budget. The purpose of the decision package is to force the program manager to critically examine the operations he is responsible for in terms of services to be delivered at different expenditure levels, alternatives to "business as usual," important results, impacts, benefits of his activity, results of closing the shop—who gets hurt, how.

The decision package is the manager's concise statement of what he is in business for, what he hopes to achieve, how, and at what cost. Let's look at how a decision package fits into the ZBB process.

The ZBB Process

The ZBB process normally consists of five steps: designating the budget units (cost centers) for which decision packages will be developed, ranking the decision packages in order of importance, consolidating the decision packages and preparing a traditional budget.

Designating the decision unit. This is normally the lowest level or cost center of an organization for which a set of decision packages and a budget are prepared. An important rule is that each decision unit must have an identifiable manager with the authority to establish priorities and allocate resources. Decision units usually follow the responsibility structure in an organization.

Formulating the decision packages. Managers prepare analyses of their activities stressing: (1) different methods of performing a function (in order

Figure 12–1.
Simplified Example of a ZBB Analysis of an Ambulance Service

Resources Added to the Budget at Each Level[a]	Added Cost at Each Level	Cumulative Cost	Consequences of Added Resources
Level 1 One ambulance manned around the clock, 365 days per year (police respond to all calls to assist driver). *Cost Items:* Salaries and fringe benefits of 4 drivers (4 are required for full protection). Annual vehicle operating costs.	$44,600	$ 44,600	Minimal quantity and quality of service. Average response time. 8 minutes Average time for arrival at hospital. 22 minutes Possibility exists that no unit would be available at certain times because it is already on call.
Level 2 A second ambulance unit. Some manning schedules as level one (police respond to all calls to assist driver). *Cost Items:* Salaries and fringe benefits of 4 more drivers. Annual costs of operating second vehicle.	$44,300[b]	$ 88,900	Improved quantity and same quality service. Average response time. 5 minutes Average time for arrival at hospital. 16 minutes Very slight possibility that both units would be in use at same time and no unit available.

Level 3
To each unit add a trained medic available around the clock 365 days per year (police need no longer respond).

$96,000 $184,900

Same quantity but better quality of service.
Average response time.   5 minutes
Average time for arrival at hospital.   16 minutes
Improved service quality may reduce complications among those requiring emergency vehicle.

Cost Items:

Salaries and fringe benefits of 8 medics.

Level 4
A third driver/medic and ambulance unit manned around the clock, 365 days per year.

$92,200 $277,100

Improved quantity of service; same quality.
Average response time.   3.5 minutes
Average time for arrival at hospital.   13 minutes
Virtually no chance of a unit being unavailable.

Cost Items:

Salaries and fringe benefits of 4 more drivers and 4 more medics.
Annualized costs of operating a third vehicle.

[a]Assumes use of police/fire radio dispatch system at no extra cost as well as free use of space in existing firehouses or the general hospital.
[b]Less than amount shown in Level 1 because of reduced average running time and consequent reduction in average maintenance cost with two units operating instead of one.

Figure 12–2.
Decision Package Example

Manager ——————— Prepared by ——————— Date ———————

2. Agency: HCFA/MSA   3. Rank: 2

1. Function: Fraud and Abuse

4. Objective: To conduct reviews of Medicaid providers in order to achieve claims reimbursement integrity

5. Method of Performance: Conduct field investigations and audits of samples of provider claims to determine validity: 10 states scheduled for audits and field reviews.

6. Expected Results: Identification of level of probable fraud and abuse in each state Medicaid Program; estimate of dollar loss; profile of abuse patterns and providers. Reports and documentation for follow-up action by state (provider review, dismissal, prosecution, etc.).

7. Consequences of Not Approving: Public criticism of inaction; continued absence of fraud and abuse controls in Medicaid; continued dollar loss from unchecked abuses.

8. Quantitative Measures	FY '77	FY '78
Claims reviewed	500	2000
Providers audited	100	500

10. Resources Required (Dollars in thousands)	FY '77	FY '78	%FY '78/77
Personnel Operations	$150	1250	500%
Lease rentals			
Capital outlay			
Total			
People (positions)	100	250	250%

Figure 12–3.
Consolidation Summary

Package Ranking	FY'76 Amount		FY'77 Amount		Cumulative Level		
	Funds	Positions	Funds	Positions	Funds	% '77/76	Positions
1 Administration (1 of 1)	32,500	3	36,400	3	36,400	3.8	3
2 Executive Admin. (1 of 1)	26,200	1	32,400	1	68,820	7.2	4
3 Grants MWSI (1 of 2)	100,000	4	150,000	4	168,820	17.7	8
4 Budget (1 of 3)	55,500	2	55,500	2	224,320	23.5	10
5 Fin. Mwst (1 of 3)	155,875	19	132,493	17	356,813	37.4	27
6 Program A (1 of 3)	100,000	15	150,000	20	506,813	53.1	47
7 Program B (1 of 3)	400,000	20	450,000	22	956,813	100.1	69
8 QC (1 of 3)	50,000	15	50,000	12	1,006,813	100.5	81
9 Grant Mngt. (2 of 2)	25,000	5	30,000	5	1,036,813	100.9	86
10 Budget (2 of 3)			100,000	10	1,136,813	119.0	96
11 QC (2 of 3)			75,000	6	11,186,813	124.3	102
12 QC (3 of 3)			100,000	10	1,286,813	134.7	112
13 Fin. Mngt. (2 of 3)			50,000	5	1,336,813	139.9	117
14 Training (1 of 2)			150,000	10	1,486,813	155.7	127
15 Fin. Mngt. (3 of 3)			50,000	5	1,536,813	160.1	132
16 Promotion (1 of 1)			200,000	5	1,736,813		137
17 Training (2 of 2)			50,000	5	1,786,813		142
Total Pkgs.	955,075	84		142			

$$\frac{356,813}{955,075} = 37.4$$

to find the best way); and (2) different levels of performing the function (in order to find the most efficient level).

Normally decision packages are prepared for three levels of expenditure (or service output). First, the "minimum level package"—a given percentage below last year's budget. Next, the "stand still package"—the same as last year's budget. Then, the "augmentation package"—an increase in last year's budget.

This process of budgeting at different levels of expenditure gives higher level managers a clear comparison of the results vs. costs of various expenditure levels.

Ranking the decision packages. Each manager ranks his decision packages in decreasing order of importance. For example, a program benefiting only 25,000 persons might be given a low ranking when compared to a program benefiting 50,000 persons. However, a program benefiting 1,000 persons—if it is their sole source of assistance—might receive a very high ranking. For example, a manager's total budget this year is $100 million and he is asked to rank all of his packages so they total only $20 million. He does this and passes his consolidated ranking up to the next level for review plus those decision packages which didn't make his dollar cut-off.

Consolidating the decision packages. As the decision packages are passed up the organization ladder from one level to another, they are further consolidated at each level. The result is that each progressively higher level of management closely reviews a list of packages which are ranked in descending order of importance and a list of the packages that failed to make the dollar cut-off point.

This approach of ranking and consolidating packages at successively higher expenditure cut-off points forces managers to perform what economists call "marginal analysis"—at this given expenditure level is an increment in program A more important than an increment in Program B or is a program element of one more important than another. Thus the higher level manager can pull a decision package out of the consolidated ranking list and replace it with one or more of the packages that his subordinate placed outside the cut-off point. The benefit of this process is that the order of priorities within a program and among the programs is made crystal clear and the decisions about the order are made by the managers responsible for the entire agency. Some commonly used criteria for ranking decision packages and trading off one against another include: impact of the package on public health and safety; numbers of people who will benefit; legislative requirements; contribution to the objectives of the agency.

Once the decision packages have been ranked and consolidated into the ZBB summary and a decision made on next year's expenditure level, the

ZBB budget is normally converted to the familiar object-class, line-item budget.

Preparing the traditional budget. The ZBB format is converted to the traditional object-class budget and operating work plans (if used) showing how the various program activities will be carried out. The ZBB format may also be linked to other management control systems such as operational work plan or production schedule.

One advantage to a budget in ZBB format is that it fully exposes the decisions of managers. For example, if a welfare agency presented its budget to its State legislature in ZBB form, the legislators could agree with the welfare administrator's recommendations; shift some programs to higher service levels and lower others to free up required resources; increase appropriations to expand services.

The process puts the welfare administrator and legislators in the enviable position of having meaningful expenditure options and knowing the consequences of each. If they are funding new service levels and are not funding existing levels, they are in a position to assess the relative merits of the programs presented by the agency. They can easily determine that the consequences of one level of service are more important than those derived from the next level. In addition a zero-base process requires that every piece of the budget be analyzed for its costs and benefits—not just high visibility programs.

Stopping the Game Players

When a ZBB system is implemented some precautions must be taken to prevent "gaming," the process by which a manager can illegitimately obtain both his low-priority and high-priority packages. A manager can do this by assigning high rankings to low-priority items and low ranking to high priority ones in the hope that upper management will quickly upgrade his low-priority packages and not down-grade his high-priority ones because they are not easily spotted in a consolidated list. Another ploy is to pad the "production function" in a particular decision package by claiming more resources than are actually required to produce a given output.

An audit system can discourage both types of gaming. Such an audit may include: keeping trend lines on unit costs to spot unusual jumps in "production function" processes; spot checking operations with work measurement audits; installing internal labor productivity measurement indices (productivity base year/productivity current year); sending in special management audit teams to uncover unusual rankings; relying on judgments of seasoned program and budget people to spot low-priority packages hidden in a consolidated ranking list.

ZBB is not suited for every enterprise. It is not well suited, for example, to manufacturing operations nor to operations requiring a five- to ten-year "blind faith" commitment, such as basic research. Basically it is ideally suited to most activities in government programs, especially those in the human services area.

Although ZBB is readily modified to fit any organization, it usually takes two to three years before the system is fully operative. Implementing ZBB is an unsettling process. It displaces an established budget process. It forces an annual identity crisis on every manager. It can go out of control, producing an avalanche of paper.

Thus management must carefully weigh the decision on where and how to implement it and then be unremitting in its support of it. Otherwise implementation will fail. Some of the questions top management must ask about implementing ZBB are: how much of the organization to cover; how deep into it should ZBB reach; over what time period should it be implemented?

Once implemented, however, ZBB is an invaluable tool whose benefits multiply with increased use. Public welfare agencies would do well to carefully examine these benefits.

Indeed, the very favorable experience of companies, such as Texas Instruments, which pioneered use of ZBB, and several government agencies, particularly the state of Georgia under Governor Carter, have shown that ZBB is highly useful. President Carter is directing much of the federal government, including HEW, to prepare its next budget in ZBB form. Thus the federal government is committed to ZBB. Will states and local agencies follow? The choice is theirs.

13. Implementing ZBB

Steps to Success
with Zero-Base Budgeting Systems

TERRELL BLODGETT

Professional judgments about zero-base budgeting (ZBB) cover the whole gamut between boundless enthusiasm and utter mistrust. President Carter ordered federal government agencies to prepare their next budgets in accordance with this technique, following the lead of at least eleven state governments and half a dozen cities. His decision was generally applauded as the solution to "budget creep," which has been putting government at all levels in increasingly difficult positions.

Yet many authorities on government management have serious doubts about ZBB. One respected professor, writing in *The Wall Street Journal*, went so far as to label it a "fraud." Concerned citizens may well wonder whether ZBB will prove to be a financial wonder drug or just snake oil.

This article will attempt to explain the workings of ZBB for government organizations, especially municipalities. It will evaluate its benefits and shortcomings. The major emphasis, however, will be placed on how to get ZBB started on the right track. For ZBB, like other management methods, can be either an extremely useful control or just another way to appear more efficient.

Why Introduce ZBB?

ZBB was formally delineated and put into practice for the first time by Texas Instruments, Inc. just fifteen years ago. Since then it has been adopted by several other noteworthy companies, including Xerox, Allied Van Lines, and Westinghouse Electric. Their objective has been to allocate resources more rationally and efficiently.

The majority of cities and states adopting ZBB (mainly in the last few years) have had a similar purpose. Most have acted under orders from

Reprinted with permission from *Management Controls* 24, no. 6 (November/December 1977): 14–23. Copyright by Peat, Marwick, Mitchell & Co.

elected governing bodies, such as city councils or legislatures, which have been motivated partly by a desire to convince their constituents that they are doing something to curb the rising costs of government.

Alternatively, the new budgetary technique may be launched by the chief executive. Reasons advanced by administrators for the changeover include:

The incremental nature of the existing budget process, in which department heads generally consider existing programs already justified and thus justify only the "new money" they ask for.

The executive probably wants more information to be developed for the budget process regarding the services of the city—their nature, the level, the beneficiaries, and the required resources.

He may very well want the information in the current budget process to be "packaged" so that decisions of reduced or increased funding can be made in a logical, informed manner and the impact of more or less money can be predicted.

And he wants to engage supervisors and foremen below the department-head level in the budget process. This emphasizes budget accountability at the sub-department level and furthers these supervisors' professional development generally.

ZBB Is a Map of Rational Change

The person generally credited with first using the term "zero-base budgeting" publicly is Arthur Burns, Chairman of the Federal Reserve Board. In 1969 he told a meeting of the Tax Foundation that "a reform of vital significance [to the control of government expenditures] would be the adoption of zero-base budgeting." Burns knew first-hand that most government agencies, at the federal, state, or local level, assumed that whatever they were currently spending was accepted as necessary and all they had to justify in each budget were the increases above the previous year's appropriation. He believed it would be healthy for every agency to make a fresh case for its entire appropriation each year.

Thus the concept of zero-base budgeting—at least theoretically—is that the managers of an activity have to justify *everything* they want to do in the new budget year. Rather than merely modifying the previous year's budget or justifying only the increases, managers must start afresh. They must develop the rationale and determine the resources required for alternative levels of service. Accordingly, all programs, new or old, and the various levels of service, are given equal opportunity to find their places in the final budget.

There are four key steps in the ZBB process: (1) the definition of "decision units," sometimes called "basic budgetary units," (2) the analysis of decision units to decide the appropriate alternative service levels and the preparation of "decision packages" to describe those various levels of service; (3) the "ranking " of the decision packages in order of priority, first by the persons directly responsible for the programs and then up through the chain of command until there is a city-wide ranking, determined largely by the people having responsibility for the entire municipality; (4) the presentation of the budget to the governing body.

Decision Units and How They Are Chosen

A decision unit, the basic ingredient of ZBB, is usually defined as a basic activity or group of activities that management considers for planning, analysis, and review. In other words, a decision unit is generally the lowest level for which budget decisions are made. In municipalities, each decision unit is normally an organizational unit, although it can also be a program, a project, a line item, or a capital project.

The selection of a decision unit is a critical step. Choosing organizational units with multiple activities and large budgets can defeat the objective of sorting out individual programs that ought to be eliminated if made to stand scrutiny by themselves. On the other hand, a decision unit that consists of too small an activity can require analysis and paperwork out of proportion to possible benefits.

ZBB has no absolute dictums, definitions, or procedures, and the selection of the decision unit is no exception. Considerations such as the size of the organization, its range of activities, and the availability of accounting and workload data should dictate the size and extent of the decision unit. In one city, for example, accounting information was available down to the section level in large departments and to the division level in smaller departments. This city chose these levels as their decision units and worked with the resulting 125 units.

Decision Packages

The first step at setting budget levels: Once the decision units are selected, each decision-unit manager is asked to analyze his activity and to consider various service levels. One might be a minimal level that can operate with appreciably smaller funds than are allocated in the current budget. Another level might be an intermediate level requiring approximately the same funds as the current level. And, finally, additional levels above the current level are worth considering.

While the name of the system is zero-base budgeting, the unit managers do not have to submit a "zero package." The essential services, e.g., fire and police protection or refuse collection and disposal, must be provided and require some level of funding. The question is at what level the service should be provided and how much funding this requires.

For each service level, the manager prepares an analysis and presents it in a "decision package," which is the aggregate of his service level's analyses. Each package generally contains a statement of the objectives for the decision unit, a description of its activities, definitions, and statistics for work-load performance, personnel and cost requirements, funding sources, alternative methods for performing the decision unit's activities, and the consequences of *not* funding the package. The description of a decision package can run from one to three pages, depending on the detail of information desired.

A minimum of three decision packages is usually prepared for each decision unit. The maximum is generally four to five, although some imaginative and eager unit managers have submitted as many as ten packages for a single decision unit.

Setting Budget Priorities

The next step is ranking the decision packages from related decision units. The ranking represents an opinion as to which level of service should get funded first, which level second, and so on. It is done by the person responsible for the different decision units, who places relative values on the decision packages submitted by the heads of the units. As he does his ranking, he prepares a "ranking sheet," which lists the packages in priority order, specifies the cost and personnel required by each package, and also specifies the cumulative cost at each level in the ranking.

For example, a manager may be in charge of three decision units. If decision unit "A" prepares three packages, decision unit "B" four packages, and decision unit "C" three packages, the manager will have ten decision packages to rank in priority order.

The manager then submits his ranking sheet to his superior who evaluates the recommendations for funding decision packages in conjunction with recommendations made by the other managers at the same level. In other words, the superior develops an overall ranking for his entire area of responsibility. He is not bound to the relative rankings assigned by his subordinates but has a free hand to rank the packages in his area as he sees fit.

Ranking continues all the way up to the chief executive, who does it for the entire budget. He might assume this responsibility personally, delegate it to a committee of top assistants or department heads, or have the budget office make preliminary judgments, which he then would review in consultation with department heads.

One of the criticisms leveled at ZBB is that the high-level managers generally have no objective or measurable criteria with which to rank the packages presented to them. This has been true in many organizations. Although it is desirable to have a clearly delineated set of goals and objectives for each of the organization's functions and units and to have some objective ranking criteria, the fact is that ranking at this point may need to take place as it has always been done—by the subjective judgment of the division and department heads on what they perceive to be the objectives, priorities, and needs of the unit and the city.

Once the decisions are made on the inclusion of packages, the detailed budget is compiled for presentation to the city council. ZBB does not require major changes in budget format, but it does provide substantially more and clearer information. For example, the major policy decisions can be identified in the front of the budget document; then the manner in which each decision package supports one or more policy decisions can be set forth in the package. Hence, the decision makers have information that helps them make more logical decisions.

Starting the Organization's First ZBB

The ZBB concept is not complex or esoteric. Indeed, it is an extremely logical approach to arriving at a budget that provides the essential services, yet ensures that an organization is staying within its means. What is difficult and requires special attention is the implementation process. A government should follow a complete and carefully defined implementation plan. The most significant requisites are: a clearly stated set of goals and objectives for the organization as a whole and for each of the component units; a well-structured set of criteria for work-load measurement; an accounting system capable of generating financial and budgetary data for the city's organizational units and program efforts; and a professional budget staff to guide the ZBB efforts and coordinate the entire changeover in the budget process, plus the ability to augment this staff with outside assistance if necessary.

Few municipalities can enjoy the luxury of having all four requisites operational before the request comes from the city council: "We want next year's budget prepared by ZBB techniques and procedures." Accounting data available at the decision unit level is vital. If the city's accounting system identifies costs only to the department-head level, for example, and the city desires to define decision units at a lower level, problems will arise in arriving at defensible costs for the lower-level units.

Next, there must be at least one adequately trained budget person who will guide and coordinate the entire ZBB effort. This person must take the lead in setting the timetable for completion of the various steps, preparing and training the department heads and supervisors in the entire ZBB process, rendering technical assistance to the departments in the actual preparation of their decision packages, checking the package submissions as they are submitted, and assisting the city-wide ranking process.

Seventeen Steps to Success

Experience shows that the following steps provide a simple, effective process for the city that has decided to implement ZBB.

1. *Fix responsibilities.* Any project of the magnitude of ZBB requires the fixing of responsibilities for the various steps among all concerned individuals and groups, e.g., the city council, the chief executive, department, division, and section heads, budget staff, and outside consultants if employed. More specifically, the responsibility for preparation of a budget calendar should probably be assigned to the budget staff, and the responsibility for approval of that calendar should be assumed by the chief executive or the city council. These responsibilities should be fixed at the beginning of the process, defined in writing, and then adhered to during the budget preparation.

2. *Develop a budget calendar.* The responsible person or group, i.e., budget staff or project team—should prepare a budget calendar. With a normal, ongoing budget process, the calendar might begin as late as six months prior to the beginning of the fiscal year. For the first year under ZBB, however, more time will be required. The budget process, rather than starting during the seventh month of the fiscal year, needs to be initiated in the third or fourth month of the year. This schedule would provide department heads and other responsible officials additional time to become familiar with the ZBB process and to prepare competent decision packages. Other reasons for starting earlier is that time will be required for ranking and the chief executive may well want to allow more time for the governing body's consideration of the recommended budget.

The earlier starting date will not always be necessary. In subsequent years, the city should be able to shorten the budget process and match the starting date of its former budget process.

3. *Define certain policies and procedures.* Before departments are able to prepare their decision packages, several preliminary questions must be answered at the city-wide level. Should the ZBB include all of the city's funds? Most cities prepare basic budgets covering only their so-called general funds. Many operations, e.g., utilities, library, and perhaps others, as well as operations financed by federal or other outside funds are not included in the general fund. At what spending levels should the units be submitting packages? This is usually stated in percentages of current expenditures, e.g., 50 percent, 75 percent, 90 percent, 100 percent. Usually, the decision is made by first defining the minimum level. This minimum level then generally determines the appropriate levels for the second, third, and subsequent packages. The decision should obviously consider the economic condition during the budget year. The tighter the situation, the lower the levels should be set. Growing cities, however, might consider mandating the minimum-level package "not to exceed 90 percent of current expenditures."

What ZBB forms are to be used? During the first year, cities will probably want to use a three-to-four page decision package form. Much can then be reduced in complexity and length in subsequent years: e.g., budgetary and accounting decisions regarding such matters as level of expense detail to be required in the decision packages; the procedure for handling capital-project items; the approach to handling salary increases; methods for recognizing nondepartmental items, such as utility costs and insurance; and minimum and maximum dollar size of packages. All of these decisions should be incorporated into a budget manual to be distributed to department heads and other key officials at the orientation session (which is discussed subsequently).

4. *Consider a pilot-project approach.* The city should consider whether it wants to adopt ZBB by having just a few departments install the system in the first year on a pilot-project basis. There are arguments pro and con. The advantages of the pilot-project approach are that the effort prepares the way for the remaining departments. It also enables a city to work out the "bugs" so that full implementation can proceed in a more orderly fashion. The disadvantages are that most city departments do not relish the idea of serving as a guinea pig, that no practical advantage is gained by segregating one or two departments from the rest, and that no ranking of packages can be accomplished with a pilot, since there is no city-wide mechanism to be ranked against. Further, a pilot-project approach can be used in an attempt to satisfy an elected official with a "we gave it a try and, see, it didn't work" response.

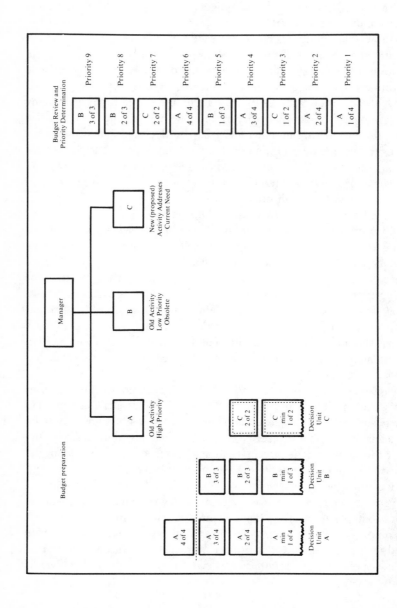

Figure 13–1.
Use of ZBB Techniques in Budget Formulation

Figure 13–2.
Early Phase of a Hypothetical Department's Decision Process

Summary assessment of community services
Stage of development

Most inadequate	More inadequate than most	Average adequacy	More adequate than most	Most adequate
Low-income housing G Group day care S Homemaking	S Financial assistance Hospital care-chronic Hospital care-mental Nursing home care Sheltering aged Visiting nurse svcs Casefinding Detention-delinquents Foster family care Legal counseling Sheltered work	G Environ-sanitation G Family counseling G Mental diagnosis S S S S Lental care G Detention-adults S Individual counseling S Protective services Rehabilitation svcs Sheltering-children Sheltering-retarded Social rehabilitation Vocational counseling S Family life education Friendly visiting Residential GRP care Sheltering-homeless Sheltering-unwed Short-term counseling Transportation Transient accommodations	G Hospital care-acute P Medical diagnosis S S Adoption G Character building P Disease control G Health education S Informal education S G P S P Camping P Disaster relief S Physical education G S S P S S	S S P P G S P P S S Social recreation S

Financial responsibility codes: G—Mostly government; P—Mostly private; S—Mostly government and private

5. *Conduct an orientation seminar.* Training of departmental personnel is another important preliminary step. It should start with an orientation seminar for department heads. This can be a two-hour department meeting to present the history, concepts, principles, and terminology of ZBB to stress the value of departmental goals, objectives, and workload measures.

The opening seminars can also be used to describe where ZBB is now being used and the benefits that have resulted. Indeed, reading material describing the experiences of other cities and organizations should be given to the officials in order that they may learn about the experiences of others. Finally, it is a good idea to ask the department heads to take time following the seminar to consider and then establish or reconfirm their department's goals, objectives, and work-load measures.

6. *Define decision units.* At this point the city is ready to define its decision units. To accomplish this critical task, we suggest a joint approach. The department heads should define their decision units following instructions from the budget staff. The budget staff should then review and suggest changes. The end result should be a reasonable number of decision units that reflect the way the city is organized to provide services.

7. *Conduct training workshops for personnel who will be preparing the budget.* The next step is to train people for their role in formulation of decision units and packages and ranking. This training should be provided for all management, including the lower-level supervisors. One of the strengths of ZBB is the involvement of personnel who are at the operating level, but who have not taken part previously in budget preparation.

The training workshop should be approximately four to six hours. The principles of ZBB should be discussed, but this should be followed by specific exercises in working with ZBB decision packages in order to give the participants a "hands on" feeling for their tasks. The workshop should also provide instructions for the completion of every block on the ZBB forms. In contrast to the orientation seminar, which is more general, the purpose of the training workshops is to impart specific information in order that the departmental officials can return to their departments and begin preparation of the ZBB packages.

8. *Prepare decision packages.* Following the training session, departmental managers should be given reasonable time to consider how the functions for which they are responsible serve the community, to decide how these services can be provided in the ensuing year, and to develop their decision packages. These instructions should be part of a budget manual containing illustrative completed forms. During this time, the budget staff should visit the departments to render technical assistance in the new procedures.

9. *Rank decision packages in the department.* The next step is for each department to rank its decision packages. In small cities the work would be

done entirely by the department head. In larger cities with divisions and sections below the department level, the division heads will first rank all of their sections; the department head will then take the divisional rankings and combine them into an overall departmental ranking for all divisions and sections in the department.

10. *Review of decision packages by budget staff.* At this point the department heads submit to the budget office all of the packages prepared by their personnel plus their own ranking sheet. The submissions should be on a staggered basis with smaller departments having earlier deadlines than the larger departments. The first step for the budget staff is to review the packages for completeness and adherence to the instructions. This can be facilitated by using a decision-package check sheet that lists each block in the ZBB form and specifies the kind of response that should be in each block. Also, since a computer is often used in the budget preparation process, photocopies of the decision package forms can be sent to the data processing center, and the computer used to check the arithmetic calculations.

11. *Analysis of decision packages by budget staff.* The next step for the budget staff is analysis of the submissions. While the decision packages and departmental ranking sheets can go directly to the chief executive of his designated group for a city-wide ranking, it is advisable to have the budget staff first review each package. They should be alert to certain recurring problems:

Departmental personnel may attempt "gamesmanship"—e.g., by ranking packages out of order. Packages that are obvious necessities are ranked low with the thought in mind that they will have to be funded even if they miss the cutoff line.

The packages may include too small or too large dollar amounts for useful analysis. These can usually be detected by identifying more than one level of service that has been compressed into a single package.

There may be obvious discrepancies in expenditure or workload estimates that do not correspond to personnel estimates to accomplish the same level of service.

12. *Estimate revenues for the new year.* During the time the department heads and budget staff are preparing and analyzing the decision packages, another individual should be making revenue estimates for the new year. Preliminary estimates can be made early to give general guidance to the preparation of decision packages, i.e., the percentages of the current year's spending at which to develop the packages. As the year moves on, the revenue estimates for the new year should be sharpened so that by the time the departmental rankings and reviews are completed, the budget staff is able to submit a fairly accurate estimate of next year's revenues.

13. *City-wide ranking of decision packages.* The task of ranking all decision packages across the complete spectrum of a city has probably brought as much criticism to ZBB as any other single step. No doubt it is difficult for a single chief executive or even a team to rank all the packages, particularly if there are several thousand.

The first consideration, therefore, is to minimize the complexity right from the start by setting an arbitrary limit on the number of packages. The next suggestion is not to be afraid to innovate when doing the city-wide ranking.

14. *Hold a training session for the governing body.* The chief executive should conduct a briefing session with whatever legislative body is going to review the budget prior to its submission. The purpose is to acquaint the members with the new process that was used to develop the budget they will be receiving, to explain what the document will look like and how they can benefit from this format, and otherwise to set the stage for their consideration of the budget document. If the council initiated the entire process, it would be well also to have a session with the group at the beginning of the process.

15. *Submit budget to the governing body.* At this point the chief executive submits his budget to the governing body. It is built from the city-wide rankings of expenditure requests and the revenue estimates. The chief executive might consider supplementing this basic recommendation with some of the documentation used to develop the budget. It would provide a foundation in case the governing body wanted to hold hearings with departments.

16. *Review and adoption of the budget by the governing body.* The role of the governing body in the budget process should be planned from the beginning. If its expectations have been properly considered and met, the review and adoption of the budget by the governing body should go quite smoothly.

17. *Subsequent years.* ZBB is still new and there is no logic that requires a city to follow the first year's procedures precisely in subsequent years. Indeed, the first city to adopt ZBB is now in its fourth year and has changed its emphasis each year. Thus, after the first year, the city's budget staff should evaluate the process and adopt modifications for improvement.

For instance, forms can generally be simplified. Analytical effort can be concentrated on internal administrative services and policies affecting the entire organization, such as wage and salary programs, data processing, telephone costs, or vehicle management, or on one functional area, e.g., the public-works area, which may seem to merit attention. Still another approach is to place emphasis on other methods of performing the service in question. This is rarely addressed adequately in the first year or two, even though it deserves substantial attention.

Practical Advice for Starting ZBB

Cities that have tried ZBB are beginning to learn much from their brief experiences. In conclusion, here is a list of the most important lessons in the form of practical advice:

Anticipate what the council wants and expects from ZBB. It may be nothing more than a slightly altered budget format, or it may be much more. If the expectations are not foreseen and planned for, a bad experience can result.

Anticipate a possibly negative reaction from the chief executive. Where the governing body has initiated ZBB, the chief executive may not be entirely friendly to the process. The executive's attitude can greatly influence success or failure.

Build on the existing budget process and forms where possible. ZBB requires enough changes in forms, procedures, and habits. Try to utilize existing procedures and forms wherever possible.

Define decision units carefully. This simple early step is vitally important. Time spent in a thorough analysis of what level of the organization should be utilized for decision units will be more than recouped later.

Question the work-load statistics presented. Few departments in few cities have developed their work-load statistics to a high degree of accuracy. The budget staff should question these statistics carefully and critically and provide technical assistance to the departments in improving the reliability of the information.

Anticipate the volume of decision packages and prepare alternative approaches to handle it.

Decide how salary increases will be budgeted. If the decision at the beginning of the process is to eliminate all salary increases, i.e., cost-of-living and merit, from initial package figures, then there should be a way at the time of city-wide rankings to insert salary considerations. If they are not inserted and the chief executive makes his priority listing without regard to salary increases, he is telling the council that to increase salaries, taxes must be increased.

One way to handle salary increases is to have four to six packages prepared that are "salary packages" only. These could be packages based on the costs of 3 percent, 5 percent, and 7 percent cost-of-living increases, and packages setting aside amounts for merit increases.

Provide space on the decision-package forms for federal and supplemental funding. One of the advantages of ZBB cited by virtually every city using it has been the additional information on supplemental funding available to the decision unit. As a result, many governing bodies are requesting chief executives to bring decision-making on all budgets—the general fund budget, the general revenue-sharing budget, and the community development budget—into one time frame so that the total needs of the city may be considered and budgeted together.

Don't be overly concerned the first year with lack of information on alternative methods for providing a service. The block entitled "Alternative methods of providing this service" has uniformly been completed in the poorest, most incomplete fashion. This is a vitally important part of the ZBB process, but can wait until subsequent years for concerted effort.

Manage the paperwork and remember to emphasize "substance over form." Perhaps the most frequent criticism of ZBB is the amount of time and paper it requires. There is no question it requires more of both the first year, although the time element decreases in subsequent years.

The essential idea is to concentrate on the quality of information gathered, not the quantity. And as ZBB grows from infancy to maturity, its true value will be judged by the extent to which it improves the quality of government.

An Approach to Zero-Base Budgeting

SHIRLEY M. BUTTRICK and VERNON MILLER

In September 1976, the University of Illinois at Chicago Circle undertook a revision of its budgeting procedures and, in that process, moved from incremental to program budgeting. In addition, four units on the campus were asked to prepare a zero-base budget. These four units comprised two instructional and two noninstructional departments. The Jane Addams College of Social Work, which offers all three degree programs (BSW, MSW, and DSW), was one of the instructional units designated.

The approach that the College of Social Work followed is the subject of this paper. Not only is the approach an interesting departure from a normative zero-base budget but, to our knowledge, no school of social work has undertaken such a preparation. In this respect, the description of the approach used should be of interest to other schools of social work as well as to human services agencies. Hopefully, this paper will make a

Reprinted from *Administration in Social Work* 2, no. 1 (Spring 1978): 45–57, with the permission of the publisher. © 1978 by The Haworth Press. All rights reserved.

contribution to the planning and budgeting procedures of both academic and nonprofit human services organizations.

The context in which the change from an incremental to a program budget took place needs some elaboration. The institution of new budget procedures coincided with the arrival on campus of a new set of administrative actors. The chancellor had been there for only one year; the vice-chancellor for academic affairs had just arrived. Most of the deans were new. The campus itself was known for its past upheavals, and accordingly, the tenure of administrators had been relatively short. The Chicago Circle Campus, one of three units of the University of Illinois (Urbana-Champaign, Chicago Medical Center), was seen as the campus that "was not able to get itself together," and some ten years after its inception there was still confusion and debate over its proper mission.

In setting up the new budget procedures, the vice-chancellor for academic affairs established an Academic Resources Board. This board, which included the major political power centers on the campus, was established as a decision-making body, not an advisory group. The vice-chancellor for academic affairs was to be a voting member of this board, but only the chancellor could overrule the decisions of the board. Given its composition, this was not a likely possibility.

The Academic Resources Board was established with the understanding that a resource/performance profile for each college, school, department, center, or institute would be developed within a two-month period. This resource/performance profile would serve as the prime data base for use by the Academic Resources Board in considering allocations for the following year. Other data such as qualitative program evaluations could be solicited as well as additional information on cost-effectiveness, research and grant development, student demand, and disciplinary trends. Efforts were also to be made to obtain comparable data for programs in other universities, both in and outside the state. Thus, it was clear that a good deal of technical expertise would be demanded of the participants of the Academic Resources Board and of the department heads in their budget presentations.

The annualized budget system that was delineated was neither original nor particularly innovative. It followed the general pattern of an accountability and program planning approach to academic resource allocation that had been instituted at several universities in recent years. For this kind of budgeting system to work well, several factors are necessary, among them a reliable data base, intensive work on the part of the heads of units as well as the campus central administration, and a high capacity for campus-wide collegial decision making in the best interest of the university.[1] . . . In theory, the advantages of this system, as compared with the more traditional type (historic rollover budget with ad hoc adjustments at the margin), are considered by many to be substantial. Primarily it assumes a clearer accountability in the use of resources and, as a result, greater campus credibility in the justness and rationality of resource allocation. It becomes possible to identify units that are significantly underfunded and to reallocate resources from other units to support programmatic developments of importance for the campus. Resource reallocation, touchy as it is, often provides the only realistic source for the funding and generating of new programmatic directions. Finally, for the Chicago Circle Campus, it was felt that "putting the house in order" and demonstrating effective use of current resources would be very important subsequently in obtaining new money for the campus.

Theoretical Framework

Our frame of reference derives from Aaron Wildavsky.[2] . . . Budgets, he says, are political documents, and budgetary decisions answer the central political questions of who gets what and how. In essence, a budget is a document that describes items of expenditure (salaries) or purposes (e.g., improving mental health), and figures are attached to each item or purpose. If the connection exists between what is written and what will happen, then the budget becomes a "link between financial resources and human behavior to accomplish policy objectives."[3] . . . Since funds are limited and have to be divided among competing uses, the budget further becomes a mechanism for making choices among alternative expenditures. When these choices are coordinated to achieve desired goals, a budget becomes "a plan."

Although a proposed budget represents the expectations and aspirations for a unit, a budget request is very often a strategy as well. As each person in the process acts on the budget, he receives information about the preferences of others and indicates his own desires through the choices he makes. What emerges is a network of communication. Equally significant is the fact that a budget, once enacted, becomes a precedent. The fact that something has been done once vastly increases the chance that it will be done again, for normally only substantial departures from the previous year's budget are scrutinized. Unchanged items are just carried along.

The purposes of budgets are quite varied, and the view one adopts of the budget depends upon one's purposes. Wildavsky's concern, for example, is with the federal budget, and therefore with the budget as a political process. We pay more attention to the technical component but are in agreement that the budget records the outcome of a political process. That outcome provides a record of who got what and whose preferences did indeed prevail.

Given the complexity of the budgetary process, there are good reasons for staying with traditional or incremental budgeting. Traditional budgeting (incremental as contrasted with comprehensive) reduces the amount of conflict because it does not focus attention on the program or on the policy implications of a particular program. It permits negotiation to take place around specific line items, and in that regard compromise is possible and policy implications can be avoided. In program budgeting, the presentation is in terms of the end product—of program packages such as public health. The virtues of this are presumed to lie in the usefulness of relating ends to means, in the emphasis upon the policy implications of budgeting, and in the ease with which consideration of the budget as a whole is permitted as each program competes with every other for funds.[4] . . . In recent years, the trend toward program-oriented budget formats has accelerated. The impetus has come from many sources. It has come from central administrators who desire to play a larger role in the programmatic decision making. It has come from demands that greater benefits, efficiencies, and accountability need to be achieved by public service enterprises. It has come from the drive toward better understanding of the purposes, goals, and objectives of universities and colleges. The result has been a reshaping of the budget format in an effort to yield more information on the output side.

The shift in emphasis toward the output side is present in the association of goals and objectives of the budgetary unit and of the "systems" approach which confronts the traditional incremental budgeting strategy. Comprehensive budgeting requires justification of the total amount spent for a program or activity. Thus, one cannot talk about comprehensive budgeting without talking about the concepts inherent in a systems approach, which requires justification of the budget/output terms and a link to long-range planning. Yet the systems approach and comprehensive budgeting introduce concepts and techniques that in many ways are antithetical to higher education as it is presently and traditionally organized.

A Note on the Planning, Programming, and Budgeting System (PPBS) and Zero-Base Budgeting (ZBB)

PPBS, the best known program budgeting technique, is one of program analysis and evaluation. It has proved extremely difficult to implement in higher education. The reasons generally given for this and the failure of academic administrators and faculty to support PPBS are many. Like any systems approach, PPBS tends to favor the central authority in the negotiation process, and this has not met with a favorable response in higher education. PPBS also requires a comprehensive date base, which is rarely available in higher education. It further requires that definitions of the outputs of higher education be expressed in quantitative terms. The problems of defining outputs for the human services and for educational institutions are well known, and it is even more difficult to find definitions that are acceptable to faculty and administrators alike. PPBS uses a cost-benefit approach to analysis; that is, the criteria for program evaluation are measures of efficiency. PPBS also requires a link between planning and budgetary decision making.

Long-range planning further implies multiyear budgeting, which is not considered productive by most universities since funding agencies are reluctant to commit themselves for more than one annual or biennial period. "Without clearly defined objectives and without sharp lines of authority and responsibility, the formal structure of PPBS serves little use beyond giving outside observers a false sense of precision and security."[5]. . .

More recently, zero-base budgeting has surfaced in popularity and has been introduced to higher education. Like PPBS, ZBB is an objectives-oriented, analytical technique designed to support a comprehensive budgeting strategy. The purpose is to force analysis and evaluation of alternatives presented in the decision-making process. It differs from PPBS, in that it exploits the decentralized decision-making structure within the organization. Initial and primary responsibility for the development of program objectives is placed at the "program manager" level (department/college, etc.). The manager utilizing this process must first justify his complete budget request in detail and then justify or prove why he should spend any money. This is accomplished by working through the two central steps of zero-base budgeting: (a) developing decision packages and (b) ranking the decision packages.[6] . . . Simply stated, ZBB is a management tool designed to assist in reevaluating all programs and expenditures each year. It is well to remember, however, that ZBB is an approach, "not a fixed procedure or a set of forms to be applied uniformly from one organization to the next."[7] . . .

The decision package consists of at least five elements: (a) purpose (goals and objectives); (b) consequences of not performing the activity; (c) measures of performance; (d) alternative courses of action; and (e) cost and benefits.

The decision package identifies and describes a specific activity in such a manner that management supposedly can evaluate it and rank it against other activities competing for limited resources and make a decision to approve or disapprove. Therefore, the information displayed on each package must provide all the needed information. Clearly, zero-base budgeting as a systems approach becomes entangled in the same thickets as PPBS, namely, problems in the definition of outputs, centralized versus decentralized authority, and the value of long-range planning.

The basic question for us was not whether to use a zero-base budget, but how to adapt it for a school of social work. The term "zero-base," although appropriately descriptive of the conceptual framework, is even in name a formidable threat that brings visions of extinction to faculty and administrators. Zero-base budgets do not, however, result in a budget of "zero" for any unit; in fact, examination of their application in various state and federal government areas demonstrates that the result is usually evaluation of something less than 100 percent of the unit's budget. It does, however, open the possibility that, from an evaluation of each activity, certain activities can be phased out and other activities phased in.

An examination of the four zero-base budgets developed by the Circle Campus units revealed that all four, while following the Peter Pyhrr guidelines for a zero-base budget, nonetheless came up with variations from that normative approach. Examination of the Jane Addams College of Social Work's zero-base budget request will not reveal the standard forms and mechanical procedures. The effort was to apply the approach in the most creative and productive way. In so doing, a set of forms and devices was developed consistent with zero-base budgeting and the reality of the social work school within the educational enterprise.

A Zero-Base Budget for Jane Addams

The Jane Addams College of Social Work was in a process of change the year it was asked to prepare a zero-base budget. It was moving from a school offering a generic social treatment master's degree and a doctorate into a complex college administering four distinct programs and projecting an applied research center. It had developed, for the first time, within the master's of social work curriculum two distinct concentrations. It was also in the process of achieving accreditation and was changing its courses and requirements to reflect its new concentrations and curricula.

Over the previous five years this school, of all units on campus, had received the largest percentage increase in its base budget. Although it had started from a low base level, the perception on the campus was that the school had been favored. It had also achieved this increase in its base budget with a decline in its enrollment (very small). It was further considered one of the "better" units on campus in that there was a high demand for admission to the school and the caliber of the students attracted was very high. As a result of this favorable position, this school had "gone its own way" within the university. It appeared at times that the university needed this school more than the school needed the university. Given the newly created Academic Resources Board, and the resultant public scrutiny, there was legitimate concern that the school would not fare well in its budget request. The zero-base budget was viewed by the new dean as an opportunity to restate the school's programmatic objectives and to solicit support and understanding for the school.

The purpose of the zero-base budget exercise was never considered to be a justification of existence nor a blueprint for elimination of the school. *Continuing activity was assumed* for the three degree programs. Consistent with zero-base budget concepts, the irreducible minimum at which each program could function was defined and the resources required for the anticipated outputs at this level of operation described.[8] The model had the further constraint of a clear and recognizable relationship between additional resource requirements and increasing levels of activity.

The first task, then—and perhaps the most difficult—was to develop a set of decision variables and policy parameters that would provide the framework for data collection and analysis. The analytical model began with a two-dimensional matrix (Figure 13–3).

Headcount Enrollment	Program Name	Program Activities					
		Instruction	Prog. Planning Curr. Devel.	Research Public serv.	Program Admin.	Field Coordination	TOTALS
	B.S.W.						
	TREATMENT						
	ADMINISTRATION/ PLANNING/ ORGANIZATION						
	D.S.W.						
	FIELD INSTRUCTION						
	JANE ADDAMS CENTER						
	COLLEGE ADMINISTRATION						
	TOTALS						

Figure 13–3.
Basic Resources Requirements Table

As can be seen in Figure 13–3, "Programs" formed one dimension and were defined by the degree programs (bachelor's, master's, doctoral), field instruction, organized research center, and administrative and support program. Definitions for each of these programs are to be found in the description of Jane Addams College as a professional school organized to provide instruction and training, advancement of knowledge in the field, and public service in the community. These program definitions presented some technical difficulties when the analysis began, but these were resolved within the framework established by other decision variables. The second dimension of the matrix was developed through an "Activities" description for each program. This description is traditional, with primary activities described as instruction, curriculum development, program administration, coordination with field agencies, and released time activities. Before resources could be associated with these programs and activities, however, a minimum set of decision variables necessary for the analysis had to be defined:

1. *Faculty work load.* The definition chosen for our analysis was the number of faculty contact hours of instruction per week. In order to account for courses with varying contact hours, a measure of standard course hours was developed.

2. *Courses offered in each program.* The definition had to be developed in a way that recognized that some courses were common to several programs, some were required of all students, some were required for particular curricular concentrations but elective for others, and some were totally elective. This definition followed from the basic assumption that there was an irreducible number of courses (required and elective) necessary for competence in an area.

3. *Section capacity.* This variable was expressed as the maximum number of students to be admitted to any particular section of each course.

4. *Structure, type, and duration of the practicum or field experience requirement.* This variable presented some unique problems of measurement which were resolved by designation of field instruction both as a program and a unique activity (see Figure 13–3).

5. *Faculty mix.* This variable defined the faculty required for each program by senior/junior level which permitted a pricing or salary policy.

6. *Projected enrollment demand.* This was complicated because of the need to account for demand for instruction, preparation at entry point, time to completion of the program, trends in curricular preferences, and the like. We assumed that the demand for the school's programs would continue and projected our ability and desire to admit particular numbers.

7. *Student support and levels of administrative support.* This involved an analysis of clerical, secretarial, and technical support levels by program,

and use of shared resources such as equipment and telecommunications. This analysis, which was developed from historical trends and a *step-function* relationship between levels of support and number of faculty associated with each program, was largely technical and involved little that was new conceptually.

The key portions of the analysis were, as might be expected, related to the instructional activity for each program. The goal was to determine the minimum full-time equivalent faculty required to support the instructional programs for one full academic year. Because faculty work load was expressed in contact hours per week, we had to define the minimum number of course sections to be offered under the assumption that each program would be continued if at least one student were enrolled at each level (i.e., a two-year program would have one first-year and one second-year student). One section of every course necessary for each program would be offered once during the academic year. This was called the irreducible minimum for the instructional function.

The model was capable of producing three vital pieces of information at this early stage: (a) a simple measure of faculty required to support the programs at an irreducible level; (b) the number of students who could be admitted by program and level; and (c) the excess capacity in each instructional program. (Excess capacity occurs when there is an imbalance between the number of spaces available in required courses and the number of spaces in elective courses. If enrollment demand is large enough, excess capacity may be reduced by offering multiple sections in some courses but not in others.) Thus, the effects of increasing or reducing course requirements and the effects of increasing enrollments in each program in terms of additional sections and faculty can be calculated if there were no changes in the work load or section capacity. These calculations were supported by an analysis of the historical course enrollments in the college to obtain an average course load per student and the patterns of enrollment in required and elective courses for each program.

The instructional function is not the only determinant of necessary resource requirements. What faculty resources, for example, are required for curriculum development, program planning, public service, administration, and research? Unlike the instructional function, these activities could not be related directly to the number of courses or students in the program at any given time. Since the faculty work load used to calculate the instructional function contains an assumption that a substantial part of the faculty member's time is devoted to such activities, only that portion that would require time over and above the baseline faculty work load was counted for these activities.

The field instruction and the doctoral programs posed many conceptual and statistical problems that had to be resolved. For field instruction the principal difficulties were statistical, and the procedure used here related students and coordinating effort directly to the number of agencies and the agency capacity for absorbing students. This indirect contribution was priced directly and could be shown to constitute a substantial part of the resources of the college. The college's direct costs could further be demonstrated to be a function of the number of agencies participating in the program.

Doctoral work involves a progressive movement from structured (class and seminar) instruction to independent study and thesis research. Because students progress at different rates with varying support needs, this program presented unique properties that made the model developed for other programs inappropriate. An independent model was developed for the doctoral program which detailed progress from admission to completion and developed attrition rates during the critical phases of the program. The model described in quantitative terms faculty effort that would be required for a given number of students in varying phases of completion of the program. It was then possible to complete the basic resources requirements table (Figure 13–3).

The basic resources requirements table is presented in terms of full-time equivalent faculty and staff, with dollar values given only for nonpersonnel items. Only after determining the appropriate ratio of senior to junior faculty could the basic resources requirements table be translated into a budget request.

The zero-base budget efforts at Jane Addams College of Social Work was directed toward a five-year plan. This plan incorporated changes in enrollment and orderly movement toward a desired faculty mix, as well as specified growth (and reduction) in certain support activities. For budgetary purposes these changes were displayed in a format identical to the basic resources requirements table. The basic resources requirements table could be expanded along either dimension to display a more detailed program budget for each year and at varying levels of enrollment. For example, the program of "College Administration" could be expanded to display subcategories, such as secretarial and other support staff, commodities and telephone, distributed across the various functions of instruction, curriculum development, program administration, and so on. This type of display permits decision-making based on various levels of support associated with expected results. Alternatively, the basic resources requirements table could be easily translated into the more traditional line item budget request focusing on personnel, materials and supplies, and the like.

Conclusions and Implications

What, if anything, was achieved by this exercise? Measured in time alone, approximately three months of a new administrator's efforts were consumed. Although the theory is that faculty participate fully, in point of fact time permitted only the key administrators (the chairpersons of the divisions) to do so. In general, faculty involvement was not gratifying. The fact that this was a transitional year with a new dean further generated fears and anxieties about the change potential. A zero-base budget demands clearly stated programmatic directions and goals, and this was not useful in fudging the conflicts that are traditionally found in schools of social work.

Interestingly, the budget exercise also presented problems for those to whom it had to be presented. Thus, members of the Academic Resources Board (whose hearings were open and recorded) found themselves asking questions based on a more traditional data base and were unable to absorb and respond to the material presented. This was true for all four presentations. Since most university units are labor intensive and expenditures are not subject to significant short-term change, the exercise seemed futile. Indeed, the argument is repeatedly made that zero-base budgets are not useful where personnel constitute the major cost item and where they cannot be quickly eliminated.

The results, however, in terms of the school and its image in the university community, were quite positive. The exercise provided an excellent opportunity for a new administrator to state a desirable and necessary five-year direction for the school. It gave an opportunity for a social work school to interpret its functions, its ways of operating, and its programmatic thrusts and needs to a skeptical and suspicious academic community.

It highlighted the issue of faculty imbalance. It was possible to demonstrate that the school might have enough faculty but still not have the properly qualified mix to carry on its desired programs. The knowledge that is required to prepare a zero-base budget is in itself convincing to those whom one must convince. It was also possible to demonstrate in what ways programmatic changes and administrative savings were being affected within the existing budget.

Far from receiving a retrenchment budget, the school received an increment in its base budget. Given the tight university situation, the school fared well. Could this result have been achieved with a simple clear statement of program objectives and the more usual 5 percent increment/decrement approach? In all probability, it would have been possible. What would have been lacking would have been the credibility and the conviction that was imparted with the zero-base document. The detailed analysis of the school's operation (both academic and nonacademic) helped change the Academic Resources Board from one predisposed to retrench the school's budget into one that voted an increase in the base budget and in a year when an increase in one unit's budget had to come at the expense of another.

The basic problems of zero-base budgeting are formidable. Already mentioned was the inability of the receiving body to shift its thinking to respond in zero-base terms. Another was the inability to bring the entire faculty along, and, as is true for any comprehensive budgeting approach, ideological differences were highlighted rather than minimized. Since, fundamentally, change takes place at the margin, zero-base concepts strike many people as idealistic, unreal, and futile. It is, therefore, not surprising that the faculty community in the second year of the existence of the Academic Resources Board voted out any further zero-base budgets. Their concern with the time involved is certainly understandable. Higher education administrators seem most comfortable with annualized budgeting and 5 percent increase/decrease projections. Since that is about all that one can reallocate in a single budget cycle, it makes pragmatic sense.

Nonetheless, there are times when this comprehensive presentation serves well a number of diverse purposes. In retrospect, it was a valuable learning experience for a new administrator, a useful time to project a new image of a school, and a time to demonstrate a technical competence which in the end had good political payoffs. Looking at who gets what, the school of social work benefited substantially from its zero-base budget.

NOTES

1. Office of the Vice-Chancellor for Academic Affairs, University of Illinois at Chicago Circle, "*Inauguration of Annualized Budget System and Establishment of Academic Resources Board*," Mimeographed, January 12, 1977.
2. Aaron Wildavsky, *The Politics of the Budgetary Process* (Boston: Little, Brown, 1964).
3. Ibid., p. 51.
4. Ibid., p. 135.
5. G. B. Weathersby and F. E. Balderston, *PPBS in Higher Education Planning and Management,* Ford Foundation Program for Research in University Administration, Paper P-31 (Berkeley: Office of the Vice-President-Planning, University of California, 1972).
6. Peter A. Pyhrr, *Zero-Base Budgeting: A Practical Management Tool for Evaluating Expenses* (New York: Wiley, 1973), p. 6.
7. Peter A. Pyhrr, "An Approach to Zero-Base Budgeting," *Society for Advanced Management Journal,* vol. 41 (3) Summer 1976, pp. 5–14.

8. "Irreducible minimum" is that level of expenditure below which continuation of the programs is not possible without changing their definition. "Resources required" includes all appropriated funds in the annual operating budget of the college. "Outputs" are measured in number of courses taught, number of students served, and quantity and type of activities engaged in by faculty and staff.

---

14. ZBB and Program Evaluation

Evaluating Program Performance

JOSEPH S. WHOLEY

Problems with Program Evaluation

The role of program evaluation . . . is to provide information on program performance for use by policymakers and managers in zero-base budgeting and other policy and management decisions. Over the past fifteen years, a new industry has been created to evaluate the performance of government programs. The federal government now spends more than $200 million per year for program-evaluation studies, and huge additional sums are spent on program evaluation at state and local levels.

To date, however, relatively little has come from the investments made in evaluation. Most evaluations are not sufficiently timely, relevant, and conclusive to be useful in policymaking or management. Policymakers and managers already get a great deal of informal feedback on program performance without evaluation—through telephone calls, letters, meetings with constituents and interest groups, the press, professional opinion, views from other levels of government, and elections (the ultimate evaluation). This informal feedback is constant, often invalid and unreliable, but still very helpful in keeping policymakers in contact with program reality. Policymakers have little time and less inclination to read program-evaluation reports, unless they respond directly to the policymakers' own questions and concerns.[1]

Reprinted by permission of the publisher, from *Zero-Base Budgeting and Program Evaluation* by Joseph S. Wholey (Lexington, Mass.: Lexington Books, D. C. Heath and Company, Copyright 1978, D. C. Heath and Company).

Although program evaluation has been a growing area of government activity, there is little evidence that evaluations are being used in policy/ management decisions or that government programs are improving as a result. In "Program Management and the Federal Evaluator," my colleagues and I concluded that the ineffectiveness of program evaluation efforts usually results from inadequate definition of the problem addressed by the program, insufficient specification or understanding of the assumed causal links between program inputs/activities and program outcomes/ impacts, or lack of management willingness or ability to act on the basis of evaluation information.[2]

In the typical government program, there is no "right" set of performance measures. Government programs often lack clear direction; program objectives are seldom defined in measurable terms. Evaluators are therefore often unclear about what information is needed for what purposes. Evaluators are uncertain about which of the many possible questions about program performance are most important and uncertain about the degree of precision required in answering evaluation questions.

Useful Program-Evaluation Approaches

The keys to effective policy control of large organizations seem to be establishing a small number of clear, realistic, measurable objectives measuring organizational performance in terms of these measures and using the feedback measurements to bring about changes in resources, activities, or objectives. In his books on well-managed private organizations, Peter Drucker shows the feasibility and value of translating vague goals into specific objectives and measurements that allow managers throughout the organization to know what they are intended to accomplish and how they are performing. General Motors, for example, uses *market share* as its key measure of performance; the Bell Telephone System created *customer-satisfaction* standards.[3] Both General Motors and the Bell System used their measures to evaluate organizational performance.

In the public sector, evaluators can do relatively little for policymakers unless policymakers take the time to clarify their priority information needs and the ways in which they intend to use evaluation information. The best vehicle we have found for accomplishing useful evaluation work is a strategy in which policymakers invest in a series of relatively quick and inexpensive evaluation efforts that produce successive increments of information about program promise and performance.

Four program-evaluation processes provide the policymaker with these successive increments of program-performance information: evaluability assessment; rapid-feedback evaluation; outcome monitoring; and intensive evaluation. In the balance of this chapter, I show the contribution that these evaluation processes can make to effective informed policymaking.

EVALUABILITY ASSESSMENT[4]

Evaluability assessment is assessment of the feasibility and likely utility of evaluation in a particular setting. Evaluability assessment clarifies what the program is intended to accomplish (in the eyes of the policymaker for whom the evaluation is to be done) and reveals what measurements of program performance would be feasible and relevant to the information needs of those policymakers. The time scale for evaluability assessment is usually one to four months; the cost, one to six man-months.

The key to useful program evaluation is agreement on relevant, feasible measures of program performance. Research on evaluation reveals that most evaluations are not used because evaluation is undertaken before the program is ready for useful evaluation.[5] In particular, the research shows that evaluation is unlikely to be useful unless certain "evaluation planning standards" are satisfied—(1) program objectives are well defined, (2) causal links between program activities and objectives are plausible and testable, and (3) intended uses of evaluation information are well defined.

1. Program objectives are *well defined* if measures of progress toward objectives have been agreed upon by those who are to use the evaluation information and measurement data are obtainable at reasonable cost and in a reasonable time frame.

2. Causal links are *plausible* if there is evidence that program activities are likely to lead to program objectives.

3. Causal links are *testable* if tests of causal assumptions have been agreed upon by those who are to use the evaluation information and comparison data are obtainable at reasonable cost and in a reasonable time frame.[6]

4. Intended uses of evaluation information are *well defined* if the intended users of the evaluation information have been identified and the users agree that the evaluation information is needed to assist them in specific decision processes.

Evaluability assessment clarifies the logic of the program (resources, activities, objectives, and causal links between activity and objectives); identifies those portions of the program which are ready for useful evaluation (well-defined objectives; plausible, testable causal links between activities and objectives; well-defined uses for evaluation information); and identifies feasible evaluation and management alternatives.

In evaluability assessment, the evaluator identifies the primary intended users of the planned evaluation; reviews program documentation and interviews program management, agency management, and higher-level policymakers to define intended program activities, objectives, assumed causal links between program activities and objectives, and likely uses of evaluation information; develops a model of the program representing the logic of program activities, objectives, and assumed causal links; reviews field operations to clarify actual program activities, operational objectives, and availability of data; applies the four previously mentioned evaluation planning standards to determine what portion of the program is ready for useful evaluation; and interacts with the intended user to determine which, if any, of the presently available or feasible evaluation alternatives would be sufficiently useful to justify the cost of data collection and analysis.[7] . . .

Evaluability assessment documents the logic of government programs, those portions of the programs which are ready for useful evaluation, and feasible evaluation/management alternatives to current operations. Presentation of evaluability-assessment results allows the intended user to agree with or correct the program logic, measures of success, and intended uses of evaluation information.

Getting agreement on clear, realistic, measurable objectives is at least half the battle in evaluating the performance of government programs. In many cases, program objectives will be input or process objectives (e.g., spend more money on education of disadvantaged children; establish special tutoring programs). In other cases, program objectives will be outcome or impact objectives (e.g., raise the educational achievement level of children served by the tutoring program; raise the average reading levels in inner-city schools).

When a program is important enough to warrant policymakers' attention and there is the possibility of special data-collection efforts to meet policymakers' information needs, evaluability assessment can be used to clarify program objectives and measures of success and clarify what additional program-performance information would be sufficiently useful to justify its cost. The time and effort required of evaluators and policymakers, however, mean that evaluability assessment will have to be used selectively.

RAPID-FEEDBACK EVALUATION[8]

All evaluation information has costs: political costs, bureaucratic costs, costs in time and money. These costs include the costs of agreeing on the measurements and comparisons to be made and agreeing on the anticipated uses of evaluation information; the costs of collecting and analyzing the data; and the costs of reviewing, understanding, and using the resulting information.

In many cases, these costs will be minimal. Some program-performance information will always be available. The types of performance information available and the decision criteria will vary from issue to issue: some programs (like general revenue sharing and some other intergovernmental revenue transfers) only have *input objectives*; some programs (like social security and public service employment) have *input and process objectives*; some programs (like manpower training and drug treatment programs) have *outcome objectives*: intended changes in those directly served by the program; some programs (like antismoking, civil rights, and immunization programs) have *impact objectives*: intended changes in the society or the environment. When a program is being managed to achieve an objective (whether it is an input objective, a process objective, an outcome objective, or an impact objective), performance information will be available on the degree of progress toward that objective. Outcome and impact information will usually be sparse, but many policy decisions do not in fact require outcome or impact information. As Exhibit 14–1 illustrates, many policy decisions can be made using the program-performance information already available.[9] In some cases, additional information will be required to assist executive or legislative decisions.

Rapid-feedback evaluation is a tool for quickly obtaining specific information on program performance, including estimates of program outcome or impact. Rapid-feedback evaluation synthesizes what is already known and what is readily knowable about program performance, in terms of measures and comparisons agreed to by policymakers who require the information for specific decisions. In addition, rapid-feedback evaluation shows what it would cost to improve on this preliminary evaluation by specifying the measures, comparisons, and resources required for more definitive evaluation.

Frequently, all that can be learned from a reasonable expenditure of resources can be learned relatively quickly and inexpensively through rapid-feedback evaluation. The time scale for rapid-feedback evaluation is usually less than six months; the cost, less than two man-years.

Rapid-feedback evaluation is accomplished through a four-step process: collecting readily available information on program performance; estimating the magnitudes of program inputs, activities, outcomes, impacts, and relationships among inputs, activities, outcomes, and impacts; preliminary evaluation; and evaluation design.

Given agreement on a set of performance measures of interest to policymakers (i.e., given the results of evaluability assessment), rapid-feedback

Exhibit 14–1.
Performance Information Needed versus Performance Information Available

Program	Types of Performance Information[a]				Possible Decisions
	Input	Process	Outcome	Impact	
Antismoking	*NNNNN* *AAAAA*	*NNNNN* *AAAAA*	*NNNNN* *AAAAA*	*NNNNN* *AAAAA*	Redesign an ineffective program.
Medicaid	*NNNNN* *AAAAA*	*NNNNN* *AAAAA*	*NNNNN*		Redesign programs to achieve outcome objectives. Increase overhead.
Medicare	*NNNNN* *AAAAA*	*NNNNN* *AAAAA*	*NNNNN*		Establish outcome monitoring system.
Community Mental Health Centers	*NNNNN* *AAAAA*	*AAAAA*			Maintain, reduce, or expand, depending on resources required for higher-priority programs.
Manpower Training	*NNNNN* *AAAAA*	*AAAAA*	*AAAAA*		Expand or cut program, depending on unemployment rates.
Safe Streets Act	*NNNNN*	*NNNNN*			Cut overhead.
(LEAA Block Grants)	*AAAAA*	*AAAAA*			Transform into special revenue sharing.
General Revenue Sharing	*NNNNN* *AAAAA*				Maintain, reduce, or expand, depending on administration and congressional priorities.

[a]*N* indicates the types of performance information likely to be needed or wanted by federal policymakers for decisions they must make to achieve their objectives; *A* indicates the type of performance information available.

evaluation uses program documentation, past evaluation and research studies, expert opinion, quick telephone surveys of program staff or clients, and a limited number of site visits to assemble readily available information on program inputs, activities, outcomes, and impacts. Data collection is limited to the relatively brief period within which evaluation planning and design is being carried out.

From the available data, the evaluator estimates the ranges of variations of, and functional relationships among, key program variables. In some cases, the evaluator will then have sufficient information to allow a preliminary evaluation of program performance. Often the program is so structured that the evaluator's estimates of program performance could not be greatly improved upon even if a full-scale evaluation were undertaken.

In any case, the evaluator will now have the information needed to allow preparation of designs for one or more feasible evaluations. The evaluator specifies the measurements that would be taken, comparisons that would be made, and the resources required, so that the policymaker has sufficient information for an informed judgment as to whether to proceed with a full-scale evaluation.

For example, in 1973 the Department of Housing and Urban Development asked the Urban Institute to design an evaluation of Operation Breakthrough, a program that was intended to demonstrate the feasibility and value of industrialized housing production.[10] We agreed to design the evaluation through our proposed rapid-feedback evaluation process. We saw rapid-feedback evaluation as a very careful evaluation design process that might develop sufficient data to permit, as a byproduct of evaluation design, a preliminary evaluation of the program.

Operation Breakthrough was initiated at nine prototype sites. Twenty-nine hundred housing units were produced under the demonstration program, and another twenty-three thousand units were built under the Department's Section 236 program. Operation Breakthrough, like many public programs, had a large number of vague goals. There was great diversity among federal officials in their interpretation of Operation Breakthrough goals and in the relative priority they assigned to different goals.

Our rapid-feedback evaluation used available program documentation, existing data, telephone surveys of those involved in or knowledgeable about Operation Breakthrough and housing production, and site visits to four of the nine prototype sites. In the telephone surveys and site visits, 73 people were interviewed.

The rapid-feedback evaluation required approximately five months, using ten man-months of effort. The preliminary evaluation revealed that under Operation Breakthrough housing units were built and marketed as intended; savings and loan institutions did not significantly change their involvement in financing industrialized housing production; Operation Breakthrough did not directly stimulate significant innovation in housing production technology; and there was no evidence that Operation Breakthrough had a measurable effect on the nation's housing production.

The rapid-feedback evaluation of Operation Breakthrough was presented to Congress. With some modifications, the Urban Institute's evaluation design was used for the full-scale evaluation. The two-stage evaluation process provided information more quickly and at lower cost than the single large evaluation originally planned by the Department of Housing and Urban Development.

Many reviewers considered that all that could be learned from evaluation of Operation Breakthrough was learned in the rapid-feedback study. As evaluators we learned, however, that larger samples would have increased users' confidence in the preliminary evaluation.

OUTCOME MONITORING[11]

If policymakers decide that more information is needed on program results than is already available or is quickly obtainable through rapid-feedback evaluation, two evaluation options are open: *intensive evaluation*, which uses the principles of research design to estimate the causal relationships between program inputs/activities and the resulting program outcomes and impacts, or *outcome monitoring*, which compares actual program results with prior or expected results but does not attempt to prove whether observed outcomes on impacts were caused by the program. Exhibit 14–2 compares and contrasts these evaluation options with traditional administrative monitoring of program expenditures, services de-

Exhibit 14–2.
Distinctions among Administrative Monitoring, Outcome Monitoring, and Intensive Evaluation

	Administrative Monitoring	Outcome Monitoring	Intensive Evaluation
Measures Used			
Input	X		X
Process	X		X
Outcome		X	X
Impact		X	X
Measures Compared With			
Expected Results	X	X	
Prior Results	X	X	
Time-Series Data			X
Comparison Groups			X
Control Groups			X

livered, and numbers served. The next section discusses intensive evaluation; here we examine outcome monitoring.

As defined here, outcome monitoring can be considered to be midway between sophisticated evaluations using experimental and control groups or time series data, on the one hand, and administrative monitoring, on the other. Outcome monitoring may measure the same variables that intensive evaluation would measure; administrative monitoring typically measures input and process only. Intensive evaluation uses control groups, comparison groups, and time-series data in attempting to determine whether program activities cause observed results; outcome monitoring compares actual program results with prior or expected results.

One of the main problems in meeting policymakers' information needs is that in the real world a conclusive evaluation of program effectiveness often is not feasible at all, given the structure of the program, or not feasible at an acceptable cost or within an acceptable time frame. All too often, evaluators are asked to carry out costly, usually inconclusive efforts to address essentially unanswerable questions. The fact that a program was not designed or operated as a controlled experiment does not stop policymakers from asking questions that could only be answered with an experiment, but it does mean that the questions may be unanswerable, given the structure of the program and the typical lack of baseline data.

The key to effective outcome monitoring is the establishment of clear, measurable objectives that clarify what the program is trying to accomplish and what information can and will be collected on program performance (e.g., reduce crime as measured by reported robberies and auto thefts; improve citizen satisfaction as measured by telephone surveys of households and neighborhood businesses; or cut red tape as measured by numbers of man-hours required to complete a particular form). If policymakers or managers wish to achieve specific outcomes/impacts and will agree on appropriate measures of success, outcome monitoring can provide timely, reliable reports on the degree of progress toward those outcome/impact objectives.

Outcome monitoring provides specific information on program outcomes/impacts while the program is still in progress. Measures of success may be quantitative or qualitative. The focus of outcome monitoring is on short-term outcome or impact measures that are related to program goals and can reasonably be expected to be influenced by the program.

Sources of monitoring data may be existing records, newly created project records, special follow-up surveys, or site visits. Data collection may involve a program reporting system in which project managers mail in the data, or may use telephone surveys or site visits to bypass intermediate management levels and deal directly with those in the field or those whom the program is intended to help.

For example, in cooperation with the District of Columbia Department of Environmental Services, the Urban Institute developed a system for monitoring the cleanliness of city streets and alleyways.[12] Monitors observed random samples of streets and alleys, compared litter conditions with those in a set of reference photographs, and assigned numerical ratings ranging from 1 (clean) to 4 (heavily littered). The resulting ratings could then be aggregated to show the cleanliness of the streets and alleys in a geographic area, used to identify problem areas, . . . and used to measure the results of regular and special cleanup activities. . . .

A number of cities have adopted and used this street-litter monitoring system in the management of sanitation department cleaning of streets, sidewalks, and alleyways. Rather than holding the sanitation department and district supervisors accountable for performance defined in terms of process measures, these cities monitor performance in terms of outcomes achieved.

Outcome monitoring moves evaluators away from sterile, academic arguments about standards of proof. In the real world, definitive or conclusive evaluation is often not feasible. Outcome monitoring is usually the least costly, most feasible, and most useful evaluation that can be done under real-world conditions. . . .

Significance

As suggested previously, program-evaluation work should be focused on specific measurements needed by the policymakers involved in specific decision processes. By providing successive increments of information on the degree to which program objectives have been defined, the extent to which data measuring program performance are available or obtainable, the range of likely costs and effects of program activities, and the extent to which relevant outcome measurements meet or deviate from standards of prior or expected performance, the evaluator can determine the extent to which specific policymakers are willing and able to use evaluation information.

Techniques are available for obtaining timely, useful information on program performance. Useful evaluation work can often be done in the absence of randomly assigned experimental and control groups. The key is agreement between policymaker and evaluator on the evidence (specific measurements and comparisons) needed for policy decisions. Policymakers who want to make government more efficient, effective, purposeful, and manageable can be helped with quick evaluations of program promise and performance, using the evaluability-assessment, rapid-feedback, and outcome-monitoring processes outlined previously.

These program-evaluation processes provide occasions for interaction between the evaluator and the policymakers to whom he provides information. On each occasion, the evaluator provides information on program activities and objectives; policymakers then either focus the evaluator's subsequent efforts in areas where evaluation work will be relevant and useful or terminate evaluation activities when further evaluation effort would be too costly.

These program-evaluation approaches will be helpful in settings in which policymakers wish to direct government programs to achieve outcomes or impacts beyond the delivery of services. These program-evaluation processes provide policymakers with information they need to set realistic objectives and measure progress or lack of progress toward program objectives. The key is policymakers' willingness and ability to set clear objectives and to allocate resources, direct program activities, and maintain or change objectives on the basis of progress or lack of progress toward priority objectives.

In a zero-base budgeting environment, the evaluator has both a better-than-average opportunity to determine policymakers' needs for information and a clearer use for evaluation products. Dialogue among policymakers and managers over decision alternatives provides important clues to relevant measures of program effectiveness; and policy decisions to fund program activities above minimum service levels will often be based on agreement that a specific set of outcomes or impacts is worth achieving (thus providing the basis for subsequent monitoring of program accomplishments). The zero-base budgeting process provides ample opportunity for use of evaluation information: evaluability assessments and rapid-feedback evaluations can assist this year's budget decisions; and outcome monitoring or intensive evaluation can assist in next year's budget decisions.

NOTES

1. As a policymaker, I rarely read evaluation reports that come to me from the outside world. I do not read two-page summaries of evaluation reports; I do not read evaluation reports that come to me with a personal cover note. When evaluation reports come to me from outside groups, I pile them up, unread. When the pile gets too high, I start another pile. Evaluations addressed to a broad audience usually don't communicate

with me. If evaluators want to communicate with me, they have to communicate through my staff when a specific decision is to be made, or get
their evaluation findings in one of the newspapers I read.

2. Pamela Horst et al., "Program Management and the Federal Evaluator,"
   Public Administration Review 34, No. 4 (July/August 1974):300–308.
3. Peter F. Drucker, *Concept of the Corporation* (New York: John Day,
   1946; revised edition, 1972); and *Management: Tasks, Responsibilities,
   Practices* (New York: Harper and Row, 1974).
4. This section is based on Richard E. Schmidt et al., *Serving the Federal
   Evaluation Market* (Washington: The Urban Institute, 1977); and Joseph
   S. Wholey et al., "Evaluation: When Is It Really Needed?" *Evaluation* 2,
   No. 2 (1975):89–93.
5. Horst et al., "Program Management and the Federal Evaluator."
6. As will be seen later, this standard need not be satisfied for useful *outcome monitoring* work, since outcome monitoring does not attempt to
   prove whether or not program activities cause the observed results.
7. The hypothetical example of evaluability assessment is based on the discussion of street-cleaning programs and systems for evaluating such programs in Louis H. Blair and Alfred I. Schwartz, *How Clean Is Our City?*
   (Washington: The Urban Institute, 1972).
8. See note 4.
9. I am indebted to John Scanlon of the Urban Institute for this example.
10. This example is based on Donald R. Weidman, Francine L. Tolson, and
    Joseph S. Wholey, *Summary of Initial Assessment and Evaluation Study
    Design for Operation Breakthrough* (Washington: The Urban Institute,
    December 1973; revised, May 1974); and Donald R. Weidman, "An Ex-
    ample of Rapid Feedback Evaluation: The Operation Breakthrough Ex-
    perience" (Washington: Urban Institute Working Paper, October 1976).
11. This section is based on John D. Waller et al., *Monitoring for Govern-
    ment Agencies* (Washington: The Urban Institute, 1976); Joseph S.
    Wholey et al., "Evaluation: When Is It Really Needed?"; and Louis H.
    Blair and Alfred I. Schwartz, *How Clean Is Our City?* (Washington: The
    Urban Institute, 1972). Further information on outcome monitoring will
    be found in Harry P. Hatry, Richard E. Winnie, and Donald M. Fisk,
    Practical Program Evaluation for State and Local Government Officials
    (Washington: The Urban Institute, 1973); Annie Millar, Harry Hatry, and
    Margo Koss, *Monitoring the Outcomes of Social Services*, Vols. I and II
    (Washington: The Urban Institute, 1977); and Joseph S. Wholey, *Evaluat-
    ing Government Performance* (Washington: The Urban Institute, in draft).
12. See Blair and Schwartz, *How Clean Is Our City?*

15. Problems of Analysis and Review

Can ZBB Work?

PAUL H. O'NEILL

MR. O'NEILL. Thank you, Mr. Chairman. . . . I appreciate the opportunity to testify before this task force.

We in the administration, following the president's strong leadership, are firmly committed to the stated purposes of these bills [H.R. 11734 and S. 2925]: "To eliminate inactive, unnecessary, duplicative, or outmoded programs, and to see to it that every dollar of the taxpayer's money is spent as efficiently as possible to produce the best possible product."

The president's commitment to these purposes is fully demonstrated in his legislative and budget program. . . .

In turning more specifically to H.R. 11734 and S. 2925, I would first like to raise a caution. Perhaps growing out of too many years of experience, I am frequently reminded of one of H. L. Mencken's pithy observations. He said: "For every human problem there is a solution: neat, simple . . . and wrong."

That is not to suggest that you put aside the legislation you are considering. But it is intended to urge caution.

I believe a good case can be made for legislative action by observing the progress that has been made under the Congressional Budget Act. But at the same time our experience with the planning-programming-budgeting (PPB) systems of the 1960s suggests we proceed with great care. In my judgment, our experience with PPB demonstrates the problems that can be created with a rigidly specified system. Those of you who were close to it will recall, as I do, the mountains of paperwork it produced. One saving grace was the fact that it was a creature of the executive branch which we were able to redirect without legislative action, preserving its fundamental ideas while doing away with its process burden. And so, I think it is extremely important, as this legislation is considered, that we try very hard to say precisely what it is we think will be accomplished by its enactment

Statement of Paul H. O'Neill, Deputy Director, Office of Management and Budget. Hearings before the House Task Force on the Budget Process, U.S. Congress, July 27, 1976.

and what its cost will be. In other words, we should apply the ideas of sunset and zero-base review in considering this legislation.

Last spring, in testimony before the Senate Government Operations Committee, we offered an analysis of S. 2925 in its original form, which at that time was identical to H.R. 11734. Those comments are, I believe, still valid and I have therefore attached them to my prepared statement.

There is one concern not covered by the attachment that I want to mention. It has become apparent that the program identification required to be made by the GAO under the existing bills may lead to a paperwork process that is mind-boggling—even by Washington standards. We have indications that the GAO approach may result in the identification of 20,000 or more programs. These programs would then become the basis for determining the number of reviews to be made and of objectives to be covered in the budget.

[The attachment referred to follows:]

Effect of Provisions of S. 2925 [Sunset Legislation]

Some of the specific provisions of S. 2925 could work at cross-purposes with the basic intent of the bill. A discussion of some of these problems follows.

LIMITING AUTHORIZING LEGISLATION TO FOUR YEARS

Title I imposes a four-year limit on authorizing legislation for most federal programs and activities. This means that these programs must be reauthorized every four years or be terminated. . . .

The provision ignores some realities. The functions of some agencies (as opposed to the efficiency with which these functions are carried out) are not subject to dispute. For example, there seems to be no disagreement that Justice must enforce federal laws, Defense must maintain the national security, and the Bureau of Census must count the population.

Tying the mandatory reauthorizations to the functional classification will insure that the programs in each category will be reviewed simultaneously. However, this does not provide for focusing review and reauthorization on government-wide issues that may cut across functions or subfunctions. In addition, it is unlikely that any fixed classification could provide for such focus. Use of the functional classification would also make restructuring of that classification more difficult to accomplish.

The processing and paperwork that would be required each year for those federal programs being reauthorized would be mountainous. The end result of this provision would be to divert time from focusing on those programs or activities for which changes should be made. The necessity to prepare detailed justifications and evaluations for all reauthorizations would impose an unnecessary workload and paperwork burden on those agencies whose functions are not subject to dispute and those agencies whose efficiency is not questioned.

The means already exist for concentrating our evaluation efforts on those areas for which they are most needed. The legislative committees of the Congress clearly have it within their power to specify that evaluation studies will be made in conjunction with new authorizing legislation or amendments and extensions of existing law. Moreover, the Government Operations Committees and Budget Committees would appear to have both the authority and the interest to suggest areas of study. Of course, the appropriations committees have a strong interest in program evaluation, too, but the horizon of the appropriations process is generally too short to encompass a complete evaluation cycle. This is not to say that progress reports to appropriations committees are not appropriate. Finally, the executive branch, particularly OMB, has ideas on where program evaluation is most needed and would welcome working with the Congress to develop program evaluation plans.

ZERO-BASE REVIEW AND EVALUATION BY THE EXECUTIVE BRANCH

Section 321 of the bill requires the executive branch to conduct zero-base review and evaluation every year for about a fourth of the federal programs. A very complex and technical evaluation would have to be conducted to assess the level of program quality and quantity that could be purchased at various expenditure levels. The results of the reviews conducted by the executive branch would be required to be transmitted to the Congress at the same time as the president's annual budget. To accomplish this each year in connection with the annual budget would either very seriously degrade the quality of the regular budget review of the programs not subject to zero-base evaluation, or it would require significantly greater resources and more time than [are] now available for the budget review process.

If the type of zero-base review and evaluation defined in . . . the bill is to be made, program impact levels must be measured accurately—in terms of service output—and related to resource inputs in terms of incremental amounts of budget authority. The initial program analysis and evaluation of this bill coupled with the reauthorization process will suffer the same data and paperwork problems experienced for the Planning-Programming-Budgeting system in the late 1960s. It proved impossible to use effectively the considerable amount of information provided by that system.

The magnitude of this task for most, if not all, programs can be illustrated by the following example of a two-step process.

Step 1: Measurement of Effort. Determination of the program impact of a specific level of budget authority is frequently so difficult that it is virtually impossible to anticipate how much time it will take to have useful results.

An excellent, though not extraordinary, example of these problems is provided by an elaborate evaluation of Title I of the Elementary and Secondary Education Act (ESEA). The measurement instruments for this evaluation are now undergoing tests. Title I of the ESEA is aimed at meeting the special needs of educationally disadvantaged children. The evaluation study is expected to take seven years—at a cost of approximately $7 million for the first two years. Design and measurement techniques in such an evaluation present a formidable task due to the diversity of projects that have been undertaken under Title I. State and local educational jurisdictions have taken highly varied and individualized approaches in designing corrective programs for the educationally disadvantaged. Moreover, the measurement of educational attainment is clouded by the absence of standard tests for which there is agreement among educators as to their validity, and by the unavailability of adequate comparison groups. All of these uncertainties about the success of this long-term expensive evaluation project are set against a background of previous efforts, which frequently have been unable to demonstrate conclusive evidence concerning the effect of such special educational programs. The difficulty and expense of measuring program effects is not to be taken lightly.

Step 2: Production Functions. Even if these vexing measurement problems can be solved—and we are constantly seeking solutions—true zero-base review and evaluation as outlined in the bill require a good deal more. [They require] relating such efforts to varying dollar and employment levels.

Even with more program impact data than it is reasonable to expect, the development of such production functions would be a challenging analytical task in itself. It is likely that sophisticated mathematical models will be required. We are not aware that such techniques have been successfully developed for any significant social programs, not because of a lack of will on the part of those who have attempted to develop them but because of the great methodological difficulties inherent in them and excessive costs alluded to previously.

At this point, it is not more evaluations but better evaluations that are needed.

There are also reservations to the indiscriminate use of the zero-base technique. This technique may be inappropriate to many federal programs, and in such cases less complex, less detailed techniques may better serve the purpose while at the same time requiring fewer resources. A study was made of the indiscriminate use of zero-base budgeting for a whole agency, the Department of Agriculture, some years ago. In the view of one writer a major conclusion of this study was that: ". . . The main result was a mountain of paperwork. The experiment failed both because no one could figure out how to make the comparisons and because no one was willing and able to make the drastic reallocations that would have been required."

It is doubtful that the basic purpose of this bill is best served by requiring in law that across-the-board zero-base evaulations be performed every four years. The resultant lack of flexibility may not be worth the added emphasis that a statute would provide. It may be that despite its noble intent, enactment of the bill as presently written would cause more harm than good. It would so systematize a very complex and sensitive process and so diffuse our current efforts to encourage quality evaluations that it might cause a net loss of usable data to evaluate and manage federal programs.

Nothing now prevents either the executive branch or the appropriate legislative committees from conducting zero-base reviews and evaluations of the basic purposes and functions of agency programs.

The Congress should allow the heads of agencies to work with the authorizing committees to determine where evaluations are needed as well as their frequency. It should be possible to impose a discipline without the rigidities and inefficiencies involved in taking the across-the-board statutory requirement approach.

ANNUAL OBJECTIVES INCLUDED IN THE PRESIDENT'S BUDGET

[The bill] . . . requires that the President's budget include specific annual objectives for each federal program or activity and an analysis of how the objectives set forth in previous budgets were met. In addition, [it requires] that the President and the Congress specify—in quantitative terms—the objectives of the programs and activities as part of the four-year reauthorization process.

Considerable care must be taken in the proper development of performance measures. Otherwise, these measures often show how busy people are rather than the cost benefit of their activity. The development of a meaningful performance measurement requires significant managerial effort and reorientation. In addition, the maintenance of the process requires that Congressional and executive decisions be based on these analyses or the process will be discredited.

This effort would be staggering. There are more than 1,000 federal domestic assistance programs alone. The amount of information to be included in the President's budget would be so great that detailed analysis by the OMB and agency staff would necessarily give way to "pro forma" examination. OMB policy officials could not possibly do an adequate job of reviewing such a large mass of material and devote the time and effort required during the already overloaded budget review process. Agency accounting systems, many of which are computer-based, would have to be redesigned and reprogrammed. These crushing data requirements would be superimposed on those added by the Congressional Budget and Impoundment Control Act, which have stretched the abilities of OMB considerably. The requirements of [the bill] are more—much more—than the system should be expected to meet.

OVERLAPPING WORK BY THE LEGISLATIVE AND THE EXECUTIVE BRANCHES

The bill requires evaluations to be conducted by Congressional committees, the GAO, the CBO, and the executive branch. . . . A great deal of overlap would be inevitable. An alternative is to reach an understanding on the design of the evaluation—which should be fully coordinated at the start—then have either the executive or the legislative branch conduct the evaulation and avoid duplication of effort.

SUMMARY

The development of an effective process that provides a systematic mechanism for periodic full-scale review and evaluation of federal programs is complex and difficult.

Legislation that provides the flexibility that is needed to make the process work could well be too broad to be meaningful. On the other hand, specificity in the legislation could result in an unduly restrictive and inflexible approach. Rather, it would appear that legislation is not necessary to accomplish needed evaluations.

A more fruitful approach would be to reach agreement with the appropriate legislative committees on a limited number of major program areas that should be evaluated, develop cooperatively a study design for evaluating the programs included in those areas, and then work closely together to make certain that the studies are completed on schedule. OMB could suggest program areas for these committees to consider. It would also make a great deal of sense if the legislative committees were to impose evaluation requirements whenever new programs are instituted or the authorizations for old ones are extended.

This approach differs considerably from the plan outlined in the bill. But it should be possible to find a more appropriate way to accomplish the objectives of this bill without a legislated mechanical and inflexible approach.

THE CHAIRMAN. Thank you very much Mr. O'Neill. I have only one question, . . . the same one that I directed to Mr. Schick. My experience in working with the budget process this year, last year, and the year before leads me to a certain amount of caution such as you mention. I don't want to see a big mountain of paper come up here and when we are finished have the same result we get now. I need to know your suggestions for alternative ways to trigger or select under this process. . . .

Now if we enshrine this into a statute of selective process what are your suggestions as to what is possible? I don't want to overpromise and under-produce in this area.

MR. O'NEILL. . . . I certainly agree with your concerns, and perhaps it would be helpful to start back up the logic stream someplace and talk about what it is this bill seeks to do that is different from what we are now doing.

I think frankly many of those who have talked with such fervor about sunset and zero-base review haven't any idea what the executive budget process is all about. . . .

In the years I have been in the executive branch I cannot recall one when the sum of spending suggested to the President when he was beginning to formulate his budget was not more than $20 billion or $30 billion more than prudent people would reasonably believe should be spent by the executive branch. Given that circumstance, which I frankly do not see changing very dramatically over the next ten or fifteen years, *I think the executive branch is always going to be in a position where it must in effect do zero-base budgeting.* [Emphasis added.]

We do not have a choice because spending demands on the President overwhelm the amount which fiscal policy indicates can reasonably be spent. I think you see the proof of that in the short list of examples in my prepared statement.

Many of the reform, restructuring, and elimination proposals that have been made by the President were not easy proposals to make. It would have been much easier to take the easy road and say, "Let's fund all of these things and not offend any interest groups or any committees or any of the other interested parties that have some attachment to these things."

But I think without regard to partisan politics, Presidents have had to, and will have to in the future, practice zero-base budgeting.

If you agree with me in that assessment then it seems to me the correct question is: What is it we are trying to accomplish with this legislation? . . .

Let me give you an example where the Congress has not been very interested in asking questions that need to be asked. It is one I know you have some experience with. That is, the Public Health Service hospital program, a program created in 1789 when admittedly we had a limited number of hospitals available in the country and we had a problem with our merchant marine bringing infectious diseases back into the country. We had a relatively low-paid merchant marine. So we thought we ought to have a special hospital care system to take care of those people and those problems. In spite of the fact we have a merchant marine that is rather handsomely paid by comparison with most other people in the economy and the fact that we have thousands of general hospitals which can take care of people and we know how to deal with infectious diseases, we still have eight Public Health Service hospitals run by the government for a purpose that escapes me. And yet, in spite of efforts beginning in 1965 with Lyndon Johnson, we have not been able to stop doing that job.

As I say, I think if this bill were successful in doing what it proposes to do, we would stop doing that, but only if this legislation were truly to cause the Congress to ask the question, "Why are we doing this at all?"

It frankly is not clear to me with all the ins and outs of the data requirements and the procedural requirements for canceling programs that that essential purpose will be accomplished by this legislation. That is to say, that the right questions will be asked which will lead to the elimination of outmoded, duplicative, or unnecessary programs.

THE CHAIRMAN. Thank you very much. I am concerned about it because of what I see occurring in the budget process this year. In a democracy you must learn from the way a process proceeds, not from some theory of what you thought or hoped it was going to do or anything else. What I see occurring is this. There are many programs already in place through either permanent legislation or because they are in areas where they have enormous political clout—and I use that again in a nonpartisan sense. When you place a ceiling on some programs as we do in the budget process, these other long-lived programs survive at the expense of the programs that are required to be appropriated each year. . . .

I am trying to determine a way to make it fair for all programs that are faced with the ceiling. I would appreciate your answer.

MR. O'NEILL. Mr. Chairman, I have thought about it quite a bit. We have been in discussions with the Senate Government Operations Committee that has been looking at this legislation since they began last February, and frankly I have come to the conclusion there is no mechanical way we can force people to ask the right questions.

To take your example, GI bill benefits for postwar volunteer armed services people: It is not clear to me that the fact of the sun setting on the GI bill program would lead to a different result than the one you suggest we may be faced with this year. That is to say, there is nothing in the notion of sunset that will cause the members of the committee to ask why are we doing this, and there is nothing in the sunset idea to force them to ask public witnesses to come forward to say that this is a rotten idea.

It really does seem to me that trying to solve what I agree is a very fundamental public problem right now doesn't seem to be subject to the kind of mechanical process that is suggested by these bills. . . . I don't think there is anything built into this legislation the way it has been drafted, nor has anyone identified a way to insure that members ask witnesses who come before them, "Why are we giving you any money at all?" When the witness says, to take a narrow example, "Because we have an infant mortality problem in the country," to press beyond that and say, "All right, I agree with you, infant mortality is too high, we are thirteenth in the world in our rates. You tell me how the dollars you are proposing to be spent in this program are going to have a direct and decided effect on the problem of infant mortality. Then tell me, Mr. Witness, how it is that we prevent the dollars the Congress appropriates for this infant mortality program from simply replacing dollars that are being spent by state or local governments or by the private sector so that we can see what is going on in the national sense."

One of the difficulties we have had for many years in the way we approach budgeting in this country from a federal level is an egocentric view that says if we appropriate $200 million for some purpose, that adds $200 million to the margin as to what the country is spending in totality. I think you can look at program after program and be hard put to draw the conclusion that dollars appropriated from the federal till actually end up being 100-cent dollars by the time they were spent through our society. We have been kidding ourselves.

Looking at the witnesses' testimony before committee after committee, I find very, very infrequently any indications where the witnesses are put on the spot beyond the kind of superficial first question I suggested.

PART V

Management Information Systems

Introductory Note

The role of *information* in management and policy making in the human services has become increasingly central. One reason for this development is the growth in the scale of operations which has made it more difficult to know what is going on. Simultaneously contemporary analytic requirements to answer the question, "what difference do programs make?" requires a massive informational base concerning organizational goals and objectives, program impacts, and the benefits and costs attached. Even short of the analysis of impacts, funding agents are demanding far more extensive reporting on the utilization and deployment of funds and of staff in terms of populations served, by what programs, services, and intervention modes. Thus, at the service delivery level, more and more agencies are struggling to implement effective information systems.

Human service organizations have always had information systems. The file cabinets with data on client dispositions, the budget, case conferences, even the humble case record are information systems. But systems of the "count and sort" type are in many ways inadequate to contemporary demands. What is significant in the current period is the growing utilization of fully automated information systems—systems that are designed for a variety of management purposes in support of operational, administrative and policy making activities, hence the term, Management Information System or MIS. Ideally, such systems are designed to deliver timely, accurate, and comprehensive information, demands that "count and sort" systems are usually unable to meet. Thus, for example, an MIS can easily "track" and locate clients as they move through and between systems, it can answer the question, "what is the unit cost of an hour of adult outpatient service as compared to the same services to a child?" or it can provide administrators with data on staff activities even down to hourly counseling sessions.

The evolution of electronic data processing in the human services has gone through two distinct phases. In the first, emphasis was on "paper pushing" operations such as payroll, or for example, the processing of client checks in public welfare agencies and the Social Security Administration. From the management of such routine procedures, management information systems are now used for comprehensive record keeping and for dealing with relatively structured problems where the data and objectives can be fairly well specified in advance. Elsewhere, in the private corporate sector, a third possible stage is pre-figured in "decision centered" design of information systems.[1] In such applications, the main focus is on improving the decision making of managers in classes of problems where there is sufficient structure for the computer to be of aid, but where management judgement is essential.

Although computerized information systems conjure images of clean, glittering efficiency, these systems are replete with technical, organizational and social problems. In private enterprise, where computer applications have been far advanced, such routine operations as billing and accounts receivable were marked by numerous fiascos when first computerized during the 1960s and even today numerous problems remain. The relationship between systems designers or information technicians and administrators may also be problematical owing to the fact that each has a different view of what the information system ought to look like. Management scientists, for example, tended in the past to drift toward "big is beautiful" dreams of large centralized systems that proved to be expensive follies.[2] Related has been the tendency of MIS specialists to consider the installation of information systems only as technical or design problems overlooking the problems of organizational change. Actually, the MIS may impede effectiveness through an overemphasis of efficiency, and in attempting to rationalize and systematize information flows in an organization, may prove to be disruptive of the informal communications system. In short, "design" considerations must not eclipse "people" considerations.[3] Finally, the MIS provokes the most vexing problems of civil liberties, privacy, confidentiality, and the protection of people against "data abuse."[4] For all of these reasons, the MIS should be under the control of the human service administrator, and toward that end it is vital that those in the human services grasp the essentials of the MIS including its pitfalls and hazards.

Beyond the generalization that an MIS is an organized set of data gathering and processing procedures designed as a supportive tool for managers, the term MIS has few agreed upon definitions. Management science, computer science, information economics, and behavioral science have their own viewpoints.[5] In this section our concern is to equip the reader with an understanding of the *overall design process* involved in the installation of the MIS as a problem of *administrative strategy* rather than focusing on the software and hardware componentry of the system. In passing, we point out that *software* componentry refers to the techniques for structuring the data base, methods of organization, languages for retrieval of data and programs for communication control, while *hardware* refers to such elements as data storage, data processing, and retrieval devices.

From an administrative perspective the key strategic issues hinge on the purposes of the system and on the management of the overall design process from first to last steps. As for the purposes of the system, it is possible to use some generic classification of data, that is, whether it is intended for day-to-day operational usage, budgetary and fiscal control, and/or planning purposes. More specific purposes of data may be defined in terms of *service utilization* (aggregate service delivered, volume by type of service, staff member, etc.) *fiscal* and *budgetary data* (total costs, unit costs, direct and indirect service costs, etc.) *client data* (characteristics, problems, status, disposition, etc.). To collect data before defining the need for it is a costly mistake, hence there is no simple taxonomy that can be overlaid on all agencies.

Turning to the readings, we will consider in sequence the overall design process, selected applications of the MIS, issues in organizational change, and finally, some of the crucial social and ethical issues raised by "information management."

Systems Development. Although as Michael I. Youchah points out, the development and installation of information processing systems is still something less than a science, it is possible to describe and specify the general phases in bringing a system to fruition. Youchah guides the reader through the five basic phases, and through discussion of the major phase-specific tasks together with graphic displays, the author provides a firm foundation for understanding the macro-process. The phases discussed are: the development of operational requirements for the system, the design specifications, production specifications, installation, and initial operation.

The MIS in Action. David Fanshel discusses the child welfare system and deals with a widespread problem: how can we prevent clients from getting lost in the system? In New York City where about 30,000 children are in foster care, the Child Welfare Information Services (CWIS) was designed. In "Computerized Information Systems and Child Care," the author notes, "It is impossible to adequately administer a system caring for large numbers of children without modern methods of information and analytic treatment of the data." Fanshel's discussion of the generation of data *usable* for planning and managerial purposes is especially noteworthy because administrators may suffer from a glut of irrelevant information rather than information deficit.[6]

P. Bruce Landon and Marian Merchant in "Treatment Information System for Feedback and Evaluation in a Mental Health Setting" describe another type of client-oriented tracking system, one that is designed to meet the needs of the administration and of the frontline worker. The aim of the system is to provide evaluation data for both clinical and administrative decision making, and ultimately for the national level for evaluation purposes. Sample data input forms are presented and the overall system is laid out graphically. As the authors note, the Treatment Information System (TIS) required more data than was originally anticipated, a not uncommon problem.

The MIS and Organizational Change. Unless administrators attend to the installation of the MIS as a problem of systems change in the organization, the MIS is likely to be resisted, underutilized or disruptive of valuable informal communications systems. Writing from the perspective of the information specialist, William R. King and David I. Clelland's discussion of MIS design as a problem of organizational change will be no less valuable for the human services administrator. In their "information analysis" approach, the authors focus first on the identification of the "user set" and secondly on the involvement of those users of the MIS in aspects of the design process typically left to technical analysts. In a tightly formalized process, managers develop a descriptive model to show how information requirements are generated, a normative model to show how the organization might be restructured for optimality of the MIS, and finally a consensus model of organizational improvement which is a byproduct of the MIS rather than one that subordinates organizational structures to the MIS.

People and Machines. By many criteria of management, the accumulation and control of information is an ideal management tool for it permits detailed monitoring and control of the organization and those within it. But, as Theodore Sterling points out, the costs of control are high. Among these costs, the procedural features of computerized MIS's can easily dominate management features, and people can come to serve the system rather than the other way around. (In the human services, for example, the way in which a social worker conducts an interview with a client may be significantly affected by the data requirements of the MIS.) While not much is yet known, says the author, about how to avoid the most dehumanizing features of information systems, he pursues this line of inquiry and provides guidelines in terms of specifications for interfacing systems and users; requirements for system flexibility; procedures for evaluating, inspecting, and correcting information about people and protecting privacy; and guidelines for systems design bearing on problems of ethics.

NOTES

1. Thomas P. Gerrity, Jr., "The Design of Man-Machine Decision Systems," *Sloan Management Review*, vol. 12 (2) Winter 1971, pp. 59–75; Peter G.W. Keen and Michael S. Scott Morton, *Decision Support Systems; An Organizational Perspective* (Reading, Mass.: Addison-Wesley, 1978).

2. Jerome Kanter, *Management-Oriented Management Information Systems*, 2d ed. (Englewood Cliffs, N.J.: Prentice-Hall, 1977); Frederick G. Withington, "Five Generations of Computer Use," *Harvard Business Review*, vol. 52 (4) July–August 1974, pp. 99–108; Gary E. Bowers and Margaret R. Bowers, *The Elusive Unit of Service*. Human Services Monograph Series, No. 1 June 1976. Project Share, U.S. Dept. of HEW No. OS–76–130 (Washington, D.C.: Government Printing Office, 1977).

3. Henry C. Lucas, Jr., *Why Information Systems Fail* (New York: Columbia University Press, 1975); C. Argyris, "Resistance to Rational Management Systems," *Innovation*, no. 10, November 1970, pp. 28–34.

4. Alan F. Westin and Michael A. Baker, eds. *Databanks in a Free Society: Computers, Record Keeping and Privacy* (New York: Quadrangle, 1972); Robert S. Boguslaw, *The New Utopians* (Englewood Cliffs, N.J.: Prentice-Hall, 1965); Ida R. Hoos, *Systems Analysis in Public Policy: A Critique* (Berkeley: University of California Press, 1972); Verne R. Kelley and Hanna B. Weston, "Computers, Costs and Civil Liberties," *Social Work*, vol. 20 (1) January 1975, pp. 15–19; *Records, Computers and the Rights of Citizens*. Report of the Secretary's Advisory Committee on Automated Personal Data Systems, U.S. Dept. of HEW, July 1973 (Washington, D.C.: Government Printing Office, 1974).

5. A useful discussion is provided in Keene and Morton, *Decision Support Systems*, pp. 33–54.

6. Russell L. Ackoff, "Management Misinformation Systems," *Management Science* (Application Series), vol. 14 (4) December 1967, pp. B-147–B-156.

16. Systems Development

An Introduction to Systems Analysis, Design, and Implementation

MICHAEL I. YOUCHAH

Introduction

The design, development, and installation of information processing systems is still something less than a science. However, the System Development Corporation, in its work in the field of information systems, has continuously developed and refined its methodology with the express purpose of making the process less of an art and more of a science. These efforts have led to the formulation of a 'systems approach' which embodies many of the aspects of the scientific method and applies them to the production of information systems.

The development of an automated information (or data) processing system is characterized by five general phases (Figure 16–1, The ADP Cycle):

Figure 16–1.
The ADP Cycle

     Phase I —Operational Requirements Development
     Phase II —Design Analysis
     Phase III—Production
     Phase IV—Installation
     Phase V —Initial Operation

This chapter discusses in detail each of these phases, their relationship to the system development process, and the products resulting from the work effort.

It should be noted that the phases listed above are not to be taken as the only possibilities, nor is the arrangement to be considered rigid. It is our intent rather to provide a clearer understanding of the nature and scope of system development. There is a great deal of overlap among the phases and

Reprinted with permission from Geoffrey Y. Cornog et al., eds., *EDP Systems in Public Management* (Chicago: Rand McNally, 1968), pp. 34–50.

the processing within a phase or step and the sequence of the steps may vary for any individual system application. The phase definitions given here, however, cover all major tasks involved in the design, development and installation of the usual information processing system.

Phase I: Operational Requirements Development

The development of Operational Requirements starts with a description of the current operational system (Figure 16–2, Phase I, Operational Requirements Development). It is further necessary to develop an understanding of the system user; his missions, goals, organization, operating techniques, and his role and responsibilities in the environment in which the proposed system is to operate. This preliminary analysis can be used to separate the user's needs into short-range and long-range requirements.

The Operational Requirements for the system to be designed must use the existing "system" as a point of departure for any developmental work; in short, the new system must be compatible with the existing system. (It is assumed that a system, no matter how rudimentary, is always in existence in any organized human endeavor.) Compatibility is not to be construed as meaning that the new system is to be limited by the old one. Rather, the designers of the new system must take cognizance of the old system and provide for a smooth transition from one to the other. The idea that on a given date, at a given time, the old system can be turned off and the new system turned on is far from the truth.

The information analysis performed in this phase involves gathering of all relevant data available on the user's problems and needs. This information is evaluated and categorized to assist in developing functional areas of operation. The relationships of these functional areas, their relative importance and their information demands are used to develop a priority scheme for the functions within the system.

The results of the preliminary analysis are used to develop descriptions of the capabilities to be provided in the new system. A detailed knowledge of how the existing system operates in combination with the information analysis permits proceeding to the next step in the process. The designers, in concert with the users, establish a set of optimal, flexible, and integrated requirements that can help meet the urgent short-range demands without sacrifice or compromise of important future goals. Taking into account the necessary constraints, the system designers and users can then organize the component functional areas and provide for transitional phasing. The transitional phasing information will provide guidelines for the planning of personnel training.

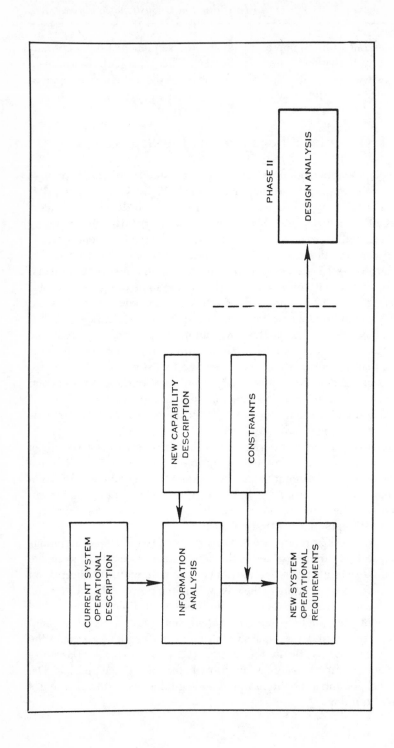

Figure 16-2.
Phase I: Operational Requirements Development

The Operational Requirements are used to develop the system functions, tasks, and support information as the design proceeds through levels of ever-increasing detail (Figure 16–3, Functional Development). The Operational Requirements Products contain detailed statements in three categories: (1) how the information is to be treated, (2) what information is to be entered into the system, and (3) what the outputs of the system will be. (Figure 16–4, Operational Requirements Products, shows the items included under each category.)

Included in the output statements will be decisions on the types of data presentation techniques to be employed. . . .

Phase II: Design Analysis

As can be seen from Figure 16–5, Phase II, Design Analysis, the Operational Requirements for the new system are used as a primary source of information to determine which portions of the system are to be allocated to each of the three operating elements of the system: the men, the machines, and the computer programs.

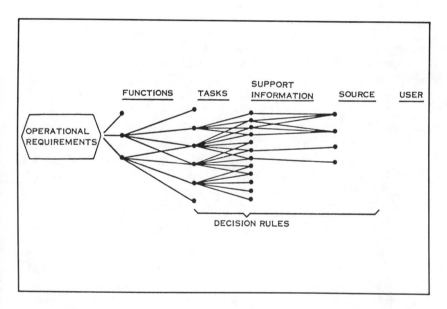

Figure 16–3.
Functional Development

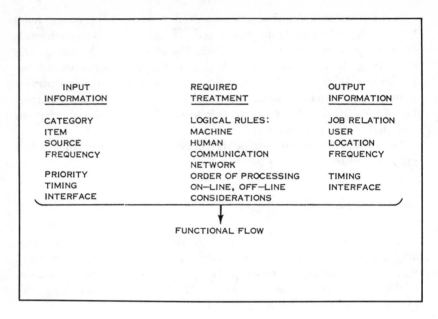

Figure 16–4.
Operational Requirements Products

Trade-off and cost analyses are performed in conjunction with the design analysis in the continuous balancing of the man, machine, and computer program requirements. (Balancing does not imply equal distribution.) The resulting equipment, organizational, and training requirements are thus also in agreement with the constraints that were introduced in the Phase I, Operational Requirements Development. The balancing of man, machine and computer program requirements is critical in assuring the ultimate successful operation of the system. The combination of equipment, organizational training, computer program, man, and machine requirements comprise the detailed design specifications. These are reviewed through the application of cost and trade-off analysis. When this process has been completed and all of the constraints have been applied and considered, the design specifications are used as the primary input to Phase III, Production.

The design specifications that result from the Phase II analysis can be arranged in three subsystems as shown in Figure 16–6. The Program Subsystem will contain descriptions of the operational computer programs, the utility (or support) programs, and the data base. The Personnel Subsystem will contain descriptions of those actions required of the humans, the requirements for new organizations or for modifying the existing organiza-

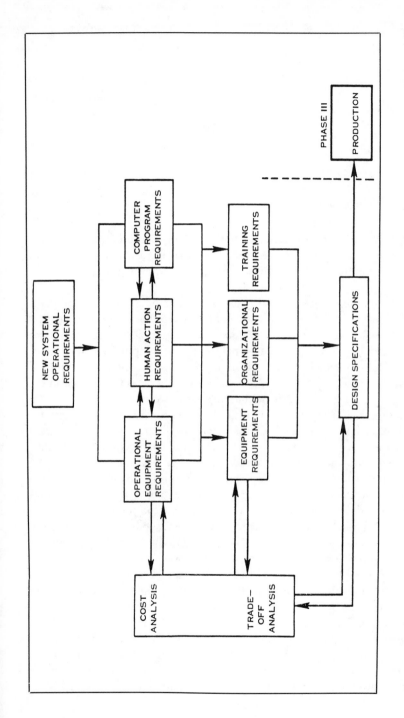

Figure 16-5.
Phase II: Design Analysis

Program Subsystem	Personnel Subsystem	Equipment Subsystem
Operational	Human Action	Core Size
Utility	Requirements	Access Time
Data Base	Human Engineering	Storage Requirements
	Training	I/O Requirements
	Requirements	
	Organizational	
	Requirements	

Figure 16–6.
Design Specifications

tions, and will indicate where additional training is required. Considerations must also be given to the human engineering aspects of the system such as equipment locations, noise levels, and maximum utility of viewing devices.

The Equipment Subsystem requirements must be specified in sufficient detail to permit the proper selection of hardware. Some of the items that must be specified are the core size of the computer, access times and size required for both internal and external storage, and Input/Output requirements. There is usually a trade-off among size, speed, and cost per unit of information stored. Generally, the smaller, slower machines have lower costs and the larger, faster machines are more expensive.

The Program Subsystem can be subdivided roughly into the categories of operational programs and utilities functions (Figure 16–7, The Program Subsystem). In the Operational Program Subsystem the Executive Program acts as a monitor and scheduler, which controls the use of the computer and the ancillary equipment. It interprets the messages that are sent to it and decides which programs and data are to be used. It brings programs and data together in the proper place in the computer, monitors the program functions through completion, then sends the outputs to the appropriate point and returns the data base and the operational programs to their normal storage area. The operational programs are those programs which are used to actually manipulate the data base. These are the programs which do the necessary arithmetic and logical functions which are associated with the processing. The data base is that body of information which is comparable to the files of any organization.

The Utility Subsystem is usually at least composed of a compiler, a data insertion capability, an error detection capability, and a recording and a retrieval capability. To avoid too much detail, it will suffice to say that these programs are the tools used in constructing any operational and executive

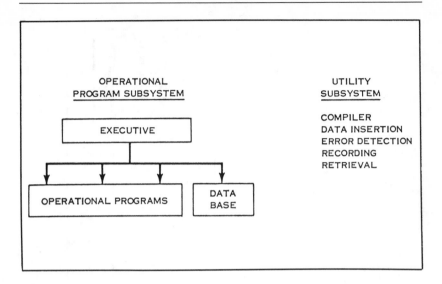

Figure 16–7.
The Program Subsystem

program system. The compiler translates the programs as they are written by the programmer into the type of instructions used within the computer. The data insertion and other programs are used to support the building and operation of the system.

Phase III: Production

The Design Specifications (Phase II) are used in Phase III (Figure 16–8, Phase III, Production) for the development of computer programs and for the structuring of operating procedures for computer personnel, handbooks for the guidance of the users of the system, and training procedures and materials to insure that proper orientation has taken place prior to installing the system.

As each of the areas is developed, it is subjected to component testing to insure the integrity of each individual segment of the system. The segments are subsequently subjected to further component testing and "debugging." (Debugging is the common jargon for the detection and correction of errors in an electronic data processing system. A "bug" in the system usually refers to a small, but bothersome, error.) The development of programs, procedures, handbooks, and training materials proceeds in parallel with each segment being subjected to a series of increasingly

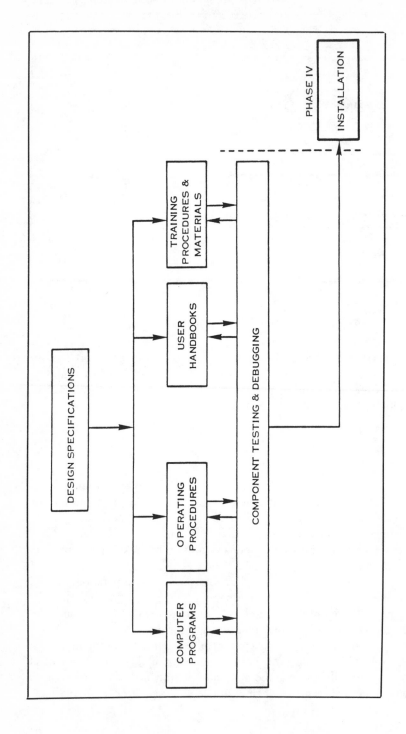

Figure 16-8.
Phase III: Production

complex and interrelated tests. Thus, at the end of the component testing task, the system will have reached a stage of development where all programs not only work independently but can work as an integrated whole.

As shown in Figures 16–8 and 16–9, coding of the computer programs is accomplished and used as the basis for the development of the procedural guides and handbooks. (Coding here means writing the computer program instructions.) These in turn are used in the development of the training materials. The individual programs are checked out and then subjected to further tests, called assembly tests, for the purpose of arriving at a fully integrated operational system. The system test and installation phase involves the introduction of the concept of operational testing (involving the training of both user and operator personnel) leading to the final operational system.

Phase IV: Installation

As can be seen in Figure 16–10, Phase IV, Installation, the tested components of the system are used to check out the operation of the equipment complex and to assure that all the components fit together into a properly coordinated and integrated system. This involves the coordination of the computer programs and procedures developed for each program to insure consistency throughout the operation, so that meaningful materials can be developed for training personnel.

The operational shakedown or checkout of essential equipment, computer programs, procedures, and personnel training materials is essential in the system testing and debugging phase which is roughly analogous to the shakedown cruise of a warship when the crew, equipment, systems and procedures get their first chance to work together. Many problems are revealed in the checkout which are not apparent in the testing and evaluation of individual components that goes on in earlier phases. The two-way flow of information (Figure 16–10) between system testing at one level, and equipment, programs, procedures, and training functions at another level is intended to indicate that there will be feedback of information and modifications as necessary to correct errors or shortcomings in the system discovered during the operational shakedown.

Once the operational shakedown is complete, the turnover procedures start during which the design and development personnel and the user personnel begin the process of disengaging the one group, the designers, and having the user take over more and more of the operations of the system.

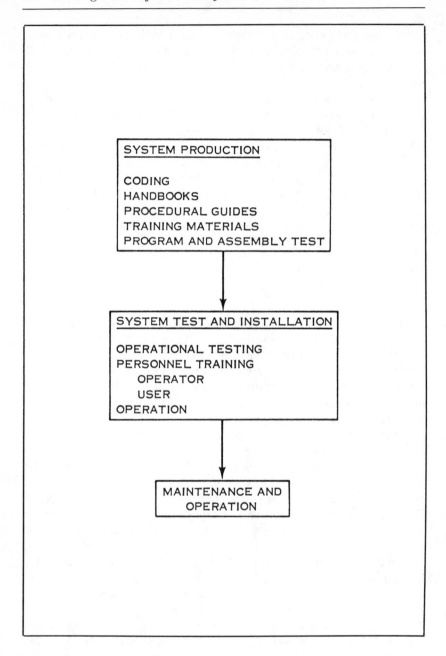

Figure 16–9.
Products of the Production and Installation Phases

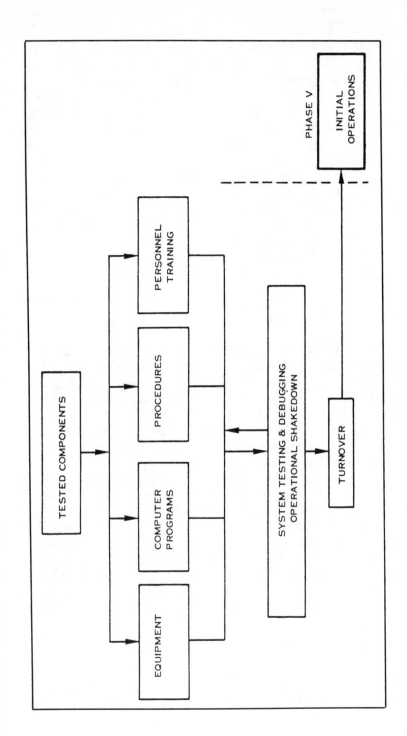

Figure 16–10.
Phase IV: Installation

The products of the System Production and Installation phases are shown in Figure 16–9. The system production products consist of the code generated for each program and the handbooks telling what information must be available in the data base for use by the programs and how the programs are to be operated. There are also procedural guides indicating how the system operates in general terms, and what program and assembly tests must be performed. The training materials that are generated are those which are necessary for training the system users and the machine operators. (The system users are the group of people who have responsibility for performing the functions which the data processing system is to support. The machine operators are those people who will be responsible for actually making the equipment function.) The operational testing of the programs and the training of the operators and users comprise system testing and the installation phase. This testing and installation brings the user personnel into the actual operation of the system.

Phase V: Initial Operation

Each component of the system is developed and tested individually and then assembled and subjected to the operational shakedown as described in Phase IV. Having reached the operational shakedown state, the newly assembled system enters Phase V, a period of initial operations (Figure 16–11, Phase V, Initial Operations).

In Phase V, the system user gets the opportunity to start stressing and testing the system in actual practice. As a result of this experience, it is not uncommon to find that certain changes are necessary to modify an existing capability of the automated system's operation or to add a new capability. In the case of modifying an existing capability, there is a need to go back to the existing design, redesign, and introduce the newly checked-out capability. In the case of adding a new capability, the entire design and implementation process is repeated, but on a smaller scale. In both cases, prior to entering into any effort of significant magnitude, the requirements for changes or additions to the system are subjected to cost analysis and trade-off analysis. These will determine whether the design and production phases have to be entered into again.

Summary

Figure 16–12, User-Designer Relationship, shows the relationship of the user to the designer of the system. The user makes known his needs which

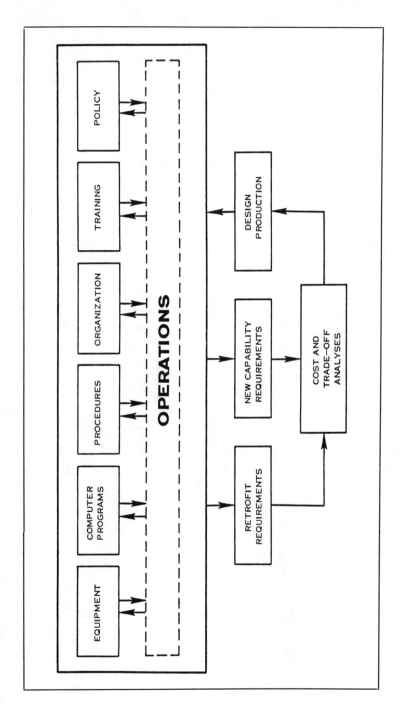

Figure 16–11.
Phase V: Initial Operations

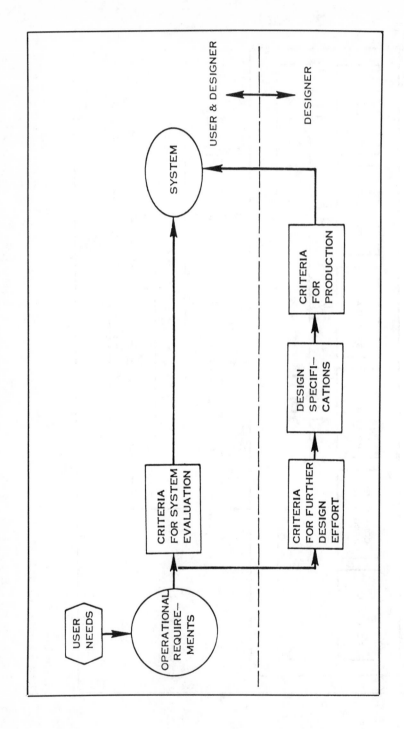

Figure 16–12.
User-Designer Relationship

help to determine Operational Requirements used to establish criteria for evaluating the system. The Operational Requirements are used as the criteria for further design efforts which yield the design specifications and criteria for production. Together, the criteria for production and the criteria for system evaluation are used in evaluating the system and in insuring its continued successful operation.

One should consider that the design and development of an information processing system is not a one-time operation, but rather a continuing and vital process in which the system, to fulfill its sole purpose of serving the user, must change to be consistent with its environment and with the needs of the user.

17. The MIS in Action

Computerized Information Systems and Foster Care

DAVID FANSHEL

Most human service systems in the United States are administered without benefit of organized information. We know woefully little about who comes to the attention of social agencies, the nature of services rendered or the outcomes of such efforts.[1] The situation has been close to scandalous and has tended to make a mockery of the notion that there has been some semblance of accountability of these systems to their supporting publics. It also appears obvious that program management and the process of social policy formulation have been badly hampered by this lack of knowledge.

Increasingly, it has been recognized that computerization of service data through the promulgation of management information systems is required to correct this problem, and such undertakings deserve a high order of priority. If the impulse to satisfy accountability obligations does not provide the impetus for computerization, the reporting requirements of Title XX are apt to result in the same quest.

Reprinted with permission from *Children Today* 5, no. 6 (November–December 1976): 14–18, 44.

The emergence of Child Welfare Information Services (CWIS) in New York City as a viable system for meeting the information needs of agencies providing foster care services for close to 30,000 children—a foster care population larger than that in any of the other states except for California— is a development of considerable importance, one that is gaining increasing national attention. Incorporated in 1972, CWIS has already demonstrated its usefulness in the management of a large social welfare enterprise through its everyday operation, its reports and the central role it has been assigned in the rationalization of service delivery.

Background

The foster care system in New York City has been subjected to severe criticism over the last two decades. A climate of suspicion has long hung over the system; it has frequently been charged that children have been unnecessarily separated from their parents and kept in care to meet the needs of agencies rather than to serve the interests of clients. With all of the charges and countercharges there has been much acrimony, but very little solid information has come forth to illuminate the issues raised. The system simply could not muster up the aggregated data needed to settle the controversy.

When it was established, CWIS was funded primarily with foundation grants but it now receives 95 percent of its budget from New York City's Human Resources Administration. Its data-gathering capability after three years of existence takes the form of an "Undercare Module" which includes only children already in care or awaiting care. An "In-Process Module" is being developed to account for the procedure by which children enter care and are deployed to agencies. The relative success of the "Undercare Module" after such a short period of existence has raised hopes in the community that even greater progress will be made in the near future, when the system becomes more comprehensive in its data capability.

Information and the Politics of Child Care

It no doubt occasions surprise that New York City should become the site of a positive advance in the administration of social programs, since it recently captured the attention of the country as a presumed example of a community guilty of profligacy, one in danger of "going down the drain." Such a picture has, of course, been exaggerated and overlooks efforts at streamlining government operations that have been going on for almost a decade.

When the organization of CWIS took place it was clear to this observer and others that a very important political decision had been made by the administration of Mayor Lindsay. Since the public social service agency was involved in either direct service to foster children or the purchase of such care from close to seventy-five voluntary agencies, activities that accounted for as much as 95 percent of the cost of providing service, the City of New York could legally have created an informational system on its own initiative and mandated compliance from the voluntary agencies. Instead, the choice was made to work cooperatively in a joint enterprise with the voluntary sector. Thus CWIS was created with an organizational format which allocated class memberships in a controlling board in a fashion that gave strong representation to both voluntary and public (city and state) agency interests.

Since the large-scale use of purchase of foster care services from voluntary child care agencies in New York City differs widely from the national pattern and has come under attack from many quarters as against the interests of children, the make-up of the CWIS governing board might be viewed as a questionable political compromise. Would it not have been more appropriate for the public agency to flex its muscle, develop its own management information system and assert its authority to secure concise information about every child it was supporting in foster care? From my observation of the process over a number of years, the validity of the decision to accommodate to the voluntary sector interests seems beyond question. The state and city social service departments had made several earlier attempts to develop a management information system (MIS) enterprise, and these efforts had turned out to be major failures.

CWIS was able to be launched successfully because the public and private agencies were able to complement each other's efforts in bringing skilled personnel and the requisite resources to bear in the design and execution of the system. Important groundwork was performed in 1972 by the Project Management Staff of the Mayor's Policy Planning Council. Executives and board members of the voluntary agencies devoted considerable time to the planning; their business contacts brought into play the skills of outside consultants such as the Price Waterhouse Company, which had impressive prior experience in the development of MIS facilities. Such expertise was crucial in the development of CWIS.

Despite the resort to an arrangement of shared power in the governance of CWIS, it has become clear that the development of a better informational capacity to describe service delivery to foster children has strengthened the role of the public agency in carrying out its administrative function. For the first time, Special Services for Children (in the Human Resources Administration) has organized information available about the characteristics of children in care, for each agency with whom it has a contractual relationship. The extent to which an agency tends to permit children to "drift" in foster care is now much more visible than heretofore, in that data can now be aggregated to show how long an agency's wards have been in care, whether discharge plans have been formulated and the extent of parents' contacts with their children and their social workers. The work of the agencies is thus more open to public view and the matter of accountability is more powerfully present as a feature of service delivery.

I believe that all the parties involved in the creation of CWIS, voluntary and public, had an intuitive sense that the field of child welfare would never be quite the same with the advent of computerization of data, and that conditions for service delivery would be radically altered. However, they were not quite sure how the change would manifest itself and how relationships between the public and private sectors would be affected.

Service Operations

CWIS already performs many operations that are characteristic of business-oriented computerized service bureaus. While this type of activity does not have the prestige within professional circles that operations which support social policy and planning functions do, it impacts in very important ways upon the efficiency of the system. One must bear in mind the fact that until the advent of CWIS all new forms required for city, state or federal purposes had to be filled out manually. Thus unfinished work often piled up so that such tasks as applying for federal reimbursement in appropriate cases were very much in arrears. It is noteworthy that in the midst of the darkest period of New York City's fiscal crisis, Mayor Abraham Beame gave strong personal support for an expanded level of city funding for CWIS before the city's Board of Estimate. Part of the enthusiasm stemmed from the following types of operational achievements by CWIS:

It was estimated that the capability of CWIS to generate forms partially filled out by the computer for children in care for the first three months of FY 1975–76 enabled the city to claim AFDC foster care payments under Section 408 of the Social Security Act as reimbursement on a level 36 percent higher than was possible without computerized assistance. The savings to the City of New York have been estimated to be well over $10 million a year. There is no doubt that computerization will pay for itself and then some.

CWIS has recently been tooled up to enable it to perform the billing function which allows the voluntary agencies to secure reimbursement from the city for care provided children. This speeds up payments and eliminates a process for the agencies which has consumed much staff time;

it also makes it possible to analyze cost data, as these relate to social planning efforts.

In February 1976 the city found it necessary to have a new state form prepared for every child in the system within a month's period of time in order to enable the state to meet its obligations under Title XX funding. The ability to design this operation and successfully carry it out without disrupting the service functions of the system represented a tour de force which evoked admiration in many quarters.

In the spring of 1976, the New York State Legislature mandated a statewide computerized information system for children in foster care in New York State. It was decided that the CWIS system would constitute the model for the state system. National recognition has also been forthcoming and it appears likely that the early success of New York City in computerizing its child care operations will lead to the system becoming the prototype for many of the states.

Role of the University Team

A special relationship has been developed between CWIS and the Columbia University School of Social Work, where I head a small research team which provides back-up support to the computerization effort. The special linkage between the two organizations has already produced a significant payoff in the form of a computer software program developed by the university team which makes it possible to produce over fifty analytic tables for the data file of any given organizational entity, i.e., the system as a whole, a federation of agencies, or an individual agency.[2] With a single pass at the computer, it is possible to summarize the information available in a CWIS data file at any point in time and generate organized reports in the form of frequency distributions and two-variable and three-variable cross-tabulations.

The first reports about the system as a whole were distributed nationally,[3] and reactions from researchers, administrators and those concerned with the formulation of social policy have been strongly positive. Enthusiasm for the system has been expressed by the leadership of Special Services for Children, which must monitor children in care who are spread among some eighty agencies. The Assistant Commissioner for Children's Services receives, on a quarterly basis, well-organized tabular reports for each agency in the system. The advent of CWIS has made it possible to learn much more about the characteristics of children in care, the nature of the recent intake of children into care, and how many and what kinds of children are discharged.[4]

Under a recently awarded grant of Title IV-B research funds from the New York State Department of Social Services, the university-based research team will extend the development of computer software programs so that CWIS will have the capacity to produce a series of analytic reports in addition to the profile of children in care (Series A) already in place. CWIS can now or will very shortly be able to produce reports on children entering or being discharged from care (Series B) and on the status changes of children in care (Series D). An important new data element in the basic CWIS data file describes the frequency of parental contact with the child during the placement experience; a basic package of about 12 tables analyzing such parental visiting (Series C) is now ready for a trial run. For the future, it is planned to develop a series of analyses emphasizing the cumulative costs of foster care for children (Series E).

Emphasis is placed upon the analytic capability of management informational systems such as CWIS because this is the area where informational systems developed for the human services have tended to perform badly. It is one thing to collect data and perform operations characteristic of service bureaus, e.g., filling out automated forms for court appearances of children or annual reviews of cases by the public department. It is yet another task to aggregate the data, to fashion reports that are useful for social planning and program management purposes. Software programs permit the aggregation of data on a routine basis without the special involvement of researchers. In addition, the computer performs all of the typing functions, turning out fifty tables for a single agency within a minute's time.

CWIS Findings

A sense of what the future holds may be gleaned from insights provided by some findings that emerged during reporting of first returns of the analysis of the system-wide data file maintained by CWIS as of May 31, 1975:[5]

The average length of time in care for some 27,000 children is calculated to be 5.4 years. About 5,500 children have been in placement for ten years or more. It is clear that the system is heavily loaded with children who have been locked into permanent care.

Among the older children in care, a high proportion of boys are in foster placement because of their own behavior difficulties. They have been placed primarily in institutions. There is another large group of teenagers who have been in care most of their lives, and they are almost exclusively placed in foster family homes.

The foster care system is thus faced with the problems of serving quite contrasting types of children, i.e., the dependent older child who poses only minor adjustment problems and the youngster who is acting out in the community, for whom adequate placement facilities are scarce.

There are some 5,600 children whose data files in the CWIS system indicate that adoption is the clearcut discharge objective. This represents a massive potential workload considering the much smaller number of children who are placed for adoption each year. Legal proceedings to terminate parental rights of all the parents who had lost contact with their children would alone require the investment of heavy financial resources in the build-up of a major-sized legal department.

A single, relatively uncomplicated element of information emerges as having powerful implications for assessing important problems of service delivery: the nature of the discharge plan established for a child. According to the social workers' specifications of discharge objectives, only one child in five currently in the system is likely to return home to his or her own parents. From the ratings of the workers, one gets the impression of rather massive failure of many parents to maintain an interest and involved role. Over 7,000 children (26 percent) are destined to be discharged to their own responsibility. Many of them will have reached young adulthood after growing up in the foster care system.

A sign of the problem of "drift" in the foster care service network in New York City is the fact that for 31 percent of the cases the social worker has indicated an inability to specify a discharge plan. Of particular note is the fact that even larger proportions of young children (under five years) were without a specified discharge plan. One should keep in mind the fact that a child entering foster care in New York City as an infant in 1971 and remaining in care for eighteen years would encumber about $122,500 in costs in the form of public fees paid to an agency.[6] The situation is aggravated by the fact that there were several hundred children under the age of five for whom the social worker specified "discharge to own responsibility" as the plan, thus openly committing the agency to have a child spend all of his childhood years in care.

There are almost 5,000 children (19 percent) in the system who are in care for circumstances related to abuse or neglect.[7]

When cases of children discharged from the system for the period June 1, 1974–May 31, 1975 are examined, it is found that more than half who had been in care for at least a year returned to their own parents, and 18 percent were discharged to their own responsibility. About 11 percent of the children were adopted, the majority of the children aged six to nine. Almost 25 percent of the children aged six to nine years left foster care by virtue of subsidized adoption being available. This form of adoption loomed larger as a resource for black Protestant children than for other children.

Choice of Data Elements

The situation of children in foster care is very complex and presents the designers of MIS systems with problems of choice about the domains to be covered. It is necessary to decide what is important to know about children in care and what kinds of outcomes must be accounted for. In studying the foster care phenomenon in longitudinal perspective,[8] two major outcomes may be identified as important to monitor: status outcomes and changes in the condition of children while in care. Included in the first category is information about the return of children to the homes of their natural parents: the length of time children are in care and the number of placements they experience; adoptive placements; and transfers of children to mental hospitals or training schools. The question of whether of not children are visited by their parents while in care also comes under the heading of status outcomes.[9] It is obviously essential that such information be gathered if policy planners and program managers are to address the problem of "drift" of children in foster care. Fortunately, the phenomena in question are relatively straightforward and measurement problems do not loom large.

A more demanding task is to develop informational forms which can be used to monitor the condition of children over the time they are in care. How to plan to secure information on children's physical health status is less of a problem than how to gather information on their personal and social adjustment. It is necessary to develop age-appropriate terms of description which are within the capacity of observers to provide and which do not tend to label children in a way that adversely affects their life opportunities. It is also not possible to ignore the problems of reliability and validity that have concerned those who construct formal tests to assess children.

The source of information for the CWIS data file is usually the social worker assigned by the agency to work with the child and his family. If the case is uncovered, a supervisor of a unit of workers is apt to fill out the forms. These arrangements are not unusual since most management information systems in the social services rely exclusively upon social workers as the primary source of information. However, this feature of CWIS acts as a constraint upon the quality and quantity of information that can be gathered.

It is estimated that about 85 percent of the social workers involved in foster care services for children in New York City do not have graduate degrees, and most come to their jobs with minimal educational preparation. The level of judgment required to fill out CWIS forms, therefore, must not require the kind of professional sophistication that comes through specialized training. It would be different if the data were to be provided by psychiatrists or psychologists on the basis of standardized examination or only from social workers with graduate (M.S.W.) degrees; if such were the case, one might ask for judgments reflecting the professional expertise of the informants.

Problems to Be Handled

The CWIS staff and board have had to give careful consideration to a number of issues which, if not handled properly, could result in problems which would undermine the system. These include: the resistance of agency executives and line staff workers to the basic concept of computerization of child welfare data; the problem of human error leading to grossly inaccurate reports; and the problem of maintaining the confidentiality of cases as applied to individual persons and agencies. These matters tend to interact so that, for example, if a worker perceives CWIS as not handling confidentiality with proper care, he is apt to be more resistant to filling out forms and more error-prone in the information he provides.

Many social workers have an instinctual distrust of computerized data systems. They perceive the phenomenon as another example of "big brother looking over your shoulder." They fear the loss of control over their cases and view aggregated data about children as reflecting the antithesis of the individualized approach they seek to incorporate in their work with children. Educational work must be undertaken to overcome such orientations so that workers will understand that CWIS effort actually supports an individualized approach. They must be persuaded that there is no greater loss of individuality for a child than to be cast adrift in a large bureaucratic system where no discharge plan has been formulated and the plight of the child is hidden from administrators of the system.

Workers who are asked to fill out forms also need assurance that something useful will result from their efforts. Too often they have been asked to fill out forms which have simply been filed, with no effort made to aggregate the data provided. Early feedback of what can be learned from the data stored in the CWIS files has helped to change the prevailing climate of opinion.

The problem of error in the data being collected and stored was anticipated as being inevitable in the beginning phase of a new system. However, a fairly high level of complaints from agency executives about the accuracy of data being stored led CWIS to engage in vigorous activity to confront the problem. During 1975, special case audits comparing agency case record data and CWIS data for the same children were conducted in the voluntary agencies. Of 169,692 data items checked at forty-four agencies, 15,362 were found to be in error for one reason or another, for an overall rate of 9.05 percent. Agency-related errors constituted 92 percent of all errors. These resulted mainly from failure to place the information, from placement of erroneous information or through failure to keep the data current. The total CWIS-related errors, mainly keypunch errors, constituted 3.3 percent of all errors.[10] Careful work with the agencies and rigorous auditing efforts give promise of radically reducing the error problem.

The issue of confidentiality has required serious attention. From the inception of the CWIS system, there has been recognition that storing information about human beings is replete with dangers. It is essential that the privacy of the individual be respected and that information secured for the purpose of delivering service not be divulged to unauthorized persons or used in a way that would victimize an individual by making him the object of public ridicule. Similarly, agencies are entitled to have some control over the information stored about their programs within the agreed-upon parameters of accountability obligations.

Concern for confidentiality is legitimate and its need well-founded in the professional literature. However, it must not be used as a screen for covering up agency failures to carry through on their obligation to provide permanency for children who enter the foster care system. The rights of children will best be safeguarded in an open system where agencies can be scrutinized with respect to their performance in meeting goals established for the children in their care.

Summary Comment

It is impossible to adequately administer a system caring for large numbers of children without modern methods of information storage and analytic treatment of the data. It is pointless to talk about goal-oriented social service systems and accountability when hand-sorting of index cards is the basis of statistical operations. The time is long overdue for computerized management information systems to be put into place to account for service delivery to children in foster care in all cities and states of the nation.

The collection of information cannot be burdensome to the point where such a task interferes with service operations. It cannot aggravate the "paperwork" problem which threatens to engulf service activities. The assumption underlying the activities of CWIS is that ultimately the computer will reduce the problem of paperwork by filling out forms where the information is redundant and also by reducing the need for long narratives in case records by introducing case descriptions in which categorical checklists are employed.

The better collection, storage and analysis of information related to service delivery is not a cure-all for problems that beset a social service system. It does not compensate for the lack of staff or the meagerness of resources to serve failing parents. It does not compensate for the lack of imagination in program development or for sluggish administrative leadership in the public or private sector. But it does make it possible to bring greater rationality to service delivery, to deploy staff more intelligently and to better utilize available resources. It can enable program managers to focus upon cases where timely intervention, with appropriate investment of staff and resources, is likely to turn situations around, to change a child's fate from one of years of foster care status to early return to his own parents or placement in an adoptive home.

NOTES

1. For a major exception, see Dorothy Fahs Beck and Mary Ann Jones, *Progress on Family Problems: A Nationwide Study of Clients' and Counselors' Views on Family Agency Services*, Family Service Association of America, 1973.

2. This program supplements the many computerized reports CWIS has been able to generate through its own staff resource.

3. See: David Fanshel and John Grundy, *Computerized Data for Children in Foster Care: First Analyses from a Management Information Service in New York City*, Child Welfare Information Services, Inc., Nov. 1, 1975.

4. According to established procedures, the public department may have access to information from the CWIS data file for a given agency whenever it desires; a duplicate copy of the requested report is always provided to the agency.

5. Fanshel and Grundy, *Computerized Data*.

6. David Fanshel and Eugene B. Shinn, *Dollars and Sense in the Foster Care of Children*, Child Welfare League of America, 1972.

7. There were 1,244 children in care where abuse was identified as a reason for placement, and 3,134 where neglect was identified.

8. David Fanshel and Eugene B. Shinn, *Children in Foster Care: A Longitudinal Investigation* (New York: Columbia University Press, 1978).

9. See David Fanshel, "Parental Visiting of Children in Foster Care: Key to Discharge?", *Social Service Review*, December 1975 and David Fanshel, "Status Changes of Children in Foster Care: Final Results of The Columbia University Longitudinal Study," *Child Welfare*, March 1976.

10. Source: *Annual Report, Fiscal Year 1976*, Child Welfare Information Services, 1976.

Treatment Information System for Feedback and Evaluation in a Mental Health Setting

P. BRUCE LANDON and MARIAN MERCHANT

The Treatment Information System (TIS) at Regional Psychiatric Centre (RPC) is designed to serve several needs. The original objective was to develop a system that would provide comprehensive and meaningful evaluation of patient treatment. Prior to developing a system, a systems analysis was performed on the Health Care System at RPC. This analysis revealed that not only was patient treatment evaluation in a global sense desperately needed but also there were requirements for: (1) descriptive reports of the patients at the Centre, (2) descriptive reports of the treatments provided by the Centre, (3) a simple method by which clinical information could be distributed to decision makers throughout the hospital, (4) a method of long-range patient follow-up that could provide information of sufficient detail to guide future treatment decisions, and lastly, (5) some timely and accurate means of keeping track of the location of patients within the hospital. Similar conclusions were reached independently by McLean and Miles (1974). The TIS developed to meet these requirements has in fact turned out to encompass more than appeared to be originally required. The TIS has been supplemented with the Problem Oriented Record (POR) method of recording patient information. Thus the TIS services two classes of customer: (1) the primary customer is the front line therapist clinician, (2) the secondary customer is the hospital administration. The TIS will be described first from the point of view of the front line therapist.

The TIS can best be described by following a patient through the system. The thirteen steps in a patient's progress through the system are illustrated in the Patient Treatment and Evaluation Flow Chart (see Figure 17–1).

1. *Patient referral by admissions assessment team or institution psychiatrist.* Patients are referred to RPC just as they would be to any other mental hospital as either a regular admission to one of the treatment

Reprinted from Barry Willer, Gary H. Miller, and Lucie Cantrell, eds., *Information and Feedback for Evaluation* (York University Communications Department, 1975), pp. 91–98.

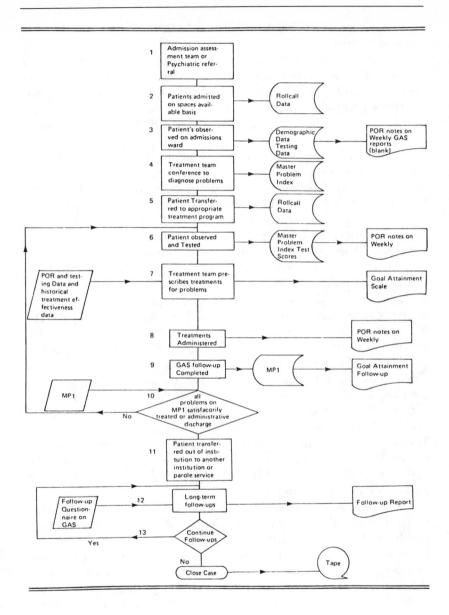

Figure 17–1.
Patient Flow through the System

programmes or an emergency admission because of a crisis such as attempted suicide.

2. *Patients admitted to the hospital*. Referrals are accepted primarily on the basis of space available at the hospital. When a patient comes into the hospital a transfer form is sent to the Research Department where the institution Roll-Call is updated to reflect the new population status. Generally patients will be housed on the admissions ward when they first come to the institution.

3. *Patients observed on the admissions ward*. During the patient's stay on the admissions ward extensive notes are made by the nursing staff in the POR . . . format.[1] These notes are made on special pages supplied by the Research Department with the patient's name and ward on the form. One or more pages are supplied every week as needed. Also during the first few days demographic data are collected and diagnostic tests, such as the Differential Personality Inventory . . . , are administered.[2]

4. *Treatment Team Conference to diagnose the problems*. Periodically during a patient's stay on the admissions ward, treatment team conferences are held to finalize diagnoses in terms of specific problems that the patient is having. These problems are entered on a Master Problem Index. The Master Problem Index (MPI) is composed of six sections: (a) the date the problem is identified; (b) the location where the problem is identified (usually the admissions ward); (c) a brief statement of the problem; (d) the date of onset of the problem; (e) the date the problem is resolved or inactive; (f) the Master Problem Index code for that problem (unique within each patient's data). The six parts appear as columns on the Master Problem Index form. Each row of the form is for a separate problem. . . . The MPI is kept on the front of the patient's file. The admissions ward is involved in primarily diagnostic functions, consequently very few patients have any problems that will be judged resolved or inactive while the patient is on the admissions ward.

5. *Patient is transferred to the appropriate treatment programme*. After the patient's problems have been adequately diagnosed it becomes a simple matter to direct that patient to the appropriate treatment programme at RPC. Currently these are programmes for psychotics, sex-offender, personality disorders, heroin addiction, and continued care. When the patient is transferred, the Research Department is notified and Roll-Call is again updated to reflect the accurate locations of the patients within the Centre.

6. *Patient is observed*. Further observations are made on the patient and new problems can be discovered. As these problems are discovered they too are entered on the MPI. Additional testing is done at this time and reports are entered on the patient's file. The test scores are also coded and

submitted to the Research Department for inclusion in a data base. Progress notes are made on the patient's Weekly Treatment Plan. A patient's Weekly Treatment Plan includes a description of each of his problems currently under treatment with an assessment of its importance. The specific treatments applicable to each problem are also recorded. The nursing notes are made on the same page. . . . At this point we are getting a little ahead of ourselves, but it is important to keep in mind that progress notes and observations relevant to particular problems of a patient are usually made prior to the decision of what treatment is appropriate for each specific problem. The Weekly Treatment Plan is the form on which those notations are recorded and thus becomes part of the POR for each patient.

7. *Treatment team prescribes treatments for patient's problems.* The team concept applied at the Centre involves the majority of the treatment team in decisions regarding which problems to treat as well as what treatments to use for those problems. The treatment team has access to the progress notes on the problems, testing results and the historical data from the TIS on how effective different treatments have been for the problem in question. It is this feedback of the cumulative experience with problem-treatment combinations that can enable the Centre to increase treatment effectiveness.

After the treatments and the importance of the problem have been decided a Goal Attainment Scale form . . . is completed for each problem under treatment (Figure 17–2).[3] The Goal Attainment Scale (GAS) form has seven portions that are of particular interest here: (a) the patient identification; (b) the start date of treatment; (c) the projected follow-up date; (d) a concise description of the problem; (e) a concise description of the specifics of the treatment plan; (f) a behavioural description of the outcomes, both good and bad, that could result from the treatment; (g) a rating of the starting level for the patient in terms of those possible outcome levels.

One copy of the completed GAS form is forwarded to the Research Department to be entered into the TIS. The contents of the Weekly Treatment Plan, previously referred to in the context of progress notes, is produced from the submitted GAS forms. This procedure serves as a record of which problems are currently being treated. Completing the GAS form requires the clinician to carefully identify the problem and specify the possible treatment outcome from the least to most likely in concrete behavioural terms. This imposed outcome orientation has proved to be a difficult transition for the mental health workers at RPC because their training was primarily directed toward the identification of the treatment procedure without explicit concern with evaluating treatment outcome.

8. *Treatments administered.* With the coordination made possible by the

NAME ——————————————————— MASTER PROBLEM INDEX NUMBER ▢▢▢
　　　　Surname　　　Initial

IDENTIFICATION NUMBER ▢▢▢▢　　　CHECK ( ) ONE　NEW PROBLEM ▢　REHASH ▢

WARD ▢▢　LOCATION ———　TREAT FROM START ▢▢▢　TO FOLLOW UP ▢▢▢
　　　　　　　　　　　　　　　　　　　　　D　M　Y　　　　　　　　　　D　M　Y

CONCISE STATEMENT OF THE SPECIFIC PROBLEM ————————————————————

CIRCLE IMPORTANCE　| Most Important　1　2　3　4　5　6　7　Least Important |

Rx: CONCISE DESCRIPTION OF SPECIFICS OF THE TREATMENT PLAN ——————————

LEVELS	BEHAVIOURAL DESCRIPTIONS OF POSSIBLE TREATMENT OUTCOMES	START LEVEL
MOST UNFAVOURABLE OUTCOME THOUGHT LIKELY		
LESS THAN EXPECTED SUCCESS		
EXPECTED LEVEL OF SUCCESS		
MORE THAN EXPECTED LEVEL OF SUCCESS		
MOST FAVOURABLE OUTCOME THOUGHT LIKELY		

CHANGES IN TREATMENT PLAN ——————————————————————————

ORIGINAL APPROVED BY ————————————————————
　　　　　　　　　　　Supervisor's Signature

START LEVEL RATER　　————————————————————
　　　　　　　　　　　Member of Treatment Team

FOR DEPARTMENT OF RESEARCH

START LEVEL　　　　　▢▢
ORIGINAL RATER　　　▢▢▢　　　RECEIVED IN C.S.B. ————
ORIGINAL APPROVED BY ▢▢▢　　INFO. BY PHONE ————————
　　　　　　　　　　　　　　　COPY XEROXED ————————

Figure 17–2.
Goal Attainment Scale

Weekly Treatment Plan the prescribed treatments for the patients are administered over the treatment period specified on the GAS form. Progress notes are made in the POR format on the Weekly Treatment Plan for each patient during the specified treatment period. Linking nursing notes to specific problems, as required by the POR system, facilitates follow-up evaluation of treatment success.

9. *Goal Attainment Scaling Follow-up*. The first follow-up of the patient's problem on the Goal Attainment Scaling form is made around the time specified in the projected follow-up date. Remainders are included on the Weekly Treatment Plan for follow-ups that are overdue. Follow-ups are made on the same form as the original rating so that the change as a result of treatment is immediately available to the treatment staff. A copy of the follow-up rating scale is forwarded to the Research Department for inclusion into the Treatment Information System. When a follow-up is received the specific problem follow-up is eliminated from the subsequent Weekly Treatment Plans for that patient. The Centre policy is that the follow-up rater should be someone other than the rater who made the initial assessment of problem severity. This procedure improves the objectivity of the data collected by the follow-up evaluation.

10. *Decision to discharge*. After all of the patient's problems have been treated and followed up to the satisfaction of the treatment staff the patient can be recommended for discharge from the Centre. A patient may also be discharged from the Centre if he requests transfer. The patient may request a transfer from the institution because he was not satisfied with the treatment he received or because his prison sentence has expired. If it is decided that not all the problems have been treated to the satisfaction of the treatment staff, the "iterative treatment loop" is re-entered at step 6 and the patient is observed again. The MPI is the final record of when problems are resolved or judged inactive. The expected length of treatment at RMC is from eighteen months to two years.

11. *Patient discharged or transferred*. Patients are transferred to other penitentiaries within western Canada or are discharged usually in the custody of the National Parole Service. Case responsibility is then assumed by a health care officer at an institution, a social worker at a halfway house or a parole officer. Knowing the address of the discharged patients and the case worker facilitates follow-up evaluation.

12. *Long-term follow-up*. Six months after the first follow-up rating is completed, a second follow-up of important problems is undertaken (see Figure 17–3). If the patient is still within the institution the follow-up is easily conducted by Centre staff. In the case of patients who have been discharged from the Centre, arrangements are made to follow-up the patient's problems with an outside rater such as a parole officer or some

Johnson, L.

February 07, 1975   Ward: N2

In order to evaluate the long-term effectiveness of the treatments used at RMC it is necessary to follow-up the patients' progress. Your cooperation in completing this form and returning it promptly to the Research Department will be greatly appreciated.

Imp MPI   *Problem*

2 002   Tendency to be seclusive—works separate from others— becomes anti-social, stays in room.

GOAL ATTAINMENT SCALE OUTCOMES

Place "X"
next to
present
level

☐ Always remains aloof, anti-social—works apart, etc.
☐ Become seclusive, anti-social 2-3 times per week
☐ Seclusive, anti-social once per week
☐ Rarely seclusive—once per month
☐ Never seclusive or anti-social

Follow-up rater: _____

Follow-up date: _____
                        Day   Month   Year

Figure 17–3.
Long-Term Follow-up Questionnaire

other person who is well acquainted with the patient. The rating is made with respect to the same treatment outcome levels that were originally proposed by the treatment team for evaluating the effectiveness of their treatment. This outside rating represents a genuine attempt at uncontaminated long-term evaluation. It is important to note that the evaluation is in the same terms as the original evaluation so that it will be meaningful to the treatment team of the Centre. The rating itself is made in one of two ways. The method of choice is a follow-up survey form in which the rater is asked to rate which one of the behaviours the patient seems to currently exhibit. The back-up method for the survey form is a personal contact over the telephone where the rater is asked to judge as best he can which of the possible outcomes most closely describes the patient's current behaviour patterns.

13. *Decision to continue long-term follow-up.* A follow-up report is produced by the TIS for the treatment staff of the former patient. This is a primary method of feeding back the information on long-term follow-up to the treatment staff. Also at this time the treatment staff are requested to indicate if the clinical data is sufficient. If the follow-up procedure is continued, the next follow-up is completed six months after the second follow-up or at a year after the original follow-up was completed. In principle, long-term follow-ups can be conducted indefinitely. With some problems such as heroin addiction it is obviously necessary to follow a patient for more than a year to know for certain if the treatment has been effective. If the treatment staff decides not to continue follow-up, the patient's case file is transferred into a historical data base for guiding future treatment.

The Treatment Information System services its secondary customer, the hospital administration, by providing several kinds of regular feedback reports on the treatment that is conducted at the Centre (see Figure 17–4). One such report is the Weekly Treatment Plan for each patient. The clinical director and director of nursing are supplied with copies of the Weekly Treatment Plan for all patients which embodies the entire planned treatment currently being administered at the Centre. In this way these two administrators can monitor the course of treatments in different treatment programmes. Also on a weekly basis the Roll-Call of the institution is distributed in the form of a list containing the number and location of each patient. This population status list is distributed to all departments in the hospital since all areas need to know the current location of each patient.

A report indicating how many GAS's were completed in the month is distributed each month. Copies are made for the director of nursing and the clinical director so they can monitor the effectiveness of the treatment in the various programme areas. This essentially provides an overview of the accomplishments in each of the treatment areas as well as the detailed analysis of the effectiveness of particular treatments for specific patients. This report will grow over time as long-term follow-ups completed during the month are added to the first follow-up records completed during a particular month.

At the end of each quarter a major evaluation report is produced. This report contains comprehensive descriptions of the patients in each of the programmes, the problems that are dealt with, the treatments that are used and the effectiveness of those treatments in GAS terms. Other Normative measures are also used to provide information in the quarterly report such as the Psychotic In-Patient Profile, . . . a behavior rating of

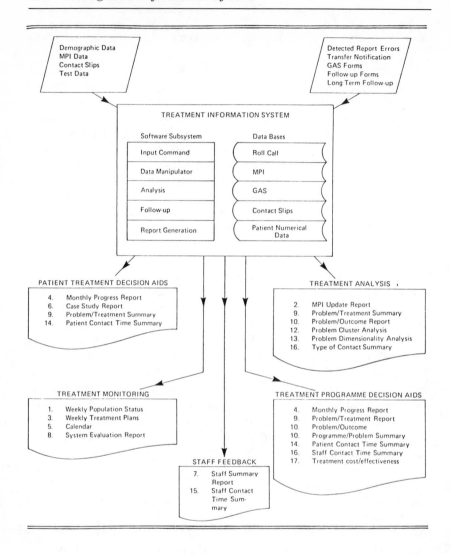

Figure 17–3.
Treatment Information System Input Output

patients by the nursing staff. In addition, several self-reports scales are used to assess the patient's level of functioning and progress from the last quarter. These scales measure such things as Ego Strength and Locus of Control. Included in the report are recommendations on the basis of the available evidence for changes or modifications in the ongoing treatment programmes. The quarterly report is sent to the director of the institution, the clinical director, the director of nursing and the psychiatrist involved in various treatment programmes. It is also submitted to National Headquarters for consideration in evaluating the institution as a whole.

In summary, the TIS provides relevant data for clinical and administrative use. The use of GAS within a POR format facilitates evaluative research about which treatments are most successful with different problems.

A more detailed description of the data collected, the computer software developed and the wide range of data generated by the system is available from the authors.

NOTES

1. L. Weed, *Medical Records, Medical Education, and Patient Care* (Chicago: Year Book Medical Publishers, 1971).
2. D. Jackson, *Differential Personality Inventory* (London, Ont.: author, 1972).
3. T. Kiresuk, "Goal Attainment at a County Mental Health Service," *Evaluation Monograph*, vol. 1 (1973), pp. 12–18.
4. M. Lore and N. Vester, *The Psychotic Inpatient Profile Manual* (Beverly Hills, Calif.: Western Psychological Services, 1968).

18. Sociotechnical Aspects of Systems Design

The Design of Management Information Systems: An Information Analysis Approach

WILLIAM R. KING and DAVID I. CLELLAND

Objective and Basic Premises

This study addresses itself to the development of a methodology for MIS design which focuses on the determination of the information require-ments of managers in a formalized, yet participatory, fashion. The approach seeks to provide an objective framework for analyzing informa-tion requirements while at the same time significantly involving the man-agers, who will be the MIS users, in the design process.

In achieving this objective, the methodology operationalizes some theoretical and research results regarding the participation of managers. This is done in a decision-oriented framework which makes use of the model-based management-analyst teamwork concepts presented in King and Cleland.[1] . . . The methodology is also built on some of the ideas of Ackoff.[2] . . .

This MIS design methodology has several important features which simultaneously enhance its value and potentially constrain the domain of its applicability.

First, it is *decision-oriented* to a degree which might preclude its use in the development of data processing or operational-level information sys-tems such as those designed to perform billing, accounting or other repeti-tive operations. The contexts in which it has been developed and tested exclusively involve nonroutine activities and decisions.

Reprinted with permission from *Management Science* 22, no. 3 (November 1975): 286–97. Processed by Professor Charles H. Kuebel, Departmental Editor for Information Systems, and Associate Editor Gordon Davis; received August 30, 1972, revised May 21, 1974. This paper has been with the authors three months for revisions.

This research was supported through Grant NI–71–096 of the National Institute of Law Enforcement and Criminal Justice. The aid of research assistants Dundar Kocaoglu and Peter Smith and the cooperation of former Commissioner Frank N. Felicetta, Commissioner Thomas R. Blair and Captain Phillip Francis of the Buffalo New York Police Department is gratefully acknowledged.

Secondly, the methodology involves participation on the part of the managers who will use the MIS. It emphasizes this manager participation to such a great degree as to require the acceptance of a *broader definition of optimality* than that usually adopted by MIS designers. Of course, many approaches to MIS design involve management participation in specifying information needs and in reviewing the system development effort. However, this approach involves user participation in basic systems design decisions which are usually thought of as "technical" in nature. Thus, the methodology can produce systems which cannot be thought of as optimum in the technical sense.

In this regard, the approach is addressed to a broader variety of optimality which considers *both* technical cost-benefit considerations *and* the manager's perception of the potential utility of the system in enhancing his decision-making effectiveness. The essence of this broader view of optimality is the belief that a technically-optimum system which goes unused is inferior to a system which is technically inferior, but perceived to be useful to the organization's managers. . . .

Information Requirements Analysis

The information analysis design methodology is conceived of as a process involving a series of steps. As in most such processes, the sequencing of the steps is in terms of the initiation rather than in terms of the execution of each. Thus, step 1 *begins* before step 2, but because of the implicit feedback loops and interdependencies in the process, step 1 may not end prior to the end of step 2.

The various steps in the process are: (1) identification of User Set and Interfacing Organizations; (2) identification of Decision Areas; (3) definition of Decision Areas; (4) development of a Descriptive Model of the System; (5) development of a Normative Model of the System; (6) development of a Consensus Model of the System; (7) decision Model Identification and Specification; (8) specification of Information Requirements.

Each of these steps will be explained using elements of a police strategic planning MIS design process for illustration. In all cases, the illustrations are from a real-world situation, but they are not intended to portray comprehensively the police system in question.[3]

IDENTIFICATION OF USER SET
AND INTERFACING ORGANIZATIONS

The "user set" for an MIS—the set consisting of those managers who are designated to be the primary users of the system's output—is in part specified by the stated objectives of the system. Such objectives must be clearly defined prior to embarking on an analysis of information requirements. For instance, a system which has the objective of supporting corporate long-range planning will have a user set which is quite different than the set for a production control system. Indeed, the user set for a corporate-level control-oriented MIS may well differ from that for a corporate-level planning MIS.

In this MIS design process, the user set is initially defined by the analyst, using the statement of objectives for the MIS, organizing charts, job descriptions and other documents, as guides. In the strategic planning MIS case, the system objectives reflect the recognition that past planning inadequacies are largely due to a lack of relevant information. Most of the information, or data, that is currently processed by the organization's information system is descriptive of the past history of the internal organizational subsystem. Most of it is outdated and inward directed. To be useful for strategic planning, such information must be prospective and focused toward those environmental and competitive elements of the organization that will most critically affect its future.

Because of this objective, this variety of MIS must consider external interfacing organizations as well as internal users. These organizations are defined in terms of specific informational inputs and outputs—i.e. those organizations with which information is communicated in support of, or as a result of, the functions which the MIS is to support.

The column headings in Table 18–2 show a list of users (by position level) and interfacing organizations for a police planning MIS. The listing shown there represents a "first pass" by the analyst, and thereby emphasizes position levels (ranks) more than specific positions. Because of the intrinsic interrelationship of positions, interfacing organizations and decision areas, further refinement of this list would take place as subsequent steps are performed.

IDENTIFICATION OF DECISION AREAS

The next step in the information analysis process involves the identification of decision areas. This step is initiated by the analyst on the basis of existing "theory" and refined by him through discussion with the appropriate managers who will be the users of the system.

Table 18–1 shows such a "decision inventory" related to the planning function of a police department. It represents one possible delineation of some of the critical decision areas involved in the planning process in any organization.

Table 18–1.

Policy Formation—Internal
Policy Formation—External
Direction of Operations
Organizing Activities
Budget
Tactical Planning
Community Relations
New Programs
Training
Personnel Selection
Allocation of Resources
Research
External Coordination
Internal Coordination

Other categorizations could be used as well. In fact, during the process of developing such an inventory, the analyst will usually begin from a theoretical point of view based on his highly abstracted view of the organization and then proceed to revise his inventory based on discussions with executives and members of the user set. This process serves to provide a good theoretical foundation and to ensure that major omissions are avoided, while at the same time avoiding the problems of confusing terminology and overlapping decision areas.

DEFINITION OF DECISION AREAS

After decision areas have been identified, they must be specified in detail. The discussions held with executives and the members of the user set, as outlined in the previous step, will assist greatly in achieving the desired level of specificity. These discussions serve a secondary purpose as well—the obtaining of support and acceptance by the people on whom ultimate success will depend.

The process involved here is, therefore, much the same as that of the previous step except that the decision areas are broken into decision elements on the basis of their (1) homogeneity, (2) need for common informational input, or (3) performance by a single individual or unit. In all cases, these assessments must be made on rather loose grounds, since rigorous formal criteria are probably unwarranted at this preliminary definitional stage.

A definition of each decision area may be in process terms such as that shown in the row descriptions in Table 18–2 for the decision area "external policy formulation" for a police department. The process of formulating policies related to the police department's environment is described as consisting of a number of general steps ranging from the analysis of data reflecting various clientele groups to the implementation and control of policy decisions.

DEVELOPMENT OF A DESCRIPTIVE MODEL OF THE SYSTEM

The third phase of the MIS design process involves the utilization of the user set and decision areas to develop a descriptive model of the organizational and environmental systems which are relevant to the MIS. This is done in a two-dimensional format which is an adaptation and extension of the concept of a "linear responsibility chart" (LRC).[4] The LRC is a simple organizational model which was originally introduced to provide a more realistic description of the operation of organizations than does the traditional heirarchical chart. The method used to accomplish this is to describe authorities, responsibilities, and roles in a matrix form which relates positions and tasks through the use of coded symbols designating the specific roles to be played by each position in the accomplishment of each task.

Although the overall use of the LRC in this methodology is normative, this phase of its use is descriptive. Table 18–2 describes the existing external policy formulation process in a police department. Similar models should be developed to describe existing organizational processes in each of the decision areas which the MIS is to support.

The entries in the chart represent a number of organizational characteristics with regard to the decision area: (1) authority and responsibility relationships; (2) initiation characteristics; (3) input-output characteristics. The codes used to describe these characteristics for internal positions are: I—Initiation, E—Execution, A—Approval, C—Consultation, S—Supervision.

Numbered subscripts on these role descriptors serve to identify the specific relationship.

For instance, the simplified macro-level chart of Table 18–2 shows on the first row that the analysis of routine complaints (E) is handled at the police captain level under the supervision of an inspector (S) with the police commissioner having approval authority (A). In performing this function, the captain has the consultation of the uniformed patrolmen (C_5, where the subscript $= 5$ indicates with whom the consultation takes place).

Table 18–2.
Descriptive Model of External Policy-Making Process

	City Council = 1	Mayor = 2	Budget Director = 3	Police Commissioner = 4	Deputy Commissioner = 5	Inspector = 6	Captain = 7	Uniformed Patrolman = 8	Police Administrator = 9	Other City Depts. = 10	Board and Agencies = 11	Federal Government = 12
Analysis of routine complaints				A	C₄	S	E	C₅				
Observ. of field practices				A	S	E						
Crime analysis												
Court analysis												
Analysis of social problems												
New legislation				A	S	E						
Issue clarification–definition				A	S	E						
Selection of alternatives				A	E	C₃						
Obtaining relevant facts												
Analysis of facts												
Review		A		E						$2^{i,o}$		
Formulation				E	C							
Articulation				A	S₄	S	E					
Training for implementation					A	S	E					
Execution and control				A	S	E	C₄					

Another consultation takes place when the Deputy Commissioner consults with the Commissioner (C₄) at the approval stage.

Various informational linkages with interfacing environmental organizations are also depicted in these charts. Table 18–3 shows only one such linkage—that involving "other city departments" who both provide input (*i*) to and receive output (*o*) from the mayor (= 2) in his approval role.

The model depicted in Table 18–2 is an abstract description of the way the system actually operates with regard to the single planning area described as "formulating external policy." While descriptive models such as this are often developed by systems analysts to provide themselves with a basis for understanding the functioning of a system, the purpose for this descriptive model in this methodology is, in fact, prescriptive. However, the use of the model in this fashion first requires that a comparable normative model be developed.

DEVELOPMENT OF A NORMATIVE MODEL OF THE SYSTEM

A descriptive model of the organizational and environmental system such as that provided by Table 18–2 and other associated charts is a useful "road map" for guiding informational analysis. It provides insights into "who does what," the interactions among organizational units and between internal and external units, the general nature of information required, the direction of information flow, and the manner in which information requirements are generated.

However, the use of a model of this variety as the sole basis for information systems design would represent an abrogation of the information analyst's proper role. Rather than creating an information system to serve an existing organizational system, he should attempt to influence the restructuring of a decision-making process so that the MIS may be oriented toward the support of a more nearly "optimal" process.

To do this, the analyst may call on the best of the knowledge and theory of management to construct a normative model of the organization which is consistent with, and comparable to, the descriptive one previously developed. For instance, a police department which is not already using a program budget structure can be stimulated and aided in developing one by the incorporation of such procedures into the normative model.

A comparable normative model for the "external policy formulative" area is shown in Table 18–3 using the same format as was used for the descriptive model of Table 18–2. It was developed by the analysts on the basis of existing theory as constrained by the unique characteristics of the organization in question.

However, just as it would be inappropriate for the analyst to design an MIS to suit the descriptive organizational model of Table 18–2, it would be unrealistic of him to focus solely on the normative model of Table 18–3. If he were to do so, he would either design a completely inappropriate MIS (as many feel analysts are wont to do in some organizations) or autocratically impose the requirement for an organizational redesign as a response to the MIS.

To meet the criterion of broad optimality based on improved effectiveness and usability, the designer must seek some consensus model which can serve as a realistic basis for systems design.

DEVELOPMENT OF A CONSENSUS MODEL OF THE SYSTEM

Although few organizations desiring an MIS would be willing to restructure their organization's authority and responsibility patterns and relationships to suit the needs of the MIS, it is generally recognized that

Table 18–3.
Normative Model of External Policy-Making Process

	City Council = 1	Mayor = 2	Budget Director = 3	Police Commissioner = 4	Deputy Commissioner = 5	Inspector = 6	Captain = 7	Uniformed Patrolman = 8	Police Administrator = 9	Other City Depts. = 10	Board and Agencies = 11	Federal Government = 12
Analysis of routine complaints				A	C_4	S	E	C_7		7^i	7^i	
Observ. of field practices				A	S	E	C_6					
Crime analysis				A	S	E	C_6			6^i	6^i	
Court analysis				A	E	C				5^i	5^i	5^i
Analysis of social problems				A	S	E	C_6			6^i	6^i	6^i
New Legislation				A	S	E	C_6			6^i	6^i	6^i
Issue clarification–definition				A	S	E	C_6					
Selection of alternatives				A	E	C_5						
Obtaining relevant facts				A	S	E	C_6	C_6		6^i	6^i	6^i
Analysis of facts				A	E	C_5						
Review	A	A		E						$4^{i,o}$	$4^{i,o}$	
Formulation				E	C							
Articulation		A	A	A	C_4	S	E			6°	6°	
Training for implementation					E	S	E					
Execution and Control	A	A		A	S	E	C_6			6°	6°	

procedural improvement is a valid by-product of MIS design. Therefore, organizations are normally willing to consider some elements of a normative organizational model such as Table 18–3 rather than to insist simply that the MIS solely service existing procedures, authorities, etc.

The development of a consensus model hinges on an objective comparison of a descriptive model such as that of Table 18–2 with a normative model such as that of Table 18–3. This comparison and evaluation must be done by managers with the aid and advice of analysts.

One possible medium for this process which has been used successfully by the authors is that of a "participataive executive development program." The program involved the MIS user as "students" and the MIS analysts as "teachers." The normative model was developed and discussed in lecture-discussion sessions. After it had been communicated fully, workshops were used to facilitate the detailed evaluation and comparison of the descriptive and normative models. Recommendations emanating from the workshops were reviewed by top management, and those which were approved were incorporated into a consensus model of the system.

A consensus model of this variety provides the basic framework for analysis of both formal and informal information requirements. It identifies specific involvements of users in each element of each decision area. Further, it indicates the direction of the information flow in each phase— both within and outside the organizational system.

Such a model can therefore serve a variety of functions. It is a general plan for an MIS. Further, it is a prescriptive model for modified organizational processes which will be supported by the MIS. However, for purposes of this discussion, the primary value of the consensus model is as a guide to the information analysis which is an integral part of data base design.

DECISION MODEL IDENTIFICATION AND SPECIFICATION

. . . The term "model" as used in this context is a broad interpretation of the usual usage. It includes not only sophisticated mathematical models, but also simple descriptive models and even the "mental models" which are a part of every decision-making process. Such models are difficult to assess in objective terms, but the necessity for doing so in MIS design has become clear. . . .

DETERMINATION OF INFORMATION REQUIREMENTS

The final step in the process is the determination of information requirements from the consensus model of the system and the specific "decision models" which have been explicated for each of the entries in the chart representing the consensus model. These decision models serve to specify specific information requirements, and the consensus systems model prescribes the linkages and relationships of these elements of information.

If, for example, an "Approval" activity is indicated in the consensus model, it would have been detailed in the previous step in terms of the specific factors and criteria which need be considered in determining whether approval is to be given—i.e. the specific levels of these factors which need be achieved for approval to be granted.

To illustrate, suppose that an "Approval" activity associated with a hiring decision is under examination. The manager might have explained his "model" for the "Approval" activity as: (1) first, check to see that all company hiring policies have been followed; (2) then, check to see that no one already in the organization desires to fill the job; (3) then, check to see if the candidate helps us to fulfill our objectives with regard to minority group hiring, and, if not, to ensure that no equally good candidates are available who will help us to achieve them.

These criteria specify a rather specific set of information requirements: (1) hiring policies, (2) data on candidate and hiring procedure relevant to each hiring policy, (3) comparable data on existing personnel, (4) data on job transfer desires of existing personnel, (5) minority group status of candidate, (6) data on other candidates. Of course, in order that these represent operational information requirements, these elements would need to be detailed much further. However, once specifications such as these have been made, the process of detailing them is a straightforward one. . . .

Conclusion

The MIS design process described here directly produces both a set of information specifications and an overall general systems design in the form of the consensus systems model. It represents a structured method for incorporating managers into those aspects of the design process which are typically left to technical analysts.

In doing this, it provides the capability of developing systems that are, in part, designed by the people who best understand the job that the systems are to do—the user managers—and it permits the development of systems which incorporate many of the informal indicators and practices that managers commonly develop and use outside of the domain of formalized information systems. This latter capability is inherent in both the systems model phase, which begins from a descriptive model, and the information requirements phase, in which managers are asked to explicate their reasoning with regard to specific functions and decisions.

Since the methodology is based on the concept that the system should be designed by those who best know the "business" and who will be users of the system, it is addressed to a broad variety of optimality which encompasses both technical cost-benefit concerns and the user's perception of the usefulness of the system. Thus, the design process involves not only managerial "input" and review, but managerial design decision making.

This approach is consistent with recent research and conceptual results in systems design as well as with many existing systems design practices. For instance, the consensus model can provide the basis for traditional input-output identification of information flows as well as providing the basis for the more sophisticated decision model information analysis.

Perhaps more importantly, the approach provides an orderly and systematic basis for participatory organizational change as well as for MIS design. The interrelationships of various organizational dimensions such as management systems and procedures, information systems, organizational structure and management practices is becoming increasingly apparent.[5] The difficulties in operationalizing comprehensive changes in these myriad dimensions are severe however. With this approach, such changes are structured by managers rather than by analysts. The greater understanding of the need for change and of the value of specific changes which this process engenders in managers may well be its greatest asset. . . .

NOTES

1. William R. King and David I. Clelland, "Manager-Analyst Teamwork in Management Information Systems," *Business Horizons*, vol. 14 (2) April 1971, pp. 59–68.
2. Russell L. Ackoff, "Management Misinformation Systems," *Management Science*, vol. 14 (4) December 1967, pp. B147–B156.
3. Law Enforcement Assistance Administration. "The Development of a Management Information System for the Overall Management of an Urban Police Department," Research Report N–71–096, U.S. Department of Justice, May 1972.
4. See David I. Clelland and William R. King, *Systems Analysis and Project Management* (New York: McGraw-Hill, 1968), pp. 193, 196–98.
5. William R. King and David I. Clelland, "Decision and Information Systems for Strategic Planning," *Business Horizons*, vol. 16 (2) April 1973, pp. 29–36.

19. People and Machines

Humanizing Computerized Information Systems

THEODORE D. STERLING

The accumulation and control of information is a crucial function for government and private, industrial and nonindustrial organizations. Yet the role of information as an organizational resource is not very well understood, especially as it is related to the organization's environment. What does appear is that computerized information systems have become a facilitating technology that interacts with organizational, historical, and environmental pressures and goals to shape not only the internal structure of an organization but also its interactions with society.[1,2] There is little doubt that the computerized or automated information system is revolutionizing the management of most, if not all, systems by which goods and services are produced or information is accumulated. This should be a source of great concern.

Weizenbaum[3] asked whether large computerized systems can be used by anybody except governments and really large corporations and whether such organizations will not use them mainly for antihuman purposes. The power of computerized information systems to control large enterprises answers the need to manage large systems and make them amenable to human control. By any criteria of management performance, computerization of a system permits its detailed control, and thus the computer is the ideal management tool. But the cost of the control is high. Start-up costs to redesign and computerize large-scale enterprises are immense. In concentrating on feasibility and workability and simultaneously minimizing costs, few systems designers seem to have been concerned about whether their products will be used for antihuman purposes.

In many ways, it is immaterial whether control over the management network is exercised by manual means or by automation. As long as official procedures are detrimental to human dignity, nothing is changed in con-

Reprinted from *Science* 190 (December 19, 1975): 1168–72. Copyright 1975 by the American Association for the Advancement of Science.

verting to automation—except that individuals may shift the blame for their oppression from the human cog to the computer cog. It may be necessary, therefore, to clarify the dehumanizing components of a management system, which may be present whether or not the system has been automated, and to provide relief for any suffering they may have caused.

In a previous analysis[4] I pointed to two design strategies that account in large part for the presence of dehumanizing features in a management system. First, the efficiency of an enterprise is commonly increased by treating the recipients of the service and participants in the system as unpaid components whose time, effort, and intelligence do not appear in the cost accounting. Then, in order to maintain the efficiency of procedures once they have been established, the system is made exceedingly rigid, permitting freedom of action at only a few, usually hidden, focal points of real control. Dehumanizing features are thus already ingrained in most systems of management, and automation of such systems simply transfers the dehumanizing practice from one means of exercising control to another, codifies it in computer programs, and expands its influence to a larger circle of recipients and participants. To provide for the smooth and efficient operation of a largely computerized management system, the automation process makes demands of its own on all participants which decrease the area of free action remaining to the individual. Rules of procedure are thus dictated by the growth of machines and not by the needs of man. As a consequence, it is possible for the machine to capture the prerogative to formulate questions important to man. If we take such developments as inevitable, we are surrendering our humanity.

The point is that an intelligent understanding of a machine mode of control may be delayed until long after this control has been exercised. Wiener[5] argued that although procedures laid down to satisfy a process of automation are subject to human criticism and modification, such criticism may be ineffective because it may not surface until long after it is relevant. It may be too late then to correct the damage to the human condition. Systems are not detached from the people they interact with and the settings they create, and people strive for a sense of dignity, have needs that should be taken seriously, like to be treated with consideration and courtesy, and occasionally act as individuals—in short, they are entitled to be treated as human beings.

Despite the overriding importance of a person's dignity and humanity, little is known in terms of "scientific" specifics about the operational meaning of these concepts or the antecedent conditions that enhance or diminish them. Relatively few analyses have been devoted to systems features that may humanize organizations.[6,7] We know of only one attempt to incorporate humanizing features in a system and to evaluate their effects.[8] Yet we cannot afford to wait for knowledge to accumulate about the procedures to be incorporated in information systems or information parts of systems to help avoid dehumanizing or add humanizing qualities to them. We live in a time of active proliferation of new and revised management procedures, and designers of information systems are organizational designers as well, who cannot avoid changing organizations.[9] This is especially true of the proliferation of management information systems, which are more than information systems in the technical sense, as they include all bureaucratic procedures and perhaps all systems components that enter into the production and distribution of goods and services and so dominate the economic, political, and social management of society. Organizational design should be taken on as an explicit activity and management information systems implemented in such a way that they create a more humane setting.

Gouldner[10] showed how rules and regulations respond to the self-interest of those who govern and are governed. But to influence the shaping of new bureaucracies and other management systems, it is first necessary to isolate the crucial categories of design features that may make manifest humanizing or dehumanizing qualities of information systems. The analysis presented here is based on the guidelines developed by the Stanley House workshop on humanizing computerized information systems[11,12] in a serious attempt to isolate such design features. The guidelines are grouped into five broad categories, as shown in Table 19–1.

Many of the Stanley House criteria make sense as procedures for softening a bureaucracy as well as making an information system less rigid. There is no real distinction between manual and automated systems, and guidelines apply whether or not computers are used.

Discussion and Guidelines

By and large, the Stanley House guidelines are self-descriptive. This discussion is designed to illuminate their less obvious aspects and point to special problems that arise in connection with their implementation.

Criterion A2 is not a commonly encountered consideration in systems design. And, indeed, courtesy is not a substitute for real rewards, high quality of service, or other qualities. However, it is possible that courtesy is a prerequisite of humane society. In a rehabilitation hospital where courteous communications were part of a specially designed hospital information system, employees were pleased with that feature and regarded it highly.[13] It is difficult to evaluate the importance of this courtesy criterion

Table 19–1.

Stanley House Criteria for Humanizing Information Systems

A. Procedures for dealing with users
1. The language of a system should be easy to understand.
2. Transactions with a system should be courteous.
3. A system should be quick to react.
4. A system should respond quickly to users (if it is unable to resolve its intended procedure).
5. A system should relieve the users of unnecessary chores.
6. A system should provide for human information interface.
7. A system should include provisions for corrections.
8. Management should be held responsible for mismanagement.

B. Procedures for dealing with exceptions
1. A system should recognize as much as possible that it deals with different classes of individuals.
2. A system should recognize that special conditions might occur that could require special actions by it.
3. A system must allow for alternatives in input and processing.
4. A system should give individuals choices on how to deal with it.
5. A procedure must exist to override the system.

C. Action of the system with respect to information
1. There should be provisions to permit individuals to inspect information about themselves.
2. There should be provisions to correct errors.
3. There should be provisions for evaluating information stored in the system.
4. There should be provisions for individuals to add information that they consider important.
5. It should be made known in general what information is stored in systems and what use will be made of that information.

D. The problem of privacy
1. In the design of a system all procedures should be evaluated with respect to both privacy and humanization requirements.
2. The decision to merge information from different files and systems should never occur automatically. Whenever information from one file is made available to another file, it should be examined first for its implications for privacy and humanization.

E. Guidelines for system design having a bearing on ethics
1. A system should not trick or deceive.
2. A system should assist participants and users and not manipulate them.
3. A system should not eliminate opportunities for employment without a careful examination of consequences to other available jobs.
4. System designers should not participate in the creation or maintenance of secret data banks.
5. A system should treat with consideration all individuals who come in contact with it.

precisely because experience with courtesy in automated systems has been so rare.

Criterion A5 has far-reaching implications for a system's cost and efficiency. One of the favorite methods for optimizing the efficiency and minimizing the cost of a bureaucratic system is to require the individuals being served to supply the necessary information at each procedural component with which they are involved. Further, in order to ensure an uninterrupted flow of work, recipients of service are required to stand in queues at each point. Yet very often the required information can be made available to each procedural component at relatively small cost. It may be particularly important to do this at times when participating individuals are under additional pressures. One pernicious example is the queuing of hospital patients before special treatment or diagnostic centers (such as physical therapy or radiology). Appointments for individual patients made through the hospital information system could eliminate the queues of sick people in drafty corridors so typical of hospital operations. Similarly, a good system could eliminate unnecessary queues and travel by job seekers. On the other side of the coin, we find that the repetitive and unrelieved need to supply a service to queues of recipients is often dehumanizing to service personnel, and the constant demands of the queue prevent trained personnel from applying their skills in a selective manner.[14]

Criteria A6 and A7 may be related. Large-scale systems tend to be converted onto computers as cheaply as possible. In order to do this a global method of design is often used in which all subprocedures are rigidly defined into a single large structure. The more flexible, albeit much more expensive, way is to build a basic system of linkages to which different procedural modules can be attached. Whenever modifications are required it is then only necessary to reprogram the one affected module. One of the side effects of the global method of design is that it is difficult to modify the system to deal with errors that had not been anticipated. Yet errors of every sort, especially those related to information input, are almost unavoidable in a system that handles a large number of transactions. There is a suspicion in the concerned data processing communities that many corporations leave some errors uncorrected because it is cheaper to lose an occasional customer than to correct for each mistake. The human interface would be a desirable component of a system, even when correction of error may not be the major need. Human contact may be needed for individuals in vulnerable positions, such as the unemployed or the sick, to answer questions about unavoidable delays in providing a service or replying to an application; or just to soften the impact of an impersonal bureaucracy.

The human interface is lacking in most systems we have examined so far, and it may well be that the interface will have to be provided from the outside. One extra-organizational scheme is to have a computer ombudsman serving a large community. Such an ombudsman service could be provided by a professional, consumer, or governmental body, or by a combination of organizations, and would be the mediating link between the perplexed citizen and the perplexing system.[15]

Related to A6 and A7 is A8, the criterion that management ought to be held responsible for the situation where faulty design causes discomfort and frustration to individuals unable to get relief or attention from a system. Poorly designed systems are often not corrected because no one is really responsible for their actions. As a consequence, Kafkaesque nightmares may be created for users and participants.

In many ways, procedures for dealing with exceptions may be the most necessary components of a humanized system. The human condition is never so homogeneous that a set of rules can be devised to cover all exigencies. Once bureaucratic procedures are structured, they tend to become rigid even though they may contain provisions to deal with human needs. Exceptions are always difficult to manage. To provide for such flexibility, it is absolutely necessary to provide access to focal points of information or control in order to accommodate a departure from the "norm" where the users' needs require it.

I do not believe that there are technical obstacles to incorporating in working systems the kind of criteria that would permit the consideration of exceptions. My main concern is that obstacles will be generated by unavoidable conflict among humanizing criteria and between such criteria and the use of the system. Consider criterion B1, for example. Some employers of manual job bank programs rely on the face-to-face system to weed out those whom they regard as undesirable applicants. Here is an unstated trade-off between flexibility and equity. Also unstated may be the need to specify whom the system serves. What defines a class of individuals depends, in each case, on the kind of services the system provides or the demands it makes on participants. It is easy to say that a system should at least be aware that affected individuals differ in many personal characteristics and needs and should be accorded correspondingly different types of treatment. However, to achieve that may require an explicit definition of the purposes of a system. For instance, does a job bank serve the job seeker or the employer? It obviously serves the needs of both, and when a conflict exists between these needs it may not be feasible to make that conflict explicit.

In a similar sense conflicts may be created by criterion B4. There is a large variety of situations in which individuals may not wish to avail themselves of services or to provide a system with information touching on their private lives. The whole idea of "choice" is foreign to most large-scale systems, whether automated or manual. The provision of choices may very well mark the border between the dehumanizing and the humanizing system. However, it will add greatly to the complexity of systems, because permitting individual choices may set up conflicts with other criteria or services, including some through which the system seeks to become less dehumanizing. For example, in Canada, Provincial Health Services send an account of services rendered to the head of household. This would seem to fulfill the requirement of keeping the user or recipient of a service informed. Other members of the family, however, might object to finding their health needs reported to the head of household (without necessarily detracting from the affection they might feel for their spouse, parent, or provider). While this problem could be alleviated by addressing the report to the concerned individual, other situations may arise that cannot be easily resolved without providing a wide variety of choices. The spouse of the head of household or the adult children may not wish to inform the head that they have sought medical services. In fact, reporting such information may be harmful to a course of therapy or may needlessly disrupt family life, as when members of a family are seeking treatment for venereal disease or drug addiction, for example.

Opinions are divided about the extent to which information about individuals ought to be withheld from them and from others. Yet there is general agreement that provisions are needed for making access to and evaluation and correction of that information possible.

Criteria concerning actions of the system with respect to information have been widely discussed, so no additional comments may be necessary except in one case criterion C4. This would make it possible for individuals to add to the system information which they think bears importantly on their background or needs, even if the information is not important for processing their files. This might not add anything to the efficiency of a system, but would add a great deal to the psychological comfort of affected individuals.

Requirements for safeguarding the privacy of individual records may seriously conflict with requirements for humanizing an automated system. In general, the more information a system has about individuals who are affected by it, the more likely it is that it can be humanized, but also the easier it becomes to misuse that information and to violate individual needs or desires for privacy and confidentiality. The extent to which individuals are entitled to privacy or even wish privacy is a matter of political or social decision, as is the extent to which individuals ought not to be dehumanized by a system. Privacy versus humanization is an issue that has not received sufficient attention, and our experience with these concepts is too limited for it to be possible to compare requirements for privacy with those for humanization or make judgments on which is more important. However, it is clear that a very private system with no humane provisions may be just as undesirable as a very humane system with no safeguards to protect the privacy of its participants.

What makes procedural features desirable or undesirable with respect to privacy or humanization can be determined only in the context of the purpose of the system and the safeguards possible. Some systems that list individuals and information about them are desirable and others are not. They may also be desirable and undesirable to different people. For instance, a detailed file on handicapped children in the community would be useful for providing individual services, allocating community resources, and directing planning for schools and recreational facilities. On the other hand, attempts have been made to keep on file the names and records of minors who have been convicted of criminal offenses and to merge such files with other record systems. This has met with opposition from thoughtful members of the community, including members of the police department, and would be very objectionable, at least until adequate safeguards against abuse of such systems have been firmly defined and can be implemented. In the final analysis, it is not only a file's existence but its use which determines its ethical value. Nevertheless, the social and political considerations underlying criterion D1 can be resolved within the context of a particular system. What we are saying is that society can decide whether and how a file of handicapped children or of juvenile offenders should be assembled, maintained, and used.

It may be much more difficult to deal with criterion D2. Central to the problem of privacy is the very much enlarged information base available to government agencies when it becomes possible to merge information from different files. Merging of information may also make many systems more efficient and might make their action more equitable or even more humane. But it may be more to the point that under the guise of humanizing systems or making them more equitable (not necessarily the same thing), the rights of individuals for privacy and freedom from government surveillance in a democratic society may be seriously compromised. For example, the new Insurance Corporation of British Columbia, which is regulated and run by the provincial government, provides compulsory insurance under the name Autoplan for all drivers and car owners and bases its rate structure on records of driver violations. It is disquieting to note the ease with which Autoplan has been able to merge court and police files with records of largely business activities of Canadians in British Columbia without a public examination of this important step. Nor has there been public opposition to the extension of Autoplan to other insurance areas. In a similar vein, Lauden[16] has shown for four U.S. police and welfare systems how easily information from many sources may be merged.

These are perfect examples of the type of activities warned against by Wiener, [17] who predicted that the needs of large-scale government systems would generate practices which would be discovered only after they were well established.

It is thus clear that the extent to which a system can or will incorporate humanizing or dehumanizing features depends on economic, social, and political decisions. There are limits to the power of managers, engineers, systems designers, and scientists to provide for the inclusion of many desirable features in systems. So we suggest a set of ethical principles, criteria E1 to E5, which, if followed, will ensure that within any set of constraints a system will tend to be humane rather than dehumanizing.

Largely because many transactions of an automated system are difficult to inspect and by their very nature are less open to view than their manual predecessors, the requirement that systems should not deceive or trick, criterion E1, becomes of paramount importance. But even when a system is restrained from deception by law, it may still try to violate the spirit if not the letter of the law. (Common examples are billing practices whereby attempts are made to hide the amount of interest that is being collected from customers or that would be collected if the customer pays only part of what he owes.)

Computerized transactions make it possible for systems to assist participants without needlessly exploiting their labor (criterion E2). The idea that users must provide supportive services in order that a system may function is deeply ingrained not only in the designers of systems but also in the individuals they serve. Members of society are conditioned from birth to stand in line and fill out forms in order to register, to pay, or to receive. They have been habituated to supply information and contribute by their labor wherever they sought to receive a service, were ill, or provided a service for the government (such as paying taxes). It is grotesque but true that when the Nazis led millions of people into concentration camps and eventually into gas chambers, the victims had to stand in lines and deliver their possessions, provide information, and perform all the necessary services required to part them from their goods, their loved ones, and finally their lives. Manual systems burden recipients of a service with a great deal of effort to make the systems function smoothly. Computerized systems do not need to do so, or not really to the same extent. However, the temptation is always there to exploit the willing and conditioned cooperation of members of society. A contrary attitude, that the system should be burdened rather than the human component, needs to be fostered.

Similarly, an attitude should be cultivated by systems designers that all individuals, including employees, who come in contact with a system should be treated with the same consideration (criterion E5). It has been established that organizational structure produces characteristic patterns of alienation. For instance, Blauner[18] has shown that workers may develop perceptions of "meaninglessness," "powerlessness," and "work estrangement," depending on how they are fitted into an industry's technology.[19]

We have chosen to group criterion E3 with ethical rather than economic and social or political considerations. Within the area of information systems and systems control through computers, there are many types of employment that are relatively pleasant and interesting and offer opportunities to large numbers of individuals which are difficult to find elsewhere. The overall cost of eliminating such jobs may be high. This is true when computerization of technology affects jobs that rely heavily on human skills and qualities of perception, attention, and intelligence. There are severe costs when sources of employment that provide interesting, challenging, and above all human types of employment are eliminated. One example of an endangered group, victims of the computerization of communication networks, is telephone operators. Is is questionable that replacement jobs for this large number of eliminated positions which offer equally acceptable work for humans are available. The cost of finding employment for the communication workers who ordinarily would have worked for the telephone system has to be borne by society and not by the telephone company, and there is no way to assess or repay the costs to individuals who are forced into less satisfactory employment because opportunities for interesting and humane jobs are eliminated. From an economic point of view, this example shows that a cost-benefit analysis of job elimination through automation should not be based on the effects on a particular industry alone, but should include society as a whole. While it is recognized that it may be difficult for the systems designer to resist the temptation to eliminate such desirable jobs, he should be the first to recognize when they are in danger of being eliminated, and it behooves him as a human being to sound the alarm.

A Final Word About Economics

Perhaps the most serious obstacle to the inclusion of humanizing modules is that they reduce the efficiency of most information systems. Their inclusion will increase overhead in terms of design effort, complexity of procedures, and execution time. It may even be necessary to add to the physical resources of central computers (to provide a larger memory, a greater ratio of input, and so on). Consequently, appreciable research along these lines is not expected to be initiated by systems designers and managers, whose primary commitment is to efficiency. While our discussion is not designed to come to grips with the concern of those who are highly cost-conscious, we are nevertheless suspicious of those who refer to humanistic features as negative externalities and who hope that some market mechanism will handle their underlying problem. There is also a "humanistic" side to the debate.[20]

Lauden[21] makes a convincing case that the arrival of the third-generation computer offered new hope for administrative reformers, and indeed many admnistrative reformers attempted to fulfill his hope almost immediately. The new computer technology promised more closely integrated (which meant centralized) elements of federal, state, and local bureaucracies. It promised better decision-making, better government, better production, better distribution, and better allocation technology. Another important factor, Lauden stressed, is that the value to society of changes in (computerized) information systems does not have to be tested through the electoral process. Similarly, technological changes in industry rarely depend on decisions by stockholders. There are thus factors that shape computerized information systems and restructure means of producing and allocating goods and services or collecting information that are determined solely by political or industrial management and are neither controlled by nor responsive to social pressures. In the case of information systems, political ends are often achieved by management under the guise of instituting cost-saving efficiencies.

The utility of humanizing procedures will not be revealed in ordinary cost-benefit calculations but in the quality of life. Should we burden ourselves and future generations with dehumanizing practices designed and implemented today? Must not the wish to keep systems humane and dignified take its place with the desire to keep the air and the water palatable as a necessary countermotive to the drive of government and industry to be as efficient and cost-conscious as possible?

Summary

Computerized management information systems increasingly determine all bureaucratic and management procedures that control the production and distribution of goods and services and the collection of information. Thus, they begin to dominate the economic, political, and social management of society. With this domination come procedural features that may dehumanize participants or users affected by the working of most public and private organizations. Yet, despite the overriding importance of a person's dignity and humanity, little is known in terms of scientific specifics about the operational meaning of these concepts or of the antecedent conditions that enhance or diminish them. It will be too late if we wait for knowledge to accumulate about procedures to be incorporated in information systems or information parts of systems to avoid dehumanizing or to add humanizing qualities to them. A set of guidelines has been developed in a series of workshops sponsored by the Canadian Information Processing Society, Canada Council, and Simon Fraser University. These guidelines may apply where organizational design needs may be met and management information systems implemented in such a way that they create a more humane setting.

NOTES

1. The most recent analysis for computerized agencies is in K. Lauden, *Computers and Bureaucratic Reform*, New York: Wiley, 1974.
2. For an example of the impact of technology (but not computerization) on an organization see Peter Blau, *The Dynamics of Bureaucracy* (Chicago: University of Chicago Press, 1963).
3. J. Weizenbaum, "On the Impact of the Computer on Society," *Science*, vol. 176, 12 May 1972, pp. 609–14.
4. T. Sterling, *Humanist in Canada*, vol. 25 (2) 1973.
5. N. Wiener, *The Human Use of Human Beings* (Garden City, New York: Doubleday-Anchor, 1954); Norbert Wiener, "Some Moral and Technical Consequences of Automation," *Science*, vol. 131, 6 May 1960, pp. 1355–58.
6. C. Argyris, *Integrating the Individual in the Organization* (Georgetown, Ontario: Irwin Dorsey, 1965); C. Argyris, "Some Limits of Rational Man Organizational Theory, *Public Administration Review*, vol. 33 (3) May–June 1973, pp. 253–67. R. Kling, "Computers in the Service of Man," *Proceedings of the Association for Computing Machinery* (New York: Association for Computing Machinery, 1973), pp. 387–91.
7. R. Boguslaw, *The New Utopians* (Englewood Cliffs, N.J.: Prentice-Hall, 1965).
8. T. Sterling, S. Pollack, W. Spencer, "The Use of an Information System to 'Humanize' Procedures in a Rehabilitation Hospital," *The International Journal of Biomedical Computing*, vol. 5 (1) January 1974, pp. 51–57.
9. J. Galbraith, *Organizational Design* (Reading, Mass.: Addison-Wesley, 1973); T. Whisler, *The Impact of Computer Organizations* (New York: Pergamon, 1970); and Boguslaw, *New Utopians*.
10. A. Gouldner, *Patterns of Industrial Bureaucracy* (New York: The Free Press, 1954).
11. The guidelines were generated during a number of workshops held at Stanley House, a small estate in the Gaspé at which Canada Council and the Canadian Information Processing Society sponsored one workshop each in 1973. Participating in various of these workshops and otherwise

contributing to the formation of these guidelines were R. Ashenhurst, computer scientist (University of Chicago); M. Bockelman, police department (Kansas City); L. Brereton, editor, *Humanist in Canada*; C. Capstick, computer scientist (Guelph University); A. Close, barrister (Law Reform Commission); G. Cunningham, assistant commissioner (Royal Canadian Mounted Police); V. Douglas, psychologist (McGill University); C. Gottlieb, computer scientist (University of Toronto); H. Kalman, historian (University of British Columbia); R. King, computer scientist (University of California, Los Angeles); T. Kuck, philosopher (Department of Health, Education and Welfare); P. Lykos, computer scientist (National Science Foundation); S. Pollack, computer scientist (Washington University); H Schlaginweit, manager (British Columbia Telephone Co.); W. Rogers, provincial auditor (Alberta); D. Seely, computer scientist (Simon Fraser University); M. Shepherd, programmer (Toronto); T. Sterling, computer scientist (Simon Fraser University); and J. Weizenbaum, computer scientist (Massachusetts Institute of Technology). For a detailed description of the guidelines see Sterling in note 12.

12. T. Sterling, "Guidelines for Humanizing Computerized Information: A Report from Stanley House," *Communications of the ACM*, vol. 17, no. 11, 1974, pp. 609–13.

13. Boguslaw, *New Utopians*.

14. Ibid.

15. The Canadian computer ombudsman scheme is developed around a joint effort of the Canadian Information Processing Society and the Consumer Association of Canada (see T. Sterling, *J. CIPS*, in press). The U.S. effort, spearheaded by the Association for Computing Machinery, has as its main concern eliminating an incorrect image of computerized systems and is thus different from the Canadian model.

16. Lauden, *Computers*.

17. Wiener, *Human Use*.

18. Robert Blauner, *Alienation and Freedom* (Chicago: University of Chicago Press, 1964).

19. For confirming evidence of Blauner's findings, see F. C. Mann and L. R. Hoffman, *Automation and the Worker* (New York: Holt, Rinehart and Winston, 1960); C. R. Walker, *Toward the Automatic Factory* (New Haven, Conn.: Yale University Press, 1957); A. N. Turner and P. R. Lawrence, *Industrial Jobs and the Worker* (Cambridge, Mass.: Harvard University Press, 1965).

20. See, for instance, K. W. M. Kapp, *The Social Costs of Private Enterprise* (New York: Schocken, 1950); E. Richardson, *Work in America* (Cambridge, Mass.: MIT Press, 1973); and Lauden, *Computers*.

21. Lauden, *Computers*.

PART VI

Problems of Rationality and "Correct Choice"

Introductory Note

Of the need for better management of the human services there can be no doubt. Numerous observers have argued convincingly for more effective, more rational decision making. Jerry S. Turem, for example, puts it in terms of a "management stance," and Monica Shapira states that "in an economy in which economic growth depends on an increased productivity rate higher than on additional resources, the allocation of public resources will be unavoidably tested against the measurement of efficiency in utilization of resources for specified purposes of social utility."[1]

Against the stern will of economics, the minimal use of the tools of rationality and intelligent choice in the human services appears a serious deficit.

> . . . welfare service organizations on the whole are not yet equipped with integrated modern information systems or devices for monitoring system performance and sensing changes in its environment. Most welfare organizations still use the incremental budgeting system instead of programed [sic] budgeting; they have no provisions for cost-benefit analysis and no modern technology for planning and programming.
>
> The general absence of modern tools of managerial analysis and control in welfare systems is all the more astounding in view of the revolutionary impact such technologies have had on increased productive capacity of other systems and on the quality and cost of goods and services produced by them.[2]

Today, the "rational decision" model associated with management science and systems approaches exercises hegemony in the human services, if more in theory than actual practice. To recapitulate the model, it pivots around that central issue in organizational rationality, the problem of choice, or what should be done with resources in specific instances of administrative decision making. In the rational model, choices are made by evaluating alternatives in terms of goals and objectives against the criteria of efficiency and effectiveness, and on the basis of available information. Through the application of a variety of management tools and techniques (PPBS, MBO, ZBB, benefit-cost analysis, MIS), it is presumably possible to improve the quality of the information used, the search for and assessment of alternatives, and the actual choices made.

Fundamental to the model is the primacy of rationality. Indeed, one of the strongest ethics in the professional culture is the ethic of rationality. For typically, individual and organizational action is justified in terms of that ethic, in terms of the analysis of means and ends. Closely related is the assumption that human service organizations are, or can be, instruments of rational action. Another assumption, put as a prescription, is that the cause of rationality will be advanced by converting vague (but politically useful) goals into clear and precise ones with metrics attached whenever possible. Presumably this will improve the quality of service delivery. For human service workers can be held accountable once objectives are specified, and with quantitative feedback, error correction is more likely. At the organizational level as well, quantification is also more desirable than judgment and intuition. With the application of the tools of rationality and intelligent choice, it will be possible to describe what has been done, with what results, and at what cost. In this model, each advance of rationality concomitantly furthers the cause of accountability.

What could be more plausible than the rational decision model? Its abstract logic and the case for the tools of rationality are so persuasive as to be almost self-validating and self-sealing. But were it so, it would be dogma, not science or rationality. Science demands an attitude of skepticism, and there are skeptics and critics when it comes to the tools of rational choice.

Descending from the world of abstract logic and model building, some criticisms find *normative flaws* and *value biases* in the tools. Others deal with *operational* issues involving the design and implementation of the tools. Some deal with larger *institutional* issues such as the social structure of decision making and the proper role of economic rationality.

Among the many specific questions that are found to arise are: Do the tools of rationality really work? If so, under what circumstances and with what costs? What are their unanticipated consequences? Are human service organizations really instruments of rational social action, or can they be better understood in terms of influence and power processes? Do the tools of rationality actually yield solutions to the problem of accountability, or does the proliferation of formalistic procedures and controls produce opposite results from those intended? Finally, if we are to speak of accountability, what role does the citizenry play in the model of rational choice?

How Rational is Rationality? Analyzing problems of resource allocation at city, state, and federal levels, Aaron Wildavsky, one of the early and most prolific critics of systems analysis in government, marshals evidence to show that MBO, PPB and ZBB inevitably fail. The Social and Rehabilitation Service is a case in point of the failure of MBO. Typically says

Wildavsky, the chief result of MBO is a long list of useless objectives, useless primarily, because they become mechanisms for avoiding choice. Since MBO subsumes critical problems of organizational design under a total emphasis on objectives, the system is seriously flawed. PPB and ZBB, also "share an emphasis on the virtue of objectives." The former relates larger to smaller objectives among different programs, the latter does the same within a single program. PPB's rationale lies in its comprehensive integration, its "bundling together" of like programs. But herein is an element of *irrationality*, because in operation, the more tightly linked program elements, the greater the system rigidity, the greater the costs of organizational error, and the less the likelihood error will be reported. Thus, PPB makes it hard to correct errors. PPB shares with ZBB a prerequisite for better information that relates inputs to outputs, the former across areas of policy, the latter within areas of policy. Neither requirement can be met. These plus other defects produce costly rationales for inevitable failures of implementation. Moreover, the tools of rational calculation, though disguised as neutral techniques are political philosophy.

On conceptual and methodological grounds, H. G. Shaffer writing on the threshold of the expansionary 1960s, takes issue with the use of benefit-cost analysis. Shaffer offers an important distinction between *investment* and *consumption* expenditures and with this distinction he develops a threefold argument against benefit-cost analysis in the educational field. In that field and others, government expenditures directed toward the realization of certain preferences, "bear no necessary relation to their economic profitability as investments." Shaffer offers several interesting and provocative examples of the socially bizarre results of attempting to use investment criteria in decision making. His assertions are consistent with the later ones of Otto Eckstein, a leading public investment theoretician and pathmaker in benefit-cost analysis. Eckstein has suggested that benefit-cost analysis be applied "only in limited cases like flood control, electric power production, the Post Office, some transportation and recreation facilities—mostly in fields where benefits are primarily economic, tangible, and measurable."[3]

Organizational Environments and Their Effects. Rationalistic approaches to management tend to give short shrift to such "extra-rational" processes as influence, power, and control. Their preoccupation is with the relationship between organizational inputs and outputs, hence they have been called "black box approaches." Both Charles Perrow and Michael Lipsky attempt to grapple with a variety of organizational dynamics and the dysfunctional consequences of rationalistic approaches.

While heretofore preoccupied with organizations as instruments of rational action, Perrow now suggests that human service organizations can be rational instruments of announced policy goals only to a quite limited extent. To assert the rationalistic position, mystifies or conceals the more important functions of organizations that are to subserve internal and external interests. If the focus would be on the ways in which human service agencies are *used*, then *power* and *influence* would be at the *center* of attention, the measurement of *efficiency* and *effectiveness* at the *periphery*. As for the workings of power and influence, Perrow observes that working-class, poor and minority people have comparatively little opportunity to formulate organizational goals and priorities. Discussions of efficiency and rationality must then ask: "In whose terms, in whose interests?"

Analyzing contemporary accountability policy, performance measurement and procedures for goal clarification, Lipsky finds manifest as "assault on the human services." Where the "black box" is empty of organizational/environmental analysis, Lipsky attempts to show that conventional accountability policy produces dysfunctional consequences. For when the technology of human service workers is essentially uncertain and requires tailoring to the case, management systems that aim toward routinization and control ultimately subvert the worker's sense of control, they displace qualitative concerns, and, in the end, must debase the rendering of service.

The Institutional Level. The "rational paradigm" polarizes decision making into two spheres. One is cognitive analysis and technical design. The other sphere is the political process, bargaining, and social interaction. In the rational paradigm, it is assumed that error is built-in to political processes and that the tools of choice are the solution to error.

An opposing viewpoint, sometimes called "democratic theory" asserts the overarching value and intelligence of political processes. Where the rational paradigm defines a concrete and limited problem of organizational choice as a purely technical problem, political theory is more apt to see larger contexts—historical action, conflicts of interest, cultural values— and to go outside the technical problem of the organizational system up to the level of the institutional system. A case in point is the observation of the economist Gunnar Myrdal. Looking at the build-up of administrative intervention in the welfare state, Myrdal saw the problem in political terms and called for an explication of the democratic ideal of the welfare state in which "the citizens themselves carry more and more of the responsibility . . . with only the necessary minimum of direct state interference."[4] Myrdal's comments are interesting in relation to the rational paradigm and the advance of administrative intervention:

> Bureaucracy, petty administrative regulations, and generally a
> meddlesome state should not be the signum of our vision of a
> more accomplished democratic Welfare State. To fight against reg-

imentation from above was always a rallying cause for the progressive elements in the Western countries. Now . . . we have every reason to use state legislation and administration for fundamental economic and social policies . . . But we should not make peace with bureaucracy. I view as short-sighted those would-be reformers, both in the United States and in other Western countries who, in their urge to improve society, place an almost exclusive trust in continual extension of state regulations, thereby presenting their fellow citizens with a sort of "etatistic liberalism."[5]

Herein lies the challenge to the advance of administration and bureaucratic accountability policy. Although thorny, the conflicts between technical and political decision making, between the form of accountability and its substance, between the citizenry and the seemingly relentless advance of bureaucracy may be soluble. In pursuit of this solution, Stafford Beer piques the managerial imagination in a synthesis of politics and technical rationality that is analogous to "social self-management" practiced in a number of other nations. Drawing from cybernetic theory, one of the original homes of management science, Beer describes a Chilean experiment in which a sophisticated information system and its program Cyberstride were put in the hands of the citizenry, a kind of "cybernetic democracy." In an eloquent plea to his fellow management scientists to "give away" their knowledge and their craft, Beer notes that "brains and brainlike systems make their decisions wherever the information relevant to those decisions comes together. . . . Any concatenation of logical elements may acquire the information relevant to the decision; therefore, any such concatenation is potentially in command."[6]

NOTES

1. Monica Shapira, "Reflections on the Preparation of Social Workers for Executive Positions," *Journal of Education for Social Work*, vol. 7 (Winter 1971), p. 58; Jerry S. Turem, "The Call for a Management Stance," *Social Work*, vol. 19 (5) September 1974, pp. 615–23.
2. Ibid., p. 60.
3. Otto Eckstein, *Public Finance*, 2d ed. (Englewood Cliffs, N.J.: Prentice-Hall, 1967), p. 28.
4. Gunnar Myrdal, *Beyond the Welfare State* (New York: Bantam Books, 1960), p. 82.
5. Ibid.
6. For an interesting account and bibliography see Ichak Adizes and Elisabeth Mann Borgese, eds., *Self-Management: New Dimensions to Democracy* (Santa Barbara, California: ABC-Clio, 1975).

20. How Rational Is Rationality?

PPB and ZBB

AARON WILDAVSKY

If the old budgeting became anti-analytical because it arrested development at the level of inputs, the new budgeting became irrational by
dwelling excessively on outputs. A fixation on what is put in has been
replaced by a compulsion over what should be taken out. Objectives
replace resources as *the* key to analysis. After decades of discussing effort
instead of accomplishment—how hard teachers work but not how well
students learn, how much money is spent on police but not how much
crime is reduced—the urge to concentrate on results rather than resources
is understandable. Unfortunately, the grip on one excess has been
loosened only to embrace another; alas, the affair with resources has been
replaced by the romance with objectives. . . .

Before turning to PPB and ZBB, it is useful to say a few words about
MBO (Management By Objectives) because it is the epitome of a method
for improving choice based on analyzing objectives. The lesson of Management By Objectives is that what may begin as puffery (Look at our wonder-
ful objectives!) often winds up as self-deception—ranking objectives equals
analyzing problems.

Management By Objectives

The idea behind Management By Objectives is that objectives should be
specified and that management and workers should agree on the results by
which workers are to be judged in accordance with these objectives. At
each level objectives are formulated, discussed, agreed to, and passed up
the hierarchy. Minor objectives are stacked like Chinese boxes within
major ones. What could possibly be wrong with so appealing an idea?
Managers should have objectives for their organizations, and workers

Excerpted from Chapter 6 of Aaron Wildavsky, *The Politics of the Budgetary Process*, Third
Edition. Copyright © 1979 by Aaron Wildavsky; copyright © 1974, 1964 by Little, Brown and
Company (Inc.). Reprinted with permission.

should be held to account for achieving results. MBO, in a word, is a restatement of good management based on rational choice for effective decision making. The trouble is that the attempt to formalize procedures for choosing objectives without considering organizational dynamics leads to the opposite of what was intended: irrational choice and ineffective action.

The main product of MBO, as experience in the United States federal government suggests, is literally a series of objectives. Aside from the unnecessary paperwork, such exercises are self-defeating because they become mechanisms for avoiding rather than making choices. Long lists of objectives are useless because rarely do resources exist to carry out more than the first few. The experience of the various federal commissions on national priorities, for instance, is that there is no point in listing 846 or even 79 national objectives because almost all the money is gone after the first three or four are funded. If choosing objectives means abandoning choice, choosing objectives is a bad idea.

The larger the number of objectives, the greater the likelihood that some organizational activity will somehow contribute to at least one, the less the need to give up one thing for another. Public agencies prefer more objectives rather than fewer, so whatever consequences they cause are more likely to fit under one of them. Everyone knows that objectives of public agencies tend to be multiple, conflicting, and vague; multiple and conflicting because different people want different things with varying degrees of intensity, and vague because objectives can thus accommodate disagreement. Reconciling these conflicts is not made easier by telling bureaucrats that their strategic behavior—staking out their own objectives as a prelude to bargaining—has become sanctified as an object of virtue, indeed, as the essence of rationality itself.

The most elaborate evaluation of an MBO operation, "The Case of the Social Rehabilitation Service," shows that MBO's chief effects are an increase in paperwork and in discussion of objectives and a decrease in time spent on programmatic activity. When asked what they would recommend as improvements beyond MBO, "Both regional and central administrators mention management accountability and responsibility . . . better teamwork . . . coordination . . . a need for clear mission goals and priorities . . . and the development of management information systems"—in other words, exactly what MBO was suppose to accomplish in the first place. Interviews with 159 top administrators reveal that MBO "is generally perceived by managers and supervisors as a system which reinforces such bureaucratic norms as centralized organizational control and decision-making, paperwork, efficiency emphasis and lack of participation."[1]

By putting all the emphasis on objectives, MBO subsumes critical problems of organizational design—how to relate people and activities so that errors become evident and are corrected—under the surface sentimentality of human relations jargon. What MBO does to program objectives, PPB does to organizational incentives.

PPB

Program budgeting contains an extreme centralizing bias. Power is to be centralized in the Presidency (through the Office of Management and Budget) at the national level, in superdepartments rather than bureaus within the Executive Branch, and in the federal government as a whole instead of state or local governments. Note how W. Z. Hirsch assumes the desirability of national dominance when he writes: "These methods of analysis can guide Federal officials in the responsibility of bringing local education decisions into closer harmony with national objectives."[2] G. A. Steiner observes that comprehensiveness may be affected by unrestricted federal grants-in-aid to the states because "such a plan would remove a substantial part of Federal expenditures from a program budgeting system of the Federal government."[3] Should there be reluctance on the part of state and local officials to employ the new tools, Anshen states "that the Federal government may employ familiar incentives to accelerate this process."[4] Summing it up, Hirsch says, "It appears doubtful that a natural resources program budget would have much impact without a good deal of centralization."[5]

Within the great federal organizations designed to encompass the widest range of objectives, there would have to be strong executives. Cutting across the subunits of the organization, as is the case in the Department of Defense, the program budget could be put together only by the top executive. A more useful tool for increasing his power to control his subordinates would be difficult to imagine.

That all decisions ought to be made by the most central person in the most centralized body is a proposition difficult to justify on scientific grounds. In fact, it cannot be justified except as reflecting a distaste of politics—for the more centralized a system, the fewer the decision-makers and the less the need to bargain.

In the literature discussed earlier there appears several times the proposition that "the program budget is a neutral tool. It has no politics."[6]

How could men make so foolish a statement? Perhaps they identify program budgeting with something good and beautiful, and politics with something bad and ugly. McKean and Anshen speak of politics in terms of "pressure and expedient adjustments," "haphazard acts . . . unresponsive to a planned analysis of the needs of efficient decision design." From the political structure they expect only "resistance and opposition, corresponding to the familiar human disposition to protect established seats of power and procedures made honorable by the mere facts of existence and custom."[7] In other places we hear of "vested interests," "wasteful duplication," "special interest groups," and the "Parkinson syndrome."[8] Somebody doesn't like politics.

Politics

Political rationality is the fundamental kind of reason, because it deals with the preservation and improvement of decision structures, and decision structures are the source of all decisions. Unless a decision structure exists, no reasoning and no decisions are possible. . . . There can be no conflict between political rationality and . . . technical, legal, social, or economic rationality, because the solution of political problems makes possible an attack on any other problem, while a serious political deficiency can prevent or undo all other problem solving. . . . Non-political decisions are reached by considering a problem in its own terms, and by evaluating proposals according to how well they solve the problem. The best available proposal should be accepted regardless of who makes it or who opposes it, and a faulty proposal should be rejected or improved no matter who makes it. Compromise is always irrational; the rational procedure is to determine which proposal is the best, and to accept it. In a political decision, on the other hand, action never is based on the merits of a proposal but always on who makes it and who opposes it. Action should be designed to avoid complete identification with any proposal and any point of view, no matter how good or how popular it might be. The best available proposal should never be accepted just because it is best; it should be deferred, objected to, discussed, until major opposition disappears. Compromise is always a rational procedure, even when the compromise is between a good and bad proposal.[9]

It will be useful to distinguish between policy politics (which policy will be adopted?), partisan politics (which political party will win office?), and system politics (how will decision structures be set up?). Program budgeting is manifestly concerned with policy politics, and not much with partisan politics, although it could have important consequences for issues that divide the nation's parties. My contention is that the thrust of program budgeting makes it an integral part of system politics.

It is hard to find men who take up the cause of political rationality, who plead the case for political man, and who are primarily concerned with the laws that enable the political machinery to keep working. One is driven to a philosopher like Paul Diesing to find the case for the political:

> . . . the political problem is always basic and prior to the others. . . . This means that any suggested course of action must be evaluated first by its effects on the political structure. A course of action which corrects economic or social deficiencies but increases political difficulties must be rejected, while an action which contributes to political improvement is desirable even if it is not entirely sound from an economic or social standpoint.[10]

There is hardly a political scientist who would claim half as much.

A major task of the political system is to specify goals or objectives. It is impermissible to treat goals as if they were known in advance. "Goals" may well be the product of interaction among key participants rather than pronouncements of some deus ex machina or (to use Bentley's term) some "spook" which posits values in advance of our knowledge of them.

Once the political process becomes a focus of attention, it is evident that the principal participants may not be clear about their goals. What we call goals or objectives may, in large part, be operationally determined by the policies we can agree upon. In a political situation, then, the need for support assumes central importance. Not simply the economic but the political costs and benefits turn out to be crucial.

The literature of economics usually treats organizations and institutions as if they were costless entities. The standard procedure is to consider rival alternatives (in consideration of price policy or other criteria), calculate the differences in cost and achievement among them, and show that one is more or less efficient than another. This way of thinking is insufficient. If the costs include getting an agency to change its policies or procedures, then these organizational costs must be taken into account. . . .

Why PPB Is Irrational

To better understand the failure of program budgeting everywhere and at all times, it is helpful to imagine what would be required for its success. Most discussion has been confined to "sufficient" conditions. The critical assumption has been that it is easy to set up PPB but difficult to implement the system. The problems presumably lie, therefore, in rooted interests, recalcitrant politicians, and hidebound bureaucrats. It has been readily acknowledged, in addition, that the implementation of PPB has been hampered by lack of trained manpower, absence of essential data, and even inadequacies in the state of the art. The point is that all these putative defects can be remedied. Unreceptive politicians and bureaucrats can be got around or replaced. Training can be stepped up, better data can surely be collected, and knowledge of analysis will undoubtedly be improved. If these were the only difficulties, it would be difficult to explain why PPB has no successes whatsoever to its credit. For surely somewhere, sometime, the right conditions for PPB to prosper should have existed. Maybe they should have, but they didn't. Why not? To answer that question we have to be prepared to accept the possibility that PPB lacks "necessary" as well as sufficient conditions, that its disabilities occur not merely in program implementation but in policy design—that, in a word, its defects are defects in principle, not in execution. PPB does not work because it cannot work. Failure is built into its very nature because it requires ability to perform cognitive operations that are beyond present human (or mechanical) capacities.

Program budgeting is like the simultaneous equation of governmental intervention in society. If one can state objectives precisely, find quantitative measures for them, specify alternative ways of achieving them by different inputs or resources, and rank them according to desirability, one has solved the social problems for the period. One has only to bring the program budget up to date each year. Is it surprising that program budgeting does not perform this sort of miracle? Planning, Programming, and Budgeting Systems require a structure in which all policies related to common objectives are compared for cost and effectiveness. Not a single theory for a particular area of policy but, rather, a series of interrelated theories for all policies is required. If we barely sense the relation between inputs and outputs in any single area of policy, however, how likely are we to know what these relationships are across the widest realm of policy? As one area of ignorance interacts exponentially with other areas, we get not an arithmetic but a geometric increase in ignorance.[11]

There is no need to blink at the inevitable conclusion: PPB is not an embodiment of rationality; PPB is irrational. If the goal is to alter the allocation of resources in a more productive way, or to generate better analyses than those that are now used, PPB does not (because it cannot) produce these results. PPB is not cost effective. It produces costly rationales for inevitable failures.

But why do seemingly rational procedures produce irrational results? By sacrificing organizational incentives in the name of economic efficiency, program budgeting serves neither. The good organization is interested in discovering and correcting its own mistakes. The higher the cost of errors—not only in terms of money but also in personnel, programs, and prerogatives—the less the chance anything will be done about them. Organizations should be designed, therefore, to make errors visible and correctable, that is, noticeable and reversible, which in turn is to say, cheap and affordable.

Program budgeting increases rather than decreases the cost of correcting error. The great complaint about bureaucracies is their rigidity. As things stand, the object of organizational affection is the bureau as serviced by the usual line-item categories from which people, money, and facilities flow. Viewed from the standpoint of bureau interests, programs to some extent are negotiable; some can be increased and others decreased while keeping the agency on an even keel or, if necessary, adjusting it to less happy times, without calling into question its very existence. Line-item budgeting, precisely because its categories (personnel, maintenance, supplies) do not relate directly to programs, are easier to change. Budgeting by programs, precisely because money flows to objectives, makes it difficult to abandon objectives without abandoning the organization that gets its money for them.

Notice I do not say it is inadvisable for analysis to take place at the level of programs and policies. On the contrary, there is every reason to encourage analytical thrusts from different directions and dimensions of policy, provided only that no single one is encased in concrete and be considered the final way. It is better that non-programmatic categories be used in formal budget categories, thus permitting a diversity of analytical perspectives, than that a temporary analytic insight be made the permanent perspective through which money is funneled.[12]

If error is to be altered, it must be relatively easy to correct. But PPB makes it hard. Its "systems" are characterized by their proponents as highly differentiated and tightly linked. The rationale for program budgeting lies in its connectedness—like programs are grouped together. Program structures are meant to replace the confused concatenations of line-items with clearly differentiated, non-overlapping boundaries; only one set of programs to a structure. This means that a change in one element or structure must result in change reverberating throughout every element in the same system. Instead of alerting only neighboring units or central control units, which would make change feasible, all are, so to speak, wired together, so the choice is effectively all or none.

Imagine one of us deciding whether to buy a tie or a kerchief. A simple task, one might think. Suppose, however, that organizational rules require us to keep our entire wardrobe as a unit. If everything must be rearranged when one item is altered, the probability we will do anything is low. The more tightly linked the elements, and the more highly differentiated they are, the greater the probability of error (because the tolerances are so small), and the less the likelihood error will be reported (because with change, every element has to be recalibrated with every other one that was previously adjusted). Why idealize an information system like PPB that causes many more mistakes than it can correct? Being caught between revolution (change in everything) and resignation (change in nothing) has little to recommend it. . . .

Zero-Base Budgeting

. . . Program managers at each level are assumed to be in the best position to make decisions on priorities and trade-offs in the programs for which they are responsible. Managers are additionally responsible for defining the specific objectives and identifying the outputs of their programs. In a document called the "decision package," the basic tool of ZBB, this description of their program is combined with an analysis of the effects of conducting the program at alternative levels of funding. Typically these funding levels include a minimum below which operation could not function, the current level above the minimum level, and a middle level between these two. Lower-echelon managers are placed in a position of great responsibility in this system, since they compute the marginal utility of changes in funding and assess the difference these changes would make. With respect to a discrete activity referred to as the "decision unit," a manager presents the activity's purpose, the consequences of not performing the activity, measures of its performance at various levels of operation, alternative courses of action at each level, and the costs and benefits of running the program at the current level.

The second stage of ZBB involves ranking the decision packages. Managers send the packages up the bureaucratic ladder to their direct superiors, who rank them according to the priority of that program within the agency. Subsequently, agency priorities are ranked within the overall department. Many different rankings are compiled as the decision packages gradually move toward the department head's desk. Superiors receive groups of ranked decision packages from those directly below them which they in turn rank, until there is one comprehensive ranking of all programs in the department. A cutoff line is drawn to delineate the expected amount of revenues for the year, or the level of "affordability." Packages that fall above the line receive funding while those below the line do not. This flexible cutoff line is reputed to facilitate accommodating late-year budget windfalls or deficits; the response to a change in expected revenues is merely to move the line and accept or reject several more decision packages.

After isolating the objectives of the program, managers are responsible for explaining the consequences of not funding certain activities. To determine these consequences, managers must thoroughly understand the effects their programs have upon other programs with which they do not normally deal in day-to-day operations. How are they to provide this information? No one knows. And, after figuring out the consequences of doing without particular activities, managers must also compute the efficiency of carrying them on at various levels below the current apportionment. They are asked, basically, "How well would this program function at another level?"; but this is a question to which there are an infinite number of possible answers. Managers must therefore decide which funding levels they wish to analyze.

In general, managers have been unable to assess programs' efficiency at that vague "other" level, and states have provided their managers with set increments at which they are to evaluate their programs. Consequently, managers are actually computing from a base above zero. Instead of trying to discover the minimum level at which to carry on a certain activity (a task posing insurmountable problems), they evaluate the program at an arbitrary low proportion of the current level, say 80 percent. However, this method removes the assumption that there is any possibility of entirely canceling funding and obviates the necessity of determining the consequences of not performing the activity. Managers are now asked, "How would your program function at this specific level of funding?" Nevertheless, managers still require specific data relating announced objectives to program performance at alternative levels of funding. . . .

The majority of the eleven states currently using ZBB in their budgeting procedures use some form of priority ranking for the programs, and most of the states make use of decision packages. In attempting to bridge the gap between upper- and lower-level managers, states have sacrificed the zero-based focus of ZBB. No states justify all programs from zero, and many have abandoned alternative funding levels. Instead, they submit budget proposals indicating the costs of the programs at set levels of operations. Arkansas, Illinois, and Texas selected 90 percent of the base level of the program for the minimum level of operation. Above that comes the current budgeted amount, and then actually a 10 percent increase over the base figure. Rather than being a Zero-Base Budget, justifying from zero, these states have introduced a 90 percent base budget.

Missouri, Idaho, and California are even further off zero base. Missouri and Idaho rank only proposed increases above the base. Similarly, California "focuses on proposed changes in the budget."[13] Ranking decision packages above the base seems indistinguishable from incremental budgeting. Tennessee has pursued another variant: each program must assess its performance at four preordained levels, which are approached in a unique manner. The levels are (1) continuation at current level of funding, (2) continuation at current level of service, (3) improvement to meet new legislative requirements and to replace lost federal aid, and (4) improvements based on departmental estimates of need.[14]

Few states have a long acquaintance with ZBB. For many, ZBB has only been used for one or two years. In these cases it is difficult to draw any definite conclusions. New Jersey encountered a number of difficulties (such as staff resistance and low-quality submissions), although it feels these problems can be overcome as its personnel become more accustomed to ZBB concepts and processes. Idaho reports that 75 percent of its first-year reports were unsatisfactory.[15] This high failure rate was due largely to budgeters' inadequate understanding of the procedures. Other states complain, as well, of agency and staff resistance to the system, lack of understanding of basic concepts, and deficient quality of data. After two years in Georgia—one year when revenues markedly decreased and one when expenditures sharply increased—ZBB was abandoned and new submissions were requested.[16] . . .

Organization

The tension between analysis, which seeks out error and promotes change, and organization, which seeks stability and promotes its existing activities, is inevitable. The bulk of analysis is rejected by the organizations for which it is intended.[17] Better information alone will not matter without incentives for organizations to use it. Struggling with organizational incentives, therefore, is a perennial (perhaps paramount) problem of policy analysis.

Ignoring the organizational levels, and the proper approaches to each, is the original sin of new budgetary systems. PPB fails because no organizational level gets information (1) that it is willing to use and (2) that is relevant to the resources at its disposal. MBO either obfuscates objectives, so higher levels will be unable to understand them, or overwhelms the upper echelons with objectives, so they cannot figure out which ones apply. After participating in a lengthy MBO exercise, as a result of which it was decided that the status quo was splendid, a business participant reported: "I suggest this is a conspiracy by the Board to prove the fruitlessness of deviation from established group practices."[18] MBO is better seen as a misguided effort to violate an analytic theorem—treating objectives apart from resources—than as a mode of analysis.

Clinging to last year's agreements is enormously economical of critical resources (particularly time and good interpersonal relations), which would be seriously depleted if all or most past agreements were reexamined yearly. If there is a mechanism for holding on to adequate solutions and sequentially proceeding to solve remaining problems—which focus on increases and decreases to the base—knowledge is more likely to result. Similarly, an agreement-producing process is more likely to work if past agreements can be retained while the system works on unresolved issues.

Only poor countries come close to Zero-Base Budgeting, not because they wish to do so but because their uncertain financial position continually causes them to go back on old commitments. Because past disputes are part of present conflicts, their budgets lack predictive value; little stated in them is likely to occur.[19] Historical practices, which are a dire consequence of extreme instability and from which all who experience them devoutly desire to escape, should not be considered normative.

Analysis aims to bring information to bear on current decisions which do have future consequences. Taking these consequences into account—acting now to do better later—is what all analysis is about. Because prediction comes at a premium, however, analysis uses history—what has been tried in the past, how past patterns have led to present problems, where past obligations limit future commitments—as a source of both limits and possibilities.

Theory

A promise underlies public policy: if the actions we recommend are undertaken, good (intended) consequences rather than bad (unintended) ones will come about. Since causal connections are strict in designing public policy—if this is done by government, then that result will follow—failure to match promise with performance is likely to be high, as is reluctance to acknowledge error. Objectives are kept vague and multiple to expand the range within which observed behavior fits. Goal substitution takes place as the consequences actually caused by programs replace the objectives originally sought. Goal displacement becomes the norm as an organization seeks to make the variables it can control, its own efforts and processes, the objectives against which it is measured. This is how organizations come to justify error instead of creating knowledge. On all sides theoretical requirements are abandoned, by considering inputs or outputs alone, until there seems to be no error (and hence no truth), and it becomes impossible to learn from experience.

If our society lacks production functions—which is to say, policy relevant theory that purports to connect resources like teaching to objectives like reading—in most areas we wish to affect, how much more profound must be ignorance of the consequences of alternative programs across areas of policy and over time.[20] PPB and ZBB make demands on theory that cannot be met. They require knowledge of relationships between governmental action and social consequences over the broadest range of issues. Who is most misled by this—the proponents who sell these budgetary systems or the politicians who buy them—is debatable. But if these systems represent the best in rational analysis, as many surely believe, and if this presumed rationality is doomed to failure, as it certainly is, then the sure loser is policy analysis, with its idea of applying intelligence to policy problems.

Learning

There is more than morbid curiosity in the study of Zero-Base and program budgeting. Though one has died and the other should, their experiences teach about better budgeting by negative example. Whatever they do, the rule is, should not be done.

ZBB and PPB embody extreme (though different) forms of comprehensive calculation. (True, they can't practice what they preach; the effort either does them in or they lose any distinctive quality.) ZBB insists on making all possible vertical calculations, from zero to base, as it were, until the most efficient ways of achieving objectives are chosen. PPB covers at least all major horizontal relationships between related programs so the most cost-effective combination for achieving objectives is chosen. Ergo, the lesson is that budgeting should not be comprehensive. Since knowledge, time, and manpower are usually in short supply, most policy analysis is concerned with reducing rather than increasing the cost of calculations. Budgeting should not hinder that effort.

PPB is ahistorical in that it is interested in comparing programs in the here and now. The past is an anachronism, a leftover remnant of an outmoded era, and there is no evolution. ZBB doesn't so much ignore as set out to abolish history; the clock is always set at zero. Budgets apparently spring newborn like Minerva from the brow of Jove. The lesson is clear: budgets should be explicitly historical, comparing what is about to be done with what has recently happened. This evolutionary approach brings insight because policies have internal logics of their own—future policies are usually reactions to the defeats of past policies—that can best be appreciated from the inside.[21] In deciding whether policies are desirable, moreover, it is usually not possible to say that a problem has been solved since objectives are multiple and contradictory where they are not vague and resources including knowledge are usually insufficient. It is wiser, instead, to ask how policies of today (including the evils not yet mitigated) compare with those they superseded yesterday. A historical approach, therefore, not only conserves calculations by focusing on increments of change but also suggests the right kinds of calculations to make for purposes of evaluating public policy.

ZBB and PPB share an emphasis on the virtue of objectives. Program budgeting is about relating larger to smaller objectives among different programs, and Zero-Base Budgeting promises to do the same within a single program. The policy implications of these methods of budgeting, which distinguish them from existing approaches, derive from their overwhelming concern with having and ranking objectives. Thinking about objectives is one thing, however, and making budget categories out of them is quite another. Of course, if one wants the objectives of today to be the objectives of tomorrow, if one wants no change in objectives, then building the budget around objectives is a brilliant idea. But if one wants flexibility in objectives (sometimes known as learning from experience), it must be possible to change them without simultaneously destroying the organization by withdrawing financial support.

The traditional line-item budget is, of course, uninterested in objectives. Budgeters may have objectives, but the budget itself is organized around activities or functions—personnel, maintenance, etc. One can change objectives, then, without challenging organizational survival. Traditional budgeting does not demand analysis of policy, but neither does it inhibit it.

Every criticism of traditional budgeting is undoubtedly correct. It is incremental rather than comprehensive; it does fragment decisions; it is heavily historical and looks backward more than forward; it is indifferent to objectives; and it is concerned about the care and feeding and control of organizations, their personnel, space, maintenance, and all that. Why, then, has traditional budgeting lasted so long? Because it has the virtue of its defects.

Traditional budgeting makes calculations easy precisely because it is not comprehensive. History provides a strong base on which to rest a case. The present is made part of the past, which may be known, instead of the future, which cannot be comprehended. Choices that might cause conflict are fragmented so that not all difficulties need be faced at one time. Because it is neutral in regard to policy, traditional budgeting is compatible with a variety of policies, all of which can be converted into line items. Traditional budgeting lasts, then, because it is simpler, easier, less stressful, and more flexible than modern alternatives like ZBB and PPB.

Needless to say, traditional budgeting also has the defects of its virtues. Though budgets look back, they may not look back far enough to understand how (or why) they got where they are. Comparing this year with last year may not mean much if the past was a mistake and the future likely to be a bigger one. Quick calculation may be worse than none if it is grossly in error. Policy neutrality may degenerate into disinterest in programs. So why has traditional budgeting lasted? So far no one has come up with another budgetary procedure that has the virtues of traditional budgeting but lacks its defects.

NOTES

1. Jong S. Jun, "Management by Objectives in a Government Agency: The Case of the Social and Rehabilitation Service." Mimeographed. The Social and Rehabilitation Service, U.S. Department of Health, Education and Welfare, August 1973.
2. Werner Z. Hirsch, "Education in the Program Budget," in David Novick, ed., *Program Budgeting*, 2nd ed. (Cambridge, Mass.: Harvard University Press, 1967), p. 370.
3. George A. Steiner, "Problems in Implementing Program Budgeting," in David Novick, ed., *Program Budgeting*, p. 347.
4. Melvin Anshen, "The Program Budget in Operation," in David Novick, *Program Budgeting*, p. 365.
5. Werner Z. Hirsch, "Education in the Program Budget," in David Novick, *Program Budgeting*, p. 203.
6. Melvin Anshen, "The Program Budget in Operation," p. 370.
7. R. McKean and Melvin Anshen, "Limitations, Risks and Problems," in David Novick, *Program Budgeting*, p. 289.
8. Ibid., p. 359.
9. Paul Diesing, *Reason in Society* (Urbana, Ill., 1962), pp. 198, 203–204, 231–32.
10. Ibid., p. 228.
11. Aaron Wildavsky, "Policy Analysis Is What Information Systems Are Not," *New York Affairs,* vol. 4 (2) Spring 1977, p. 16.
12. Ibid., p. 17.
13. Allen Schick and Robert Keith, "Zero-Base Budgeting in the States," Library of Congress Congressional Research Service (August 31, 1976), p. 38.
14. Ibid., p. 14.
15. Ibid.
16. George S. Nimier and Roger H. Hermanson, "A Look at Zero-Base Budgeting—The Georgia Experience," *Atlanta Economic Review* (July-August 1976), pp. 5–12. In 1974 there was an increase in available funds and in 1975 a decrease.
17. David H. Stimson and Ruth H. Stimson, *Operations Research in Hospitals, Diagnosis and Prognosis* (Chicago, Hospital Research Trust, 1972), which evaluates several hundred analyses of hospital administration and

suggests that a good 90 percent were ignored or opposed by the sponsoring agency.

18. John Brandies, "Managing and Motivating by Objectives in Practice," *Management by Objectives*, vol. 4, 1 (1974), p. 17.
19. See Aaron Wildavsky, *The Politics of the Budgetary Process*, 2nd ed. (Boston, 1974).
20. See Aaron Wildavsky, "Policy as Its Own Cause," in *Speaking Truth to Power: The Art and Craft of Policy Analysis* (Boston, forthcoming).
21. Ibid.
22. Ibid.

A Critique of the Concept of Human Capital

H. G. SHAFFER

The treatment of currently or potentially productive human beings as capital and/or wealth has a long history in economic literature.[1] But during the first half of the twentieth century, certainly the overwhelming majority of economists, following Alfred Marshall,[2] . . . have shown a tendency to use the concept of capital as applicable only to that portion of the non-human, material, man-made stock of wealth which is utilized directly in further production.

In spite of 'majority opinion' the application of the capital concept to man has not disappeared from economic literature[3] and the past few years especially have witnessed a revival of the idea in U.S. economic journals. In the forefront of scholarly efforts in this direction stands the work of Theodore W. Schultz.[4] . . .

I shall grant unequivocally that theoretical models, incontestable from an abstract or mathematical point of view, can be built on the basis of the application of the capital concept to man. Yet, I shall contend that it is generally inadvisable to treat man as human capital.

Schultz believes that the main reason for the opposition to the human capital concept is based on a somewhat irrational fear that to accept the concept would be morally wrong and degrading to free man.[5] . . . This, however, is not the reason for my opposition. It is my contention that,

Reprinted with permission from *American Economic Review* 52, no. 5 (December 1961): 1026–35.

mainly for three reasons, economics has little to gain and much to lose by the universal application of the capital concept to man.

First, "investment in man" is essentially different from investment in nonhuman capital. The difference arises largely from the fact that, as a general rule, at least a part of any one direct expenditure for the improvement of man is not investment as the term is usually used, i.e. it is undertaken for reasons other than the expectation of a monetary return, it has not traceable effects on future output and it satisfies wants directly. To the extent to which any part of such an expenditure is investment in this sense it is rarely if ever "rational" investment based on a careful comparison of alternate investment opportunities, with the anticipated monetary return and the degree of safety as guiding rods. Furthermore, any such part is inseparable from other parts which, not being classified as investment, are then conveniently referred to as consumption expenditure.

Secondly, where it is possible to separate consumption expenditure from investment in man it would still remain a virtual impossibility to allocate a *specific* return to a *specific* investment in man (though aggregate expenditures for the improvement of man's skill, abilities, and productive capacities certainly have a positive influence of indeterminable magnitude on man's efficiency as a productive agent and, hence, on his output).

Finally, if consumption expenditure could be separated from investment in man, and if it were possible to compute the part of man's income that results from a given investment-in-man expenditure, it would in most instances still be ill-advised—from the point of view of social and economic welfare—to utilize the information thus obtained as the exclusive or even the primary basis for policy formation, public or private.[6]

I shall attempt to illustrate how these three arguments are applicable to expenditures on education. I shall then indicate briefly that the same arguments are applicable to direct expenditures on man for purposes other than his education.

I. Education: Consumption Expenditure or Investment?

Few U.S. social scientists today will argue with the basic spirit of Marshall's statement that: "There is no greater extravagance more prejudicial to the growth of national wealth than that wasteful negligence which allows genius that happens to be born of lowly parentage to expend itself in lowly work."[7] . . . But Marshall did not utilize this realization to treat expenditures for education as "investment in man" and neither should we.

Up to a certain age, public school attendance is compulsory and any private expenditures connected therewith (such as expenditures for notebooks, gym clothes, etc.) are taken out of the area of private decision making (except for whatever influence the parent may have as a voter or vote-getter). Some parents decide to incur additional expenses, beyond those required by law, for their children's education. They may send their children to "better" private schools or to parochial schools, they may provide them with private dancing or piano lessons, they may employ the services of a French governess. But such expenditures, more often than not, are at least in part consumption expenditures as far as both the economic motivation of the investor and the economic effects on the individual and on society are concerned. Due to the inseparability of the consumption and the investment part of such expenditures (and for other reasons discussed below) the return on any incremental expenditure to either the individual or society is not computable.

When we turn from legally required minimum education to voluntary private expenditures for education at the high school and the college level, it still seems quite impossible to explain human behavior in terms of capital investment (as we have been using the term). Many a parent who would not think of spending thousands of dollars to establish his son in business or who would at least require a partnership in such a business, does not hesitate to spend an equal amount on his son's education without expecting any monetary return for himself (and with higher anticipated life income for his son often at best one of several motivating factors). The young college student who finances his own education will probably enroll in many courses and read many books that would bear only a remote relation, if any, to future expected or realized income. Although some of these may be required for graduation and therefore may be of indirect economic value, it is in all probability still a fair evaluation of human motivation that "the prospects of achieving more subtle satisfactions from mastering a higher education are more compelling to many people than the prospects of greater financial success."[8] . . . Any attempt to show that rational individuals tend to undertake expenditure on education up to the point where the marginal productivity of the human capital produced by the process of education equals the rate of interest—a point at which the marginal expenditure on education yields a return equal to the return on marginal expenditure for any other factor of production—would be a mockery of economic theory.

At best, we can go along with Schultz's contention that ". . . *some* individuals and families make decisions to invest in *some* kinds of education, either in themselves or in their children, with an eye to the earnings that they expect to see forthcoming from such expenditures on education."[9] And Schultz has to admit that in the case of expenditures on human beings, those for consumption and those for the purpose of increasing income are quite interwoven, "which is why the task of identifying each component is so formidable and why the measurement of capital formation by expenditures is less useful for human investment than for investment in physical goods."[10] . . . He therefore proposes yield (measured in increased earnings) as an alternate method for estimating human investment.

II. Education and Income

Studies showing a close correlation between schooling (measured in numbers of years of attendance and/or type of school attended) and success (measured in terms of social position and/or annual or life earnings) antedate the turn of the century.[11] "Some recent studies attempt to measure the financial return to 'investment' in education. The value of a college education in the late 1950s, for instance, has been estimated anywhere from $100,000 to almost $180,000.[12] . . . However, the present value of a lifetime income differential of nearly $106,000 between a high school and a college graduate amounts to a mere $3,305 when figured after taxes and when discounted at 8 percent[13] . . . —not an unreasonable rate of discount if one considers the risk involved in "investing" in a college education.

To obtain valid figures for lifetime incomes (on the basis of present actuarial tables), to correlate such figures with years of schooling, to compute the cost of such schooling in terms of private expenditures, public expenditures, and opportunity costs (*without* any attempt to segregate "consumption" from "investment in education" expenditures), to compute the rate of discount which will equate the expenditures with lifetime income differentials, and, finally, to compare this rate with the rate of return on investment in nonhuman capital—all these do not present insurmountable difficulties. But to establish a cause–effect relationship, to prove, in other words, that the income differential is the result of the additional education is quite a different matter. To do so, one would have to assume that the more educated individual does not differ from the less educated in any characteristic (other than education) that could explain part or all of the income differential. Such an assumption would be highly unrealistic as it is evident that there is a close correlation between intelligence and years of schooling (especially at the higher levels). There are also good indications of at least some correlation between the financial standing of parents and the years of schooling of their children. Finally, there is the possibility, if not the strong probability, that other factors such as connections, residence (urban *vs* rural, North *vs* South, etc.), occupational and cultural level of parents, health, etc., have some influence on years of school attendance. And surely all these factors have a direct bearing on income, independent of years of preparation.

In the early forties, Elbridge Sibley studied the case records of 2,158 Pennsylvania students and discovered that, at the below-college level, intelligence had a greater influence on years of education than parental status. However, as to the probability of spending at least one year in an institution of higher learning, "while the most intelligent boys have only a 4 to 1 advantage over the least intelligent, the sons of men in the highest occupational category enjoy an advantage of more than 10 to 1 over those from the lowest occupational level."[14] . . . In his study of the relationship between income (annual and lifetime) and education from the years 1939–59, Herman P. Miller noted that at least part of the higher income of those with more education could probably be accounted for by differences in intelligence, home environment, family connections and other factors.[15] . . . D. S. Bridgman points to evidence that "unearned" (property) income of college graduates is higher than that of noncollege-trained individuals and he expresses the view that factors such as ability and property income have been given insufficient recognition in the past as causal agents of higher income of the more educated.[16] . . .

In 1958, Jacob Mincer constructed a model to account for personal income distribution in terms of differential "investment" in education.[17] . . . He started out with many admittedly oversimplified assumptions, one of which was the assumption of identical abilities. But when he relaxed this unrealistic assumption, the plausibility of a positive correlation between ability traits and amount of education (with the obvious effect on income distribution) became apparent.[18] . . . To this he added that "when incomes rather than earnings are considered, the positive association of property incomes with occupational level . . . magnifies income differences" (thus accentuating whatever effects the training factor *per se* might have).[19] . . . Therefore, he could not and did not claim that a quantitative estimate of the effect of training on personal income distribution could be derived using his model.

J. R. Walsh, in his early (1935) study of the applicability of the capital concept to man explained that in order to isolate the effect of education he would have to eliminate all other influences (such as ability, age, occupation, health, etc.) but that he had attempted no such elimination as he considered it impossible.[20] . . . Indeed, it is so completely impossible to eliminate all other influences[21] that one has to agree with Houthakker that ". . . we cannot even be sure that the apparent effect of education on income is not completely explicable in terms of intelligence and parents' income, so that the *specific* effect of education would be zero or even negative."[22] . . .

There is another factor that enhances the difficulty of determining the return on "investment in education." This factor I shall call "maintenance costs."

Certainly, whenever the financial return on any investment in nonhuman capital is computed, maintenance costs of the capital good are considered. But, to the best of my knowledge, such maintenance costs have been utterly neglected in the case of human capital by all economists who have advocated the application of the capital concept to man. These maintenance costs first arise during the investment period. The tuxedo, the evening dress, the more frequent haircuts may not be absolutely necessary for the increase in subsequent earning capacity but they are *de facto* expenses connected with higher education (and they might be indirectly necessary for the intended investment goals lest the anxiety and the loss of tranquility caused by their absence interfere with scholastic accomplishments). But maintenance costs by no means end with the completion of the investment period. A part of these continuous maintenance costs (such as the more expensive car, the more luxuriously dressed wife, and the more lavishly furnished home of the "organization man," or the more frequently washed shirt and the more frequently dry-cleaned suit of the white collar worker) are almost unavoidably connected with the retention of the position which yields the higher income to the more educated.

Another part of these maintenance costs, perhaps less compulsive but still widely prevalent, relates to increased qualitative (and to some extent also quantitative) consumption demands resulting from higher education, higher income, or both.[23] To the extent to which increased consumption expenditure results from increased income *per se* (which it will whenever the marginal propensity to consume is more than zero) it is independent of the case of the increase in income. To the extent, however, to which increased consumption expenditure results from the educational development of greater cultural, aesthetic, and discriminating tastes (which is not a separable part but rather a result of the aggregate education process), it reflects an increased expenditure directly and uniquely attributable to the specific type of investment (in education).[24] In time, these education-created expenditures will probably tend to become essential for the former student's efficient performance as a producer and, thus, part of the maintenance costs of the education-created human capital.[25]

III. Public Policy in Relation to Expenditure on Education

At present, the investment-in-human-capital concept appears to be gaining in favor among "liberals" who apparently intend to utilize it as a rationalization of federal aid to education (and, secondarily, other government investment-in-man expenditures). Walter Heller, Chairman of the Council of Economic Advisers to the President, for instance, refers to the human mind as America's greatest resource and points to the "vast implications for public policy" embodied in the development of the investment-in-human-capital concept.[26] . . . But nothing is more dangerous to the very position of the liberals, I fear, than to attempt to defend government expenditures for education as a type of collective business investment which will yield economic returns attractive to the investing society in term of maximum increase in GNP over and above costs. To cite just one example of the untenable position to which such argumentation could lead: Schultz sees a direct correlation between the lower incomes of Negroes in the United States (as compared with whites) and their relatively lower productivity resulting from inadequate educational preparation.[27] . . . and he considers an 'investment' in their education as financially sound. But more specific studies clearly show that due to greater vocational opportunities, the income differential correlated with additional education is considerably higher for whites than for Negroes.[28] Were we to agree that the government should treat expenditures for education as investment, could not a good case be made for the decrease, if not the discontinuation, of governmental subsidization of nonwhite students and a consequently higher subsidization of the financially more remunerative white students?

By the same token, should society discourage advanced studies by women unless they can give some reasonable assurance that their "human capital" will be used even after they are married? Or should we—COULD WE???—compute the indirect, long-range value of such women to society in terms of increased future productivity of their children whom they would perhaps rear more efficiently? The education of many young men and women who choose to prepare themselves for professions which they expect will yield them comparatively low monetary but comparatively high psychic incomes (such as teaching) might be of great value to society. But if we were to take return on investment as the guiding rod, how would we proceed? A teacher's *immediate, direct* contribution to GNP (equal to his gross income) would not be a true reflection of his value to society, and his *indirect, long-run* effect (expressed in terms of his influence on the income of others) is not measurable. Marshall proclaimed that: "All that is spent during many years in opening the means of higher education to the masses would be well paid for if it called out one more Newton or Darwin, Shakespeare or Beethoven."[29] . . . Was Marshall wrong? I do not think he was. Yet, how would one obtain empirical evidence that such investment would be "well paid for?" How would one go about computing a significance rate of return on such an investment?

Indeed the advocate of more governmental aid to education who attempts to defend his proposal exclusively on an "it's sound investment policy" basis stands on shaky ground, for he would logically have to advise expenditures on education up to the point where the marginal productivity of the human capital created equaled the marginal productivity of other nonhuman capital, as well as the rate of interest. And what would this advocate of more government aid to education do if he were confronted with a study such as Becker's which reaches the conclusion that ". . . it would appear that direct returns alone cannot justify a large increase in expenditures on college education relative to expenditures on business capital?"[30] . . . He could find support in arguments such as Schultz's that Becker failed to take into consideration that a part of the expenditure on education is always for education as a pure consumer's good, that Becker therefore underestimated the return on investment in education, and that it is reasonable to assume that there has been underinvestment in education.[31] . . . But, on the other hand, our advocate of more government aid to education might also have to cope with the argument that Becker, perhaps, overestimated the return on investment in education, as no allowance was made in Becker's study for such parts of total returns as may have been attributable to factors other than education (as discussed in section II above) or offset by increased "maintenance costs." And once the advocate of increased government aid to education reaches the conclusion that it is impossible to compute a scientifically unassailable rate of return for such investment, he loses even his theoretical basis for *any* government "investment" in education, forcing him once more to utilize arguments other than "it's sound investment policy" to defend his proposals.

IV. Expenditures on Human Beings Other Than for Education

For essentially the same reasons as presented in sections I and II above, it seems for most purposes impractical, inconvenient, and of relatively little use to attempt the explanation of direct expenditures on man, other than for his education, in terms of investment in human capital concept. And for essentially the same reasons as presented in section III above, it seems ill-advised to base governmental policy on such a concept.

Whether we deal with outlays on food, improved medical care, housing, recreational facilities, or other "investments in man," we once again are faced with the impossibility of separating consumption from investment in any of those areas and with the impossibility of computing scientifically valid marginal returns on any of these expenditures. And once again it might prove detrimental to the best interests of society (measured in terms other than aggregate economic returns on investment) to have governmental policy determined (or even substantially influenced) by an investor's point of view. Governmental programs, for instance, providing for medical care or financial assistance to individuals beyond the retirement age (individuals thus fully depreciated as human capital) would be difficult to defend from the point of view of profitable investment *per se* (except, perhaps, in terms of the greater tranquility and therefore productivity of those still serviceable as human capital); and slum clearance projects might be considered poor investments as compared with the improvement of golf courses that would aid in steadying the nerves of more productive human capital.

V. Conclusions

Whether productive human beings should be treated as capital and whether some direct expenditures intended for or resulting in an increase in their productive capacities should be treated as investment in human capital are not questions of principle. There is no "right" or "wrong" way, because what constitutes *capital* and what constitutes *investment* is a matter of definition. Should one decide to include under "investment in human capital" everything that tends to increase man's productivity, the overwhelming part of all expenditures to which we usually refer as consumption expenditures would have to be considered investments. A substantial part of all expenditures for food, shelter, and clothing, many expenditures for recreation, entertainment, and travel, and even some expenditures for mere conveniences and luxuries would certainly need to be reclassified as investments to the extent to which they contribute, directly or indirectly, to the enhancement of a person's productivity.

While it is undeniable that the sum total of countless sensible expenditures on man (including expenditures for his education, health, proper nourishment, etc.) will tend, on the average, to have a beneficial impact upon his productivity, present and future, each of these expenditures individually and all of them in the aggregate consist of inseparable and indistinguishable parts of consumption and investment expenditures. The spender's motivation is essentially different from that of the investor in nonhuman capital. The return on the investment cannot be computed satisfactorily as both the amount of pure 'investment' and the return to be allocated thereto are conjectural. And in society's allocation of productive resources for the advancement of economic and noneconomic welfare, the question of the financial wisdom of any direct expenditure on man must be reduced to one of secondary importance. We have come to accept as axioms that health is preferable to illness, knowledge preferable to ignorance, freedom (whatever the term may mean) preferable to slavery, peace preferable to war, etc. Governmental expenditures directed towards the realization of these preferences bear no necessary relation to their economic profitability as investments.

This paper's opposition to the application of the capital concept to man, then, is not based on any argument that such application is "wrong" but only that, more often than not, it would confuse more than elucidate, it would create more problems than it would solve, and—as a basis for public policy—it would be of questionable value.

NOTES

1. Sir William Petty, "Political Arithmetic," in Charles Henry Hull, ed., *The Economic Writings of Sir William Petty*, vol. 1 (Cambridge, 1899), pp. 233–313; Adam Smith, *The Wealth of Nations* (New York, 1937), pp. 265–66; Irving Fisher, *The Theory of Interest* (New York: 1930), p. 13; Irving Fisher, *The Nature of Capital and Income* (New York, 1906), p. 65.

2. Alfred Marshall, *Principles of Economics*, 8th ed. (London, 1946).

3. J. R. Walsh, "Capital Concept Applied to Man" *Quarterly Journal of Economics*, vol. 49 (1935), pp. 255–85. A short bibliography of articles in British, German, French, and Italian journals during the first three decades of the twentieth century.

4. Theodore W. Schultz, "Capital Formation by Education," *Journal of Political Economy*, vol. 68 (1960), pp. 571–83; Theodore W. Schultz, "Education and Economic Growth," in H. G. Richey, ed., *Social Forces Influencing American Education* (Chicago, 1961); Theodore W. Schultz, "Human Capital: A Growing Asset," *Saturday Review*, January 21, 1961, pp. 37–39; Theodore W. Schultz, "Investment in Human Capital," *American Economic Review*, vol. 51 (1961), pp. 1–17; Theodore W. Schultz, "Investment in Man: An Economist's View," *Social Service Review*, vol. 33 (1959), pp. 109–17.

5. Schultz, "Capital Formation by Education," p. 572; Schultz, "Investment in Human Capital," p. 2; Schultz, "Investment in Human Capital," p. 2; Schultz, "Investment in Man," p. 110.

6. Joan Robinson sees the main difference between investment in acquiring earning power and investment in income-yielding property in the fact that in a capitalist society the earning power is not a salable commodity in the sense in which the income-yielding property is—a point not stressed in this paper. From this, she reaches the conclusion that "the present capital value of future personal earnings has a metaphorical, not an actual financial meaning." While this seems a valid comment, her view that "from the point of view of the economy as a whole, the similarity is more impor-

tant than the difference" is one contested in this paper. Joan Robinson, *The Accumulation of Capital* (Homewood, Ill., 1956).

7. Alfred Marshall, *Principles of Economics,* 8th ed. (London, 1946).
8. P. C. Glick and H. P. Miller, "Educational Level and Potential Income," *American Sociological Review,* vol. 21 (1956), pp. 307–12.
9. Schultz, "Capital Formation by Education," pp. 572–73. Emphasis mine.
10. Schultz, "Investment in Human Capital," p. 8.
11. See Ellis A. Caswell, "The Money Value of Education," *Bureau of Education, Bulletin,* no. 22 (1917). Washington, D.C.: U.S. Dept. of the Interior, for a discussion of many of these early studies and a bibliography of more than 125 books and journal articles on the subject published between 1898 and 1917.
12. D. S. Bridgman, "Problems in Estimating the Monetary Value of College Education," *Review of Economic Statistics,* Supplement, vol. 42 (1960), pp. 180–84; H. S. Houthakker, "Education and Income," *Review of Economic Statistics,* vol. 41 (1959), pp. 24–28; H. P. Miller, "Annual and Lifetime Income in Relation to Education: 1939–1959," *American Economic Review,* vol. 50 (1960), pp. 962–86.
13. H. S. Houthakker, "Education and Income," p. 28.
14. Elbridge Sibley, "Some Demographic Clues to Stratification," *American Sociological Review,* vol. 7 (1942), pp. 322–30. Sibley's study was published in 1942. Since then (in the United States, at least) increased numbers of scholarships and public subsidization of education have certainly diminished the dependence of schooling on parental status.
15. Miller, "Annual and Lifetime Earnings in Relation to Education," p. 964; P. C. Glick and H. P. Miller, "Educational Level and Potential Income," *American Sociological Review,* vol. 21 (1956), pp. 307–12.
16. Bridgman, "Problems in Estimating the Monetary Value of College Education."
17. Jacob Mincer, "Investment in Human Capital and Personal Distribution of Income," *Journal of Political Economy,* vol. 66 (1958), pp. 281–302.
18. Mincer, "Investment in Human Capital," p. 286.
19. Ibid., p. 302.
20. J. R. Walsh, "Capital Concept Applied to Man," *Quarterly Journal of Economics,* vol. 49 (1935), pp. 255–85.
21. Theoretically it would not be necessary to eliminate all other influences as partial (or multiple) correlation methods could be employed to allow for the effects of some other variables. However, amount of education is at least partly a matter of personal choice. As long as this is true, no matter how many factors have been considered, one can never be certain that there are not some unanalyzed variables influencing this choice which in themselves are responsible for the income differential attributed to education.
22. Houthakker, "Education and Income," p. 28.
23. Other causes of increased consumption, if any, are disregarded as irrelevant to the main argument.

24. That there is *some* education-created increase in consumption (and not just substitution of one kind of consumption for another) appears evident from observation.
25. Schultz does not count such education-created consumption expenditures as maintenance costs. On the contrary, while acknowledging their existence, he suggests that the part of the cost of education that induces them be classified as consumption expenditure. By so decreasing the cost base for investment in education Schultz arrives at a higher rate of return on the investment than he would otherwise. Schultz, "Investment in Human Capital," pp. 12–13.
26. *Time Magazine*, March 1961, p. 22.
27. Schultz, "Investment in Human Capital," pp. 3–4; Schultz, "Investment in Man," p. 109.
28. In 1949, for instance, the difference in income between nonwhite college graduates and nonwhite males with one to three years in college (for the 45–54-year age group) was about $500 for the year while the corresponding differential for white males was about twice as great. Glick and Miller, "Educational Level and Potential Income," p. 309.
29. Marshall, *Principles of Economics*, p. 216.
30. G. S. Becker, "Underinvestment in College Education," *American Economic Review*, Proceedings, vol. 50 (1960), pp. 346–54.
31. Schultz, "Investment in Human Capital," p. 15.

---

21. Organizational Environments and Their Effects

Inside and Beyond Demystifying Organizations

CHARLES PERROW

It is a mystery why the many advances in organizational theory have not had an appreciable impact upon health service organizations. Wave on wave of sophisticated theory, from human relations techniques to the latest in contingency theory have been applied, proved to have a small effect in research studies, and virtually no effect in actual usage. They all *should*

Excerpted from Rosemary Sarri and Yeheskel Hasenfeld, eds., *The Management of Human Services* (New York: Columbia University Press, 1978), ch. 5. Reprinted with the permission of the publisher.

work, if we know anything at all about human behavior organizations. But none seem to work well. Why?

It seems possible that an extreme answer is worth pursuing—our theories are mystifications of reality and need to be demystified. The theories are mystifications because they are designed to disguise what I will claim are the real functions of organizations and to assert a counter reality. The reality being asserted in mainstream theory is that organizations are, or can be, rational instruments of announced goals. Of course some mainstream theories such as systems[1] and human relations theories oppose a mechanical, rationalistic notion of organizations when they stress natural adaptations, human needs, informal groups, and so on. But these natural characteristics are perceived as constraints on the organization, as problems to be overcome, or opportunities to be utilized in making the organization more effective (rational) in achieving its legitimate, announced goals. The hospital should cure, the training program train, the prison reform, the welfare program help people to become independent. Deviations from these goals are due to such things as poor motivation, faulty communications, misperceived goals, poor coordination, inadequate resources, poor management, or faulty structures, according to most theories.

No doubt these play a role. But an alternative position is worth exploring: announced goals are one of the least important constraints on organizational behavior; organizations can be rational instruments of announced goals only to a very limited extent. They have more important things to do. Instead, organizations are resources for a variety of group interests within and without the organization; they are used by a multitude of interests, and the announced purposes, while they must be met to some limited degree in most cases, largely serve as legitimating device for these interests, or a mystification of the reality.

There is nothing novel in the view that organizations serve many functions; what may be novel is to take this view so seriously as to put it at the center of our theory, rather than leave it as a peripheral routine observation or qualifier while we vigorously explore the impact of technology on structure or leadership on productivity. To expose these uses and the low priority of legitimate goals is a part of the demystifying process. To stop there would merely be sophisticated muckraking. To complete the demystifying process means to present an alternative definition of organizations and explain how well-meaning people and institutions participate in the fiction of intended rationality in the service of official goals. . . .

The implication of this view that I wish to draw out is not that society is mean or capitalism exploitative, or that organizations are poorly functioning and their goals are displaced. All that may be true. But the important point for organizational theory is that it is on the basis of the regulatory functions that organizations are judged, not their announced service goals. Wardens are not fired for not rehabilitating prisoners; psychiatric administrators or therapists for not curing the insane; welfare administrators for not getting people to work or mending broken homes or raising their allotments. The criteria is more likely to be "how many people did you regulate at what cost per person." The effective administrator knows that failure to meet announced goals will not mean his or her demise, and certainly not the demise of the organization. But failure to control, buy off, or segregate his or her charges will bring trouble. Furthermore, the administrator knows that announced goals are hard to achieve, because of poor technologies, poor organizational structure, inadequate training facilities, low quality employees, inadequate budgets, or recalcitrant charges. Therefore, it is not worth much effort to attempt to achieve them; no one really expects much. He or she will be interested in improvements that make life easier or more predictable for the staff, or that increase the degree of regulation, if that is called for. But the announced service goals are primarily legitimating devices for regulation and serve their purpose even if unmet.

A second function of HSOs [Human Service Organizations] is to absorb a part of the work force of the nation. It is not a function that organizational theory recognizes and takes into account, although certainly it is on the minds of politicians and government officials at all levels. It is quite clear that the private sector of business and industry cannot absorb the daily increases in those seeking employment; all firms prefer to maximize capital and minimize labor, and our tax laws favor that. Thus, the public sector has been forced to grow rapidly to absorb the worthy job seekers. Presumably, at some time there will be what James O'Conner (1973) calls the fiscal crisis of the state that will force elites to confront this inherent dilemma of advanced capitalism.[2] The growing role of for-profit firms in the public sector (the "welfare-industrial complex") will ease the crisis somewhat, but the public sector must continue to grow. To do this, we need public facilities that employ a lot of people. Using public funds, we train large numbers of people to be clerks, social workers, psychiatrists, judges, hospital administrators, and so on.

The emerging field of organization-environment relations is silent on this function, but one example should indicate its importance. It would be a disaster for New York City if the public welfare department found some social scientist who could simplify and reorganize that mess so that half of the twenty to thirty thousand employees could be laid off. Large amounts of federal and state funds would be lost, the retail economy would suffer, and large numbers of generally vocal and politically mobilizable people would be protesting the lack of jobs. It would be as if the Man in the White

Suit, having invented an indestructible garment, sought the capital to produce the garment from cotton growers, textile firms, and retail clothing stores. Inefficient public organizations have always been a part of a continuing war on poverty and will continue to be so. Current proposals to subsidize labor intensive firms in the private sector to discourage the substitution of capital for labor indicates how severe the problem is.

A third function of HSOs that is not placed at the center of organizational theories is the most important: to provide resources for other organizations. These resources are provided at the public expense but are not calculated as such in the balance sheets. They also have the advantage of being easily accessed, have little accountability in their use, and much flexibility to meet changing situations. Lloyd Ohlin (1960) drew attention to this some years ago in a piece about the environment of HSOs.[3] In one example, he described the attempt of an economy-minded executive to close down a quarry that was losing money for the prison. But the quarry, worked by the prison, provided free construction materials for private firms in the area, and so it was kept. The example could be multiplied a thousand times. The Mafia is reportedly well into the New York school system, which purchases hundreds of millions each year in supplies and contracted services and has been under no realistic constraint to save money; the hospital equipment industry and supply industry, not to speak of the drug companies, could not survive without extravagant waste, duplication, and inefficiency in hospitals; land holders and real estate firms have enjoyed considerable largess through New York City's poverty programs and day care centers with twenty-year leases at several times the market value; the political system evades civil service regulations to staff HSOs, and sometimes extracts kickbacks and campaign contributions; a substantial number of legitimate organizations benefit from police corruption and inefficiency; private employees found the agencies serving the handicapped a convenient reservoir that they could dip into in time of labor shortages and then could discharge the handicapped back to the agencies in times of labor surplus, thus smoothing production and retaining their normal workers; job training programs proved to be a bonanza to private employers, the more so the more inefficient the programs were, and so on and on. I recommend this as a central topic for those studying interorganizational relations. To my knowledge, it has not been accorded more than a footnote in the major statements.

The message here is not that private business, politicians, and so on are corrupt and indifferent to the needs of the poor and the stigmatized, or that agency executives should have more guts. As true as that might be, it tells us little about organizations. What these examples do tell us about public organizations is that they must be viewed as resources for other groups,

groups with more well organized and powerful members or constituencies. If this view is moved to the center of organizational theory, rather than being a footnote offering some unknown degree of qualification to all that follows in the study, then variations in efficiency or official goal achievement can be moved to the periphery. The footnote would then read: "Of course there are some variations in performance depending upon leadership techniques, the fit between technology and structure, innovations in technologies, number of shared programs or telephone contacts between organizations, and so on. But these are quite minor and we need not spend much time studying them. The way the organization is used by other interests is much more important for understanding internal efficiency or organizational networks." . . .

But on the other hand, one might reply, these organizations do cure the ill, succor the disturbed, deter the criminal, and sometimes make life somewhat easier for the poor, the retarded, and the maimed. Of course they do. It is one of their many outputs. It is a constraint upon the use of these organizations by other organizations that these public-regarding service goals cannot be completely neglected. But it is also a constraint upon the service goals of HSOs that outside interests can't be neglected. I think the conventional phrase, multiple goals, does not capture this reality at all. I prefer the phrase multiple usages, and I would stress the adjective "multiple." There are many more usages than conventional theory will admit. Each group's usage is a constraint on each other group; in such a situation, power—group power—is likely to play an important role. Organizational theory is shy of the word power, preferring to mystify it by calling it authority, but it should be one of the key words in the perspective I am trying to develop.

The Internal Uses

. . . In all this, then, the usual functions of the executive that we find in organization texts, management programs, social work schools, and so on, loom rather small. It does not take a great deal of "organizational skill," in the sense of ability to plan ahead, formulate goals, make wise decisions on technical matters, summon the energies of the staff, and so on to be a successful executive. Perhaps you have noticed that many of them do not seem to be too bright, or energetic, or dynamic, or considerate. But it does take consummate political skills in extracting resources from a sometimes stingy environment, delivering goods to interested parties without having scandals, and meeting at a minimal level—the going rate for the locality— the official goals of the agency. But even this is too rationalistic a view; later

I will argue that much of this success is due to sheer luck and accident.

Turning now to managers and workers in the organization, mainstream theory tells us they must be motivated, informed of the goals, shown their part in the process, properly trained, rewarded, and punished. Our surveys test their understanding or commitment to the goals of the organization.

Were we to take seriously some of the marginal or incidental observations about employees, we might have a survey that would ask: the extent to which they support their superiors in covering up scandals, conform to political directives, service suppliers and others that make use of the organization, falsify records in subtle ways, and generally behave as loyal vassals of the executive irrespective of official directives or goals. We should also ask, not "how is your morale," or how satisfied are you with professional advancement opportunities, but can you minimize the personal costs of working in this place; can you manage to make the work fairly light; can you avoid unpleasant duties or clients; can you find time for relaxing conversation with friendly co-workers; can you exercise some of the skills or knowledge you laboriously picked up so as to make it seem worthwhile and give you some sense of control over your work; can you daydream and withdraw if you feel like it; can you manage to pick up office supplies or food from the kitchen or pieces of furniture for your own use; does the organization provide good cheap lunch facilities, recreation center, a retirement plan, credit union, counseling services, and so on? Can you get your friend or relative a job here? Most important of all, can you be sure of having a job here as long as you need it?

Such an "employee committment," "employee motivation," "participation scale," or whatever would be unthinkable in the normal survey. As I have noted elsewhere, high morale means that people find it gratifying to do what the organization wants them to do, not what they want to do (Perrow, 1977).[4] But there are enough good ethnographic accounts of organizations, to suggest that the goals of the organization, or efficiency, effectiveness, universalism, and so on are not what is on the workers mind. Or the minds of most managers. Why do we not have such a scale? Because, despite our asides, we not take seriously the notion that employees too use the organization. We assume they are a part of it, or are it, and therefore, if organizations have goals, they must share them. If they don't, it is a pathology and should be corrected. But it is not a pathology. It is a fundamental characteristic of organizations that employees too use them for their own ends. Why should they act differently from other groups?

Of course, executives, and superiors in general, do a great deal either to minimize this usage or to find some way to make sure that the ends of the employees and their own ends coincide. There may not be a great deal of conflict if we recall that executives are not particularly weighted down by a commitment to the official goals, so common ground can be found wherein employee comfort and security is not too inconsistent with survival and a little growth. Where there is conflict between the uses to which the employees wish to put the organization and those the executive wishes— and there will be some—the executive does his best to manipulate, threaten, and punish. She or he can manipulate more effectively than she or he can punish or threaten. Civil service regulations (and political patron- age positions where there is no effective civil service) effectively remove the threat of dismissal for cause. The lack of power the executive has over the daily running of the organization, of which we will speak shortly, makes threats of poorer jobs, harder work, no raises, no promotions, and so on fairly ineffective. Anger—direct, personal anger and hostility—is the best she or he can do, and while it works for a while, as with one's children, it invites retaliation and loses its effect after a time. . . .

But if all actors are powerful, what happens to notions of "they"—the elites, executives, or of power in organizations, and so on? The answer seems to be that elites simply have more resources and thus more power than others. But they are to a large extent also victims of the world they and others have created and are unable to achieve even a moderate degree of effectiveness in realizing their goals. They have an edge and are more effective than nonelites, but it gives them considerable trouble to get their way, even in part. In a complex, postindustrial society, that may be all that is allowed them. Furthermore, the nonelites, and especially the working class and the poor and the minorities, are no better and a bit worse at establishing what their own priorities should be, formulating their own goals, and realizing their own inherent powers in the system. Much of what they get may come as a result of accident. They too are subject to random events, unpredictable collisions of poorly articulated subsystems, only more so than the elites.

Thus, in this view, we should expect little out of our Human Service Organizations. In a society of organizations, they are part of the resources of other organizations, of elites, and of employees, and the complexity, uncertainty, and ambiguity of all organizations are visited on them at least at full measure. Only minimal functioning, in terms of our extravagant expectations, is to be expected. As users, we are all prone to ask all organizations to be more goal oriented (to our own goals), efficient (for us, in terms of the resources we put in) and rational (in terms of our own interests only) than they can ever be. Thus, organizational reform is transitory even if not misdirected. The State Department, Warwick (1975) tells us, eliminated several "superfluous" levels and specialized units and decentralized; a few years later all the levels and units had mysteriously appeared again. He notes that the bureaucrats need bureaus, even as they inveigh against bureaucracy.[5]

The executive who finds social science theory unrealistic is correct. Explaining a tiring day to his wife or his sociologist, he stresses the enormous complexity and unpredictability of his organization, its unique-ness, the role of individual peculiarities, its ability to exasperate and veer off in unpredictable directions, and he is correct in his own constructed world. We press him and he offers to us explanations we consider simplis-tic—people are like that; individuals make a big difference; leadership counts, or dedication, hard work, intelligence, or loyalty, or whatever. We find these things elusive or impossible to measure, or commonplace, and offer him alternative concepts we have taken decades to formulate. We test them, constructing measures which are largely self-confirming, predicting relationships that are nearly tautological (group cohesiveness is associated with value homopholy, for example), and still find that when we move beyond a small sample that the variance our loaded dice explains is still only 20 percent. Worse still, we are gratified by this result, even though our conclusions are largely irrelevant to the executive. (Perhaps it is well that we do not work for the worker or the poor; our conclusions would be even worse for them.) We have constructed our own social reality, and are wounded when men of practical affairs don't recognize it, and won't use it. They are correct not to use it. We are just one other group trying to use a multi-use collectivity, getting paid to do so, and building our careers on it.

Is all this a counsel of despair? It certainly is in terms of our usual expectations as citizens, and certainly in view of our advertisements for ourselves as craftsmen and our use of public funds for research and con-sultation. But suppose we took the periphery seriously and placed it at the center. We then would ask, not why nothing works, but why anything works. Why have the elites not walked away with everything, instead of just a good deal more than the nonelites? Why do people in institutions get any care at all? Why do we have public-regarding foundations? Why don't we just shoot juvenile offenders instead of allowing them to live so that most of them will become adult nonoffenders? True, the poor suffer more from juveniles when they are offending than the rich suffer, but they are still of some inconvenience to the rich. Why do we have retirement programs, dental plans, fair employment laws, and so on?

We might, in discovering the answers to these questions, discover a capacity for constructing social structures that we have taken for granted, and thus little explored. As we did make that discovery, we could explore that capacity more and think of ways to increase it manyfold. What is problematic for mainstream theory is the best way of organizing to meet official goals—what kind of leadership, structure, communication, training, and so on. If we took for granted that official goals were not that important, only one constraint among many, and a weak one at that, and that the organizational variables should be seen as constructions to mask what was really going on, then we might better find out why anything at all is achieved. As we do that, we are free from our own constructions, and can ask "how might it otherwise be done?"

I can't even phrase that last question well enough to direct my inquiry as yet. It will take me a long time to get out of the box I have so willingly let myself into and worked so long in trying to tidy up. If many of us tried to redirect our inquiry, we might really have a paradigm shift in organizational theory.

NOTES

1. [The term system is used somewhat differently here from its use in systems approaches to planning and administration. In organizational theory, the systems view treats organizations as dynamic, coping entities, whereas the goal-oriented view takes the organization as an instrument of rational action.—Editor's note]
2. James O'Conner, *The Fiscal Crises of the State* (New York: St. Martin's Press, 1973).
3. Lloyd Ohlin, "Conflict in Interests in Correctional Objectives." In R. Cloward et al., eds., *Theoretical Studies in the Social Organization of Prison* (New York: Social Science Research Council, 1960), pp. 111–29.
4. Charles Perrow, "Three Types of Effectiveness Studies." In Paul S. Goodman, Johannes M. Pennings, and Associates, *New Perspectives on Organizational Effectiveness* (San Francisco: Jossey-Bass, 1977), pp. 96–105.
5. Donald P. Warwick, *A Theory of Public Bureaucracy* (Cambridge, Mass.: Harvard University Press, 1975).

The Assault on Human Services: Street-Level Bureaucrats, Accountability, and the Fiscal Crisis

MICHAEL LIPSKY

This chapter examines the current application of administrative measures to secure accountability among lower level workers in certain public agencies. I argue that bureaucratic accountability is virtually impossible to achieve among lower level workers who exercise high degrees of discretion, at least where qualitative aspects of the work are involved. Nonetheless, public managers are pressured to secure or improve workers' accountability through manipulation of incentives and other aspects of job structure immediately available to them. When considered along with other objectives public managers seek, the result is not simply ineffectiveness but an erosion of the foundations of service quality.

People are accountable when there is a high probability that they will be responsive to legitimate authority or influence. This definition of accountability directs attention to two important aspects of the concept. First, accountability is a relationship between people or groups. One is always accountable *to* someone (or groups), never in the abstract. Although the term is sometimes used loosely confusion results unless we specify both parties in the accountability relationship.[1] . . .

Accountability to Clients

The essence of street-level bureaucracies is that they require people to make decisions about other people. Street-level bureaucrats have discretion because the nature of service-provision calls for human judgment

Reprinted from *Accountability in Urban Society: Public Agencies Under Fire* (Urban Affairs Annual Review, vol. 15), Scott Greer, Ronald Hedlund and James L. Gibson, editors, copyright © 1978, pp. 15–38 by permission of the publisher, Sage Publications, Inc. (Beverly Hills/London). The author's notes have been omitted, and the notes at the end of the reading are textual citations. Ed.

which cannot be programmed and for which machines cannot substitute. Street-level bureaucrats have responsibility for making unique and fully appropriate responses to individual clients and their situations. It is the nature of what we call human services that the unique aspects of people and their situations will be apprehended by public service workers and translated into courses of action responsive to each case, within (more or less broad) limits imposed by their agencies. They will not, in fact, dispose of every case in unique fashion. The limitations on possible responses are often circumscribed, for example, by the prevailing statutory provisions of the law, or the categories of welfare services to which recipients can be assigned. However, street-level bureaucrats still have the responsibility *at least to be open to the possibility* that each client presents special circumstances and opportunities which may require fresh thinking and flexible action.

If this is the case, street-level bureaucrats must irreducibly be accountable to the client and for an appropriate response to the client's situation and circumstances. These cannot sensibly be translated into authoritative agency guidelines. It is a contradiction in terms to say that the worker should be accountable to an agency to respond to each client in unique fashion appropriate to the presenting case. For no accountability can exist if the agency does not know what response it prefers, and it cannot assert a preferred response if each worker should be open to the possibility that unique and fresh responses are appropriate. It is more useful to suggest that street-level bureaucrats are ordinarily expected to be accountable to two sources of influence—agency preferences *and* clients' claims.[2]

There are other sources for the assertion that street-level bureaucrats are ordinarily expected to be accountable to clients, in possible opposition to the agencies for which they work. The most important of these is that most street-level bureaucrats are professionals or work in occupations aspiring to professional status. In either case a fundamental expectation attached to the job is that client needs are primary and that the extension of public trust depends upon reciprocal accountability to people as individuals, when they are encountered in the course of work. Social workers, teachers, and of course doctors and lawyers, are expected to respond to the individual and the presenting situation, however much their work situations mitigate against flexible responses.

This is a great strength and also a great weakness of the public services. It provides a measure of responsiveness to clients when the organization of bureaucratic service tends toward neglect or rigidity. But, by virtue of providing another focus of accountability, it also means that street-level bureaucrats are less controllable.

Holding Workers to Agency Objectives

Despite the dual focus of accountability inherent in the street-level bureaucrats' roles, public managers are drawn to making street-level bureaucrats more accountable by reducing their discretion and constraining their alternatives. They write manuals to cover contingencies. They audit the performance of workers to provide retrospective sanctions in anticipation of which it is hoped future behavior will be modified. They insist workers specify objectives in the hopes that accountability can be more effectively monitored. These management tools at times may be effective in controlling workers. Manuals specifying proper procedures may help standardize responses and provide instruction. Performance audits may create greater awareness that management is observing performance, and may thus lead to workers taking greater care. Specifying objectives is always likely to be instructive, and to direct workers' attention to the relationship between the available resources and the goals they are trying to achieve.[3]

However, street-level bureaucrats may subvert efforts to control them more effectively in the name of accountability. In these and other examples of attempts to increase control it is relatively easy for workers to tailor their behavior to avoid accountability. For one thing, they are likely to be the source of information management receives concerning their performance. They are fully able to provide information about the presenting situation which makes the action taken appear to be responsive to the original problem when it may not be. This involves blatant falsification less than auspicious shading of the truth and sincere rationalization.

It is extremely difficult for management to contradict workers' reports, for several reasons. A critical piece of information is the state of mind of the worker and his or her analysis of the presenting situation. Since street-level decisions are made in private, it is extremely difficult to second-guess workers, since the second guessers are not at hand to evaluate the intangible factors which may have contributed to the original judgment. The records kept by street-level bureaucrats are almost never complete or adequate to the task of post-hoc auditing for this reason, and when records are kept, they are written sketchily and defensively to guard against later adverse scrutiny.[4]

Record-keeping can help insure that certain procedures are followed (since falsification is normally not the issue). Health practitioners can be made to run certain tests, social workers to ask certain questions, police officers to follow certain procedures. But the records cannot force accountability on the appropriateness of the actions to the presenting situation.

Another major difficulty with obtaining accountability through management control efforts arises because of the dependence of street-level bureaucracies on their workers. Since the services delivered by schools, police departments, or legal services offices fundamentally consist of the actions of teachers, police officers, and lawyers, these agencies are constrained from controlling workers too much, particularly in challenging their performance, for fear of generating opposition to management policies and diminishing accountability even further. The weakness of management incentives to sanction negative performance contributes to a climate in which vigorous challenges to street-level bureaucrats' autonomy in decision-making is presumed to have possible negative net consequences for service delivery, by destroying morale and inhibiting worker initiative.[5]

Are there negative aspects to management control efforts, or are these efforts simply generally ineffective? There are several respects in which such practices can actively subvert service quality.

First, specification of methods of client treatment, under the guise of obtaining accountability, may actually result in reductions in client services. There is often a thin line between inducing workers' behavior to better conform to agency preferences, and inducing workers to be open to fewer options and opportunities for clients. For example, attempts by the Nixon Administration to increase welfare employees' accountability by auditing their error rate in accepting clients for welfare reduced services by providing incentives for welfare workers only to reduce errors which favored clients. Federal guidelines did not call for reduction in error rates for the potential welfare population as a whole. If it had, the applications of all who applied for welfare would have been audited, weighing equally those accepted and those rejected. Scrutiny of welfare workers' decisions strictly in terms of whether or not they were too lenient amounts to narrowing the role of welfare workers, reducing their accountability to clients and to professional standards of conduct. The important point is not that welfare rolls were tightened, but that tightening was accomplished in the name of accountability.

Second, supervision of subordinates with broad discretion and responsibilities requires assertions of priorities in attempting to increase accountability. Police departments may scrutinize traffic tickets, vice arrests, or interracial encounters between police and citizens. But they cannot meaningfully hold officers accountable for everything all the time. If everything is scrutinized, nothing is. Thus efforts to control street-level bureaucrats not only affect those areas which are management targets, but also those areas which are not the focus of management efforts, since by implication those efforts will not come up for surveillance. The danger is that efforts to increase accountability in some areas may come to be regarded as the only areas in which accountability will be sought and behavior scrutinized.

Third, many management control efforts provide a veneer of accountability without in fact constraining behavior very much. Management control systems have symbolic value, providing concerned publics with reassurances that employees are accountable even when they are not. Introduction of management systems at least temporarily permits deflection of criticism of street-level bureaucrats' behavior as citizens find it very difficult to challenge the emperor whom officials say is fully clothed, appearances and personal experiences to the contrary notwithstanding.[6]

Goal Clarification

One of the conspicuous features of many public services is the ambiguity and multiplicity of objectives. How can accountability be achieved, ask the critics, if public officials are unclear about their objectives? The desirability of clarifying (and then operationalizing) agency objectives in order to increase accountability stems from the force of this observation, and the recognition that a bureaucratic accountability policy requires specification of objectives (as suggested above).

It is difficult to take issue with the desirability of clarifying objectives if they are needlessly and irrelevantly fuzzy or contradictory. Surely it is easier to run an effective agency if you know what you are supposed to be doing. However, the management orientation to clarifying objectives raises an important issue for public service quality.

The issue is this: agency goals may be unclear or contradictory for reasons of neglect and historical inertia. But they may also be unclear or contradictory because they accurately reflect the contradictory impulses and orientations of the society the agencies serve. Schools attempt to instruct, but also inculcate attitudes toward social behavior and citizenship, not because educators are fuzzy but because these objectives are both favored by the clienteles of schools (and because the case that they are mutually incompatible has not and probably cannot be made convincingly). Criminal justice institutions are oriented toward punishment and rehabilitation not because judges and corrections officials are simple-minded, but because the society has impulses toward reforming as well as deterring criminals.

The public service areas of education, corrections, and welfare in recent years have all been subject to efforts to increase accountability through goal clarification. Educators have wanted to concentrate on reading to the exclusion of other educational objectives; corrections analysts have sought to clarify the role of punishment and make it more certain at the expense of emphasis on rehabilitation; welfare reformers have successfully separated decisions on income support from social service provision. The dilemma for accountability is to know when goal clarification is desirable because continued ambivalence and contradiction is unproductive, and when it will result in a reduction in the scope and mission of public services. The problem of goal ambiguity has contributed to the discrediting of services in social work, corrections, youth offenders programs, and mental health, and to the dismantling of many programs to provide assistance to those who seek it in these areas. But it requires the most serious inquiry to determine the long-term implications of requiring the clients of these institutions and agencies to have recourse exclusively to community and personal resources.

Performance Measures

The development of performance measures is critical to a bureaucratic accountability policy. Without knowing how to measure performance, organizations cannot hold employees accountable for the performance. For this reason administrators expend considerable resources attempting to develop performance measures in order to control employees' behavior.

There is no question that public services can be enhanced when valid performance measures are developed. In such cases public service workers can be held accountable for producing results in the same way that machine operators can be charged with producing a certain volume of output in a given period of time. However, public service workers, like machine operators, must also be assessed for quality control, since producing a volume of items is meaningless without consideration of the standard maintained in production. Here, paradoxically, the search for performance measures can interfere with the quality of public service.

In theory, quantitative measures of performance should be fairly easy to obtain, and consent on their validity reasonably uncontroversial. This is not always the case in street-level bureaucracies, however, for several reasons.

First, street-level bureaucrats will concentrate on the activities measured. If police officers are assessed on traffic ticketing or vice arrests, activity in these areas will increase. This is entirely predictable when we recognize that police have control over their search activities, and can choose to concentrate on one dimension of their job or another. By virtue of simply putting attention on some tasks over others, street-level bureaucrats can improve their performance on most quantitative measures managers introduce. If welfare workers are assessed on their error rate, the error rate will go down because workers pay more attention to it. If teachers are assessed on the proportion of their charges who pass year-end examinations, more will pass as teachers "teach the test." This is neither surprising nor in itself deplorable, but simply highly probable. Whenever management undertakes to concentrate on measuring a dimension of performance, workers correctly accept this as a signal of management priority. A problem is created when the measure induces workers to reduce attention to other aspects of their jobs, and when there is no control on the quality of work produced.[7]

Relatedly, street-level bureaucrats will make choices and exercise discretion by directing their activities in ways which will improve their performance scores. This phenomenon did not begin and end with Peter Blau's classic report of the employment counselors who made greater efforts for easy-to-place clients at the expense of more difficult cases when they began to be assessed in terms of successful placement ratios rather than the caseload they carried.[8] The phenomenon of "creaming" in recruiting for social programs, has similar dynamics. Workers select for their programs clients who are likely to do well in them, in order to improve the appearance of success. As James D. Thompson has put it, "Where work loads exceed capacity and the individual has options, he is tempted to select tasks which promise to enhance his scores on assessment criteria.[9] This generalization obtains for individuals and also for the work units of which they are a part.

Fraud and deception can also intrude into performance measurement. The Washington, D.C. police were quite proud of their record of reducing serious crimes until a study revealed that police officers were inexplicably reporting that most burglars involved items valued at less than $50. Significantly, the definition of a felony for this crime is defined in part as involving the theft of over $50 in value.[10] The incentives to underreport the value of items in burglaries are the same as those which induced New York City sanitation men to water their garbage so that their trucks would weigh the expected amount when they appeared at the landfill site, even though the drivers had not completed their runs.

It may be claimed that these problems—of inducing behavior to conform to the measure, neglecting other responsibilities, and unauthentically performing according to the measured standards—are simply difficulties that skilled management experts can overcome. In particular, management often seeks measures of resource deployment, depending on the inference that the provision of resources is a surrogate for (and, to be sure, a prerequisite to) service delivery. This inference is acceptable when the qualitative issue is resource deployment, as in the case of police dispatch, ambulance response time, and neighborhood shift allocations in sanitation services.[11]

The difficulty arises in the inferences that resource deployment of a particular sort bear a relationship to the quality of service delivery. For example, caseload activity might be used as a quantitative measure of performance, since it indicates formal relationships between street-level bureaucrats and clients. Class size indicates associations between teachers and children. Court dispositions indicate relationships between defendants and judicial personnel. But in all these instances there may be inverse relationships between the quality of street-level bureaucrats' involvement and the number of clients they process. If simply having people processed, or having them attached to public service workers were the issue, these measures would bear a meaningful relationship to desired service. But our expectations of these public services are different. It is not sufficient that people are assigned a social worker, sit in a classroom, or have their cases heard. We also expect that they will be processed with a degree of care, with attention to their circumstances and potential. Thus there may be no relationship, or an inverse relationship, between quantitative indicators of service and service quality.

The more discretion is part of the bureaucratic role, the less one can infer that quantitative indicators bear relationship to service quality. Even in such an apparently straightforward measure as the number of arrests made by policemen, or the number of people treated in emergency rooms, we have no idea whether the arrests were made with care, or that treatment met appropriate standards. Sophisticated management specialists acknowledge the problems of inferring quality from quantitative indicators.[12] But this does not prevent utilization of quantitative measures as surrogates for service quality and the common practice of ignoring the problems of inference in their utilization.[13]

Of course the reason quantitative measures are used so often is that actual performance is virtually impossible to measure. It is perhaps useful to put this quite bluntly: we cannot measure the quality of street-level bureaucrats' performances, particularly in terms of the most important aspects of their jobs. Aspects of performance can be measured and assessed, and many surrogates for performance measures can be developed with important implications as management tools. But the most important dimensions of service performance elude our calibration.

Measures of performance quality are elusive for reasons analogous to the difficulty in circumscribing street-level bureaucrats' discretion. If clients or presenting cases should be treated as if they might present unique situations, then it is impossible to reduce responses to sets of appropriate and previously indicated reactions. To put it another way, the more street-level bureaucrats are supposed to act with discretion, and the broader the areas of discretionary treatment, the more difficult it is to develop performance measures. If we are not agreed as to what comprises good teaching, how can we measure it? If we are not willing to deprive police officers of discretion because on the street they need to be able to make judgments based upon an appraisal of the total situation, how can we propose measures of quality arrests and interventions with citizens? If every client should be treated as if he or she may require responses tailored to the individual, how can we specify of what a good interview consists?

It may be argued that we may still assess service quality by developing outcome indicators. But here similar questions arise. First, service quality measures are meaningless without adequate controls to assess levels of difficulty. The same outcome may have required radically different service because of the difficulties presented. For example, the same student achievement levels might represent excellent work on the part of a teacher of students with learning difficulties, and poor work on the part of a teacher with bright and motivated students.

Without controls there can be no comparability of units of analysis, unless the often unwarranted assumption is made that levels of difficulty are equal. Thus teachers resist being measured by the progress of their pupils unless adequate provision is made to control for their students' previous levels of achievement (and, more importantly) for their students' capacity to learn. Thus police officers would object to utilizing arrests per capita per available officer as a measure of performance unless controls were introduced for the propensity of criminal behavior in the district. Comparing districts by outcome measures tends to be useless because of the inadequacy of such controls.

Some advocate that measures such as these be deployed in order to discover deviations from normal practice, so that measures to workers who deviate from the norm can be brought into line. Here the problem is that unless one is confident that the best workers or districts are doing a good job, such comparisons may simply institutionalize mediocrity.

Street-level bureaucrats' interactions with clients tend to take place in private or outside the scrutiny of supervisors. Interviews are held in private offices and/or under norms of confidentiality. Teaching is done in classrooms which principals and supervisors do not normally enter, and if they do, provide notice, so that the teaching, like a performance, may be changed by the presence of an audience. Police officers, although taking action in public, normally do so in the absence of the observations of other officers or supervisors. The exception is the officer's partner, who is compelled by police norms to shield his partner from criticism. Of the street-level bureaucrats we have studied, only judges tend to make their important decisions in public.

This fact provides a barrier to performance measurement, for it tends to reduce the viability of an important potential source of performance measurement. It might be possible for street-level bureaucrats to scrutinize each others' work and provide assessments of quality. But, given the structure of these agencies, such scrutiny would be highly obtrusive in relations between workers and clients, and very costly if engaged in on a widespread basis. Thus public service agencies rarely engage in direct observation of their line workers, but depend upon the written record supplied by their workers. (The reliability of such records is discussed above.)

Accountability and Productivity

Thus far I have focused discussion on some of the major difficulties in developing an administrative accountability policy. But are there any negative effects of such policies? For example, what is the harm of attempting to develop performance measures? It may be difficult to measure performance, but perhaps we are simply at the beginning of the development of a management tool. Perhaps the current measures of performance are not entirely adequate, but they may have their uses, and they may be increasingly refined.

This is the rhetoric of those who are committed to achieving bureaucratic accountability, recognize the inadequacy of current measures, but apparently have faith that their approach is ultimately correct.[14] This line of discussion would have us believe that there are some benefits to current efforts to develop accountability through improved performance measurement, that these benefits are likely to increase, and that there are no significant costs. Surely management benefits from operationalizing and attempting to develop measures of worker performance. Even if the preferred behavior cannot be adequately measured performance measurement and monitoring can signal workers powerfully concerning which aspects of performance are most salient. However, in the current period bureaucratic accountability policies also have negative consequences because of the competing demands on, and of, administrators.

In the current period public agencies are under enormous pressures to minimize costs and increase productivity. They are under pressure to reduce government expenditures or keep them from rising. They are under pressure to increase productivity in order to maintain, or claim that they are maintaining, services in the face of financial stringency. And they are under pressure to increase productivity in order to justify employee pay increases, which they are under pressure to grant. (The only way to stabilize government budgets when services cannot be reduced beyond a certain level and costs are rising is to increase the productivity of the present work force. Organized workers argue that they have no incentive to increase productivity unless they can share in the gains made because they work harder and cooperate with the reorganization of work often entailed by productivity reforms.)[15]

Productivity in the public sector summarizes the relationship between the utilization of resources and the resulting "product" in providing public services. Productivity may improve when costs remain the same, or when costs increase but services increase still more. Schematically, there are two dimensions to public services implied here—one qualitative, the other quantitative. If the quantity increases or remains the same, but services have declined qualitatively, productivity increases have not actually taken place.[16] If more garbage is picked up on the streets by the same crews, but half is strewn on the streets, productivity has not increased. The debasement of service is what infuriated New Yorkers recently when transit workers were given an increase in pay based upon gains in productivity, but it then came out that the Transit Authority had been able to provide services with fewer personnel only by increasing the time between trains and reducing the number of cars in operation.[17] In this view, the transit workers had been falsely credited with improved productivity.

These are the essential elements of productivity. In practice, however, debasement of services is rarely taken into account in productivity practices, although the problem is given lip-service by productivity theorists. First of all, if the quality of service is difficult to measure, so is reduction in service quality. Second, there are many ways to save money by eroding the quality of service without appearing to do so. They include offering services on a group rather than individual basis, substituting paraprofessionals (often paid from other sources) for regular staff, and, conversely, forcing professionals to handle clerical and other routine chores which reduce the time they have to interact with their clients.[18] Additionally, street-level bureaucrats can narrow the range of situations in which they will act. Examples include a legal services office which decides to take only emergency cases, police departments which decide to neglect selected infractions, and schools which offer a reduced program of learning opportunities. Each of these techniques permits managers to give the appearance of maintaining services while reducing costs.

Third, in the current period, pressures experienced by public managers to reduce the budget and improve productivity are pressing and general, while the constituency for maintaining service quality is disorganized, quite weak, or nonexistent. Only clients experience service quality reduction, and they are severely constrained in comparing their experiences with others, and organizing collectively to oppose service quality debasement. Ironically, the greatest opponents of service quality debasement are street-level bureaucrats themselves, for whom debasement often means harder work, less job satisfaction, and greater individual problems with clients. Yet they are cross-pressured by the interest they have in helping their agencies appear financially responsible, and their collusion with public officials to share financially in productivity increases.

But there is more to the debasement of public services than pressures and interests. A large part of the problem stems from the orientation toward measurement, precision, and scientific management itself. Consider the formula *productivity = service quantity and quality/cost*. Two of the terms, service quantity, and cost, are easy to measure; the third is virtually impossible. Managers under pressure to improve productivity are likely to try to cut personnel or obtain more work from existing personnel because these are the terms of the equation for which measures are available and which managers can manipulate. Thus staffs are reduced to bare bones without reduction in responsibilities. Thus staffs are asked to do more without increases in personnel.

Street-Level Bureaucrats and the Fiscal Crisis

. . . At best the term fiscal crisis is reserved for situations in which financial agreements and long-standing patterns of practice can no longer be honored, as when a political jurisdiction cannot meet its payroll or honor its commitments to lenders. But the term is also used much more loosely to mobilize people to believe that there is something wrong or there is a problem associated with current and projected expenditures relative to available revenues and other income. If political and economic elites are successful in promulgating a sense of crisis, they are able to make manifest and set the terms of confrontation between governmental expenditures and income. If in other times social services (for example) grew in response to perceived societal needs, in a fiscal crisis the imperatives for service development are subordinated to the demands of perceived revenue limitations.

Like other political confrontations, the management of fiscal crises have redistributive consequences. The costs of responding to the needs of expenditure constraints do not fall evenly or randomly on the population as a whole, but rather affect different segments of the population differential-ly. The fiscal crisis of the cities provides a focus and an apparently benign rationale for attacking and injuring the provision of public services. And they demonstrate the vulnerability to attack of maintaining high levels of public service quality. . . .

Who speaks for service quality in the era of performance measurement, productivity campaigns, and fiscal crisis? Public managers, with better control over costs and resource deployment than over the quality of the "product," sacrifice service quality in the name of efficiency and productivity. Street-level bureaucrats more and more are reduced to production units whose work is speeded up and whose managers appear content to sacrifice quality in order to maintain volume. In the process the conditions of work are eroded and workers are unable to utilize many of the coping mechanisms and attitudes which helped sustain their jobs under difficult conditions in earlier periods. Thus, the fiscal crisis raises the salience of the wage relationship and diminishes the salience of service. This is ironic since the wage and benefit demands of organized public employees have been widely regarded as one of the primary causes of the fiscal crisis in the first place.

This paper has drawn attention to the contributions of bureaucratic accountability policies to exacerbating problems of the quality of service delivery. But there is more. Such policies set the stage for future management of service delivery, and future conceptions of the role of human services. If current administrative practices erode workers' sense of responsibility for clients, then establishing nonmanipulative, responsive worker/client relationships will be that much harder to establish in the future. When qualitative aspects of service delivery are neglected, cost reductions and volume receive more attention as workers and managers accommodate their behavior to agency signals of priorities. This contributes to the self-fulfilling prophecy of the ineffectiveness and ultimate irrelevance of social services, even though the human needs for nurturing, protection, support, and assistance remain unanswered. Thus the tones of the fiscal crisis may linger even if the budgetary alarms of the current period are eventually quieted.

NOTES

1. Edward Wynne, "Accountable to Whom?" *Society*, vol. 13 (2) January–February 1976, pp. 30–37.
2. This is not the case with all "buffer" roles, played by people who represent organizations to the public. For example, salesmen are not expected to be responsible to buyers in anything like the same sense that, say, social workers are expected to be responsible to clients. See the discussion

of buffer roles in James D. Thompson, "Organizations and Output Trans-actions," in E. Katz and B. Danet, eds., *Bureaucracy and the Public* (New York: Basic Books, 1973), pp. 191–211.

3. I am not arguing that discretion never can and should be reduced. On the contrary, where lower-level workers usurp discretionary powers it is obviously appropriate for management to intervene. (For example of such usurpation, see Irwin Deutscher, "The Gatekeeper in Public Housing," in I. Deutscher and E. J. Thompson, eds., *Among People: Encounters with the Poor* [New York: Basic Books]), pp. 38–52.

4. For a discussion of the problems of record-keeping and accountability in medicine, see Elliot Friedson, "The Development of Administrative Accountability in Health Services," *American Behavioral Scientist*, vol. 19 (3) January–February 1976, pp. 286–98.

5. The best discussion of the effects of weak management sanctions on de-veloping norms of reciprocity supportive of low levels of effectiveness is Eric Nordlinger, *Decentralizing the City: A Study of Boston's Little City Halls* (Cambridge, Mass.: M.I.T. Press, 1972).

6. Murray Edelman discusses the symbolic implications of administration and bureaucracy for mass democracy in *The Symbolic Uses of Politics* (Urbana, Ill.: University of Illinois Press, 1964), chap. 3.

7. James Q. Wilson describes this tendency for police departments. "The police supervisor . . . would have to judge his patrolmen on the basis of their ability to keep the peace on the beat, and this . . . is necessarily subjective and dependent on close observations and personal familiarity. Those departments that evaluate officers by 'objective' measures (arrests and traffic tickets) work against this ideal." J. Q. Wilson, *Varieties of Police Behavior* (Cambridge, Mass.: Harvard University Press, 1968), p. 291.

8. See Peter Blau, *The Dynamics of Bureaucracy*, rev. ed. (Chicago: Uni-versity of Chicago Press, 1963), pp. 36–56.

9. See James D. Thompson, *Organizations in Action* (New York: McGraw-Hill, 1967), p. 123.

10. See David Seidman and Michael Couzens, "Crime, Crime Statistics and the Great American Anti-Crime Crusade: Police Misreporting of Crime and Political Pressures," Paper presented at the annual meeting of the American Political Science Association, Washington, D.C., 1972. Perhaps because they are subjected to considerable scrutiny, illustrations of ma-nipulation of statistics by the police are more likely to come to public attention than other public service agencies. See, for example, the criti-cism of an experiment in Orange County, California, which provided in-centive pay increases to police officers for crime reduction. A report on this experiment alluded to the "possibility that the increase in larceny represents a shifting of criminal activities or a reclassification of burglaries into a closely related category which will not harm prospects for an incen-tive reward" (*New York Times*, Nov. 10, 1974, p. 77.)

11. Significantly, the literature on productivity in public service provision draws its most persuasive examples from these and similar cases of resource deployment. See, for example, E. K. Hamilton, "Productivity: The New York City Approach," *Public Administration Review*, vol. 32 (6) November–December 1972, pp. 784–95.

12. A good discussion of the problems of inference is found, for example, in Harry Hatry, "Issues in Productivity Measurement for Local Governments," *Public Administration Review*, vol. 32 (6) November–December, 1972, pp. 776–84.

13. Hamilton previously cited, specifically commends the utilization of quantitative measures "output is very hard to measure . . . to improve the deployment of resources so as to maximize the probability that our resources will be available at the time and place they are needed most." This may be useful for fire protection where the *presence* of fire fighters is the critical aspect of service provision. But it cannot be adequate for street-level bureaucracies, when resource availability may not be related to service quality. See E. K. Hamilton, "Productivity," p. 787.

14. Consider the following paragraph: "Admittedly, there is an unevenness to productivity measurement. Some measures are relatively sophisticated, others crude. But in the common absence of any yardstick of productivity, even crude information is of value. At least it is a means of introducing systematic quantitative analysis into the decision-making process. Once that precedent is established, incremental refinements will undoubtedly lead to more sophisticated measures. Quantifications should only be attempted, however, if the organization has the qualitative and technical capability to interpret and apply data meaningfully." M. Holzer, *Productivity in Public Organizations* (Port Washington, N.Y.: Kennikat Press, 1976), p. 19.

15. If pay increases for workers and the cost of city services depend upon productivity, then productivity measurement and assessment obviously become highly political phenomena. For example, New York City workers seek to measure the size of productivity savings in terms of the net savings to the city from higher worker output. Fiscal managers, however, argue that productivity savings should be assessed in terms only of lower salary costs resulting from the need for a smaller workforce to accomplish the job (see the *New York Times*, March 26, 1977).

16. For a discussion of these elementary aspects of productivity, see, e.g., Nancy S. Hayward, "The Productivity Challenge," *Public Administration Review*, vol. 3 (5) September–October 1976, pp. 544–50.

17. See the *New York Times*, October 22, 1976, p. A26.

18. For a discussion of some of these service rationing practices, see R. Weatherly and M. Lipsky, "Street Level Bureaucracy and Institutional Innovation: Implementing Special Education Reform," *Harvard Education Review*, vol. 47 (2) May 1977, pp. 171–97.

22. The Institutional Level

On Heaping Our Science Together

STAFFORD BEER

Just two years ago I should have been here to act as joint chairman of your first meeting. Most unfortunately, all you had from me on that occasion was a telegram from the other side of the world regretting my unavoidable absence and wishing you the very good meeting you undoubtedly had in the event. Ten days ago Professor Hanika summoned me here today. And so he has made good the prophecy he may not remember making those two years ago: *aufgeschoben ist nicht aufgehoben.*

The reason for my defection on the last occasion was in fact an urgent recall to Santiago from the late President Salvador Allende of Chile. We had embarked six months earlier upon a programme so ambitious as to have had at least a chance of revolutionizing the form of government on a cybernetic basis that would match the revolutionary political intentions of that democracy. This endeavor took precedence with me for two years, and I emerged from the experience very much changed. I changed in my awareness of myself, of my fellow men, and of political realities; but these are not the topics that I shall discuss today. I changed also as a technologist, in terms of confidence. For I now know that it is possible to do what I have advocated for so many years—things which many used to say, and some still do say, are impossible. . . .

Consider the workers' committee that is trying to run a factory. What do they need to know? Now, of course, if our anxiety about effectiveness and freedom is real, the immediate response to this question is: what they need to know is entirely a matter for them—let them find out. Some would say that to give that answer leaves us innocent; I would call it downright oppressive. Who are we to deny to the workers' committee the tools of modern science? So, right from the start, we began an active campaign to explain to the people that science is simply ordered knowledge which can be communicated and which is part of their cultural inheritance. To make

From *Systems and Management Annual*, 1st edition, edited by C. West Churchman. © 1975 by Litton Educational Publishing, Inc. Reprinted by permission of Van Nostrand Reinhold Company.

that communication effective, the knowledge obviously must be conveyed in terms that people can understand. And we confront the cultural absurdity that no real attempt has ever been made to do it. When I say "real," I do not mean the lucrative sale of potboiling books nor the patronizing display of miraculous scientific fireworks delivered to an amazed public on television. I mean something founded in the reality of people's own experience, and in this case the factory itself.

We wanted to show workers how they could themselves make a model of their factory; therefore, there is simply no sense in conceiving of the type of model which has to be expressed by differential equations. Instead, we developed a set of rules for devising iconic representations of the dynamics of the business, which we called quantified flowcharts. To set them up in the first place, operational research teams visited all the firms, creating the rules as they went along. The important point was to create a technique that anyone could learn and that would make the relative importance of different flows and the critical measurements which govern their dynamics instantly recognizable by anyone *who actually knows the business*. So we gave them the rules; we gave them initial flowcharts; we marked initial sets of key indicators; and we explained how to express the numerical quantities in the form of indices.

Why the rules, and why the indices, and why hand over charts and create initial indicators? It is obvious that all these things are specified by the logical design of some metasystem. But in truth this is no more than to specify a language that people are asked to use inside the industrial economy so that everyone can understand everyone else. If every factory were to develop a different set of linguistic conventions, there would be no effective communication. But having made this start, we were careful to say that the quantified flowchart could be elaborated, or totally redrawn, by the workers' committee at any time; that they could add to the list of indicators as they pleased, not even saying what the new daily figures referred to, so long as they were formulated as indices—pure numbers ranging between 0 and 1; and that they could do anything else they wished provided they spoke the language provided.

Now the most interesting point about this is that if they were to find the language itself defective, then obviously they would be able to propose its elaboration, too. In this way there is nothing whatever to stop a self-organizing system that is also self-aware from joining in the process of specifying its own metasystem. Indeed, each of us does this as a human individual, insofar as he exercises choice over his environment. Note the word insofar; no individual has the chance *totally* to specify his metasystem, much of which is a genetical inheritance, more of which is socioeconomically restrained. For identical reasons, it seems to me, no unit of society—such as a workers' committee—can expect to operate without any constraint from some metasystem. But it can demand maximum freedom within it, and it can claim a democratic share in its specification. To argue for greater freedom than this seems to me a plea for anarchy; to accept less freedom than this is to abdicate responsibility and embrace dependency.

Let me now complete the example, and reveal—against this background—a feature of the Chilean work which has frightened some observers. We wanted to make science available to that workers' committee, and with it the tools of science—especially the electronic computer. There was no way of purchasing more computers because of the economic stranglehold in which the entire country was held by the rich world—which cut off its supplies, its spare parts, and its credit. There was no way of training workers in their instant use. So we set out to link up all the factories down the three-thousand-mile length of Chile to a single computer in Santiago. Again, we could not afford a genuine real-time system, because there was no teleprocessing equipment available. But using Telex and existing microwave links, we had 75 percent of the social economy in touch with this computer on a daily basis inside four months. *"Centralization,"* opponents have screamed. Not at all. If there is only one computer available, you have to use it.

Into this computer came a daily flow of indices reported from each factory. What should the computer now do with these data? Add them up? Report them? File them away in a massive data bank? Certainly not. Think of all the work that cybernetics has put in over a quarter of a century to questions of artificial intelligence. Is it not about time that managements and governments used a little human intelligence in deploying computers as the logical engines which men like Leibnitz and Babbage intended them to be, and not as glorified adding machines? This is what we set out to do, in a modest but potent way, and again—for the same reasons as before—it meant specifying a metalanguage. This, in brief, was a computer program that automatically undertook the . . . examination of every index from every plant every day.

The first question answered by the program suite called Cyberstride was this: Has the value arrived, and is it statistically plausible? Secondly, if so, is it to be viewed as a statistically random sample from the population from which it is supposed to be drawn? If it is not—that is to say, if there is a strong probability that the inspected value does not lie within the normal limits of variation about the average—then someone must be told. Who must be told? Why, the workers' committee running the factory concerned, of course—*and no one else*. . . .

I have dealt in this address, much too briefly, with key cybernetic issues as they were reflected in the practical context of the Chilean work: . . .

There is yet [another] fundamental cybernetic concept, the most real of all in terms of the Chilean experience, to which I must refer. It was taught to us by the great Warren McCulloch: the concept of redundancy of potential command.

According to this concept, brains and brainlike systems make their decisions wherever the information relevant to those decisions comes together. Therefore, it is unphysiological to appoint permanent centres where the decisions must lie. Any concatenation of logical elements may acquire the information relevant to the decision; therefore, any such concatenation is potentially in command. And since the combinatorial properties of a brain or brainlike regulator are exponentially explosive, such potential command is highly redundant. Cyberneticians know the theory. Managers very well know the practice. It is only the culture that tells us we are all wrong. The culture says that the responsibility for decision lies inside a room whose doors bear the legend "Production Director" or "Sales Director" or "President." The culture encourages the people in those rooms to beat the bounds of their estates of responsibility, keeping out trespassers, and declaring "this is where the buck stops." Not for nothing has the culture produced highly placed executives who write letters headed "From the desk of So and So." The friend I have who replied to such a letter "Dear Desk" produced his own cultural reaction; in fact, he was making a profound cybernetic point.

Decisions do not lie on this desk in this room, nor hang like an albatross around the neck of this man. As McCulloch disclosed, decisions really *are* taken where information collects in a concatenation of informed nodes. Now I have explained how we set up a virtually real-time informational network in Chile, and how we were teaching its use as a nervous system of societary management. It quickly became clear that this facilitated potential command in quite unexpected ways, and also that the nodal redundancy provided a flexibility in handling problems that no one concerned had ever experienced before. This was a revelation, and indicates that we should take our cybernetics seriously—believing what we discover as scientists, and not hesitating to apply our results in the real world.

As I said at the start, our science is an organizational science. Our studies of the brain or any other animal system, our studies of automata or any other artefacts, our studies of society itself, and the studies of everyone here at this conference—all have relevance to the nature of effective organization. Therefore, I would like to make a personal appeal to everyone here. It is to ask you to take the trouble to survey your own work from the standpoint of the world's need—political and socioeconomic—for better organizational modes. I have read all the titles under which the speakers are speaking. In some cases people are working directly on this problem, but in most they are not. To them I say, can it be that you have not asked that larger question, can it be (if you have) that you see no relevance, can it be (if you do) that you see no outlet? I do not believe that there is no relevance between your work and the world's problem of effective organization. I could easily believe that there is no outlet. But in that case we must all get together and find one. We simply must find a way to assemble all our contributions into a critical mass that will effect substantial, life-saving change.

Three organizations are involved in the running of this Conference. I was a founder-member of one; I am a past president of another. And I wonder why it is that we who study effective organization, who can effectively organize a meeting of friends to *talk* effectively *about* effective organization, seem unable to organize ourselves effectively to assault the ineffectiveness of organizations throughout the world—at every level of recursion. For we have much to say, and much to do.

As I also said at the start, we have not changed the world so far because managers and ministers do not understand what we are talking about. They would not understand this address, which does not matter—because I am not talking to them, but to you. This is one of those rare and amiable occasions when our own jargon ought to be admissible. But here comes the second appeal: Please consider whether you cannot explain what you personally cybernetically know to the people who desperately need those insights, in words that they can understand. Some of you I know are good at this; some of you apply yourselves to the study of this very problem; but mostly we do not bother.

I suggest to you that bothering about this, in a world that has become wildly unstable in almost every dimension of its organization, is now an ethical imperative for all of us cyberneticians. To use my last example from Chile: We were setting out to make films, to publish booklets, to paint slogans on the walls, and to sing songs about the scientific inheritance that belongs to the people, *and* about the effective organization of a free state, in words that all could understand. In saying "all," I mean *all*; not simply the élite, but the people themselves—with whom decisions ought to lie, but alas in Chile, finally, did not.

To them, their loved Chilean folklore singer and my friend used to sing a song called "Litany for a Computer and a Baby about to be Born." Its chorus said:

> So let us heap all science together
> before we reach the end of our tether.

I can say no better to you, today, and once again:

> Hay que juntar toda la ciencia
> Antes que acabe la paciencia.

Index

204; participation in, 37; planning
in, 26, 28; priorities in, 37; problems with, 224, 226; program decisions in, 31; program definition
process in, 46–56; program evaluation in, 34; program structure, 47–
56; programming in, 26, 38; steps
in, 34; special studies in, 31; top-
to-bottom approach in, 46, 47

Quade, E. S., 7, 15 (n.6)
Quantification in management, 60,
61, 63, 72, 133, 134, 136, 139, 149,
347; dysfunctions and limits of,
5–6, 10, 125, 134, 176, 347–51
Quantitative orientation, 3

Raia, A. P., 100, 101, 107 (n.3)
Rational decision model, 303–307;
accountability in, 304, 306; and
political theory, 306; and tools of
rationality, 303; criticisms of, 304–
307; institutional issues in, 304,
305, 306–307; mystifications in,
306; normative and value biases in,
304, 305; operational problems of,
304, 305, 306; role of political processes in, 306
Rationality, 3, 10, 11, 319, 334, 335–
36; 339; in human service organiza-
tions, 334; search for, 3–15 passim.
See also Rational decision model
Rational management, 156. *See also*
Rational decision model
Rational man theory, 71
Reddin, W. J., 104, 107 (n.13)
Redistributive function of social pro-
grams, 125
Reporting systems, 56. *See also* Man-
agement Information Systems
Resource allocations 59, 62. *See also*
Budgeting; Program-Planning-
Budgeting System
Ridley, Clarence E., 70, 73 (n.3)
Rosenzweig, J. A., 151, 157 (n.2)

Sayre, Wallace, 14
Scarcity; effects of, 353–54; percep-
tion of, 3, 174
Schick, Allen, 94, 95, 96 (n.7), 230
Scientific management, 12, 71, 94

Shaffer, H. G., 305
Services: children's, 53–54, 62, 63,
64, 255–65; education, 47, 48, 53–
54; health care, 76, 81, 86–96; job
training, 139, 140, 141; mental
health, 58–66, 158–69 passim
Shultze, Theodore W., 322, 324, 329,
331 (n.4, n.5)
Sibley, Elbridge, 326, 332 (n.14)

Taylor, Frederick, 12, 94, 96 (n.4)
Taylorism, 70
Theory Y, 94, 95
Title XX, Social Security Act, 8, 10
Tosi, Henry L., 108, 119 (n.3)
Traditional budgeting. *See* Budgeting;
Incremental budgeting
Treatment Information System, 237,
266–75
Turem, Jerry S., 156, 157 (n.9), 303

U.S. Bureau of Budget, 128
U.S. Senate Government Operations
Committee, 225, 226
United Way, 32–45 passim; Services
Identification System (UWASIS),
36–45
Urban Institute, 218, 221, 223, (n.4,
n.7, n.10, n.11)

Walsh, J. R., 326, 332 (n.20)
War on Poverty, 58
Weiner, Norbert, 288, 295, 298 (n.5)
Weizenbaum, J., 287, 298 (n.8)
Welfare State: administrative in-
tervention in, 5, 306–307; and
search for rationality, 3–15 passim;
irrationality in, 4–5; structural con-
tours of, 4–5; systems view in, 3
White, Donald D., 73
Wholey, Joseph, 175, 176
Wildavsky, Aaron, 174, 176 (n.5),
202, 304, 305
Williams, Alan, 156, 157 (n.12)

Young, E. Hilton, 173, 176 (n.1)

Zero-base budgeting (ZBB), 3, 8, 11,
173–230, passim, 303, 315–17, 319–
20; a historical quality of, 319–20;
analytical aspects of, 175; and pro-